**Fodor's**

# Las Vegas

The Ultimate Guide

Casinos and Shows

Winning Tips
and Strategies

Where to Stay,
Where to Eat

Shop 'til You Drop

Save Money
Have More Fun!

Excerpted from *Fodor's Las Vegas*

Fodor's Travel Publications • New York, Toronto, London, Sydney, Auckland
**www.fodors.com**

## Las Vegas

**EDITOR:** Carissa Bluestone, Mary Beth Bohman

**Editorial Production:** Ira-Neil Dittersdorf

**Editorial Contributors:** Bill Burton, Gregory Crosby, Fred Couzens, Lenore Greiner, Satu Hummasti, Heidi Knapp Rinella, Sarah Sper, Mike Weatherford

**Maps:** David Lindroth *cartographer;* Bob Blake and Rebecca Baer, *map editors*

**Design:** Fabrizio La Rocca, *creative director;* Guido Caroti, *art director;* Melanie Marin, *senior picture editor*

**Production/Manufacturing:** Robert B. Shields

**Cover Photo** (Las Vegas Strip): Corbis

## Copyright

## Special Sales

Fodor's Travel Publications are available at special discounts for bulk purchases for sales promotions or premiums. Special editions, including personalized covers, excerpts of existing guides, and corporate imprints, can be created in large quantities for special needs. For more information, contact your local bookseller or write to Special Markets, Fodor's Travel Publications, 1745 Broadway, New York, NY 10019.

## Important Tip

Although all prices, opening times, and other details in this book are based on information supplied to us at press time, changes occur all the time in the travel world, and Fodor's cannot accept responsibility for facts that become outdated or for inadvertent errors or omissions. So **always confirm information when it matters,** especially if you're making a detour to visit a specific place.

PRINTED IN THE UNITED STATES OF AMERICA

10 9 8 7 6 5 4 3 2 1

# CONTENTS

# ABOUT THIS BOOK

Once you've learned to find your way around this book, you'll be in great shape to find your way around Las Vegas.

You can go on the assumption that everything you read about in these pages is recommended wholeheartedly by Fodor's writers and editors. It goes without saying that no properties—no restaurants, no hotels, no casinos, nor any other establishment—has paid to be included in this book.

## The Experts Behind the Tips

There's no doubt that the best source for travel advice is a like-minded friend who's just been where you're headed. But with or without that friend, you'll have a better trip with this guide in hand, thanks to the hard work of our extraordinary writers.

**Bill Burton** is the casino gambling guide for About.com and is our gambling tutor. He writes for several national gaming publications, including *Chance & Circumstance* magazine and two newsletters, *The Crapshooter* and *Viva Las Vegas*. His book *Getting the Edge at Low Limit Texas Hold'em* was published in January 2002.

**Fred Couzens** clocked some serious car time while updating the Side Trips chapter. A Las Vegas resident, Fred has experience roaming the state as a freelance writer for the *Las Vegas Mercury* and for the *Nevada Business Journal*—not to mention all of the trips taken with golf clubs or his camera in the back seat.

**Gregory Crosby** took over the Where to Stay chapter this year. Gregory contributes a Vegas history column to the *Las Vegas Mercury* and is a docent at the Guggenheim-Hermitage Museum.

**Lenore Greiner** frequently crosses the Mojave from her home in San Diego to visit the excellent shops and spas of Las Vegas. Sometimes she does gamble but considers it just a waste of valuable shopping time. Besides contributing to Fodor's guides, she has written for *Newsday*, the *San Francisco Examiner*, and *Healing Retreats and Spas*, among others.

**Heidi Knapp Rinella** has been reviewing restaurants for the better part of 20 years and currently is the restaurant critic for the *Las Vegas Review-Journal*. She has also spent plenty of time at the kids' table, while writing the *The Lobster Kids' Guide to Exploring Las Vegas*.

**Mike Weatherford** came to us well prepared for the task of revising the Nightlife and the Arts chapter of this book. He is an entertainment reporter for the *Las Vegas Review-Journal,* so he sees all the shows and visits all the clubs. He has lived in Las Vegas since 1987.

## Features to Know

### CHOICES & RATINGS

Our goal is to cover the best properties, sights, and activities in their category, as well as the most interesting communities to visit. We make a point of including local food-lovers' hot spots as well as neighborhood options, and everything we've chosen to cover warrants recommending. A ★ denotes our top picks.

### TIME IT RIGHT

Wondering when to go? Check **When to Go** in Smart Travel Tips for weather and crowd overviews and best days and times to visit.

### BUDGET WELL

Hotel and restaurant price categories from ¢ to $$$$ are defined in the opening pages of the Where to Eat and Where to Stay chapters—expect to find a balanced selection for every budget. For attractions, we always give standard adult admission fees; reductions are usually available for children, students, and senior citizens. Look in **Discounts & Deals** in Smart Travel Tips for information on destination-wide ticket schemes.

### BASIC INFO

**Smart Travel Tips** lists travel essentials for the entire area covered by the book; city- and region-specific basics end each chapter. To find the best way to get around, see the **Transportation Around Las Vegas** section. We assume you'll check Web sites or call for particulars.

## SYMBOLS

You'll find various symbols throughout this book. For explanations of the dollar signs in the margins of hotel and restaurant reviews, see the price category charts that begin the Where to Eat and Where to Stay chapters. Here's what the other symbols mean.

★ Our special recommendations
✕ Restaurant
🏠 Lodging establishment
🐤 Good for kids (rubber duck)
☞ Sends you to another section of the guide for more information
✉ Address
☎ Telephone number
🕐 Opening and closing times
🎟 Admission prices (those we give apply to adults; substantially reduced fees are almost always available for children, students, and senior citizens)

## Don't Forget to Write

Your experiences—positive and negative—matter to us. If we have missed or misstated something, we want to hear about it. We follow up on all suggestions. Contact the *Fodor's Las Vegas* editor at editors@fodors.com or c/o Fodor's, 1745 Broadway, New York, New York 10019. And have a fabulous trip!

THE EDITORS

# Nevada

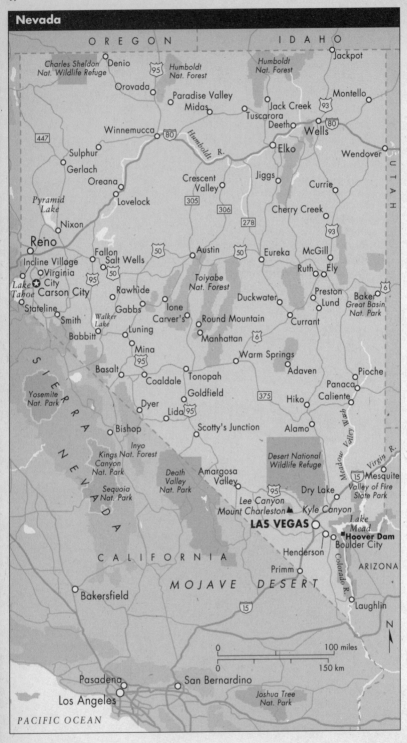

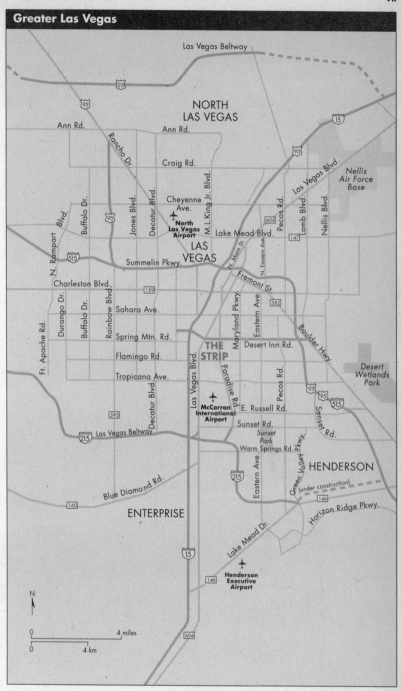

**Greater Las Vegas**

# Las Vegas

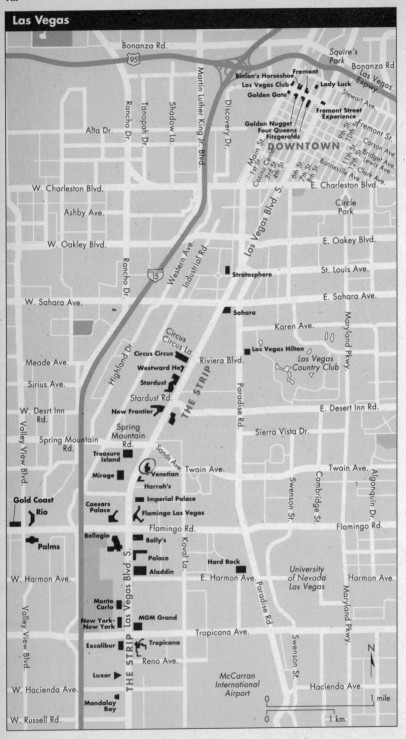

Bonanza Rd.

95

Squire's Park

Bonanza Rd

Las Vegas Expwy.

Binion's Horseshoe

Fremont

Las Vegas Club

Lady Luck

Golden Gate

Stewart Ave.

Fremont St.

Fremont Street Experience

Golden Nugget

Four Queens

Fitzgeralds

DOWNTOWN

Alta Dr.

Martin Luther King Jr. Blvd.

Shadow la.

Tanopah Dr.

Rancho Dr.

Discovery Dr.

Main St.

Casino Center

1st St.

3rd St.

4th St.

6th St.

7th St.

8th St.

9th St.

10th St.

11th St.

12th St.

Carson Ave.

Bridget Ave.

Lewis Ave.

Clark Ave.

Bonneville Ave.

E. Charleston Blvd.

W. Charleston Blvd.

Circle Park

Ashby Ave.

W. Oakley Blvd.

E. Oakey Blvd.

Las Vegas Blvd. S.

St. Louis Ave.

Western Ave.

Industrial Rd.

15

Stratosphere

E. Sahara Ave.

W. Sahara Ave.

Rancho Dr.

Sahara

Karen Ave.

Maryland Pkwy.

Circus Circus La.

Las Vegas Hilton

Las Vegas Country Club

Circus Circus

Riviera Blvd.

Meade Ave.

Westward Ho

THE STRIP

Highland Dr.

Stardust

Sirius Ave.

Stardust Rd.

Paradise Rd.

W. Desrt Inn Rd.

New Frontier

E. Desert Inn Rd.

Valley View Blvd.

Spring Mountain Rd.

Sierra Vista Dr.

Spring Mountain Rd.

Sands Ave.

Twain Ave.

Twain Ave.

Treasure Island

Venetian

Algonquin Dr.

Swenson St.

Cambridge St.

Mirage

Harrah's

Gold Coast

Rio

Imperial Palace

Caesars Palace

Flamingo Las Vegas

Palms

Flamingo Rd.

Flamingo Rd.

Bellagio

Bally's

Palace

Koval La.

Hard Rock

Aladdin

W. Harmon Ave.

E. Harmon Ave.

University of Nevada Las Vegas

Harmon Ave.

Valley View Blvd.

Monte Carlo

New York-New York

MGM Grand

Tropicana Ave.

Las Vegas Blvd. S.

Excalibur

Tropicana

Paradise Rd.

Swenson St.

Reno Ave.

THE STRIP

Maryland Pkwy.

N

Luxor

W. Hacienda Ave.

McCarran International Airport

Hacienda Ave.

Mandalay Bay

0          1 mile

W. Russell Rd.

0          1 km

# ESSENTIAL INFORMATION

## ADDRESSES

The Greater Las Vegas area is in Clark County Nevada and encompasses four cities: Las Vegas, North Las Vegas, Henderson, and Boulder City.

## AIR TRAVEL TO &
## FROM LAS VEGAS

McCarran International Airport (LAS) is well served by many nonstop and direct flights.

### BOOKING

When you book, **look for nonstop flights** and remember that "direct" flights stop at least once. Try to avoid connecting flights, which require a change of plane. Two airlines may operate a connecting flight jointly, so ask whether your airline operates every segment of the trip; you may find that the carrier you prefer flies you only part of the way. To find more booking tips and to check prices and make on-line flight reservations, log on to www.fodors.com.

### CARRIERS

All of the major airlines operate frequent service from their hub cities and between them offer one-stop connecting flights from virtually every city in the country. In addition to nonstop service to the "usual" hub cities (i.e., Atlanta, Chicago, Dallas, Denver, Houston, Minneapolis, St. Louis, Salt Lake City), nonstop service is offered to other destinations by some smaller airlines. Southwest remains the dominant airline (with highest number of passengers carried), and it offers frequent flights to many cities in the south and west, including San Diego, Los Angeles, Oakland, Seattle, and Phoenix. Many international carriers serve Las Vegas as well; their schedules include direct flights from Canada and the UK.

➤ MAJOR AIRLINES: Air Canada (☎ 800/776–3000, WEB www.aircanada. ca). American (☎ 800/433–7300, WEB www.aa.com). America West (☎ 800/ 235–9292, WEB www.americawest. com). Continental (☎ 800/525–0280, WEB www.continental.com). Delta (☎ 800/221–1212, WEB www.delta.com). Japan Airlines (☎ 800/525–3663, WEB www.jal.co.jp/en/). Northwest (☎ 800/225–2525, WEB www.nwa. com). Southwest (☎ 800/435–9792, WEB www.southwest.com). United (☎ 800/241–6522, WEB www.united.com). US Airways (☎ 800/428–4322, WEB www.usairways.com).

➤ SMALLER AIRLINES: Alaska Airlines (☎ 800/426–0333, WEB www. alaskaairlines.com). Allegiant Air (☎ 877/202–6444, WEB www. allegiant-air.com). Aloha (☎ 800/ 367–5250, WEB www.alohaairlines. com). American Trans Air/ATA (☎ 800/435–9282, WEB www.ata. com). Frontier Airlines (☎ 800/432– 1359, WEB www.frontierairlines.com). Hawaiian Airlines (☎ 800/367– 5320, WEB www.hawaiianair.com). Midwest Express (☎ 800/452–2022, WEB www.midwestexpress.com). Sun Country Air (☎ 800/359–6786, WEB www.suncountry.com).

### CHECK-IN & BOARDING

Always ask your carrier about its check-in policy. Plan to arrive at the airport about two hours before your scheduled departure time for domestic flights and 2½ to 3 hours before international flights. You may need to arrive earlier if you're flying from one of the busier airports or during peak air-traffic times.

Las Vegas used to be the premiere destination for remote check-in facilities, a service that allowed passengers to check-in for flights at various hotels on the Strip and head straight for the departure gate with seat assignment and boarding pass. At press time, however, all non-airport check-in was suspended until further notice due to heightened airport security measures.

To avoid delays at airport-security checkpoints, try not to wear any metal. Jewelry, belt and other buckles, steel-toe shoes, barrettes, and under-wire bras are among the items that can set off detectors.

Assuming that not everyone with a ticket will show up, airlines routinely overbook planes. When everyone does, airlines ask for volunteers to give up their seats. In return, these volunteers usually get a several-hundred-dollar flight voucher, which can be used toward the purchase of another ticket, and are rebooked on the next flight out. If there are not enough volunteers, the airline must choose who will be denied boarding. The first to get bumped are passen-gers who checked in late and those flying on discounted tickets, so get to the gate and check in as early as possible, especially during peak periods.

Always **bring a government-issued photo I.D. to the airport;** even when it's not required, a passport is best.

## CUTTING COSTS

It's smart to call a number of airlines and check the Internet; when you are quoted a good price, book it on the spot—the same fare may not be available the next day, or even the next hour. Always check different routings and look into using alternate airports. Also, price off-peak flights, which may be significantly less ex-pensive than others. Travel agents, especially low-fare specialists (☞ Discounts and Deals), are helpful. Always ask for package rates as these tend to be the best bargains to Las Vegas—airfare that includes hotel and sometimes car rental.

Consolidators are another good source. They buy tickets for scheduled flights at reduced rates from the airlines, then sell them at prices that beat the best fare available directly from the airlines. Sometimes you can even get your money back if you need to return the ticket. Carefully read the fine print detailing penalties for

changes and cancellations, purchase the ticket with a credit card, and **confirm your consolidator reservation with the airline.**

➤ CONSOLIDATORS: **AirlineConsolidator. com** (☎ 888/468–5385, WEB www. airlineconsolidator.com); for interna-tional tickets. **Best Fares** (☎ 800/576–8255 or 800/576–1600, WEB www.bestfares.com); $59.90 annual membership. **Cheap Tickets** (☎ 800/377–1000 or 888/922–8849, WEB www.cheaptickets.com). **Expedia** (☎ 800/397–3342 or 404/728–8787, WEB www.expedia.com). **Hotwire** (☎ 866/468–9473 or 920/330–9418, WEB www.hotwire.com). **Now Voyager Travel** (✉ 45 W. 21st St., 5th fl., New York, NY 10010, ☎ 212/459–1616, FAX 212/243–2711, WEB www. nowvoyagertravel.com). **Onetravel. com** (WEB www.onetravel.com). **Orbitz** (☎ 888/656–4546, WEB www. orbitz.com). **Priceline.com** (WEB www. priceline.com). **Travelocity** (☎ 888/709–5983; 877/282–2925 in Canada; 0870/876–3876 in the U.K., WEB www.travelocity.com).

## ENJOYING THE FLIGHT

State your seat preference when purchasing your ticket, and then repeat it when you confirm and when you check in. For more legroom, you can request one of the few emergency-aisle seats at check-in, if you are capable of lifting at least 50 pounds—a Federal Aviation Administration requirement of passengers in these seats. Seats behind a bulkhead also offer more legroom, but they don't have under-seat storage. Don't sit in the row in front of the emergency aisle or in front of a bulkhead, where seats may not recline.

Ask the airline whether a snack or meal is served on the flight. If you have dietary concerns, request special meals when booking. These can be vegetarian, low-cholesterol, or kosher, for example. It's a good idea to pack some healthful snacks and a small (plastic) bottle of water in your carry-on bag. On long flights, try to main-tain a normal routine, to help fight jet lag. At night, get some sleep. By day, eat light meals, drink water (not alcohol), and **move around the cabin** to stretch your legs. For additional jet-lag tips consult *Fodor's FYI: Travel Fit & Healthy* (available at bookstores everywhere).

All airlines flying into Las Vegas prohibit smoking.

### FLYING TIMES

To Las Vegas: From New York, 5 hours; from Dallas, 2 hours; from Chicago, 4 hours; from Los Angeles, 1 hour; from San Francisco, 1½ hours; from London, 11 hours; from Sydney, 18 hours.

### HOW TO COMPLAIN

If your baggage goes astray or your flight goes awry, complain right away. Most carriers require that you **file a claim immediately.** The Aviation Consumer Protection Division of the Department of Transportation publishes *Fly-Rights,* which discusses airlines and consumer issues and is available on-line. You can also find articles and information on mytravelrights.com, the Web site of the nonprofit Consumer Travel Rights Center.

➤ INFORMATION: **Aviation Consumer Protection Division** (✉ U.S. Department of Transportation, C-75, Room 4107, 400 7th St. NW, Washington, DC 20590, ☎ 202/366–2220, WEB www.dot.gov/airconsumer). **Federal Aviation Administration Consumer Hotline** (✉ for inquiries: FAA, 800 Independence Ave. SW, Room 810, Washington, DC 20591, ☎ 800/322–7873, WEB www.faa.gov).

### RECONFIRMING

Check the status of your flight before you leave for the airport. You can do this on your carrier's Web site, by linking to a flight-status checker (many Web booking services offer these), or by calling your carrier or travel agent.

### AIRPORTS & TRANSFERS

The gateway to Las Vegas is McCarran International Airport (LAS), 5 mi south of the business district and immediately east of the southern end of the Strip. Some people choose to fly into Los Angeles International (LAX), rent a car, and drive the five hours to Las Vegas. Fares are usually lower into LAX but after adding the car rental it averages to about the same.

➤ AIRPORTS: **McCarran International Airport (LAS)** (☎ 702/261–5733, WEB www.mccarran.com).

### AIRPORT TRANSFERS

By shuttle van: this is the cheapest way from McCarran to your hotel. The service is shared with other riders, and costs $4–$5 per person to the Strip, $5–$7 to downtown, and $5–$21 to outlying "locals" casinos. The vans wait for passengers outside the terminal in a marked area, near the cabs. Since the vans stop at many of the major hotels, it's not the best means of transportation if you're in a hurry.

By taxi: the metered cabs awaiting your arrival at McCarran are the quickest way of getting to your destination. The fare is $2.70 on the meter when you get in and $1.80 for every mile, plus an airport surcharge of $1.20. The trip to most hotels on the Strip should cost $11–$18; the trip downtown should be about $20–$25.

➤ TRANSFERS: **Bell Trans** (☎ 702/739–7990, WEB www.bell-trans.com). **Checker/Yellow/Star Cab** (☎ 702/873–2000). **Gray Line** (☎ 702/739–5700, WEB www.grayline.com).

### BUSINESS HOURS

Las Vegas is a 24-hour city, 365 days a year. Casinos, bars, supermarkets, almost all gas stations, even some health clubs and video stores cater to customers at all hours of the day and night (many people work odd hours here).

### MUSEUMS & SIGHTS

Most museums and attractions are open seven days a week.

### PHARMACIES

Most pharmacies are open seven days a week from 9–7.

➤ 24-HOUR PHARMACIES: **Walgreens** (✉ 3765 Las Vegas Blvd. S, ☎ 702/739–9645).

### SHOPS

Most stores are open weekdays 10–9, Saturday 9–6, and Sunday 11–6. The souvenir shops on the Strip and downtown remain open until midnight and some are open 24 hours. Grocery stores are open around the clock.

## BUS TRAVEL TO & FROM LAS VEGAS

Greyhound runs bus service in and out of Las Vegas; the bus terminal is downtown.

### FARES & SCHEDULES

Call Greyhound or visit their Web site for fare and schedule information.

### PAYING

Cash, travelers checks, and credit cards are accepted.

### RESERVATIONS

Reservations are not accepted on Greyhound. Seating is on a first-come, first-served basis. The most frequently plowed route out of Las Vegas is the one to Los Angeles, with departures approximately every two hours around the clock. Arriving at the bus station 30 to 45 minutes before your bus departs to purchase tickets nearly always ensures you a seat. On Sunday evening and Monday morning, arriving an hour or more before departure is recommended as buses fill up quickly on those days.

➤ BUS INFORMATION: **Greyhound** (✉ 200 S. Main St., Las Vegas, ☎ 800/231–2222, WEB www.greyhound.com).

## BUS TRAVEL WITHIN LAS VEGAS

The municipally operated Citizens Area Transit (CAT) runs local buses throughout the city and to most corners of the sprawling Las Vegas Valley. The overall quality of bus service along the main thoroughfares is decent. Most visitors only ride CAT buses up and down the Strip, between Mandalay Bay and the Stratosphere. Some continue on to the Downtown Transportation Center. If you're heading to outlying areas, you may need to change buses downtown. Mornings and afternoons the buses are frequently crowded, with standing-room only.

The Las Vegas Strip Trolleys are a bit more charming with their old-fashioned appearance, and they'll deliver you right to the door of most of the major casinos on the Strip. Bear in mind, however, that this door-to-door delivery makes them a little slower, as they have to fight the knots of cabs, limos, airport shuttles, and private vehicles that collect at every casino at any hour of the day.

### FARES & SCHEDULES

The fare for CAT buses on the Strip is $2 (exact change required; one-dollar bills are accepted). The buses stop on the street in front of all the major hotels every 15 minutes (in a perfect world), 24 hours a day. Since traffic is quite haphazard along the Strip, however, delays are frequent. Buses supposedly running every 15 minutes can take 25 to 30 minutes to show up. Other routes serve the Meadows and Boulevard shopping malls and Sam's Town Hotel and Casino on Boulder Highway. The schedule for all buses other than those along the Strip is 5:00 AM–1:00 AM daily; the fare is $1.25.

From 9:30 AM to 1:30 AM, the Las Vegas Strip Trolley travels every 15 to 20 minutes among Strip hotels, with stops at Fashion Show Mall and Wet 'n Wild. The exact fare of $1.65 is required.

➤ BUS INFORMATION: **Citizens Area Transit** (☎ 702/228–7433). **Las Vegas Strip Trolley** (☎ 702/382–1404).

## CAMERAS & PHOTOGRAPHY

Only a few casinos allow people to photograph or videotape the games or machines. This is a holdover from the bad old days, when gambling was considered a vice and people were ashamed to be caught doing it. Some players are still sensitive about having their picture taken while gambling, so the casinos generally prohibit it, though you may take pictures at Harrah's, Excalibur, and the Four Queens.

The *Kodak Guide to Shooting Great Travel Pictures* (available at bookstores everywhere) is loaded with tips.

➤ INFORMATION: **Kodak Information Center** (☎ 800/242–2424, WEB www.kodak.com).

### EQUIPMENT PRECAUTIONS

Windy and dusty conditions are not infrequent in Las Vegas, and your photo lenses can be quickly covered with a layer of sand. Always carry your equipment tightly sealed in protective covering and bring extra lens cleaner solution to wipe off lenses.

**Don't pack film and equipment in checked luggage,** where it is much more susceptible to damage. X-ray machines used to view checked luggage are extremely powerful and therefore are likely to ruin your film. Try to ask for hand inspection of film, which becomes clouded after repeated exposure to airport X-ray machines, and keep videotapes and computer disks away from metal detectors. Always keep film, tape, and computer disks out of the sun. Carry an extra supply of batteries, and be prepared to turn on your camera, camcorder, or laptop to prove to airport security personnel that the device is real.

## CAR RENTAL

Rates in Las Vegas average about $23 a day and $115 a week for an economy car with unlimited mileage. This does not include the 7.25% state sales tax and a 6% "license tag" fee. If you rent your car at the airport an additional 10% tax applies.

➤ MAJOR AGENCIES: **Alamo** (☎ 800/327–9633, WEB www.alamo.com). **Avis** (☎ 800/331–1212; 800/879–2847 or 800/272–5871 in Canada; 0870/606–0100 in the U.K.; 02/9353–9000 in Australia; 09/526–2847 in New Zealand, WEB www.avis.com). **Budget** (☎ 800/527–0700; 0870/156–5656 in the U.K., WEB www.budget.com). **Dollar** (☎ 800/800–4000; 0124/622–0111 in the U.K., where it's affiliated with Sixt; 02/9223–1444 in Australia, WEB www.dollar.com). **Hertz** (☎ 800/654–3131; 800/263–0600 in Canada; 0870/844–8844 in the U.K.; 02/9669–2444 in Australia; 09/256–8690 in New Zealand, WEB www.hertz.com). **National Car Rental** (☎ 800/227–7368; 0870/600–6666 in the U.K., WEB www.nationalcar.com).

### CUTTING COSTS

Owing to the large number of visitors who rent cars, there are many deals to be had at the airport for car rentals. During special events and conventions rates frequently go up as supply dwindles, but during other times bargains are to be had in Las Vegas.

For the best deals, check with the various on-line services, or contact a representative of the hotel where you'll be staying, as many hotels have business relationships with car-rental companies.

Although there are several local car rental companies along the Strip itself, they tend to be more expensive than those at the airport or elsewhere in the city.

For a good deal, book through a travel agent who will shop around. Also, price local car-rental companies—whose prices may be lower still, although their service and maintenance may not be as good as those of major rental agencies—and research rates on the Internet. Remember to ask about required deposits, cancellation penalties, and drop-off charges if you're planning to pick up the car in one city and leave it in another. If you're traveling during a holiday period, also make sure that a confirmed reservation guarantees you a car.

➤ LOCAL AGENCIES: **Allstate/Payless** (☎ 702/736–6147). **Brooks Rent-A-Car** (☎ 702/735–3344). **Dream Car Rentals** (☎ 702/731–6452, 702/895–6661 or 877/373–2601). **Rent-A-Vette** (☎ 702/736–2592 or 800/372–1981).

### INSURANCE

When driving a rented car you are generally responsible for any damage to or loss of the vehicle. You also may be liable for any property damage or personal injury that you may cause while driving. Before you rent, see what coverage you already have under the terms of your personal auto-insurance policy and credit cards.

For about $10 to $25 a day, rental companies sell protection, known as a collision- or loss-damage waiver (CDW or LDW), that eliminates your liability for damage to the car; it's always optional and should never be automatically added to your bill. In most states you don't need a CDW if you have personal auto insurance or other liability insurance. Some states, including Nevada, have capped the price of the CDW and LDW.

## REQUIREMENTS & RESTRICTIONS

In Nevada you must be 21 to rent a car, and several of the major car rental agencies (such as Hertz) have a minimum age of 25. Those agencies that do rent to those under 25 may charge you higher rates. There is no upper age limit for car rental. Non-U.S. residents will need a reservation voucher, a passport, a driver's license, and a travel policy that covers each driver, when picking up a car.

## SURCHARGES

Before you pick up a car in one city and leave it in another, ask about drop-off charges or one-way service fees, which can be substantial. Note, too, that some rental agencies charge extra if you return the car before the time specified in your contract. To avoid a hefty refueling fee, **fill the tank just before you turn in the car,** but be aware that gas stations near the rental outlet may overcharge. It's almost never a deal to buy the tank of gas that's in the car when you rent it; the understanding is that you'll return it empty, but some fuel usually remains. Surcharges may apply if you're under 25 or if you take the car outside the area approved by the rental agency. You'll pay extra for child seats (about $6 a day), which are compulsory for children under five, and usually for additional drivers (about $10 per day).

## CAR TRAVEL

Las Vegas is an easy city to navigate. The principal north–south artery is Las Vegas Boulevard (I–15 runs roughly parallel to it, less than a mile to the west). A 3½-mi stretch of Las Vegas Boulevard South is the Strip, where a majority of the city's hotels and casinos are clustered. Many of the major streets running east–west (Tropicana Avenue, Flamingo Road, Desert Inn Road, Sahara Avenue) are named for the casinos built at their intersections with the Strip.

Because the capacity of the streets of Las Vegas has not kept pace with the city's incredible growth, traffic can be slow in the late afternoon, in the evening, and on the weekend. At those times, **drive the streets that**

**parallel Las Vegas Boulevard:** Paradise Road to the east, and Industrial Road to the west. The Industrial Road shortcut (from Tropicana Avenue almost all the way to downtown) will save you an enormous amount of time. You can enter the parking lots at Caesars Palace, the Mirage, Treasure Island, the Stardust, the New Frontier, and Circus Circus from Industrial Road.

Visitors from Southern California should at all costs try to avoid traveling to Las Vegas on a Friday afternoon and returning home on a Sunday afternooon. During these traditional weekend-visit hours, driving times can be twice as long as during other, non-peak periods.

## EMERGENCY SERVICES

You can call 911 from most locations in Nevada to reach police, fire, or ambulance assistance. Otherwise, dial the operator. If you have a cellular or digital phone, dial *647 to reach the Nevada Highway Patrol.

## PARKING

You can't park anywhere on the Strip itself, and Fremont Street in the casino district downtown is a pedestrian mall closed to traffic. Street parking regulations are strictly enforced in Las Vegas, and meters are continuously monitored, so whenever possible it's a good idea to **leave your car in a parking lot.** Free parking is available at virtually every hotel, although you may have to hunt for a space and you can wind up in the far reaches of immense parking lots. To avoid this, simply make use of valet parking. Parking in the high-rise structures downtown is generally free, as long as you validate your parking ticket at the casino cashier.

## ROAD CONDITIONS

It might seem as if every road in Las Vegas is in a continuous state of expansion or repair. Orange highway cones, road-building equipment, and detours are ubiquitous. But once the roads are widened and repaved, they're efficient and comfortable. The city's traffic-light system is state-of-the-art, and you can often drive for miles on major thoroughfares, hitting green lights all the way. Signage is excellent, both on surface arteries and freeways. The local driving style is fast.

For information on weather conditions, highway construction, and road closures call the Department of Transportation for the state you're traveling in.

➤ INFORMATION: **Arizona Department of Transportation** (☎ 888/411–7623). **California Department of Transportation** (☎ 916/445–7623). **Nevada Department of Transportation** (☎ 877/687–6237).

## RULES OF THE ROAD

The speed limit on residential streets is 25 mph. On major thoroughfares it's 45 mph, though drivers often get impatient with people who obey the speed limit and pass on either side. On the interstate and other divided highways within the city the speed limit is a fast 65 mph; outside the city, the speed limit on I–15 is 70 and 75 mph. California's speed limit is 70 mph. Right turns are permitted on red lights after coming to a full stop in Arizona, California, Nevada, and Utah.

Always **strap children under age five or under 40 pounds into approved child-safety seats.** In Nevada, children must wear seat belts regardless of where they're seated.

## CHILDREN IN LAS VEGAS

Of the roughly 35 million visitors to Las Vegas each year, 12% are under 21. If you're the parent of one of these too-young-to-gamble tourists, you know that the hotel pool will only occupy them for so long. Fortunately, there's lots for kids to do in Vegas. Other than in the casinos, children are welcome anywhere.

If you are renting a car, don't forget to arrange for a car seat when you reserve. For general advice about traveling with children, consult *Fodor's FYI: Travel with Your Baby* (available in bookstores everywhere).

## BABY-SITTING

One reliable independent local agency is Nanny's and Granny's, which charges a variable rate depending on the number of children (fees for one child begin with a minimum $50 for the first four hours). Baby-sitters are cleared through the FBI and local sheriff's department.

Several casinos also provide child care services, but they tend to be those that appeal to locals. The facilities at Castaways, Sam's Town, and Gold Coast are free for casino patrons, two-hour maximum; you must stay in the building. At the Gold Coast and Sam's Town, children must be potty-trained. There's an hourly rate and a 3½-hr limit at Kids' Quest, the mega play areas at Texas Station, Boulder Station, Palace Station, and Sunset Station. Kids' Quest offers sprawling, elaborate play structures; video games; and some structured activities. It's available to kids up to 12 years old.

➤ AGENCIES: **Nanny's and Granny's** (✉ 6440 W. Coley Ave., Las Vegas, NV 89117, ☎ 702/364–4700, WEB www.nanny4u.com).

➤ CASINOS: **Boulder Station** (✉ 4111 Boulder Hwy., Boulder Strip, ☎ 702/432–7569). **Castaways** (✉ 2800 Fremont St., Boulder Strip, ☎ 702/385–9123). **Gold Coast** (✉ 4000 W. Flamingo Rd., West Side, ☎ 702/367–7111). **Orleans** (✉ 4500 W. Tropicana Ave., West Side, ☎ 702/365–7111). **Palace Station** (✉ 2411 W. Sahara Ave., West Side, ☎ 702/367–2411). **Sam's Town** (✉ 5111 Boulder Hwy., Boulder Strip, ☎ 702/456–7777). **Sunset Station** (✉ 1301 W. Sunset Rd., Henderson, ☎ 702/547–7773). **Texas Station** (✉ 2101 Texas Star La., Rancho Strip, ☎ 702/631–8355).

## FLYING

Experts agree that it's a good idea to use safety seats aloft for children weighing less than 40 pounds. Airlines set their own policies: If you use a safety seat, U.S. carriers usually require that the child be ticketed, even if he or she is young enough to ride free, because the seats must be strapped into regular seats. And even if you pay the full adult fare for the seat, it may be worth it, especially on longer trips. Do **check your airline's policy about using safety seats during takeoff and landing.** Safety seats are not allowed everywhere in the plane, so get your seat assignments as early as possible.

When reserving, request children's meals or a freestanding bassinet (not available at all airlines) if you need them. But note that bulkhead seats, where you must sit to use the bassinet, may lack an overhead bin or storage space on the floor.

## LODGING

Most hotels in Las Vegas allow children under a certain age to stay in their parents' room at no extra charge, but others charge for them as extra adults; be sure to **find out the cutoff age for children's discounts.** Hotels will usually provide cribs for babies and "rollaways" (cots) for children. Children are actively discouraged at the Bellagio, and they are allowed on the property only if they are accompanied by their parents and staying at the hotel.

Most major Las Vegas hotels provide extensive video-game arcades for their underage guests (though leaving children under the age of 14 or 15 alone in arcades and game rooms is not recommended). The Orleans is the casino closest to the Strip with a commercial child-care facility, Kids Tyme. An especially comprehensive child-care program can be found at MGM Grand's Youth Center. Guests of the Grand take precedence, but guests at any hotel can take advantage of this large day-care facility if space is available. Children ages 3–12 play, snack, and eat meals from 11 AM until 11 PM (midnight Friday and Saturday), starting at $8 an hour per child (up to $10.50 an hour for nonguests). Activities include basketball, Foosball, Nintendo, arts and crafts, and air hockey.

➤ BEST CHOICES: **Orleans Hotel and Casino** (⊠ 4500 W. Tropicana Ave., ☎ 800/675–3267). **MGM Grand's King Looey's Youth Center** (☎ 702/891–1111).

## SIGHTS & ATTRACTIONS

The free spectacles, the thrill rides (both big and small, actual and virtual), the many movie theaters, bowling alleys, video-game arcades, amusement and water parks, children's museums, and other activities make Las Vegas a fun place for youngsters. Places that are especially appealing to children are indicated by a rubber-duckie icon (☺) in the margin.

In addition, Mountasia Family Fun Center in Henderson, a fast-growing suburb in southeastern Las Vegas, has two 18-hole miniature-golf courses, a roller-skating rink, go-carts, bumper boats, and an arcade with 75 video games. A special $13 package includes unlimited minigolf or roller skating, two rides (bumper boats or go-carts), and five arcade tokens. Scandia Family Fun Center has three 18-hole miniature-golf courses, a video arcade with more than 100 games, 11 batting cages, bumper boats, and the Li'l Indy Raceway for miniature-car racing. You can pay by the ride/activity or purchase an $11.95 Supersaver package (one round of miniature golf, two rides, and five arcade or batting tokens) or a $16.95 wristband (unlimited rides, golf, and 10 arcade or batting tokens). The Zoological–Botanical Park is five minutes from downtown. Here you'll find the last family of Barbary apes in the United States, along with chimpanzees, eagles, ostriches, emus, parrots, wallabies, flamingos, endangered cats (including tigers), and every species of venomous reptile native to southern Nevada.

Also, check out the Side Trips chapter for everything from visiting a Wild West town to scrambling around in Red Rock.

➤ INFORMATION: **Mountasia Family Fun Center** (⊠ 2050 Olympic Ave., Henderson, ☎ 702/454–4386). **Scandia Family Fun Center** (⊠ 2900 Sirius Ave., West Side, ☎ 702/364–0070). **Zoological–Botanical Park** (⊠ 1775 N. Rancho Dr., Rancho, ☎ 702/648–5955).

## CONCIERGES

Concierges, found in many hotels, can help you with theater tickets and dinner reservations: a good one with connections may be able to get you seats for a hot show or prime-time dinner reservations at the restaurant of the moment. You can also turn to your hotel's concierge for help with travel arrangements, sightseeing plans, services ranging from aromatherapy to zipper repair, and emergencies. Always, **always tip** a concierge who has been of assistance (☞ Tipping).

## CONSUMER PROTECTION

Whether you're shopping for gifts or purchasing travel services, **pay with a major credit card** whenever possible, so you can cancel payment or get reimbursed if there's a problem (and you can provide documentation). If you're doing business with a particular company for the first time, contact your local Better Business Bureau and the attorney general's offices in your state and (for U.S. businesses) the company's home state as well. Have any complaints been filed? Finally, if you're buying a package or tour, always consider travel insurance that includes default coverage (☞ Insurance).

➤ INFORMATION: **Council of Better Business Bureaus** (✉ 4200 Wilson Blvd., Suite 800, Arlington, VA 22203, ☎ 703/276–0100, FAX 703/525–8277, WEB www.bbb.org). **Better Business Bureau of Southern Nevada** (✉ 2301 Palomino La., Las Vegas, NV 89107, ☎ 702/320–4500, FAX 702/320–4560, WEB www.vegasbbb.org).

## DINING

When planning your dining-out excursions in Las Vegas, try to hit at least one or two places off the Strip. For one thing, it's kind of educational: some visitors are surprised to learn that Las Vegans don't all live in hotels! For another, you will likely find that prices are lower—and food quality sometimes just as high—as in the places that cater to tourists. The pace is usually more relaxed, too, and you can often leave your car just steps from the door.

The restaurants we list are the cream of the crop in each price category. Properties indicated with an ✕🏠 are lodging establishments whose restaurant warrants a special trip.

### RESERVATIONS & DRESS

Some restaurants require reservations (and you should make them well in advance). You'd be well advised to call ahead to just about any popular restaurant, however, to inquire about reservation policies, because waits can be long.

We mention reservations for particular restaurants only when they're essential or not accepted. Book as far ahead as you can, and reconfirm as soon as you arrive. (Large parties should always call ahead to check the reservations policy.)

We mention dress only when men are required to wear a jacket or a jacket and tie.

## DISABILITIES & ACCESSIBILITY

Las Vegas gets a B-plus when it comes to accommodating travelers with disabilities. It's not perfect, but because so much major construction— from sidewalks to megaresorts—is recent, accessibility is very good for most places. Also, Las Vegas is well laid out for people who use wheelchairs: flat, wide sidewalks (especially in the tourist areas) and curb cuts, ramps, and wheelchair elevators and lifts are almost everywhere. Only the crowds make it at all difficult for people in wheelchairs to get around efficiently.

HELP of Southern Nevada refers callers to the proper social agency. Assistance is also available from the Las Vegas Convention and Visitors Authority ADA coordinator.

➤ INFORMATION: **HELP of Southern Nevada** (✉ 953-35B E. Sahara Ave., Las Vegas 89104, ☎ 702/369–4357).

**Las Vegas Convention and Visitors Authority ADA Coordinator** (✉ 3150 Paradise Rd., Las Vegas 89109, ☎ 702/892–7525.).

### LODGING

Despite the Americans with Disabilities Act, the definition of accessibility seems to differ from hotel to hotel. Some properties may be accessible by ADA standards for people with mobility problems but not for people with hearing or vision impairments, for example.

If you have mobility problems, ask for the lowest floor on which accessible services are offered. If you have a hearing impairment, check whether the hotel has devices to alert you

Smart Travel Tips A to Z

visually to the ring of the telephone, a knock at the door, and a fire/emergency alarm. Some hotels provide these devices without charge. Discuss your needs with hotel personnel if this equipment isn't available, so that a staff member can personally alert you in the event of an emergency.

If you're bringing a guide dog, get authorization ahead of time and write down the name of the person with whom you spoke.

Generally, the layouts of most Las Vegas hotels and casinos are such that you have to cross long distances to get from one place to another. These resort-casinos are so big— 3,000 rooms, a dozen restaurants, extensive retail areas, and huge gambling halls—that they're no less than minicities under one roof. Whether you're walking or moving around in a wheelchair, you have to cover a lot of ground.

The Imperial Palace has the most facilities accommodating people with disabilities, including a hydraulic lift at the pool, an Amigo chair in the pit, and more than 100 accessible rooms, many of which feature roll-in showers and transfer chairs. Shake-awake alarm clocks also are available. Most hotels have some rooms that are accessible to travelers in wheelchairs.

➤ WHEELCHAIR-ACCESSIBLE ACCOM-MODATIONS: **Aladdin Resort and Casino** (✉ 3667 Las Vegas Blvd. S, ☎ 702/736–0111). **Caesars Palace** (✉ 3570 Las Vegas Blvd. S, ☎ 702/731–7110). **Excalibur Hotel and Casino** (✉ 3850 Las Vegas Blvd. S, ☎ 702/597–7777). **Lady Luck Casino and Hotel** (✉ 206 N. 3rd St., ☎ 702/477–3000). **Luxor Resort & Casino** (✉ 3900 Las Vegas Blvd. S, ☎ 702/262–4000). **Mandalay Bay Resort & Casino** (✉ 3950 Las Vegas Blvd. S, ☎ 702/632–7777). **MGM Grand Hotel and Casino** (✉ 3799 Las Vegas Blvd. S, ☎ 702/891–1111). **Mirage Hotel and Casino** (✉ 3400 Las Vegas Blvd. S, ☎ 702/791–7111). **Riviera Hotel and Casino** (✉ 2901 Las Vegas Blvd. S, ☎ 702/734–5110).

## RESERVATIONS

When discussing accessibility with an operator or reservations agent, ask hard questions. Are there any stairs, inside *or* out? Are there grab bars next to the toilet *and* in the shower/tub? How wide is the doorway to the room? To the bathroom? For the most extensive facilities meeting the latest legal specifications, **opt for newer accommodations.** If you reserve through a toll-free number, consider also calling the hotel's local number to confirm the information from the central reservations office. Get confirmation in writing when you can.

## SIGHTS & ATTRACTIONS

All major attractions in Las Vegas are accessible for persons with physical disabilities, in accordance with the Americans with Disabilities Act. Call ahead for specific information.

## TRANSPORTATION

**Citizens Area Transit** (☎ 702/228–4800) operates buses in Las Vegas that accommodate persons with disabilities.

➤ COMPLAINTS: **Aviation Consumer Protection Division** (☞ Air Travel) for airline-related problems. **Departmental Office of Civil Rights** (✉ for general inquiries, U.S. Department of Transportation, S-30, 400 7th St. SW, Room 10215, Washington, DC 20590, ☎ 202/366–4648, FAX 202/366–9371, WEB www.dot.gov/ost/docr/index.htm). **Disability Rights Section** (✉ NYAV, U.S. Department of Justice, Civil Rights Division, 950 Pennsylvania Ave. NW, Washington, DC 20530, ☎ ADA information line 202/514–0301, 800/514–0301, 202/514–0383 TTY, 800/514–0383 TTY, WEB www.ada.gov). **U.S. Department of Transportation Hotline** (☎ for disability-related air-travel problems, 800/778–4838 or 800/455–9880 TTY).

## TRAVEL AGENCIES

In the United States, the Americans with Disabilities Act requires that travel firms serve the needs of all travelers. Some agencies specialize in working with people with disabilities.

➤ TRAVELERS WITH MOBILITY PROBLEMS: **Access Adventures** (✉ 206

Chestnut Ridge Rd., Scottsville, NY 14624, ☎ 585/889–9096), run by a former physical-rehabilitation counselor. **Accessible Vans of America** (✉ 9 Spielman Rd., Fairfield, NJ 07004, ☎ 877/282–8267, 973/808–9709 reservations, FAX 973/808–9713, WEB www.accessiblevans.com). **Care-Vacations** (✉ No. 5, 5110–50 Ave., Leduc, Alberta, Canada, T9E 6V4, ☎ 780/986–6404 or 877/478–7827, FAX 780/986–8332, WEB www.carevacations.com), for group tours and cruise vacations. **Flying Wheels Travel** (✉ 143 W. Bridge St., Box 382, Owatonna, MN 55060, ☎ 507/451–5005, FAX 507/451–1685, WEB www.flyingwheelstravel.com).

➤ TRAVELERS WITH DEVELOPMENTAL DISABILITIES: **New Directions** (✉ 5276 Hollister Ave., Suite 207, Santa Barbara, CA 93111, ☎ 805/967–2841 or 888/967–2841, FAX 805/964–7344, WEB www.newdirectionstravel.com).

## DISCOUNTS & DEALS

Some hotels offer "funbooks" with gambling coupons (bet $5 and win $7 on an even-money wager, for example) and discounts for food and attractions. Inquire at the front desk when you check in. The Las Vegas Convention and Visitors Authority has coupon books for discounts and deals at hotels, restaurants, and casinos.

Be a smart shopper and compare all your options before making decisions. A plane ticket bought with a promotional coupon from travel clubs, coupon books, and direct-mail offers or purchased on the Internet may not be cheaper than the least expensive fare from a discount ticket agency. And always keep in mind that what you get is just as important as what you save.

### DISCOUNT RESERVATIONS

To save money, look into discount reservations services with Web sites and toll-free numbers, which use their buying power to get a better price on hotels, airline tickets (☞ Air Travel), even car rentals. When booking a room, always **call the hotel's local toll-free number** (if one is available)

rather than the central reservations number—you'll often get a better price. Always ask about special packages or corporate rates.

➤ AIRLINE TICKETS: **Air 4 Less** (☎ 800/AIR4LESS); low-fare specialist.

➤ HOTEL ROOMS: **Accommodations Express** (☎ 800/444–7666 or 800/277–1064, WEB www.accommodationsexpress.com). **Hotels.com** (☎ 800/246–8357 or 214/369–1246, WEB www.hotels.com). **Quikbook** (☎ 800/789–9887, WEB www.quikbook.com). **RMC Travel** (☎ 800/245–5738, WEB www.rmcwebtravel.com). **Turbotrip.com** (☎ 800/473–7829, WEB www.turbotrip.com).

## PACKAGE DEALS

Don't confuse packages and guided tours. When you buy a package, you travel on your own, just as though you had planned the trip yourself. Fly/drive packages, which combine airfare and car rental, are often a good deal. In cities, ask the local visitor's bureau about hotel packages that include tickets to major museum exhibits or other special events.

## HEALTH

The dry desert air in Las Vegas means that your body will need extra fluids, especially during the punishing summer months. Always drink lots of water even if you're not outside very much. When you're outdoors wear sunscreen in summer and always carry water with you if you plan a long walk.

### DIVERS' ALERT

Do not fly within 24 hours of scuba diving.

## HOLIDAYS

Major national holidays are New Year's Day (Jan. 1); Martin Luther King Day (3rd Mon. in Jan.); Presidents' Day (3rd Mon. in Feb.); Memorial Day (last Mon. in May); Independence Day (July 4); Labor Day (1st Mon. in Sept.); Columbus Day (2nd Mon. in Oct.); Thanksgiving Day (4th Thurs. in Nov.); Christmas

Eve and Christmas Day (Dec. 24 and 25); and New Year's Eve (Dec. 31).

## INSURANCE

The most useful travel-insurance plan is a comprehensive policy that includes coverage for trip cancellation and interruption, default, trip delay, and medical expenses (with a waiver for preexisting conditions).

Without insurance you'll lose all or most of your money if you cancel your trip, regardless of the reason. Default insurance covers you if your tour operator, airline, or cruise line goes out of business. Trip-delay covers expenses that arise because of bad weather or mechanical delays. Study the fine print when comparing policies.

U.K. residents can buy a travel-insurance policy valid for most vacations taken during the year in which it's purchased (but check preexisting-condition coverage).

Always **buy travel policies directly from the insurance company**; if you buy them from a cruise line, airline, or tour operator that goes out of business you probably won't be covered for the agency or operator's default, a major risk. Before making any purchase, review your existing health and home-owner's policies to find what they cover away from home.

➤ INFORMATION: In the U.S.: **Access America** (✉ 6600 W. Broad St., Richmond, VA 23230, ☎ 800/284–8300, FAX 804/673–1491 or 800/346–9265, WEB www.accessamerica.com). **Travel Guard International** (✉ 1145 Clark St., Stevens Point, WI 54481, ☎ 715/345–0505 or 800/826–1300, FAX 800/955–8785, WEB www.travelguard.com).

## LODGING

Hotels book up quickly in Las Vegas. The city is filled with people every weekend, and there are even more visitors during holiday weekends, big conventions, and when prizefights and other major sporting events are held here. Make your hotel reservations as far in advance as possible.

Overbooking is not common; if you have a reservation, you'll get a room.

Call a hotel's toll-free number and ask what package deals it has for your vacation dates. Checking the hotel's Web site is always a good idea as many specials are offered on the Internet only. Another useful guide to bargain rates is the Sunday "Calendar" section of the *Los Angeles Times*, where most Las Vegas hotels advertise.

The lodgings we list are the cream of the crop in each price category. We always list the facilities that are available—but we don't specify whether they cost extra: when pricing accommodations, always ask what's included and what costs extra. Properties marked ✕⊡ are lodging establishments whose restaurants warrant a special trip.

Assume that hotels operate on the **European Plan** (EP, with no meals) unless we specify that they use the **Continental Plan** (CP, with a Continental breakfast), **Breakfast Plan** (BP, with a full breakfast), **Modified American Plan** (MAP, with breakfast and dinner), or the **Full American Plan** (FAP, with all meals).

### APARTMENT & HOME RENTALS

If you're staying in Las Vegas for a week or more, you might want to book a motel suite with a kitchenette at a weekly rate. The savings over a daily rate can be as high as 50%, and with a refrigerator, stove, and microwave, you can also save plenty on meals. Some "snowbirds" stay in these suites throughout the winter and pay monthly rates. **Budget Suites of America** has seven locations—and nearly 4,000 such two-room suites with full kitchen—around the city.

Vacation rentals in Las Vegas are not very common since the abundance of inexpensive hotel rooms and all-suite hotels eliminates the demand. But some **vacation home rentals** (WEB www.vacationrentals.com.) are listed on the Internet. **Hideaways International** is another resource; membership is $129.

➤ CONTACTS: **Budget Suites of America** (☎ 866/877–2000) **Hideaways International** (✉ 767 Islington St., Portsmouth, NH 03802, ☎ 603/430–4433 or 800/843–4433, FAX 603/430–4444, WEB www.hideaways.com).

## HOSTELS

There is only one hostel in Las Vegas. On Las Vegas Boulevard South between downtown and the Strip, Las Vegas International Hostel is easily accessible, although the neighborhood is not the safest at night. It has 55 beds in men's and women's dorms (six beds per dorm room), a handful of very basic private rooms, shared baths (that could use some sprucing up), and a communal kitchen and lounge.

➤ INFORMATION: **Las Vegas International Hostel** (✉ 1208 Las Vegas Blvd. S, ☎ 702/385–9955).

## HOTELS

In general, rates for Las Vegas accommodations are far lower than those in most other American resort and vacation cities, but the situation is a wacky one indeed. There are a hundred different variables, depending on who's selling the rooms (reservations, marketing, casino, conventions, wholesalers, packagers); what rooms you're talking about (standard, deluxe, minisuites, standard suites, deluxe suites, high-roller suites, penthouses, bungalows); demand (weekday, weekend, holiday, conventions or sporting events in town); and management whim (bean-counter profit models, revenue-projection realities, etc.). When business is slow, many hotels reduce rates on rooms in their least desirable sections, sometimes with a buffet breakfast or even a show included. Most "sales" occur from early December to mid-February and July through August, the coldest and hottest times of the year. Members of casino slot clubs often get offers of discounted or even free rooms, and they can almost always reserve a room even when the rest of the hotel is "sold out."

In the larger hotels, it's generally not possible to haggle over room rates, as in, "Well, will you take sixty dollars for the room, instead of seventy-five?" However, prices change continuously: you can call the same hotel several times within a short span and be quoted several different rates. So you should always ask for a lower-priced room.

If the hotel reservations clerks continually tell you they're sold out, try the Las Vegas Convention and Visitors Authority (Daily 6 AM–9 PM PST) room reservations center, which has access to a good selection of the rooms available for any given day. A good source of available rooms and discounts is the Las Vegas Reservations Bureau. They may be able to place you in the hotel of your choice.

➤ CONTACTS: **Las Vegas Convention and Visitors Authority** (☎ 800/332–5333). **Las Vegas Reservations Bureau** (☎ 800/831–2754).

## MAIL & SHIPPING

The main post office is open from 7:30 AM to 9 PM weekdays, 8 AM to 4 PM on Saturdays. Lines are often long. There are drop boxes for overnight delivery services all over town and Mail Boxes Etc. offices in nearly every strip mall.

➤ POST OFFICE: **Main post office** (✉ 1001 E. Sunset Rd., Las Vegas 89193, ☎ 702/361–9472).

➤ SHIPPING: **FedEx** (☎ 800/463–3339). **UPS** (☎ 800/742–5877).

## MARRIAGE LICENSES

When wide-open gambling was legalized in 1931, Nevada also adopted liberal divorce and marriage laws as part of the strategy to attract tourists. The rules haven't changed in seven decades: a divorce can still be obtained after only six weeks of residency and a wedding can be arranged without a blood test or a waiting period; once you have a license, a justice of the peace can unite you in marital bliss in five minutes.

Weddings are big business here, to the tune of more than $4 million in marriage licenses alone. To be among the 123,000-plus couples who tie the knot in Las Vegas every year, simply appear at the Clark County Marriage License Bureau with $55, some identification, and your beloved. It's open between 8 AM and midnight from Monday through Thursday and 24 hours Friday, Saturday, and holidays. New Year's Eve and Valentine's Day are the most popular wedding dates. Even celebrities (including Jon Bon Jovi, Bette Midler, Joan Collins, Michael Jordan, and Richard Gere) have found it handy to pop into a chapel for a quick ceremony.

For a no-frills, justice-of-the-peace nuptial ceremony, visit the Commissioner of Civil Marriages, where a surrogate-J.P. deputy commissioner will unite you in holy matrimony for $35. For a more traditional ambience—flowers, organ music, photos—head to one of Vegas's renowned wedding chapels, where the average nuptials cost $200 to $700 (though you can spend a lot more or a bit less); hotel chapels tend to cost more.

The Candlelight Wedding Chapel opened its doors in 1967; it's small, elegant, and churchlike. Weddings are reasonably priced; the most expensive package comes in at $500. The Little Church of the West is listed on the National Register of Historic Places; the cedar and redwood chapel is one of the most famous chapels in Vegas, sitting on an acre of land at the south end of the Strip. The Little White Chapel, one mi north of the Sahara hotel, is where you can get married in a pink Cadillac while an Elvis impersonator croons. The world-renowned chapel is one of only two that offer drive-through weddings (the other is A Special Memory).

Weddings at Star Trek: The Experience are held on the bridge of the Enterprise-D from Star Trek: The Next Generation; costumed characters, from Federation officers to Klingon warriors, bear witness to the proceedings. The Venetian Resort-Hotel-Casino offers weddings in a recreation of St. Mark's Square, on a replica of the Rialto Bridge or on the Venetian's canal in a gold-and-white gondola. The Viva Las Vegas Wedding Chapel offers theme weddings ranging from Elvis's Blue Hawaii to Egyptian to Fairy Tale. Ever dream of a wedding themed for Charo? Here's where you'll find it.

➤ CONTACTS: **Clark County Marriage License Bureau** (⊠ 200 S. 3rd St., ☎ 702/455–4415, WEB www.co.clark.nv. us). **Commissioner of Civil Marriages** (⊠ 309 S. 3rd St.).

➤ WEDDING CHAPELS: **Candlelight Wedding Chapel** (⊠ 2855 Las Vegas Blvd. S, North Strip, ☎ 702/735–4179 or 800/962–1818, WEB www. nos.net/candlelight). **Little Church of the West** (⊠ 4617 Las Vegas Blvd. S, South Strip, ☎ 702/739–7971 or 800/821–2452). **Little White Chapel** (⊠ 1301 Las Vegas Blvd. S, North Strip, ☎ 702/382–3546 or 800/545–8111, WEB www.littlewhitechapel. com). **Star Trek: The Experience** (⊠ 3000 S. Paradise Blvd., North Strip, ☎ 702/697–8750 or 800/774–1500, WEB www.startrekexp.com). **Venetian Resort-Hotel-Casino** (⊠ 3355 Las Vegas Blvd. S, Center Strip, ☎ 702/414–4280 or 800/883–6423, WEB www.venetian.com). **Viva Las Vegas Wedding Chapel** (⊠ 1205 Las Vegas Blvd. S, North Strip, ☎ 702/384–0771 or 800/574–4450, WEB www.vivalasvegasweddings.com).

## MEDIA

### NEWSPAPERS & MAGAZINES

The morning *Las Vegas Review-Journal* is the largest daily newspaper in Nevada; its Friday entertainment section is called "Neon." The *Las Vegas Sun* is an afternoon daily. It is smaller, but has good local coverage. The *Las Vegas Mercury, City Life,* and *Las Vegas Weekly* are free alternative papers.

Published bi-monthly, *Las Vegas Magazine* offers fashion, food, entertainment, and news articles for locals and visitors. The monthly *Las Vegas Style Magazine* focuses primarily on the hotel-casino business and features gossip and articles on food and entertainment. Published by the state, the bi-monthly *Nevada Magazine* is one of the oldest magazines in the west (since 1936); it has a large section covering Las Vegas events.

### RADIO & TELEVISION

Local AM radio stations include KDWN 720 (talk, news, sports), KXNT 840 (talk), KBAD 920 (sports), KNUU 970 (news, talk), and KENO 1460 (sports, talk).

Among the local FM radio stations are KNPR 89.5 (National Public Radio), KOMP 92.3 (rock), KWNR 95.5 (country), KKLZ 96.3 (classic rock), KLUC 98.5 (Top 40), KJUL 104.3 (classic adult), KHWY 98/99 (contemporary, highway news), and KQOL 93.1 (oldies).

The network television stations are KVBC (3, NBC), KVVU (5, Fox), KLAS (8, CBS), KTNV (13, ABC), KVWB (21, cable 12, WB) and KTUD (25, cable 14, UPN). The public TV station is KLVX (10).

### MONEY MATTERS

The prices of typical items in Las Vegas range from gratis to outrageous. For example, you can get a good deli sandwich at one of the rock-bottom casino snack bars (Riviera, Westward Ho) for $2–$3, or you can spend $12 for a skyscraper special at the Stage Deli in the Forum Shops at Caesars. A cup of coffee in a casino coffee shop will set you back $2–$2.50, while that same cuppa is free if you happen to be sitting at a nickel slot machine when the cocktail waitress comes by. A taxi from the airport to the MGM Grand goes as low as $10 if you tell the driver to take Tropicana Avenue and there's no traffic, or runs as high as $25 if you take the Airport Connector and there's a wreck on the freeway. The more you know about Las Vegas, the less it'll cost you.

The Strip is expensive and if you're on a budget then consider having meals at the buffets in downtown Las Vegas which are generally more of a bargain. For shopping, the locals save money by driving 5 mi south of the Strip to the **Belz Factory Outlet World** (⌂ 7400 Las Vegas Blvd. S, ☎ 702/896–5599), where you'll find 155 shops where you can purchase items such as designer wear at reduced prices.

Prices throughout this guide are given for adults. Substantially reduced fees are almost always available for children, students, and senior citizens. For information on taxes, *see* Taxes.

### ATMS

ATMs are widely available in Las Vegas; they're at every bank and at most casinos, hotels, minimarts, convenience stores, and gas stations as well. In addition, all casinos have cash-advance machines, which take credit cards. You just indicate how large a cash advance you want, and when the transaction is approved you pick up the cash at the casino cashier. But beware: you'll pay up to a 12% fee in addition to the usual cash-advance charges and interest rate for this convenience; in most cases, the credit card company begins charging interest the moment the advance is taken, so you will not have the usual grace period to pay your balance in full before interest begins to accrue.

### CREDIT CARDS

Throughout this guide, the following abbreviations are used: AE, American Express; D, Discover; DC, Diners Club; MC, MasterCard; and V, Visa.

➤ REPORTING LOST CARDS: **American Express** (☎ 800/441–0519). **Diners Club** (☎ 800/234–6377). **Discover** (☎ 800/347–2683). **MasterCard** (☎ 800/622–7747). **Visa** (☎ 800/847–2911).

## NATIONAL PARKS

Look into discount passes to save money on park entrance fees. For $50, the National Parks Pass admits you (and any passengers in your private vehicle) to all national parks, monuments, and recreation areas, as well as other sites run by the National Park Service, for a year. (In parks that charge per person, the pass admits you, your spouse and children, and your parents, when you arrive together.) Camping and parking are extra. The $15 Golden Eagle Pass, a hologram you affix to your National Parks Pass, functions as an upgrade, granting entry to all sites run by the NPS, the U.S. Fish and Wildlife Service, the U.S. Forest Service, and the Bureau of Land Management. The upgrade, which expires with the parks pass, is sold by most national-park, Fish-and-Wildlife, and BLM fee stations. A percentage of the proceeds from pass sales funds National Parks projects.

Both the Golden Age Passport ($10), for U.S. citizens or permanent residents who are 62 and older, and the Golden Access Passport (free), for those with disabilities, entitle holders (and any passengers in their private vehicles) to lifetime free entry to all national parks, plus 50% off fees for the use of many park facilities and services. (The discount doesn't always apply to companions.) To obtain them, you must show proof of age and of U.S. citizenship or permanent residency—such as a U.S. passport, driver's license, or birth certificate—and, if requesting Golden Access, proof of disability. The Golden Age and Golden Access passes are available only at NPS-run sites that charge an entrance fee. The National Parks Pass is also available by mail and via the Internet.

➤ PARKS INFORMATION: **National Park Foundation** (⊠ 11 Dupont Circle NW, 6th floor, Washington, DC 20036, ☎ 202/238–4200, WEB www. nationalparks.org). **National Park Service** (⊠ National Park Service/Department of Interior, 1849 C St. NW, Washington, DC 20240, ☎ 202/208–6843, WEB www.nps.gov). **National Parks Conservation Association**

(⊠ 1300 19th St. NW, Suite 300, Washington, DC 20036, ☎ 202/223–6722, WEB www.npca.org).

➤ PASSES BY MAIL & ON-LINE: **National Park Foundation** (WEB www. nationalparks.org). **National Parks Pass** (⊠ Box 34108, Washington, DC 20043, ☎ 888/467–2757, WEB www. nationalparks.org); include a check or money order payable to the National Park Service, plus $3.95 for shipping and handling, or call for passes by phone.

## PACKING

Ever since the original Frontier Casino opened on the Los Angeles Highway (now the Strip), visitors to Las Vegas have been invited to "Come as You Are." The warm weather and informal character of Las Vegas render casual clothing appropriate day and night.

Always wear comfortable shoes; no matter what your intentions may be, you'll find yourself covering a lot of ground on foot.

In your carry-on luggage, pack an extra pair of eyeglasses or contact lenses and enough of any medication you take to last a few days longer than the entire trip. You may also ask your doctor to write a spare prescription using the drug's generic name, as brand names may vary from country to country. **In luggage to be checked, never pack prescription drugs, valuables, or undeveloped film.** And don't forget to carry with you the addresses of offices that handle refunds of lost traveler's checks. Check *Fodor's How to Pack* (available at on-line retailers and bookstores everywhere) for more tips.

To avoid customs and security delays, carry medications in their original packaging. Don't pack any sharp objects in your carry-on luggage, including knives of any size or material, scissors, and corkscrews, or anything else that might arouse suspicion.

To avoid having your checked luggage chosen for hand inspection, don't cram bags full. The U.S. Transportation Security Administration suggests packing shoes on top and placing personal items you don't want touched in clear plastic bags.

## CHECKING LUGGAGE

You're allowed to carry aboard one bag and one personal article, such as a purse or a laptop computer. Make sure what you carry on fits under your seat or in the overhead bin. Get to the gate early, so you can board as soon as possible, before the overhead bins fill up.

Baggage allowances vary by carrier, destination, and ticket class. On international flights, you're usually allowed to check two bags weighing up to 70 pounds (32 kilograms) each, although a few airlines allow checked bags of up to 88 pounds (40 kilograms) in first class. Some international carriers don't allow more than 66 pounds (30 kilograms) per bag in business class and 44 pounds (20 kilograms) in economy. On domestic flights, the limit may be 50 pounds (23 kilograms) per bag. Most airlines won't accept bags that weigh more than 100 pounds (45 kilograms) on domestic or international flights. Check baggage restrictions with your carrier before you pack.

Airline liability for baggage is limited to $2,500 per person on flights within the United States. On international flights it amounts to $9.07 per pound or $20 per kilogram for checked baggage (roughly $640 per 70-pound bag) and $400 per passenger for unchecked baggage. You can buy additional coverage at check-in for about $10 per $1,000 of coverage, but it often excludes a rather extensive list of items, shown on your airline ticket.

Before departure, **itemize your bags' contents** and their worth, and label the bags with your name, address, and phone number. (If you use your home address, cover it so potential thieves can't see it readily.) Include a label inside each bag and pack a copy of your itinerary. At check-in, make sure each bag is correctly tagged with the destination airport's three-letter code. Because some checked bags will be opened for hand inspection, the U.S. Transportation Security Administration recommends that you leave luggage unlocked or use the plastic locks offered at check-in. TSA screeners place an inspection notice inside searched bags, which are re-sealed with a special lock.

If your bag has been searched and contents are missing or damaged, file a claim with the TSA Consumer Response Center as soon as possible. If your bags arrive damaged or fail to arrive at all, file a written report with the airline before leaving the airport.

➤ COMPLAINTS: **U.S. Transportation Security Administration Consumer Response Center** (☎ 866/289–9673, WEB www.tsa.gov).

## REST ROOMS

Free rest rooms can be found in every casino.

## SAFETY

The well-known areas of Las Vegas are among the safest places for visitors in the world. With so many people carrying so much cash, security is tight inside and out. The casinos have visitors under constant surveillance, and hotel security guards are never more than a few seconds away. Outside, police are highly visible, on foot and bicycles and in cruisers. But this doesn't mean you can throw all safety consciousness to the wind. You should take the same precautions you would in any city—be aware of what's going on around you, stick to well-lighted areas, and quickly move away from any situation or people that might be threatening—especially if you're carrying some gambling cash. **It's wise not to stray too far off the three main streets downtown: Fremont, Ogden, and Carson between Main and Las Vegas Boulevard.**

Be especially careful with your purse and change buckets around slot machines. Grab-and-run thieves are always looking for easy pickings, especially downtown.

## WOMEN IN LAS VEGAS

Apart from their everyday vulnerability to aggressive men, women should have few problems with unwanted attention in Las Vegas. If something does happen inside a casino, simply go to any pit and ask a boss to call security. The problem will disappear in seconds. Outside, crowds are almost always thick on the Strip and downtown, and there's safety in numbers.

Men in Las Vegas need to be on guard against predatory women. "Trick roller" is the name of a particularly nasty breed of female con artist. These women are expert at meeting single men by "chance." After getting friendly in the casino, the woman joins the man in his hotel room, where she slips powerful knockout drugs into his drink and robs him blind. Some men don't wake up.

## SENIOR-CITIZEN TRAVEL

Las Vegas is such a bargain town in general that special subsidies and discounts for seniors are uncommon. Some casinos—Four Queens, Boulder Station—give seniors special deals through their slot clubs; ask when you join.

To qualify for age-related discounts, **mention your senior-citizen status up front** when booking hotel reservations (not when checking out) and before you're seated in restaurants (not when paying the bill). Be sure to have identification on hand. When renting a car, ask about promotional car-rental discounts, which can be cheaper than senior-citizen rates.

➤ EDUCATIONAL PROGRAMS: **Elderhostel** (✉ 11 Ave. de Lafayette, Boston, MA 02111-1746, ☎ 877/426-8056, 978/323-4141 international callers, 877/426-2167 TTY, FAX 877/426-2166, WEB www.elderhostel.org).

## SIGHTSEEING TOURS

### BOAT TOURS

The *Desert Princess*, a 250-passenger Mississippi River–style stern-wheeler, cruises Lake Mead. Tours include 90-minute sightseeing cruises, two-hour dinner cruises, and three-hour dinner and dancing excursions.

➤ INFORMATION: *Desert Princess* (✉ Lake Mead marina,, ☎ 702/293-6180).

### BUS TOURS

Gray Line offers city tours, trips to Red Rock Canyon, Lake Mead, and Valley of Fire, and longer trips to the Grand Canyon and Death Valley.

➤ BUS INFORMATION: **Gray Line Tours** (✉ 4020 E. Lone Mountain Rd., Las Vegas 89031, ☎ 702/384-1234 or 800/634-6579).

## HELICOPTER TOURS

Helicopters do two basic tours in and around Las Vegas: a brief flyover of the Strip and a several-hour trip out to the Grand Canyon and back.

➤ TOUR INFORMATION: **Sundance Helicopters** (✉ 5596 Haven St., Las Vegas 89119, ☎ 702/736-0606, WEB www.helicoptour.com).

## STUDENTS IN LAS VEGAS

No special discounts or considerations are offered students in Las Vegas. No one under 21 is allowed in the casinos.

➤ I.D.s & SERVICES: **STA Travel** (✉ 10 Downing St., New York, NY 10014, ☎ 212/627-3111 or 800/777-0112, FAX 212/627-3387, WEB www.sta.com). **Travel Cuts** (✉ 187 College St., Toronto, Ontario M5T 1P7, Canada, ☎ 416/979-2406, 800/592-2887, 866/246-9762 in Canada, FAX 416/979-8167, WEB www.travelcuts.com).

## TAXES

Las Vegas and Reno-Tahoe international airports assess a $3 departure tax, or passenger facility charge. The hotel room tax is 10% in Las Vegas.

### SALES TAX

The sales tax rates for the areas covered in this guide are: Las Vegas, 7.25%; Arizona, 5%; and Utah, 4.75%.

## TAXIS

Las Vegas is heavily covered by taxicabs. You'll find cabs waiting at the airport and at every hotel in town. If you dine at a restaurant off the Strip, the restaurant will call a taxi to take you home.

The fare is $2.70 on the meter when you get in, plus $1.80 for every mile. Taxis are limited by law to carrying a maximum of four passengers, and there is no additional charge per person. No fees are assessed for luggage, but taxis leaving the airport are allowed to add an airport surcharge of $1.20.

➤ TAXIS: **Desert Cab** (☎ 702/386–9102). **Whittlesea Henderson Cab** (☎ 702/384–6111). **Checker/Yellow/Star** (☎ 702/873–2000).

## TIME

The states of Nevada and California are in the Pacific time zone. Arizona and Utah are in the Mountain time zone. Arizona does not observe daylight saving time.

## TIPPING

More so than in other U.S. destinations, workers in Las Vegas are paid a minimum wage and rely on tips to make up the primary part of their income. At restaurants, a 15% tip is standard for waiters; up to 20% may be expected at more expensive establishments. The same goes for taxi drivers, bartenders, and hairdressers. Coat-check operators usually expect $1; bellhops and porters should get 50¢ to $1 per bag. Maids should receive at least 4%–5% of the room-rate total, before taxes, for rooms that cost $100 a night or more. If the room is less than $100 per night, then 3%–4%. If the hotel charges a service fee, be sure to ask what it covers, as it may include this gratuity. A 50¢ or $1 tip per drink is appropriate for cocktail waitresses, even when they bring you a free drink at a slot machine or casino table. On package tours, conductors and drivers usually get $10 per day from the group as a whole; check whether this has already been figured into your cost. For local sightseeing tours, you may individually tip the driver-guide $1 if he or she has been helpful or informative. Tip dealers with the equivalent of your average bet once or twice an hour if you're winning; slot-machine change personnel and keno runners are accustomed to a buck or two. Ushers in showrooms may be able to get you better seats for performances for a gratuity of $5 or more. Tip the concierge 10%–20% of the cost for a ticket to a hot show. Tip $5–$10 for making dinner reservations or arrangements for other attractions.

## TOURS & PACKAGES

Because everything is prearranged on a prepackaged tour or independent vacation, you spend less time planning—and often get it all at a good price.

### BOOKING WITH AN AGENT

Travel agents are excellent resources. But it's a good idea to collect brochures from several agencies, as some agents' suggestions may be influenced by relationships with tour and package firms that reward them for volume sales. If you have a special interest, **find an agent with expertise in that area**; the American Society of Travel Agents (ASTA; ☞ Travel Agencies) has a database of specialists worldwide.

Make sure your travel agent knows the accommodations and other services of the place being recommended. Ask about the hotel's location, room size, beds, and whether it has a pool, room service, or programs for children, if you care about these. Has your agent been there in person or sent others whom you can contact?

Do some homework on your own, too: local tourism boards can provide information about lesser-known and small-niche operators, some of which may sell only direct.

### BUYER BEWARE

Each year consumers are stranded or lose their money when tour operators—even large ones with excellent reputations—go out of business. So check out the operator. Ask several travel agents about its reputation, and try to **book with a company that has a consumer-protection program.** (Look for information in the company's brochure.) In the United States, members of the National Tour Association and the United States Tour Operators Association are required to set aside funds to cover payments and travel arrangements in the event that the company defaults. It's also a good idea to choose a company that participates in the American Society of Travel Agents' Tour Operator Program; ASTA will act as mediator in any disputes between you and your tour operator.

Remember that the more your package or tour includes, the better you can predict the ultimate cost of your vacation. Make sure you know exactly what is covered, and beware of hidden costs. Are taxes, tips, and transfers included? Entertainment and excursions? These can add up.

➤ TOUR-OPERATOR RECOMMENDATIONS: **American Society of Travel Agents** (☞ Travel Agencies). **National Tour Association (NTA)** (✉ 546 E. Main St., Lexington, KY 40508, ☎ 859/226–4444 or 800/682–8886, FAX 859/226–4404, WEB www.ntaonline.com). **United States Tour Operators Association (USTOA)** (✉ 275 Madison Ave., Suite 2014, New York, NY 10016, ☎ 212/599–6599 or 800/468–7862, FAX 212/599–6744, WEB www.ustoa.com).

## TRAIN TRAVEL

You can't take a train to Las Vegas, but Amtrak can get you there via a Thruway bus from Los Angeles. You can pick up a timetable at any Amtrak station or request one by mail. Amtrak accepts all major credit cards and personal checks. You can purchase tickets aboard trains; however, an additional charge applies if the ticket office is open at your time of departure.

➤ TRAIN INFORMATION: **Amtrak** (☎ 800/872–7245, WEB www.amtrak.com).

## TRANSPORTATION AROUND LAS VEGAS

Though you can get around Las Vegas fine without a car, the best way to experience the city may be to drive it. A car gives you easy access to all the casinos and attractions, lets you make excursions to Lake Mead and elsewhere at your leisure, and gives you the chance to cruise the Strip and bask in its neon glow.

Parking on and around the Strip, although free, is not so easy. You'll have to brave some rather immense parking structures and walk up and down stairs or escalators. Valet parking is available if you're willing to

wait your turn and tip the valets. Taxis are an easy way to go door to door, although the downside is that you can't hail one off the street, so waiting in line at hotels is the only way to get a cab. During busy weekends, the wait can run anywhere from 10 to 30 minutes. Buses don't always run on time and they're frequently crowded. If you're not covering great distances, and when the weather is decent, the best way to get around Las Vegas is on foot.

## TRAVEL AGENCIES

A good travel agent puts your needs first. Look for an agency that has been in business at least five years, emphasizes customer service, and has someone on staff who specializes in your destination. In addition, **make sure the agency belongs to a professional trade organization.** The American Society of Travel Agents (ASTA)—the largest and most influential in the field with more than 20,000 members in some 140 countries—maintains and enforces a strict code of ethics and will step in to help mediate any agent-client disputes involving ASTA members if necessary. ASTA (whose motto is "Without a travel agent, you're on your own") also maintains a Web site that includes a directory of agents. (If a travel agency is also acting as your tour operator, *see* Buyer Beware *in* Tours and Packages.)

➤ INFORMATION: **American Society of Travel Agents(ASTA)** (✉ 1101 King St., Suite 200, Alexandria, VA 22314, ☎ 703/739–2782 or 800/965–2782 24-hr hot line, FAX 703/739–3268, WEB www.astanet.com). **Association of British Travel Agents** (✉ 68–71 Newman St., London W1T 3AH, ☎ 020/7637–2444, FAX 020/7637–0713, WEB www.abtanet.com). **Association of Canadian Travel Agents** (✉ 130 Albert St., Suite 1705, Ottawa, Ontario K1P 5G4, ☎ 613/237–3657, FAX 613/237–7052, WEB www.acta.ca). **Australian Federation of Travel Agents** (✉ Level 3, 309 Pitt St., Sydney, NSW 2000, ☎ 02/9264–3299, FAX 02/9264–1085, WEB www.afta.com.au). **Travel Agents' Association of New Zealand** (✉ Level 5, Tourism and Travel House, 79 Boulcott St., Box 1888, Wellington 6001,

☎ 04/499–0104, FAX 04/499–0786, WEB www.taanz.org.nz).

## VISITOR INFORMATION

Before you go, contact the city and state tourism offices for general information. When you get there, visit the Las Vegas Convention and Visitors Authority, next door to the Las Vegas Hilton, for brochures and general information. Hotels and gift shops on the Strip have maps, brochures, pamphlets, and free events magazines—*What's On in Las Vegas, Las Vegas Today,* and *Tourguide*—that list shows and buffets and offer discounts to area attractions.

The *Las Vegas Advisor,* a 12-page monthly newsletter, keeps up-to-the-minute track of the constantly changing Las Vegas landscapes of gambling, accommodations, dining, entertainment, Top Ten Values, complimentary offerings, and more, and is an indispensable resource for any Las Vegas visitor. Send $5 for a sample issue.

➤ CITY TOURIST INFORMATION: **Las Vegas Convention and Visitors Authority** (✉ 3150 Paradise Rd., Las Vegas, NV 89109, ☎ 702/892–0711, FAX 702/892–2824, WEB www.lvcva. com). **Las Vegas Chamber of Commerce** (✉ 3720 Howard Hughes Pkwy., Las Vegas, NV 89109, ☎ 702/735–1616, FAX 702/735–2011). **Las Vegas Advisor** (✉ 3687 S. Procyon Ave., Las Vegas, NV 89103, ☎ 702/252–0655 or 800/634–6753).

➤ STATE TOURIST INFORMATION: **Nevada Commission on Tourism** (✉ 401 N. Carson St., Carson City, NV 89701, ☎ 800/638–2328, FAX 702/687–6779).

➤ GOVERNMENT ADVISORIES: **Consular Affairs Bureau of Canada** (☎ 800/267–6788 or 613/944–6788, WEB www.voyage.gc.ca). **U.K. Foreign and Commonwealth Office** (✉ Travel Advice Unit, Consular Division, Old Admiralty Building, London SW1A 2PA, ☎ 020/7008–0232 or 020/7008–0233, WEB www.fco. gov.uk/travel). **Australian Department of Foreign Affairs and Trade** (☎ 02/6261–1299 Consular Travel Advice Faxback Service, WEB www. dfat.gov.au). **New Zealand Ministry of Foreign Affairs and Trade** (☎ 04/439–8000, WEB www.mft.govt.nz).

## WEB SITES

Do check out the World Wide Web when planning your trip. You'll find everything from weather forecasts to virtual tours of famous cities. Be sure to **visit Fodors.com** (WEB www.fodors. com.), a complete travel-planning site. You can research prices and book plane tickets, hotel rooms, rental cars, vacation packages, and more. In addition, you can post your pressing questions in the Travel Talk section. Other planning tools include a currency converter and weather reports, and there are loads of links to travel resources.

The Web site of the **Las Vegas Convention and Visitors Authority** (WEB www.lvcva.com) has travel tips, events calendars, and other resources, as well as links to other visitor-oriented Nevada-based Web sites. The **Las Vegas Chamber of Commerce** (WEB www.lvchamber. com) has lots of useful information, including visitor tips, local businesses, even relocation advice.

**LasVegas.com** (WEB www.lasvegas. com) has a partnership with the *Las Vegas Review-Journal,* and it offers travel information and reservations.

**VEGAS.com** (WEB www.vegas.com) advertises that, in Las Vegas, "it's who you know." Part of the Greenspun Media Group that also publishes the *Las Vegas Sun,* VEGAS.com offers information about and instant booking capabilities for everything from hotels to shows.

One of the oldest sites is **Las Vegas Leisure Guide** (WEB www.pcap.com), full of hotel, restaurant, and nightlife info. **Las Vegas Online Entertainment Guide** (WEB www.lvol.com) has listings for hotels and an on-line reservations system, plus local history, restaurants, a business directory, and even some gambling instruction.

## WHEN TO GO

Las Vegas is a year-round destination. Except for the first three weeks in December and weekdays during July, you can assume that Las Vegas will be running at full speed. Weekends, always crowded, are especially jam-packed for the Super Bowl,

Valentine's Day, President's Day, the NCAA Final Four, Easter, Cinco de Mayo, Memorial Day, July 4, and Labor Day. The week between Christmas and New Year's is the most crowded week of the year. In addition, nearly 50 conventions of more than 10,000 participants are held here every year; prices skyrocket, availability plummets, and the hordes fill every open space. Sporting events, such as boxing matches, golf tournaments, the National Finals Rodeo and the NASCAR Winston Cup Las Vegas 400, also have a major impact on the crowd situation. It's a good idea to contact the **Las Vegas Convention and Visitors Authority** (☎ 702/892–0711, WEB www.lvcva.com) to find out who or what will be in town at the time you're planning to visit.

During a "normal" week—that fairly rare time of no conventions, holidays, title fights, or local events—you can count on Sunday through Thursday being less crowded, less expensive, and less stressful than the weekend. During even a routine weekend, however, traffic jams—along with competition for room, restaurant, and show reservations, as well as spots at the slots or tables—can be ferocious.

## CLIMATE

The most comfortable times to be in Las Vegas are the spring and fall. In April and May, daytime temperatures are delightful, between 70 and 90°F. In September and October, the summer heat has abated, and the pools remain open.

Winter is a distinctly different season, with snowcapped mountains in the distance, windy and chilly days, and surprisingly cold nights. The three weeks before Christmas find Las Vegas nearly deserted, with rooms going for bargain rates and hardly a traffic jam on the Strip.

Summer is a time of dry, uncomfortably hot weather (sometimes literally 110°F in the shade), when lounging at an outdoor pool requires protection from the relentless desert sun. You'll probably find yourself continuously thirsty. At the height of the heat, however, hotels offer their lowest rates.

➤ FORECASTS: **Weather Channel Connection** (☎ 900/932–8437, 95¢ per minute from a Touch-Tone phone, WEB www.weather.com).

| Jan. | 60F | 16C | May | 89F | 32C | Sept. | 95F | 35C |
|------|-----|-----|------|------|-----|-------|-----|-----|
|      | 28  | −2  |      | 51   | 11  |       | 57  | 14  |
| Feb. | 66F | 19C | June | 98F | 37C | Oct. | 84F | 29C |
|      | 33  | 1   |      | 60   | 16  |       | 46  | 8   |
| Mar. | 71F | 22C | July | 102F | 39C | Nov. | 71F | 22C |
|      | 39  | 4   |      | 68   | 20  |       | 35  | 2   |
| Apr. | 80F | 27C | Aug. | 102F | 39C | Dec. | 60F | 16C |
|      | 44  | 7   |      | 66   | 19  |       | 30  | −1  |

## ON THE CALENDAR

Las Vegas is not known for specific celebrations—the Strip is the venue for a never-ending parade. Still, a number of annual events do attract wide attention. They are listed below, along with the major conventions that take place annually in Las Vegas, which affect everything from room rates and rental car availability to lines at buffets and crowds at the crap tables.

➤ EARLY DEC.: **National Finals Rodeo,** the Super Bowl of rodeos, brings together 15 finalists to compete in each of seven events; there are 10 performances in nine days at the Thomas and Mack Center. When the rodeo comes to town, the showrooms all feature country music, and it seems as though everyone on the street is wearing jeans, boots, and a cowboy hat. ☎ 702/731–2115.

➤ MID DEC.: In the **Parade of Lights,** boats large and small, all decked out in holiday lights, come together in a flotilla of illumination on Lake Mead. It's most fun to be on a boat, but it's also exciting to watch from the shoreline along Lakeshore Drive. ☎ 702/293–8947 or 702/293–8907.

➤ DEC. 31: **New Year's Eve** is celebrated with fireworks over various casino-hotels all along the Strip and in downtown Las Vegas. ☏ 702/892–0711.

➤ EARLY JAN.: The **Consumer Electronics Show** is a convention that attracts upwards of 125,000 participants.

➤ LATE JAN.: The **Las Vegas International Marathon** draws more than 5,000 runners. The starting line changes from year to year, but the finish line of the 5K race is Vacation Village, 2 mi south of Mandalay Bay. ☏ 702/294–1588.

➤ MID-FEB.: The early spring **Men's Apparel Guild Convention,** aka MAGIC, attracts some 100,000 participants.

➤ EARLY MAR.: The **NASCAR Winston Cup Race** is the largest sporting event of the year in Nevada. Some 135,000 racing fans converge on Las Vegas to watch the grueling 400-mi race on the 1½-mi track, with top national drivers competing for $3 million in prize money. ☏ 702/644–4444.

➤ MID-MAR.: The triennial **Conexpo** trade show is the largest show of its kind in the western hemisphere, focusing on construction products (e.g. cement) and drawing over 150,000 attendees over four days. The next show is scheduled for 2005.

➤ MAR. 17: **St. Patrick's Day** in Las Vegas is a festive occasion, with many of the casinos decorated in green and serving bargain corned-beef-and-cabbage dinners.

➤ EARLY APR.: **NHRA Drag Racing** is one of the newer racing events in Las Vegas. The National Hot Rod Association races take place at the Las Vegas Motor Speedway, which recently completed a ¼-mi drag strip and 80,000-seat grandstand. ☏ 702/644–4444.

➤ APRIL: The **LPGA Invitational golf tournament** draws top women golfers. ☏ 702/894–9746.

➤ MID-APR.: The **National Association of Broadcasters** convention fills the town with 125,000 attendees, including a bevy of major TV and movie celebrities.

➤ APRIL: The **Clark County Fair** takes place 60 mi north of Las Vegas in Logandale. ☏ 702/398–3247.

➤ APR.–MAY: The **World Series of Poker** draws crowds to the Binion's Horseshoe casino to watch the poker faces of players from around the world. This month-long tournament culminates in a four-day final round in which nearly 300 players each invest $10,000 in the hope of winning first prize: $1 million. ☏ 702/382–1600.

➤ MAY: The **Gay Pride Parade** is a five-day event, including a lighted night parade in downtown Las Vegas, plus parties and concerts. ☏ 702/395–4938.

➤ JUNE: **CineVegas Film Festival** is a nine-day event featuring works by local filmmakers (including film students at UNLV) as well as movies about Las Vegas. ☏ 702/368–2890 or 800/675–8482.

➤ EARLY JUL.: **Damboree Days** is a weekend-long festival in Boulder City that coincides with the July Fourth holiday. It culminates in the largest fireworks event in the area. ☏ 702/293–2034.

➤ LATE AUG.: The early fall **Men's Apparel Guild Convention,** aka MAGIC, attracts 100,000 participants.

➤ SEPT.: The **International Las Vegas Triathlon** draws top competitors to Lake Mead National Recreation Area.

➤ SEPT.: Masses of hot-air balloons take to the sky for the **Las Vegas Balloon Classic.** ☏ 702/247–6905.

➤ MID-SEPT.: **Football season** begins at the University of Nevada–Las Vegas. ☏ 702/895–3900.

➤ MID-SEPT.: The **World Gaming Congress and Expo** only attracts 25,000–30,000 attendees, so it barely makes a dent in hotel occupancy rates. But all the new-generation slot and video-poker machines, table games, and casino paraphernalia are on display at the Las Vegas Convention and Visitors Authority. ☏ 702/892–0711.

➤ EARLY OCT.: **Art in the Park,** one of the largest events of the year in Boulder City, is an early Christmas crafts fair, with artists and craftsmen displaying their wares in Bicentennial Park in downtown Boulder City. ☏ 702/293–2034.

➤ MID-OCT.: The **Las Vegas Invitational golf tournament,** a five-day event, is played on three courses, with television coverage. ☎ *702/242–3018.*

➤ EARLY NOV.: The **AAPEX/Automotive After-market Products** is a huge trade show bringing in over 90,000 participants.

➤ MID-NOV.: The **Comdex** computer hardware, software, and electronics convention, held the week before Thanksgiving, is one of the largest conventions of the year in Las Vegas. It attracts 225,000 participants and fills the town to the gills.

➤ NOV.: The **Pro Bull Riders Finals** is the two-day Super Bowl of the bull-riders circuit. The top 50 bull-riders compete for a $1-million purse. ☎ *800/739–0339.*

# 1 DESTINATION: LAS VEGAS

Bright Lights, Gambling, Growth

What's Where

Pleasures and Pastimes

# BRIGHT LIGHTS, GAMBLING, GROWTH

**ILLUSION IS EVERYWHERE** in Las Vegas. A 50-story Eiffel Tower looms over the Strip, gondoliers "o sole mio" their way down an ersatz Grand Canal, and acres of neon turn night into multicolored day. Gamblers defy reason (and the considerable odds against winning) in their attempts to seduce the goddess of chance, while onstage extravaganzas manipulate reality with mind-bending special effects. Even a meal can be an adventure, whether at an over-the-top, all-you-can-eat buffet or in a house of haute cuisine that you wouldn't expect to find in the Nevada desert. Head out of town and you'll come across otherworldly landscapes that nature has etched over the years. Yes, a trip to Las Vegas offers a chance to surrender to fantasy—and you'll have the time of your life doing it.

The Las Vegas of the Strip and downtown is the Rockettes and Cirque du Soleil. It's cards, dice, roulette wheels, and slots. It's harried keno runners and leggy cocktail waitresses, grizzled pit bosses and nervous break-in dealers. It's cab and limo drivers, valet attendants, and bellmen. Las Vegas is showgirls with smiles as white as spotlights and head wear as big and bright as fireworks. It's a place where thousands of people earn their living counting billions in chips, change, bills, checks, and markers.

Gimmicks, glitz, and gigawatts of electrical power are what keep Las Vegas humming day and night, not to mention the more than 36 million casino-bound visitors who arrive every year and bed down in some of the world's largest, showiest hotels (the city has 18 of the 21 biggest in the world). Vegas Vic and Vicky, the 50-ft-tall ambassadors of Glitter Gulch, are forever duded up in high western style to give gamblers a flashy welcome. Locals aren't spinning yarns when they say you can hear the buzz of Las Vegas neon in the quiet of the Mojave Desert, as far as 10 mi beyond the city limits.

While the Strip and downtown are the best known and principal tourist areas of the city, more than 1 million people live—and lead "normal" lives—within 10 mi of them. Endless subdivisions enclose rows and rows of pink-stucco and red-tile, three-bedroom-two-bath houses, most of them fewer than five years old and occupied by transplants hoping to cash in on the boom. "Lost Wages" is a city of dreamers: gamblers hoping to beat the odds and get rich; dancers, singers, magicians, acrobats, and comedians praying to make it in the Entertainment Capital of the World; and increasingly realtors, supermarket cashiers, computer techs, credit card accounting clerks, shoe salesmen, and librarians seeking a better way of life.

For all the local talk about Las Vegas citizens being average people who just happen to live and work in an unusual city, living here is undeniably different. The town is full of people whose jobs involve catering to strangers 24 hours a day, 365 days a year. Las Vegas probably has the largest graveyard shift in the world. And the notion that locals never gamble and rarely see a show or eat at a buffet is also largely a myth—residents are a large and active part of the total market that relishes 99¢ breakfasts and $5 prime ribs, slot clubs, casino paycheck-cashing promotions, and free lounge entertainment. Indeed, the casinos that cater primarily to locals (Palace Station, Boulder Station, Texas Station, the Rio, Gold Coast, Orleans, Santa Fe, Arizona Charlie's, and Fiesta) are among the most successful in town. Surprisingly, Las Vegas is also a religious town—about a third of the 450 congregations here are Mormon—which adds a somewhat incongruous conservative dimension to local politics and morals.

**GAMBLING AND TOURISM** are not the only games in town. Nellis Air Force Base employs thousands of people. The construction industry is huge. Large corporations and small manufacturing firms frequently relocate to southern Nevada, which offers tax incentives as well as a lower cost of living. But local life is merely a curiosity to the tens of millions of tourists whose primary concern is choosing among over 60 major hotel-casinos, dozens of shows, a mind-boggling list of gambling options, limitless dining, and spectacular day trips.

The largest city in Nevada, Las Vegas is 2,030 ft above sea level. It's one of the most remote large cities in the country: the nearest major population center to the west is Barstow, California, 2½ hours away; St. George, Utah, is two hours to the east. Through the years Las Vegas has wrested the political and economic power of Nevada away from Reno, 448 mi to the northwest, the city where legalized gambling first became popular and where the early casinos were built.

Las Vegas is surrounded by the Mojave Desert, and Las Vegas Valley is flanked by mountain ranges. Among them are the Spring Mountains, including Mount Charleston (11,918 ft), which has downhill skiing, and Red Rock Canyon, characterized by stunning Southwest sandstone. The Las Vegas Wash drains the valley to the southeast into Lake Mead and the Colorado River system.

Average high temperatures in Las Vegas rise to 105°F in July and August; lows drop to 30°F in January and February. The heat is saunalike throughout the summer, except during electrical storms that can dump an inch of rain an hour and cause dangerous flash floods. Heavy rains any time of year exacerbate two of Las Vegas's major problems: a lack of water drainage and a surplus of traffic. The summer blaze often makes it very uncomfortable to be outside for any length of time. Winters can be surprisingly chilly during the day and especially cold after the sun goes down. But in September and October and April and May it doesn't get any better.

Las Vegas is the largest U.S. city founded in the 20th century—1905 to be exact. Some might argue that the significant year was 1946, when Bugsy Siegel's Fabulous Flamingo opened for business. But the beginnings of modern Las Vegas can be traced back to 1829, when Antonio Armijo led a party of 60 on the Old Spanish Trail between Santa Fe and Los Angeles. While his caravan camped about 100 mi northeast of the present site of Las Vegas, an advance party set out to look for water. Rafael Rivera, a young Mexican scout, left the main party, headed due west over the unexplored desert, and discovered an oasis. The abundance of artesian spring water here shortened the Spanish Trail to Los Angeles by allowing travelers to go directly through, rather than around, the desert and eased the rigors of travel for the Spanish traders who used the route. They named the oasis Las Vegas, Spanish for "the meadows."

The next major visitor to the Las Vegas Springs was John C. Fremont, who in 1844 led one of his many explorations of the Far West. Today he is remembered in the name of the principal downtown thoroughfare—Fremont Street.

Ten years later a group of Mormon settlers were sent by Brigham Young from Salt Lake City to colonize the valley. They built a large stockade; a small remnant of it—a 150-square-ft, adobe-brick fort— still stands today. The old fort is the oldest building in Las Vegas. The Mormons spent two years growing crops, mining lead, and converting the local Paiute natives, but the climate and isolation defeated their ambitions and by 1857 the fort was abandoned.

THINGS DIDN'T START HOPPING here until 1904, when the San Pedro, Los Angeles, and Salt Lake Railroad laid its tracks through Las Vegas Valley, purchased the prime land and water rights from the handful of homesteaders, and surveyed a town site for its railroad servicing and repair facilities. In May 1905 the railroad held an auction and sold 700 lots. Las Vegas became a dusty railroad watering stop with a few downtown hotels and stores, a saloon and red-light district known as Block 16, and a few thousand residents. It remained just that until 1928, when the Boulder Canyon Project Act was signed into law, in which $165 million was appropriated for the building of the world's largest antigravity dam, 40 mi from Las Vegas.

Construction of Hoover Dam began in 1931, a historic year for Nevada. In that year Governor Fred Balzar approved the "wide-open" gambling bill that had been introduced by a Winnemucca rancher, Assemblyman Phil Tobin. Gambling had been outlawed several times since Nevada became a state in 1864, but it had never been completely eliminated. Tobin maintained that controlled gaming would be good for tourism and the state's economy; people were going to gamble anyway, so why shouldn't the state tax the profits? Thus, he was able to convince lawmakers to make gambling permanently legal. Also in 1931, the Legislature reduced the residency requirement for divorce to a scandalous six weeks, immediately turning Nevada into a "divorce colony."

The early 1930s marked the height of the Great Depression and Prohibition. The construction of the dam on the Colorado River (bridging the gap between Arizona and Nevada) brought thousands of job seekers to southern Nevada. Because the federal government didn't want dam workers to be distracted by the temptations of Las Vegas, it created a separate government town, Boulder City—still the only community in the state where gambling is illegal.

At this time Nevada's political and economic power resided in the northern part of the state: the capital in Carson City and the major casinos (notably Harold's Club and Harrah's) in Reno. But the completion of the dam in 1935 turned southern Nevada into a magnet for federal appropriations, thousands of tourists and new residents, and a seemingly inexhaustible supply of electricity and water. In addition, as the country mobilized for World War II, tens of thousands of pilots and gunners trained at the Las Vegas Aerial Gunnery School, opened by the federal government on 3 million acres north of town. Today this property is Nellis Air Force Base and the Nevada Test Site.

By the early 1940s downtown Las Vegas boasted several luxury hotels and a dozen small but successful gambling clubs. In 1941, Thomas Hull, who owned a chain of California motor inns, decided to build a place in the desert just outside the city limits on Highway 91, the road from Los Angeles. El Rancho Vegas opened with 100 motel rooms, a western-motif casino, and, right off the highway, a large parking lot with an inviting swimming pool in the middle. El Rancho's quick success led to the opening a year later of the Last Frontier Hotel, a mile down the road. Thus, the Las Vegas Strip was established.

Benjamin "Bugsy" Siegel, who ran the New York mob's activities on the West Coast, began to see the incredible potential of a remote oasis where land was cheap and gambling was legal. He struggled for two years to build his Fabulous Flamingo, managing to alienate his local partners and silent investors with his lavish overspending. He opened the joint prematurely, on a rainy night, the day after Christmas 1946. Although movie stars attended and headliners Jimmy Durante, Xavier Cugat, and Rose Marie performed, the Flamingo flopped; the casino paid out more money than it took in. This made Siegel's partners not only unhappy but also suspicious, and six months later Bugsy was dead. Once he had been bumped off, business at the Flamingo boomed—Siegel's gangland assassination had made front-page news across the country, and people flocked to see the house that Bugsy built.

The success of the Flamingo paved the way for gamblers and gangsters from all over the country to invest in Las Vegas hotel-casinos, one after another. The Desert Inn, Horseshoe, Sands, Sahara, Riviera, Dunes, Fremont, Tropicana, and Stardust were all built in the 1950s, financed with mob money. Every new hotel came on like a theme park opening for the summer with a new ride. Each was bigger, better, more unusual than the last. The Sahara had the tallest free-standing neon sign. The Riviera was the first high-rise building in town. The Stardust had 1,000 rooms and the world's largest swimming pool.

That the underworld owned and ran the big joints only added to the allure of Las Vegas. And the town's great boom in the 1950s couldn't have happened without the mob's access to millions of dollars in cash. Under the circumstances, no bank, corporation, or legitimate investor would have touched the gambling business.

In time, however, the state began to take steps to weed out the most visible undesirables. The federal government assisted in the crackdown, using its considerable resources to hound the gangsters out of business. And, finally, an eccentric man arrived on a train and soon revolutionized the nation's image of Las Vegas.

Howard Hughes had just sold Trans World Airlines for $546 million, and he either had to spend half the money or turn it in as taxes. During a three-year stay in Las Vegas he bought the Desert Inn, Frontier, Sands, Landmark, and Silver Slipper hotels, a television station, an airfield, and millions of dollars' worth of real estate. His presence in Las Vegas gave gambling its first positive image: As a former pilot and aviation pioneer, Hollywood mogul, and American folk hero, Hughes could in no way be connected with gangsters.

Hughes's presence also opened the door to corporate ownership of hotel-casinos. In 1971, Hilton Corporation purchased the International (now the Las Vegas Hilton) and the Flamingo, becoming the first major publicly traded hotel chain to step onto the Las Vegas playing field. Ramada, Holiday Inn, Hyatt, Sheraton, and others have since followed suit.

Las VEGAS FELT THE EFFECTS of both the legalization of gambling in Atlantic City in the late 1970s and of the national recession of the early 1980s—but not for very long. Through the years the city has carved a secure niche for itself as a destination for national and international tourists, a winter sojourn for snowbirds from the north; a weekend getaway for gamblers and families from California, Arizona, and Utah; and convention central. Las Vegas has expanded at a ferocious pace for the past 10 years, during which more than 65,000 hotel rooms have been added and more than a half million people have moved to the area, many of them fleeing California.

And why not? Though inching up, room rates are lower than in any other major U.S. city. There are lavish gourmet spots, but the inexpensive restaurants and buffet dining here can be cheaper than preparing a meal at home. Entertainment is abundant and reasonably priced. Las Vegas is possibly the easiest place in the world to receive freebies—the ubiquitous "comps." And best of all, gambling promotions such as coupons, slot clubs, paycheck bonuses, and drawings provide a fighting chance to win in the casino. In the back of everyone's mind is the idea that a trip to Las Vegas can be free or even a money-making vacation. That kind of thinking keeps the corporations smiling as they add a few more finishing touches to their $2-billion hotels.

# WHAT'S WHERE

## The Strip
Officially titled Las Vegas Boulevard South, the Strip runs north–south through the city. Without leaving this street you could sample all that's best in Las Vegas: the food, the shows, and of course the gambling. Almost all the major casinos are either on or just off the Strip. In fact, there's so much to see and do on the Strip that we've broken it down into South, Center, and North to help you navigate through the options.

## Four Corners
If there is one part of the Strip that is worthy of special mention, it would have to be the Four Corners. The intersection of Las Vegas Boulevard and Flamingo Road has set the standards for excess ever since Bugsy Siegel first set up shop here with his Flamingo in 1946. Caesars, the Mirage, and now Bellagio have upped the stakes in their turn, and, as of yet, there appears to be no betting maximum at the hub of the Strip.

## Downtown
You'll find the heart of downtown Vegas where Fremont Street meets Las Vegas Boulevard. It's also the epicenter of the Fremont Street Experience, the world's greatest collection of neon signs, covered by the world's largest electric sign. The hotels and casinos on Fremont tend to be older and less expensive than those on the Strip.

## Paradise Road
The Paradise Road corridor parallels the Strip and increasingly is becoming an echo of its big brother to the west. Near and along Paradise you'll find shops and lots of good-quality restaurants, as well as such landmarks as the Hard Rock Hotel, Las Vegas Hilton, and Las Vegas Convention Center. Paradise also is generally less congested than the Strip—making it a good alternative route—but construction on the monorail has impeded traffic there to some extent.

## West of the Strip
If you're looking for a place that's away from the often-crazy Strip traffic but retains much of the legendary street's glittery glamour, consider the area just to

the west across I–15. The Rio and Palms are known for their hipster appeal—in Bikinis at the Rio, and Rain and Ghostbar at the Palms. The Gold Coast is primarily a locals casino, but its corporate sister, the Orleans, draws big-name entertainment to its intimate showroom and brand-new arena.

### Summerlin

Howard Hughes left his mark on Las Vegas in many ways, and one of the biggest—and the one with the best chance for posterity—is Summerlin, named for Hughes' grandmother. He acquired the 22,500-acre chunk of desert in the far western part of the valley during the early '50s; today it's a sprawling, upscale planned community and the site of many shops, restaurants, and casinos, such as the Rampart Casino at JW Marriott Las Vegas, that draw residents and savvy visitors.

### Henderson

It's said that Henderson was "born in America's defense." It was the site of the Basic Magnesium Plant, which supplied the U.S. War Department during World War II. Henderson almost died at the end of the war; the whole town was offered for sale in 1947. It managed to survive, and for a couple of decades wore its blue collar proudly. In the '80s, however, upscale developments began to spring up, and Henderson today is home to a mix of income groups and vies with Reno as the second largest city in the state. Two of the valley's best locals' casino-hotels are here, Sunset Station and Green Valley Ranch Station Casino.

### Red Rock Canyon

You have probably seen Red Rock in the movies: it's a very popular location for Hollywood. A 13-mi scenic road loops through the red rock formations and unusual high-desert scenery of southern Nevada, only 20 minutes from the heart of the city.

### Mt. Charleston

The eighth-highest peak in Nevada, Mt. Charleston is the perfect retreat for a day or two away from the madness of Las Vegas. It's also an ideal escape from the heat of summer, because temperatures on the mountain tend to be 15 to 20 degrees cooler than those in the valley. In wintertime, it's a local ski haven, and in the summer

hikers, mountain bikers, and campers hit the slopes.

### Hoover Dam & Lake Mead

About 35 mi southeast of Las Vegas lies one of the seven man-made wonders of the world, the monster Hoover Dam. This 4.4-million-cubic-yard concrete beast dams the Colorado River, creating the 229 square mi of Lake Mead, the largest man-made lake in the country. This is your destination for water sports if your ambitions extend beyond swim-up blackjack. Nearby Boulder City, built in the early 1930s to house workers who were constructing Hoover Dam, is the only community in Nevada where gambling is illegal.

### Valley of Fire State Park

Nevada's first state park is about 55 mi northeast of Las Vegas. The name comes from the distinctive coloration of its rock formations, which range from lavender to tangerine to bright red. The lights of Las Vegas pale in comparison to the rays of sunset on this fantastic natural backdrop.

# PLEASURES AND PASTIMES

### Downtown Neon

It is a simple (and free) pleasure in downtown Las Vegas to bear witness to the extraordinary powers of electricity. The area has a collection of neon signs that only downtown Tokyo can claim to match. The 50-foot-tall neon cowboy Vegas Vic is perhaps the most famous sign. Once an hour, after dark, the modern-day wizards of odds fire up the Fremont Street Experience, all 2 million lightbulbs and 500,000 watts and four blocks of it, for a light-and-sound show unequaled anywhere on (and possibly off) the planet.

### The High Rollers

If you get a chance—that is, if it happens in one of the casinos' public rooms—just stand (in Las Vegas, chairs are for gamblers only) and watch one of the bigger players (aka, high rollers or whales) take on the tables. You have nothing to lose, but if the player hits a big streak and those chips start piling up, you can ride his or her adrenaline rush for free. This experience has become more rare in recent years, as the newest casinos shelter their biggest spenders in high-limit rooms, away from the eyes of the hoi-polloi.

## The Las Vegas Buzz

Besides the renowned enticements of Las Vegas, there are other, more subtle ones. There's the twisting of time, noticeable, for example, in coffee shops, when at any hour some people are having breakfast, others lunch or dinner, and still others snacks or coffee. There's the unmistakable air—sounds, smells, sights—of a casino. And there's the phenomenon of a city that never closes or seems to sleep, that galvanizes and emblazons the familiar activities of daily life.

## Magic & Song

Nobody ever came to Las Vegas to see Shakespeare. The city has made famous a certain brand of entertainment based on big name entertainers, spectacular production values, sex, and illusion—the old Siegfried & Roy extravaganza was long the biggest draw here. Wayne Newton continues to pack them in, and you can still catch a scantily dressed chorus line if you want. At some of the major hotels, however, a newer breed of show, the high-tech spectacular, has been packing them in and each one competes with the others for even more amazing special effects. They include Celine Dion's *A New Day* at Caesars Palace, the Cirque du Soleil productions *O* at Bellagio and *Mystère* at Treasure Island, *Blue Man Group* at the Luxor, and Bally's *Jubilee,* which with its topless showgirls and high-tech effects, bridges the gap between old and new.

## Poolside Lounging

As Las Vegas hotel-casino properties lavish ever more attention on their amenities, pool expansions have been part of the wave. And some of them are spectacular, such as the interconnected pools surrounded by lush tropical gardens at the Flamingo; the beach, wave pool, and lazy river at Mandalay Bay; the Roman-theme pool complex at Caesars Palace; the eight-acre rooftop pool area at the Las Vegas Hilton; and the five separate pools, including the 1,000-foot-long Backlot River pool, at the MGM Grand.

## Shopping

Time was when Las Vegas was a great source for shocking-pink wigs, dice clocks, life-size Wayne Newton dolls—and not much else. Today, upscale shopping destinations such as the Forum Shops at Caesars, the Grand Canal Shoppes at the Venetian and Via Bellagio have brought Chanel, Tiffany, and Versace to Las Vegas. The Fashion Show mall on the Strip offers six upscale department stores, and more proleterian offerings are available at the valley's three regional malls.

## Wining & Dining

Dining out in Las Vegas is an adventure in variety. The fun lies in choosing from the vast array of styles and price ranges, from cheap prime rib joints to hip and happening eateries to big-name-chef restaurants. Every major hotel has at least four or five eating places, and independent restaurants are scattered about town. The fabulous buffets are a traditional treat, where you find yourself, plate in hand, standing before a mountain of all-you-can-eat food—some for as little as $4.99. But the big news in Las Vegas is the arrival of excellent—albeit expensive—new restaurants offering everything from the latest California fusion to the best aged steaks.

## Winning & Losing

Times may change, but gambling is still the thing to do in Las Vegas. The first-timer is faced with a terrifying choice of possible bets—what seems like 1,001 different ways to part with your hard-earned dollars. But once you know your way around the casino, you'll quickly settle on your wagering thrill of choice. Blackjack, baccarat, and video poker offer the best odds for winning in a Las Vegas casino. The average bankroll of a Las Vegas gambler is $500, but you can experience either the excitement of winning or the frustration of losing for a lot less. The smaller casinos off the Strip are often the best bet for the amateur gambler; the pressure is less intense, the minimums are reasonable, and the staff is friendlier.

# 2 EXPLORING LAS VEGAS

The Las Vegas you knew no longer exists. This holds true even if you last visited America's most dynamic city a week ago. Even longtime residents have a difficult time of keeping up with Vegas' rapid growth, and it's quite likely that you'll see something new—and better—every time you come to town. A whole new world of casinos, attractions, museums, souvenir stands, and historical landmarks is out there, waiting to be explored. See it now—it'll be completely different next time.

Revised and
updated by
Heidi Knapp
Rinella

**F**OR 50 YEARS, up until the early 1990s, the name Las Vegas was synonymous with adult entertainment. It existed for one reason and one reason only: gambling. Then the city attempted to remake itself as a family destination, adding roller coasters, animal attractions, and arcades to its predominantly adult lineup. The strategy didn't really take, as an explosion of topless shows and after-hours nightclubs over the past two or three years would seem to indicate. But the legacy of Las Vegas' family "experiment" lingers: fabulous theme hotels such as the Luxor, New York–New York, the Venetian, the Aladdin, and Paris Las Vegas, as well as amusement parks such as Wet 'n Wild and the Adventuredome provide a minivacation's worth of excitement—no slot machines or blackjack tables required.

Whatever the current state of its on-again, off-again attitude toward families, Las Vegas has never—and probably will never—become a family destination in the sense that Orlando or Cape Cod are. Every year, about 35 million people come to Las Vegas for the traditional reason—to gamble, plain and simple. There are few supermarkets, post offices, video-rental stores, or other conveniences of everyday life on the Strip—just casinos, wedding chapels, gift stores, strip clubs, and discotheques. Las Vegas is a fantasyland—a very adult fantasyland.

The Strip, the 3½-mi stretch of Las Vegas Boulevard South between Russell Road and Sahara Avenue, is the heart of Las Vegas. Its soul is the downtown area north of the Strip, whose core is Fremont Street. By exploring these two areas, you'll experience both the commercial lifeblood and pioneer spirit of this most flamboyant of American cities.

## Getting Your Bearings

It's easy to get around Las Vegas by car. Note, however, that driving up and down the Strip to get to where you're going might take only five minutes on a Tuesday morning but could take almost an hour on a Friday or a Saturday night. Parking at the hotel garages on the Strip is free; that's the case downtown as well, if you have your ticket validated by a casino cashier.

Getting around on foot can be a challenge, as distances here are deceiving. Although all the casinos in the center of the Strip, for example, may be within a mile of each other, walking from the street to and around the hotels, especially the large ones, can easily triple that distance. Some of the newer casinos have moving sidewalks, trams, and elevated crosswalks to make it easier to get around on foot. A monorail that will run from the MGM Grand to the Sahara is expected to be completed in 2004. The Strip Trolley, which runs every 15 minutes, is the most convenient means of hotel-hopping, because it picks up and drops off passengers at hotel front doors. The local buses are more frequent, though less convenient to the actual hotels, and usually crowded to overflowing.

We've organized the Strip exploration into three good walks: south, center, and north. A fourth walk covers downtown. Most of the sights in Las Vegas are casinos, so you can start exploring any time of the day or night. But the earlier you set out, the fewer crowds and the less heat (in the summer) you'll face along the way. To see the museums and historical sights, you'll have to coordinate your tour with hours of operation.

# SOUTH STRIP

The southern end of the Strip has been the beneficiary of the lion's share of Las Vegas's family boom. In 1989 the only hotel-casino to anchor this part of the Strip was the Tropicana, which had stood alone for more than 30 years. But then came the San Remo and Excalibur (1990), Luxor and MGM Grand (1993), Monte Carlo (1996), New York–New York (1997), and Mandalay Bay (1999). To better manage the expected millions of tourists, these properties joined forces with the county in 1994 to install four overhead pedestrian walkways, complete with escalators and elevators, at a cost of $10 million. These walkways not only facilitate exploring, they provide good views (through a protective wire mesh). The intersection of Las Vegas Boulevard and Tropicana Avenue is one of the most magnetic tourist intersections in the world.

## What to See

☾ **Excalibur Hotel and Casino.** Before they opened this spectacular property in 1990, the executives of the Circus Circus Resort Group—now the Mandalay Resort Group—visited castles in England, Scotland, and Germany in search of inspiration. The result might be described as "King Arthur does Las Vegas." The pseudo-Bavarian castle, which has been called "the greatest hole in God's own miniature golf course," has plenty of turrets, spires, belfries, a moat, and a 265-foot bell tower. The over-the-top medieval theme is continued inside, with staff members in elaborate royal-court costumes and such place names as the Court Jester's Stage and Sir Galahad's Pub and Prime Rib House.

Downstairs from the 100,000-square-foot casino is **Fantasy Faire Midway,** with carnival games and international gifts. A spin on **Merlin's Magic Motion Machine Film Rides,** which include a spooky roller-coaster ride with Elvira, self-proclaimed Mistress of the Dark, plus a ride with a Greek-mythology theme, and a race-track, lasts about 5 to 10 minutes.

Upstairs from the casino are shops, theme restaurants, a huge buffet, and a roving Renaissance Faire with jugglers, puppeteers, and magicians.

Families enjoy the *Tournament of Kings* extravaganza in the showroom, and *Thunder from Down Under* is big with bachelorette parties. The Excalibur also offers more than 4,000 guest rooms and plenty of ways to win (or lose) a buck. ⊠ *3850 Las Vegas Blvd. S, South Strip,* ☎ *702/597–7777 or 800/937–7777,* WEB *www.excaliburcasino.com.* ☒ *Film Rides $4 per ride.* ☉ *Fantasy Faire open daily 10–10.*

★ **Hard Rock Hotel and Casino.** A haven for the young and hip, the Hard Rock is a high-class rock 'n' roll museum, with memorabilia from every rock decade adorning its walls. The multimillion-dollar collection is undoubtedly one of the best on display in the country—you can see everything from Kurt Cobain's guitar to one of Britney Spears' many outfits. And since the Hard Rock is a favorite hiding spot for many of the music and film stars of today, you've got a pretty good chance of bumping into one. Navigating the property is simple: it's completely circular. On the inside of the circle is the small but accommodating gaming floor, and on the outside, various shops, restaurants, and the Hard Rock's intimate concert venue, the Joint. Down one hallway is the Hard Rock's pool area, a tropical beach–inspired oasis featuring a floating bar, private cabanas, and poolside blackjack—a favorite filming location for MTV and hip TV shows. The logo shop is large, so you won't have to wait in Hard Rock's signature long, slow-moving line to buy a T-shirt. ⊠ *4455 Paradise Rd., Paradise Road,* ☎ *702/693–5000 or 800/693–7625,* WEB *www.hardrockhotel.com.*

**James R. Dickinson Library.** The special-collections department of this library of the University of Nevada–Las Vegas has the best collection of materials about Las Vegas and gambling that you'll find anywhere. ✉ *4505 Maryland Pkwy., University District,* ☎ *702/895–3285.* 🖼 *Free.* ◷ *Weekdays 9–5.*

★ **Liberace Museum.** Costumes, cars, photographs, even mannequins of the late entertainer make this museum the kitschiest place in town. In addition to Lee's collection of pianos (one of them was played by Chopin; another, a concert grand, was owned by George Gershwin), you can see his Czar Nicholas uniform and a blue-velvet cape styled after the coronation robes of King George V. Be sure to check out the gift shop—where else can you find Liberace soap, ashtrays, and other novelties? ✉ *1775 E. Tropicana Ave., East Side,* ☎ *702/798–5595,* WEB *www.liberace.com.* 🖼 *$8.* ◷ *Mon.–Sat. 10–5, Sun. 1–5.*

**Luxor Resort & Casino.** In Luxor, the folks at Mandalay Resort Group have built one of the modern wonders of the world—and made sure it could be seen from anywhere in the valley at night. Luxor, a 36-story black glass and bronze pyramid, is made with 13 acres of black glass and topped with a beam that burns brighter than any other in the world. It's composed of 45 xenon lights, and it projects enough light to be visible from space. Standing right at the base of one of the exterior walls and looking up, you'll get a glimpse of infinity. Inside is the world's largest atrium, with 29 million cubic feet of open space soaring to the building's apex. You get the full impact of the space from the second floor, also known as the Attractions Level.

The "Passport to Adventure" for the entertainment attractions in the Luxor's **Pharaoh's Pavilion** is all-inclusive—it gets you two IMAX movies, "In Search for the Obelisk" ridefilm, the reproduction of King Tutankhamen's tomb, and your choice of a virtual roller coaster ride or AE's movie *The Great Pharaohs.* Stop by the vast two-story video arcade, too.

Luxor has more than 4,000 guest rooms. The rooms in the pyramid building (there are two hotel towers as well) are reached by four "inclinators," elevators that travel along the 39-degree incline of the pyramid. ✉ *3900 Las Vegas Blvd. S, South Strip,* ☎ *702/262–4000 or 800/288–1000,* WEB *www.luxor.com.* 🖼 *Pharaoh's Pavilion attractions $4–$8.95, Passport to Adventure $23.95.* ◷ *Pharoah's Pavilion open Sun.–Thurs. 9 AM–11 PM, Fri.–Sat. 9 AM–midnight.*

★ **Mandalay Bay Resort and Casino.** The 43-story, $950-million Mandalay Bay Resort has 3,700 rooms, including a 400-room **Four Seasons Hotel** on the 36th through 39th floors (with its own parking, entrance, pool, health club, express elevators, restaurants, and meeting area). The name is a curious one—Mandalay is an ancient inland temple city in Myanmar, the country formerly known as Burma, which has no bay. And while the real Mandalay is in Southeast Asia, the hotel-casino is decked out like a South Seas beach resort, complete with the scent of coconut oil drifting through the casino. In fact, there's a 10-acre lagoon complete with a huge wave pool (8-foot waves, roughest waters on the Strip), a ¾-mi-long "lazy river" pool, and a man-made beach where concerts are held periodically. The **House of Blues,** an 1,800-seat theater and a 600-seat restaurant, is also here; the restaurant walls are covered with Louisiana Delta folk art.

The most distinctive attraction at Mandalay Bay is **Shark Reef.** The 105,000-square-foot facility holds some 2 million gallons of seawater housing exotic creatures large and small. The journey begins in temple ruins, where the heat and humidity may be uncomfortable for the humans but is quite nice for the golden crocodiles, water monitors, and tropical fish. Two glass "hallways" allow you to get up close and personal with sea life. Other notable exhibits: A shallow pool offers you a chance to give a one-finger pet to small stingrays, small sharks, and starfish; and jellyfish swim a rhythmic dance in a specially designed environment. The tour saves the best for last—from the bowels of a sunken galleon, watch sharks swim below, above, and around the skeleton ship.

This megaresort also houses a 12,000-seat arena complex that hosts major sporting contests, superstar concerts, and special events; a 1,700-seat showroom; a convention center; the Coral Reef Lounge, surrounded by virtual vegetation, rock waterfalls, and lily ponds; the four-story "wine tower" at the signature restaurant Aureole; and rumjungle, one of the hottest nightspots in town. Under construction is a shopping mall that will link Mandalay Bay and sister property, Luxor. ⊠ *3950 Las Vegas Blvd. S, South Strip,* ☎ *702/632–7777 or 877/632–7400,* WEB *www.mandalaybay.com.* ☒ *Shark Reef $13.95.* ☉ *Daily 10 AM–11 PM.*

🕑 **MGM Grand.** With over 5,000 rooms, the MGM Grand is one of the the largest hotels in the world, a self-proclaimed "City of Entertainment" sprawling over 112 acres. The front of the property is adorned with a 100,000-pound bronze lion statue that stands 45-feet tall and sits atop a 25-foot pedestal, making it the largest bronze statue in the United States. Inside you'll find a full half-mile of restaurants, ballrooms, nightclubs, and shops—even a research center for CBS Television, where you can screen potential new shows for parent company Viacom's networks, which also include Nickelodeon and MTV.

The MGM Grand also has a $9-million, 3,000-square-foot **Lion Habitat.** More than 12,000 visitors a day see the lions owned by feline expert and exotic-animal trainer Keith Evans. A see-through tunnel runs through the habitat, allowing you to watch the big cats prowl above and below. The enclosure was designed to replicate the lions' natural habitat as closely as possible and has stone, trees and foliage, four waterfalls, and a pond. The lions are trucked in each day; they really live 12 mi from the MGM Grand on an 8½-acre ranch. Admission is free. ⊠ *3799 Las Vegas Blvd. S, South Strip,* ☎ *702/891–1111 or 800/929–1111,* WEB *www.mgmgrand.com.* ☉ *Lion Habitat daily 11–10.*

**Monte Carlo Resort and Casino.** This elegant megaresort is modeled after the *real* Monte Carlo—the Place du Casino in Monaco. The $350-million hotel-casino is like a sumptuous palace, filled with arches, chandeliers, marble, statuary, and fountains. Note the Gothic glass registration area overlooking the lush pool area—a touch that resort co-creator Steve Wynn dubbed "popular elegance."

In addition to the massive gaming floor and 3,000-plus rooms, the property includes an avenue-style shopping mall dubbed the **Street of Dreams.** There you can find everything from Monte Carlo logo wear to fine jewelry, as well as a number of eateries. Perhaps the most popular restaurant here is the Monte Carlo Brew Pub, which features live nightly entertainment, decent pub-style food, and six specialty ales made on the premises. Sports fans will especially love the 35 big-screen TVs regularly broadcasting various athletic events and the state-of-the-art sound system. Also along the Street of Dreams is a high-tech arcade with more than 60 games.

The resort's most popular attraction—world-class illusionist Lance Burton—performs five nights a week in an opulent, 1,200-seat, $27-million custom-built theater modeled after the opera houses of Europe.

✉ *3770 Las Vegas Blvd. S, South Strip,* ☎ *702/730–7777 or 800/311–8999,* WEB *www.monte-carlo.com.*

★ **New York–New York Hotel and Casino.** When it opened in 1997, the stunning, $460-million complex raised the bar for theme hotels, in Las Vegas and worldwide. The exterior is a mini-Manhattan skyline, complete with a 48-story Empire State Building; a 150-foot Statue of Liberty; and smaller versions of the Chrysler, Seagram, and CBS buildings and the New York Public Library, Grand Central Terminal, and the Brooklyn Bridge. Poignant among the glitz is an impromptu memorial to the 9/11 victims, which sprung up on a wrought-iron fence near the model of a New York fireboat; items, donated by people from all over the world, are being catalogued and preserved. A Coney Island–style roller coaster, the Manhattan Express, encircles the property. The Big Apple flavor continues inside, with an art deco lobby, a Central Park–theme casino pit, an arcade reminiscent of Coney Island, and a food court patterned after Greenwich Village. And last but not least is ESPN Zone, the mother of all sports cafés, with plush seats for armchair quarterbacks and an arcade filled with sports games.

Roller-coaster aficionados take note: the **Manhattan Express** is a real rocker. While being whisked past great views of the faux New York skyline, you climb 15 stories, dive 75 feet, climb then dive 144 feet, do a 360-degree somersault, twirl through a "heartline twist" (that simulates the sensation one gets in a jet doing a barrel roll), rocket over a dizzying succession of high-banked turns and camel-back hills, and finally zip along a 540-degree spiral before you pull back into the station. ✉ *3790 Las Vegas Blvd. S, South Strip,* ☎ *702/740–6969 or 800/693–6763,* WEB *www.nynyhotelcasino.com.* ✎ *Roller coaster $10.* ☼ *Roller coaster daily 10 AM–11 PM (weather permitting).*

☾ **Showcase Mall.** This mall has several specialty shops, a movie theater, and Gameworks, a multi-level young-adult arcade.

**M&M's World** is four stories of fun that will melt in your mouth, not in your hand. The store offers plenty of candy-coated treats (including an **Ethel M. Chocolates** outlet for more upscale sweet tooths) plus everything from T-shirts to limited-edition lithographs. There's also the **M&M Academy,** featuring interactive exhibits and a free 3-D movie, "I Lost My M in Las Vegas."

**Gameworks,** a joint venture between Steven Spielberg and Sega, more than lives up to its hype—it's the biggest, most boisterous arcade in town. Gameworks has more than 300 arcade-style games, a 21-and-over bar with pool tables and live entertainment, a casual fast-food eatery, and the world's largest free-standing rock-climbing structure. ✉ *3785 Las Vegas Blvd. S, South Strip,* ☎ *702/736–7611 M&M's World, 702/432–4263 Gameworks.* ✎ *M&M Academy free entry; Gameworks free entry, $25 per 2 hrs of play.* ☼ *Showcase Mall and M&M's World Sun.–Thurs. 9 AM–midnight, Fri.–Sat. 9 AM–1 AM. Gameworks Sun.–Thurs. 10 AM–midnight, Fri.–Sat. 10 AM–2 AM. M&M Academy Sun.–Thurs. 10 AM–6 PM, Fri.–Sat. 10 AM–8 PM.*

**Tropicana Resort and Casino.** The most eye-popping sight here is the 4,000-square-foot stained-glass dome that sparkles above one section of the casino. Be sure to take a look at the lush, 5-acre pool area, where the famous swim-up blackjack game is played. The Tropicana hosts Las Vegas's longest-running show, the *Folies Bergere,* as well as a great comedy club featuring well-known and up-and-coming comedians.

A must-see at the Trop is the **Casino Legends Hall of Fame.** Portions of the world's largest collection of Nevada casino memorabilia have been displayed at several casinos through the years, but the collection has finally found a permanent home here. Thousands of items are on display, including Las Vegas chips, photographs, movie posters, postcards, slot machines, entertainer contracts and paychecks, menus, album covers, and more. There's a mock-up of a showgirl's dressing room and numerous video monitors run documentaries about the casino implosions, celebrities, hotel fires, and onetime association with organized crime figures—all the iconic people and events that shaped this town's legend. ⊠ *3801 Las Vegas Blvd. S, South Strip,* ☎ *702/739–2222 or 800/634–4000,* WEB *www.tropicanalv.com.* ⊠ *Hall of Fame $4 (look for free-entry coupons throughout the casino).* ⊙ *Hall of Fame Sun.–Thurs. 8 AM–9 PM, Fri.–Sat. 8 AM–midnight.*

WELCOME TO LAS VEGAS. Two blocks south of Hacienda Avenue, at the south end of the Strip, is this welcome sign, a familiar part of the landscape since the early 1950s and quite possibly Las Vegas's most-photographed element. It makes a great photo or video backdrop, but wait for an ebb in the traffic: the sign is on an island in the middle of the boulevard. Also of note: nearby is the Glass Pool Inn, whose signature elevated swimming pool has appeared in dozens of television shows and movies.

# CENTER STRIP

This entire part of the Strip is historic. Here you'll find the Flamingo Las Vegas, which stands on the site of Bugsy Siegel's original Flamingo, as well as Caesars Palace, whose name has been synonymous with opulence and excess for years. Casino mogul Steve Wynn raised even Caesars's high stakes with the 1989 opening of the lush Mirage, but another Wynn creation, the $1.8-billion Bellagio, with its European elegance and gorgeous fountains, set a standard that has yet to be equalled.

## What to See

**Aladdin Resort and Casino.** It took Queen Scheherazade 1,001 nights to woo her husband with tales of Ali Baba, Sinbad the Sailor, and the Enchanted Garden before he learned how to love again—nearly five months longer than it took to build the $1.4-billion, 2,567-room Aladdin. The *Arabian Nights* motif is immediately evident in the 50-foot waterfall cascading down a sandstone cliff fronting the property. You walk directly inside from the Strip—one of the many elements of the Aladdin designed for convenience—but into a shopping mall rather than a casino.

The **Desert Passage** is a $300-million complex of 135 shops ensconced in minarets, onion domes, and other Moorish architecture. Merchants' Harbor, a North African village with a huge anchored steamer ship, treats mall goers to regularly scheduled thunderstorms. Among the many restaurants in the mall and hotel are a branch of New Orleans's famous Commander's Palace.

Cocktail waitresses in harem garb glide through the 100,000-square-foot casino, which is bedecked with a 36-foot-long Aladdin's lamp. London Clubs International operates a separate casino-within-a-casino, a luxurious hideaway for high rollers. At night, Broadway shows and headliner concerts fill the 7,000-seat Aladdin Theatre for the Performing Arts. ⊠ *3667 Las Vegas Blvd. S, Center Strip,* ☎ *702/736–0111 or 877/333–9474,* WEB *www.aladdincasino.com.*

**Bally's Casino Resort.** During the day it doesn't look like much, but at night Bally's facade is one of Las Vegas's most colorful: Its Epcot-esque colored lights in green, red, purple, and blue are a throwback to the '60s space age. Four 200-foot moving walkways ferry people between the Strip and the casino—a plus for the foot-sore. The shopping arcade on the lower level sells everything from fine furs to ice cream. Bally's also hosts the $10-million showgirl spectacular *Jubilee!*. A mile-long monorail connects the resort to the MGM Grand. ⊠ *3645 Las Vegas Blvd. S, Center Strip,* ☎ *702/739–4111 or 800/644–0777,* WEB *www. ballyslv.com.*

**Barbary Coast Hotel and Casino.** Decorated with dark woods, stained glass, brass, and crystal, the Barbary Coast evokes turn-of-the-20th-century San Francisco. Downstairs, Drai's is one of Vegas's hottest restaurants. While its after-hours club launched a raft of such Strip spots, Drai's bar, with its comfortable seating and candlelit red decor, captures the opulence of the Old Vegas. One of the smallest hotels on the Strip, with only 200 rooms, the Barbary Coast is nonetheless a popular place to stay because of its central location and affordable rates. ⊠ *3595 Las Vegas Blvd. S, Center Strip,* ☎ *702/737–7111 or 888/227–2279,* WEB *www.barbarycoastcasino.com.*

★ **Bellagio Las Vegas.** The $1.8-billion, 3,000-room Bellagio is one of the most opulent and expensive hotel-casinos ever built. Scores of full-grown evergreen and deciduous trees line the "shore" (actually, the Strip sidewalk) of the 12-acre lake that fronts the hotel and reflects its Tuscan village architecture.

Stretching 900 feet across Bellagio's lake is a signature outdoor spectacle: the $30-million **Fountains of Bellagio** water ballet, made famous by an appearance in the 2001 remake of "Ocean's Eleven." More than 1,000 fountain nozzles, 4,500 lights, and 27 million gallons of water combine to dazzle audiences with dancing waters choreographed to music. Some jets launch spray nearly 250 feet in the air. There's a show every 30 minutes from 3 PM (noon on weekends) until about 7 PM, after which the shows run every 15 minutes until midnight. The best view is from the observation deck of the Eiffel Tower, directly across the street.

Walking into the lobby of the Bellagio, you're confronted with a fantastic and colorful, 2,000-square-foot glass sculpture called *Fiori di Como,* by famed artist Dale Chiluly. It's composed of more than 2,000 individually blown glass pieces and cost upwards of $10 million.

Beyond the lobby is a 12,500-square-foot conservatory, the **Bellagio Botanical Gardens,** full of living flowers, shrubs, trees, and other plants. All the horticulture in the conservatory and throughout the hotel is fresh and live, grown in Bellagio's 5-acre greenhouse, and changes with the seasons.

Through the conservatory is the **Gallery of Fine Art.** Although MGM has sold off most of the gallery's permanent collection (the pieces in the restaurants remain), the gallery remains operational, displaying rotating exhibits arranged with museums, other galleries, and private collectors. Recent exhibits have included the works of Alexander Calder and the private collection of Steve Martin.

The resort also includes a $75-million showroom where Cirque de Soleil performs its spectacular *O.* As elegant as the decor and entertainment in this resort are, the shops nearly outdo them. Bellagio has some of the most exclusive and beautiful stores in the world, including Giorgio Armani, Chanel, Gucci, Prada, and Tiffany & Co. Note: no one under 18 is allowed in Bellagio unless they are staying at the hotel. ⊠ *3600 Las Vegas Blvd. S, Center Strip,* ☎ *702/693–7111 or 888/744–*

7687, WEB *www.bellagio.com.* ✉ *Gallery of Fine Art $12.* ☉ *Sun.–Thurs. 10–6, Fri.–Sat. 10–9.*

★ **Caesars Palace.** A 20-foot statue of Caesar, which stands in front of the driveway to the main entrance, greets visitors to this iconic hotel-casino. Behind him, 18 fountains and 50-foot-high cypress trees adorn the approach to the door. Nearby is a replica of one of Thailand's most popular shrines, with a 4-ton, gold-plated Brahma (the gift of a Thai tycoon). Among the other sculptures that adorn the palatial property is a full-size reproduction of Michelangelo's *David.* The newest jewel in Caesars' crown is the Colosseum, where Celine Dion performs five shows a week. Having undergone major expansions in its long history, Caesars Palace covers a vast area, including two casinos, **Cleopatra's Barge** lounge (which actually sits on water), the **Garden of the Gods** pool area, and numerous restaurants and entertainment venues.

A particular highlight is the ultra-exclusive **Forum Shops at Caesars,** a shopping mall/entertainment complex designed to resemble an ancient Roman streetscape. It houses roughly 100 retailers and eateries, including Abercrombie & Fitch, Emporio Armani, Gucci, Hugo Boss, Louis Vuitton, Virgin Megastore, FAO Schwartz, and Spago. Overhead is a painted sky that changes from airy clouds to stunning sunsets to star-studded nights. The mall also has a number of entertainment options, including two pretty astounding animatronic statue shows. Every hour on the hour, the Festival Fountain and the Atlantis shows spring into action; the former features robotic statues of Bacchus, Pluto, Venus, and Apollo, the latter the royal family of the doomed kingdom of Atlantis.

**Race for Atlantis** is the most sophisticated digital thrill ride in Las Vegas, combining motion simulation, computer-generated 3-D graphics, and a dome-shape IMAX film format. An electronic headset comes with a personal sound system and state-of-the-art 3-D goggles. If you can only experience one virtual ride, this is the one. ✉ *3570 Las Vegas Blvd. S, Center Strip,* ☎ *702/733–7900 or 800/223–7277,* WEB *www. caesarspalace.com.* ✉ *Race for Atlantis $10.* ☉ *Forum Shops and Race for Atlantis: Sun.–Thurs. 10 AM–11 PM, Fri.–Sat. 10 AM–midnight.*

**Flamingo Las Vegas.** Prior to 1946, when Benjamin (Bugsy) Siegel imported Miami luxury to the desert, Las Vegas was still trying to keep alive the last little sliver of the Wild West. But Bugsy was intent on introducing a class joint to the new casino town, a place where his Hollywood buddies and Manhattan partners could gamble legally, where the lure of big-time entertainment would bring the beautiful people to play, and where the ordinary Joe would show up because he wanted to feel like a big shot. Although things didn't work out exactly as Bugsy planned (☞ Close-Up: Bugsy Siegel), the Flamingo of today is the classy joint that he dreamed of, glitzy and elegant—if relentlessly pink. A highlight of the property is the lovely 15-acre pool park, with pools connected by water slides. The park also includes a wild-animal habitat with a flock of live Chilean flamingos, African penguins, swans, ducks, koi, goldfish, and turtles. All of the animals live on islands and in streams surrounded by sparkling waterfalls and lush foliage. The last remnant of the complex originally built by Bugsy Siegel was torn down, but a monument in the pool park pays respect to the Flamingo's notorious founder. ✉ *3555 Las Vegas Blvd. S, Center Strip,* ☎ *702/733–3111 or 800/732–2111,* WEB *www.flamingolv.com.*

**Harrah's Las Vegas Casino & Hotel.** A carnival theme pervades Harrah's, with the festive motif carried throughout to the outdoor Carnaval Court entertainment and shopping area, which occupies a patio near the front entrance. Carnaval Court includes Carnaval Corner, an international food mart; Ragin' Cajun, a Cajun country-inspired gift shop; and the Ghirardelli Chocolate Company. During the summer months, live bands play almost continuously, well into the night. And more upscale entertainment is available in Harrah's showroom, where Clint Holmes performs six nights a week. ⊠ *3475 Las Vegas Blvd. S, Center Strip,* ☎ *702/369–5000 or 800/427–7247,* WEB *www.harrahs.com.*

☞ **Imperial Palace Hotel and Casino.** The Imperial Palace is festooned with carved dragons and wind-chime chandeliers and has a distinctly Asian feel. It rests on a postage-stamp-size parcel, so the facilities rise instead of sprawl. On the first floor are the casino and shopping plaza. On the second are the coffee shop and buffet. The third houses the showroom, race and sports book, and meeting rooms. And on the fifth floor are the hotel restaurants.

On the fifth level of the hotel's parking garage (catch the elevator at the back of the casino) is the **Imperial Palace Automobile Museum,** a collection of more than 350 antique, classic, and special-interest vehicles. Because the vehicles are all for sale, the displays change from time to time, but among the cars, trucks, and motorcycles you might see a 1976 Cadillac Eldorado owned by Elvis Presley or the world's largest Duesenberg collection, comprising 25 vehicles built between 1925 and 1937.

Imperial Palace also offers unique entertainment, including *Legends in Concert,* a multimillion-dollar stage production featuring look-and-sound-alike performers portraying stars such as Madonna, the Temptations, Liberace, Ricky Martin, Shania Twain—and, of course, Elvis. ⊠ *3535 Las Vegas Blvd. S, Center Strip,* ☎ *702/731–3311 or 800/634–6441,* WEB *www.imperialpalace.com.* 🎟 *Museum $6.95; coupons for free admission are usually handed out in front of the hotel-casino or are available on-line.* ☉ *Museum daily 9:30 AM–11:30 PM.*

★ **Mirage Hotel and Casino.** When it opened in November 1989, the Mirage launched a decade-long (and counting) building boom the likes of which the world has rarely seen. Every 15 minutes from dusk to midnight, the signature volcano in front of the Mirage erupts, shooting flames and smoke 100 feet above the water below. Just inside the resort's front entrance is a lush rain forest. Palm trees, cascading waterfalls, meandering lagoons, and exotic tropical flora are housed under a 100-foot-high dome, and a 20,000-gallon aquarium provides a stunning backdrop to the front desk.

Behind the Mirage, eight Atlantic bottlenose dolphins live in a 2.5-million-gallon saltwater **Dolphin Habitat,** the largest in the world. The 15-minute tour, which leaves from the large and lush pool area, passes through an underwater observation area and winds up in a video room where you can watch tapes of two dolphin births at the habitat. A gift shop sells dolphin souvenirs, and there's a snack bar next door.

A major attraction at the Mirage is the **Secret Garden of Siegfried and Roy,** a palm-shaded sanctuary for a collection of the planet's rarest and most exotic creatures, including snow-white tigers, white lions, and an Asian elephant, all of which appeared in the Siegfried and Roy illusion extravaganza in the showroom until it closed indefinitely in October 2003. Both attractions are free for children under 11. Danny Gans, a impressionist par excellence, also performs here. ⊠ *3400 Las Vegas Blvd. S, Center Strip,* ☎ *702/791–7111 or 800/627–6667,* WEB *www. themirage.com.* 🎟 *Secret Garden and Dolphin Habitat $10, Dolphin Habitat alone $5 on Wed. and Thurs.–Sun. after 3.* ☉ *Secret Garden Mon.–Tues. and Thurs.–Fri. 11–5, weekends 10–5; Dolphin Habitat weekdays 11–7, weekends 10–7. Secret Garden closed Wed.*

★ **Paris Las Vegas.** This $785-million homage to the City of Lights tries to reproduce all the charm of the French capital. Outside are replicas of the Arc de Triomphe, the Paris Opera House, the Hôtel de Ville, and the Louvre, along with an *Around the World in Eighty Days* balloon marquee. Also out front is the Mon Ami Gabi café, offering rare alfresco dining right on the Strip. The main gaming area sits on Monet-style floral carpeting beneath a re-creation of Paris's wrought-iron art nouveau arches. Even the sinks in the rest rooms are French porcelain. Be sure to check out the dozen original LeRoy Neiman paintings that grace the walls of the high-roller pit. Paris Las Vegas offers several entertainment venues, including Le Théatre des Arts, a 1,200-seat Parisian-style theater that has hosted everything from French hip-hop groups to a musical version of *The Hunchback of Notre Dame.*

The 50-story **Eiffel Tower,** built almost exactly to a half-size scale, rises above it all; the Eiffel Tower Restaurant is on the 11th floor, and three legs of the tower come right through the casino roof, resting heavily on its floor. A glass elevator ascends to the tower's small observation deck (a caged catwalk) at the 460-foot level. While you can catch a better, bigger view of the Las Vegas Valley and have more walk-around room at the top of the Stratosphere, the Eiffel Tower offers an incomparable view of mid-Strip. After dark, hang around long enough to catch the dancing-waters show at Bellagio directly across the street.

Cobblestone "streets" meander through **Le Boulevard** shopping district, where you can purchase everything from fine jewelry to freshly baked breads and pastries; bread delivery men ride through on bicycles, singing "Alouette" in operatic voices. Both sweet and savory crepes are sold from a storefront window. ⊠ *3655 Las Vegas Blvd. S, Center Strip,* ☎ *702/739–4111 or 888/226–5687,* ⓦⒺⒷ *www.paris-lv. com.* ⌸ *Eiffel Tower $9.* ⊙ *Eiffel Tower daily 10 AM–1 AM.*

**Treasure Island Las Vegas (TI).** Shifting its focus from a family-oriented clientele to the adult market, Treasure Island has become TI. The buccaneer theme is being phased out in favor of more stylish trappings. The pool area is large and lush, and sits next to a tropical-theme restaurant and bar, Kahunaville. A short tram connects the hotel to the Mirage next door. Treasure Island hosts the Cirque du Soleil production *Mystère,* a spectacular display of strength, dance, acrobatics, and singing.

The free **Treasure Island Pirate Show,** performed several times a night (weather cooperating) is set to be revamped as well. In the old, Disneyesque version, the British Navy frigate HMS *Britannia* sailed around Skull Point from its mooring spot near Spring Mountain Road into Buccaneer Bay on the Strip. There it encountered the pirate schooner *Hispaniola,* and a live battle ensued. The show raged with spectacular pyrotechnics, an impressive sound system, and major stunts. Planned changes include the addition of female cast members, to be called "the Sirens of Treasure Island," and Broadway-caliber dance routines. ⊠ *3300 Las Vegas Blvd. S, Center Strip,* ☎ *702/894–7111 or 800/944–7444,* ⓦⒺⒷ *www.treasureislandlasvegas.com.* ⌸ *Pirate Battle free.* ⊙ *Pirate Battle performances every 90 minutes Sun.–Thurs. 5:30–10, Fri.–Sat. 5:30–11:30.*

★ ⓒ **Venetian Resort-Hotel-Casino.** The 44-year-old Sands was imploded in 1996 to make room for this $1.5-billion resort complex. This meticulously themed hotel re-creates Italy's most romantic city with reproductions of various Venetian landmarks. From the Strip, you enter through a reproduction of the Doge's Palace, set on a walkway over a 585,000-gallon lagoon. Inside, reproductions of famous paintings with gilded frames adorn a 65-foot dome ceiling above the casino lobby. Hanging behind the front desk is a giant pictorial overview of 17th-century Venice. The geometric design of the flat-marble floor provides an M. C. Escher–like optical illusion of climbing stairs. Renaissance characters roam the public areas, singing opera, performing mime, jesting, even kissing hands.

The centerpiece of the **Grand Canal Shops,** a 90-store mall, is the 1,200-foot-long reproduction of Venice's Canalozzo enclosed by brick walls and wrought-iron fencing. Gondolas (ride for $10 per person, same-day reservations usually required) ply the waterway, steered by serenading gondoliers. The canal ends at a colossal reproduction of St. Mark's Square, authentic right down to the colors of the facades. And it's also worth noting that the Venetian houses Venus—the first new Tiki Bar to be built in Las Vegas since the Stardust's classic Aku-Aku closed in the early 1980s.

**Madame Tussaud's Celebrity Encounter** displays more than 100 wax figures, many celebrating Sin City's past—classic Las Vegas crooners such as Tom Jones, Frank Sinatra, and Tony Bennett are among those replicated here.

The main draw at the **Guggenheim-Hermitage Museum** is a 7,660-square-foot "jewel box," whose high-concept iron-oxide walls form part of the Venetian's lobby and display masterworks from the Guggenheim and Hermitage collections. It was designed by Dutch architect Rem Koolhas, and would be worth seeing even if completely bereft of art. Guided tours are available; periodically, tour guides linger and give mini-tours for free. ⊠ *3355 Las Vegas Blvd. S, Center Strip,* ☎ *702/733–5000, 702/642–6440 wax museum, 800/494–3556,* WEB *www.venetian.com.* ⊠ *Wax museum $12.50, Hermitage-Guggenheim Museum $15.* ☉ *Wax museum daily 9:30–11; Hermitage-Guggenheim museum daily 9:30–8:30.*

# NORTH STRIP

The northern end of the Strip hasn't kept pace with the latest developments of the southern and center parts. In fact, the only large vacant lots on the Strip are in this area.

But with casino mogul Steve Wynn's plans to reopen the old Desert Inn as Wynn Las Vegas in 2005 (he is promising things that even Las Vegas has never seen before), the northern end of the Strip seems poised for a rebirth. Just consider the luxury condominiums cropping up next to, and across the street from, the venerable Sahara hotel.

## What to See

**Bonanza "World's Largest Gift Shop."** Those who are determined to visit only one gift shop in Las Vegas will want to make it this one. If it's not really the world's largest, it is the biggest and best in town, with an impressive collection of Las Vegas kitsch (this is where you'll find your life-size Wayne Newton blow-up doll), the most extensive selection of Las Vegas T-shirts and postcards, along with jewelry, gambling supplies, Western memorabilia, film, fudge, and aspirin. ⊠ *2460 Las Vegas Blvd. S, North Strip,* ☎ *702/385–7359.* ☉ *Daily 8 AM–midnight.*

**Candlelight Wedding Chapel.** Its central location helps to make this the town's busiest wedding chapel. Couples often line up here waiting to tie the knot (Saturday is especially busy). Anyone can watch a Las Vegas wedding ceremony; just walk in and take a seat. Some weddings take place in the gazebo outside the chapel. ⊠ *2855 Las Vegas Blvd. S, North Strip,* ☎ *702/735–4179,* WEB *www.nos.net/candlelight.*

☺ **Circus Circus.** Circus Circus opened in 1968, with the then-unique idea of appealing to the families that showed up in the adult fantasy land of Las Vegas. To this day, Circus Circus remains family central in Las Vegas—enticing to children, surreal to parents weaned on Hunter S. Thompson's "Fear and Loathing in Las Vegas." Under the pink-and-white big top, the clowns, trapeze stars, high-wire artists, unicyclists, and aerial dancers perform daily every 30 minutes from 11 AM to midnight. Also for the family market, Circus Circus has the only RV park on the Strip.

The **Circus Circus Carnival Midway** has old-time fair games (dime toss, milk can, bushel basket) along with clown-face painting, a video arcade with more than 200 games, fun-house mirrors, corn dogs, and pizza. Many parents park their teens on the midway while they go off to gamble, pull handles, and press buttons downstairs.

Behind the hotel-casino is the **Adventuredome**, a 5-acre indoor amusement park covered by a pink dome. Inside are the world's largest indoor roller coaster (the double-loop, double-corkscrew Canyon Blaster), a flume ride, a laser-tag room, bumper cars, four kiddie rides, a carnival midway, an arcade, and a snack bar. The roller coaster has two 360-degree loops and a corkscrew; it's a rough 105-second ride, but quite a thrill. If thrill rides are your thing, also check out the Inverter, 360 degrees of constant G force, and the Fun House Express, an IMAX motion-simulator experience. Designed exclusively for Circus Circus, the Fun House Express uses computer-generated images to portray a fast-paced roller coaster ride through a spooky world called Clown Chaos. ✉ 2880 Las Vegas Blvd. S, North Strip, ☎ 702/734–0410 or 800/634–3450, WEB www.circuscircus.com. 🖾 Adventuredome free, individual rides $2–$5, all-day wristbands $16.95. ☉ Amusement park Mon.–Thurs. 10–6, Fri.–Sat. 10 AM–midnight, Sun. 10–8; carnival midway daily 10 AM–midnight.

**Elvis-A-Rama Museum.** The quintessential Elvis experience can be found at this spot on Industrial Road (behind the Fashion Show Mall). The must-see museum (for Elvis fans, at least) houses four of the King's cars, including his purple Lincoln and his 1955 Fleetwood limo. More than 2,000 of Elvis's personal items are on display, including his jewelry, clothing, letters, and records. Every hour an Elvis impersonator croons to fans on a small stage; various impersonators cover different decades of his career. Buy Elvis clocks, key chains, pins, books, and other collectibles in the gift shop. Call the museum to arrange for a free shuttle pick-up from any major hotel on the Strip. ✉ 3401 Industrial Rd., North Strip, ☎ 702/309–7200, WEB www.elvisarama. com. 🖾 $9.95. ☉ Daily 10 AM–7 PM.

★ **Fashion Show Mall.** With Saks Fifth Avenue, Neiman Marcus, Nordstrom, Dillard's, Robinsons-May, and Bloomingdale's Home as anchor stores, plus boutiques and specialty shops, you'll be sure to find what you're looking for—and more. A fashion runway, new restaurants, and more airy space are some of the features that are appearing as the mall expands, and a Lord & Taylor will be included in the next phase. ✉ 3200 Las Vegas Blvd. S, North Strip, ☎ 702/369–8382, WEB www. thefashionshow.com. ☉ 10–5 daily.

**Guardian Angel Cathedral.** The cathedral often has standing room only on Saturday afternoons, as visitors pray for luck—and sometimes drop casino chips into the collection cups during a special tourist mass. Periodically, a priest known as the "chip monk" collects the chips and takes them to the respective casinos to cash them in. Those staying on the south end of the Strip might find the **Shrine of the Most Holy**

Redeemer, (✉ 55 E. Reno Ave., ☎ 702/891–8600) more convenient; it has one Saturday afternoon and three Sunday masses. ✉ *336 E. Desert Inn Rd., North Strip,* ☎ *702/735–5241.* ☉ *Sat. mass 2:30, 4, 5:15; Sun. mass 8, 9:30, 11, 12:30, 5.*

♻ **Guinness World of Records Museum.** The Las Vegas version of the best, biggest, and most bizarre has colorful displays, video footage (including clips of elaborate tumbling-dominoes layouts from around the world), and computer data banks of various Guinness world records covering sports, science, nature, and entertainment (the most-married man, the largest snowplow). There are models of the world's tallest man and shortest woman and the person with the world's longest neck. The Las Vegas display alone, which includes information on celebrities married here, the Stratosphere, and Hoover Dam, is worth the price of admission. ✉ *2780 Las Vegas Blvd. S, North Strip,* ☎ *702/792– 3766,* WEB *www.guinnessmuseum.com.* ⛶ *$6.* ☉ *Daily 9–5:30.*

**Las Vegas Convention Center.** More than 4 million people attend the more than 1,000 conventions of varying sizes that are held every year in this 3.2-million-square-foot space that's one of the country's largest convention centers. One of the most attractive aspects for conventioneers is its proximity to all the hotels and the airport, and there's a visitors center right off the parking-lot lobby. ✉ *3150 Paradise Rd., North Strip,* ☎ *702/892–0711,* WEB *www.lasvegas24hours.com.*

♻ **Las Vegas Hilton.** Barbra Streisand opened this hotel (then the International) with a four-week gig and was followed by Elvis Presley, who made the Hilton his official Las Vegas venue throughout the 1970s. You can still stay in the Elvis Suite on the 31st floor, where the king of rock and roll resided when he played here. Though the Hilton, which is adjacent to the Las Vegas Convention Center, no longer holds the title of largest hotel in town, it's still a sight to see—best of all by standing at its foot and staring up at the 29-story three-wing tower.

The biggest attraction at the Hilton is **Star Trek: The Experience** (WEB www.startrekexp.com), a $70-million museum and interactive theater/motion-simulator ride. Trekkies will go nuts over the museum, which has a Star Trek time line of future history, costumes and props, and video loops from the shows. During the theater/ride, the audience is kidnapped by the Klingons and beamed into the 24th century and onto the bridge of the Starship *Enterprise*; it's up to the crew to get everyone safely back to the 21st-century Hilton. ✉ *3000 W. Paradise Rd., North Strip,* ☎ *702/732–5111 or 800/774–1500,* WEB *www.lv-hilton.com.* ⛶ *Star Trek $24.99 (all-day pass).* ☉ *Star Trek daily 11–11.*

**New Frontier Hotel and Casino.** The New Frontier is the oldest hotel-casino on the Las Vegas Strip, beating out the Flamingo by a full five years. In 1942, Hollywood producer D. W. Griffith opened the Last Frontier, the second hotel on the Los Angeles Highway (soon to be known as the Las Vegas Strip). It was sold in 1951 and renamed Last Frontier Village. The original building was torn down and replaced in 1955; the new hotel-casino was named the New Frontier. That structure was torn down and replaced again in 1967 and the property was named simply the Frontier. In 1998 it was sold again and renamed the New Frontier. (Confused yet?) The vestibule of the Atrium (all-suite) Tower is gardenlike, with a waterfall, creek, and pools. ✉ *3120 Las Vegas Blvd. S, North Strip,* ☎ *702/794–8200 or 800/634–6966,* WEB *www.frontierlv.com.*

**Riviera Hotel and Casino.** Here's a piece of old Las Vegas: the Riviera has been gracing the Las Vegas Strip since 1955, when it became the famous street's ninth resort (and one of the few of those nine remaining). The Riviera is mostly known for its multitude of lights that brighten up this part of the Strip—and for its entertainment. It's the home of those *Crazy Girls* whose near-bare behinds grace cabs and billboards all over town; *An Evening at La Cage,* whose female impersonators include Joan Rivers look-alike Frank Marino; *Splash*, the only show on the Strip with ice-skating; and a popular comedy club. Film buffs may recognize the hotel-casino as the backdrop for dozens of Las Vegas films, including *Casino, Diamonds are Forever,* and *Austin Powers: International Man of Mystery.* ✉ *2901 Las Vegas Blvd. S, North Strip,* ☎ *702/734–5110 or 800/634–6753,* WEB *www.theriviera.com.*

**Sahara Hotel and Casino.** The line between old Las Vegas and new is clear at the Sahara. The former Rat Pack haunt manages to encompass both old school swank and the popular NASCAR café, themed for the hottest sports franchise in recent years.

Near the NASCAR Cafe is **Cyber Speedway,** a $15-million virtual reality race car–driving experience, where 3-D motion-simulator rides make audience members feel as though they're driving on the Las Vegas Motor Speedway or the Las Vegas Strip.

The Sahara's signature roller coaster, **Speed—The Ride,** uses magnetic technology to propel riders through a tunnel, around a loop, and in and out of the building at speeds of more than 70 mph. Then you do the entire thing again—backwards. And magician Steve Wyrick performs 10 shows a week in the Sahara Theater—each of them including the appearance of a twin-engine aircraft, for the largest stage illusion in this over-the-top town. ✉ *2535 Las Vegas Blvd. S, North Strip,* ☎ *702/737–2111, 800/634–6666, 702/737–2750 NASCAR Cafe,* WEB *www.saharavegas.com.* ✇ *Rides $8.* ☉ *Speed—The Ride weekdays 10–10, weekends 10 AM–midnight; Cyber Speedway weekdays 10–10, weekends 10 AM–11 PM.*

**Stardust Hotel and Casino.** The Stardust has one of the best facades on the Strip: pink and blue neon tubes run down the front of the hotel, leading to a 183-foot programmed sign that erupts in bursts of neon stars. On its debut in 1958, the sign was the largest and brightest in Las Vegas, its glow visible for miles. The vision for the Stardust came from mobster Tony Cornero, who in the 1930s ran gambling ships off the southern California coast; he owned a small club out on Boulder Highway and dreamed of building the biggest, classiest casino in town. Cornero didn't live long enough to realize his dream, however; one morning, while shooting craps at the Desert Inn, he had a heart attack, dying with the dice in his hands. Today the Stardust is known for its sports book and has the distinction of exclusively hosting Wayne Newton, "Mr. Las Vegas" himself, in a showroom named for him. ✉ *3000 Las Vegas Blvd. S, North Strip,* ☎ *702/732–6111 or 800/634–6757,* WEB *www.stardustlv.com.*

---

NEED A
BREAK?

Between the Stardust and the Westward Ho is a **McDonald's** (✉ 2880 Las Vegas Blvd. S, North Strip, ☎ 702/731–1575) with the golden arches all decked out in neon and flashing lights. The window seats inside this frantic franchise provide a good view of the automobile, pedestrian, and pigeon traffic on the Strip.

---

★ ☺ **Stratosphere Casino Hotel & Tower.** The view from the tower and the thrill rides at the top make it worth the extra effort to get to this hotel-casino, which occupies a sort of no-man's land a few blocks beyond the traditional northern end of the Strip.

The aforementioned view has no peer—you'll be looking down at Las Vegas from the top of the the tallest **observation tower** in the United States, dominating the Las Vegas skyline at 1,149 feet. Although the view is impressive enough during the day, save a trip to the tower for the evening.

High above the Las Vegas Strip are the Stratosphere's two **thrill rides:** the Big Shot and the High Roller. The Big Shot would be a monster ride on the ground, but being high atop the Stratosphere Tower makes it twice as wild. Four riders are strapped into chairs on four sides of the needle, which rises from the Stratosphere's observation pod (the base of the ride is on the 112th floor). With little warning, you're flung 160 feet up the needle, then dropped like a rock. The whole thing is over in less than a minute, but your knees will wobble for the rest of the day. The High Roller is a roller coaster that, although tame by ground standards, is quite thrilling owing to its perch high atop the tower.

For the less daring, the Stratosphere also has the revolving Top of the World restaurant and lounge, set 900 feet above the valley. The restaurant makes a complete revolution once every hour or so, and both offer big views. The shopping plaza between the casino and entrance to the tower houses more than 50 eateries and retail stores. The Strat-O-Fair, at the base of the tower, has a small Ferris wheel and other rides suitable for children, and the new events center periodically hosts concerts. ⊠ *2000 Las Vegas Blvd. S, North Strip,* ☎ *702/380–7777 or 800/380– 7732,* WEB *www.stratospherehotel.com.* ☎ *Big Shot $11, High Roller $9, prices include admission to the tower elevator both rides and tower admission $15 Strat-O-Fair rides $3.* ☉ *Rides Sun.–Thurs. 10 AM–1 AM, Fri.–Sat. 10 AM–2 AM.*

**Westward Ho.** The Westward Ho is a rarity on the Strip: a sprawling low-rise motel. With 1,000 rooms (some of them three-room suites), the Ho claims to be the largest motel in the world. It has seven pools and no elevators. The casino is for gamblers, not gawkers, and has a dizzying array of slot machines and low-minimum table games. The snack bar is a local favorite, serving a huge strawberry shortcake. ⊠ *2900 Las Vegas Blvd. S, North Strip,* ☎ *702/731–2900 or 800/634– 6803,* WEB *www.westwardho.com.*

🄲 **Wet 'n Wild Water Park.** This 26-acre water park provides family-oriented recreation in a 500,000-gallon wave pool, three water flumes, a water roller coaster, slides, cascading fountains, and lagoons. Showers, changing rooms, and lockers are available, and inner tubes and rafts are for rent. Shops and concession stands sell souvenirs and food. ⊠ *601 Las Vegas Blvd. S, North Strip,* ☎ *702/737–3819,* WEB *www. wetnwildlasvegas.com.* ☎ *$25.95.* ☉ *May–Oct., opens daily at 10 AM, closing times vary.*

**Wynn Collection.** Steve Wynn enjoys two things: building bigger and better resort hotels, and collecting art. While he indulges his first passion on the lot next door—Wynn Las Vegas, a 3,000-room luxury hotel currently scheduled for completion in 2005—he shares his other joy in a gallery inside one of the former Desert Inn hotel wings. The Wynn Collection is world-class and includes works by Matisse, Van Gogh, and Modigliani and Picasso's "Le Reve." His collection equals the Guggenheim-Hermitage in quality. ⊠ *3145 Las Vegas Blvd. S, North Strip,* ☎ *702/733–4100.* ☎ *$10.* ☉ *Weekdays 10–9, Sat. 10–7, Sun. noon–6.*

# DOWNTOWN

If you've never traveled north of the Stratosphere Tower, you're missing a vital piece of Vegas legacy: Downtown Las Vegas is where Sin City was born. Las Vegas's first telephone was installed here; its first concrete building was built here (the Golden Gate Casino, opened in 1906 and still going strong); its first train station was at the tip of Fremont Street. And the notorious "Block 16," a block of gambling halls, bars, and legal brothels, remained in business until 1941. That was the last time prostitution was legal within city limits.

The pioneering spirit of those days lives on Fremont Street. Even though the world-famous "Glitter Gulch" was closed to automobiles and transformed into a pedestrian mall in the mid-'90s, the hotels of Fremont still seem like they should have hitching posts in front of them. The lights down here literally turn night to day, and the street's patron saints, the 50-foot-tall neon cowboy Vegas Vic and his gal, Sassy Sally, still welcome all comers with a sincere "howdy." And Fremont Street has one of Las Vegas's most spectacular sights—the four-block long Fremont Street Experience light canopy. The shows that run on it hourly, though a bit corny, are ever-changing and have to be seen to be believed.

The best way to see Fremont Street is to go with its flow—accept the free slot pulls and roulette spins you're offered, watch the shows on the light canopy, shop the weird souvenir stands, accumulate free souvenirs, and enjoy the inexpensive food and drink.

## What to See

**Binion's Horseshoe Hotel and Casino.** The late Benny Binion wanted the Horseshoe to be a gambler's haven. So while other casinos are morphing into family attractions, Binion's is still holding true to its founder's vision. With low ceilings and an Old Vegas charm, Binion's Horseshoe is a place to lay your money on the table, as many do for a living: Binion's hosts the World Series of Poker, an event that draws professional poker players from all over the world each spring. If you're keen to participate, all you need is a $10,000 ante and a lot of guts. But don't think of making a grab—Binion's also has one of the few remaining displays of guns in a casino in Nevada (including several of Benny's custom-gilt rifles and pistols). For a glimpse of what Las Vegas used to be, there's no other place than Binion's. ⊠ *128 E. Fremont St., Downtown,* ☏ *702/382–1600 or 800/237–6537,* WEB *www.binions.com.*

**California Hotel and Casino.** While it isn't so very different from most other downtown casinos (low ceilings and old-school charm), there is one quirk about this place: the California is the chief hangout for Hawaiians in Vegas. Though there's no real island theme, this hotel-casino has built a reputation for serving tourists from America's 50th state with enthusiastic hospitality. Saimin is served at the snack bar, the dealers wear Hawaiian shirts, and the carpeting is patterned with tropical flora. Upstairs is a karaoke bar; the later it gets in the evening (and the more inebriated the performers), the more fun it can be. A pedestrian bridge connects to Main Street Station across the street, with a few shops on either side. ⊠ *12 E. Ogden Ave., Downtown,* ☏ *702/385–1222,* WEB *www.thecal.com.*

**Cashman Field.** For a look at Las Vegas's other convention center, which doubles as a sports venue, drive a mile north from Fremont Street on Las Vegas Boulevard. The attractive facility has a 100,000-square-foot exhibit hall, 17,000 square feet of meeting space, and the 2,000-seat auditorium that was used as the courtroom for the trial of Wayne Newton's libel suit against NBC News. ✉ *850 Las Vegas Blvd. N, Downtown, (2 mi north of its corner with Fremont St. downtown),* ☎ *702/386–7100.*

**El Cortez Hotel.** Bugsy Siegel showed up in Las Vegas in 1942 and immediately began to muscle into whatever downtown joints didn't resist him. He started out at the El Cortez, then sold his share and bought into the El Rancho Vegas, then sold that for $1 million, his seed capital to build the Flamingo. Though nothing from that time remains of the other joints, the original El Cortez still stands on the corner of Fremont and 6th streets—including the 60-year-old marquee. Inside, the old wing is delightfully frayed around the edges (contrary to appearances and popular opinion, the carpeting *has* been replaced since it opened) and is a great place to people-watch. The coffee shop serves the last round-the-clock $1 bacon-and-eggs breakfast special in town. The "new" wing, built in the early 1980s, houses the race and sports book, hotel lobby, and Roberta's, one of Las Vegas's great "bargain gourmet" restaurants. ✉ *600 E. Fremont St., Downtown,* ☎ *702/385–5200 or 800/634–6703,* WEB *www.elcortez.net.*

**Fitzgeralds Hotel and Casino.** It's hard to miss this place. With a sweeping, illuminated rainbow stretched across its front facade, Fitzgeralds is easy to spot along Fremont Street's packed pedestrian mall. Inside, the entire casino is decked out in green, money and otherwise—pieces of the Blarney Stone are on display, direct from Ireland's famous Blarney Castle. Lucky's Lookout (off the Sports Bar) has the only second-floor outdoor balcony along Fremont Street. Arrive early to grab one of the patio lounge chairs and land one of the best spots to see the Fremont Street Experience light-and-sound shows. ✉ *301 E. Fremont St., Downtown,* ☎ *702/388–2400 or 800/274–5825,* WEB *www.fitzgeralds.com.*

**Four Queens Hotel and Casino.** In the heart of Fremont Street, the Four Queens' radiating neon rivals the canopy's lightbulb display. Inside, the casino is dark and lushly appointed. A "Big Bertha" slot machine attracts attention at the 2nd Street entrance; at the 3rd Street entrance there's usually a free-pull promotion going on. Otherwise, the Four Queens is typical of the downtown joints: the gambling is the thing. ✉ *202 E. Fremont St., Downtown,* ☎ *702/385–4011 or 800/634–6045,* WEB *www.fourqueens.com.*

**Fremont Hotel and Casino.** A downtown staple since original owner Sam Levinson switched on its fiery neon back in 1956, the Fremont is a Vegas landmark. It was the first high-rise hotel on Fremont Street. Wayne Newton made his Las Vegas debut here. Even after Boyd Gaming bought the hotel in 1985, the Fremont has remained one of the city's cornerstones. Inside, the old-style casino is reminiscent of many of the other gambling halls downtown, although the neon surrounding the main pit is unique. The poker room walls are graced with interesting Western murals. ✉ *200 E. Fremont St., Downtown,* ☎ *702/385–3232,* WEB *www.fremontcasino.com.*

★ **Fremont Street Experience.** In an effort to revive downtown Las Vegas, a partnership consisting of 10 hotels, the city, a privately owned corporation, and the Las Vegas Convention and Visitors Authority created the $70-million Fremont Street Experience, which debuted in 1995. The resulting pedestrian mall is festooned with souvenir stands and cafés, and features live entertainment ranging from mimes to rock bands, but the real attraction is overhead. The sign above this pedestrian mall is the largest electric sign in the world. (The next-largest sign, at the Las Vegas Hilton, is a 50th of its size.) The display is the length of 4½ football fields; the 2.1 million lightbulbs can produce 65,000 colors; the electricity required to run it could power nearly 2,000 homes; 208 speakers operate independently but combine for 540,000 watts of sound—and improvements are under way to beef things up even more. Six-minute light shows are presented on the hour after dark; it takes 31 computers and 100 gigabytes of memory to run the shows, and it's a don't-miss, only-in-Las Vegas experience. ⊠ *Fremont St. from Main to 4th Sts., Downtown,* ☎ *702/678–5600,* WEB *www.vegasexperience.com.*

**Golden Gate Hotel.** This is, without a doubt, the city's most historic hotel. It stands proudly, though dwarfed by the high-rises that have been built around it during its 95-year history. The tiny hotel-casino opened in 1906 (as the Hotel Nevada) and not much has changed here since then. Many of the original fixtures are still in place. The inspiration is San Francisco, as evidenced by the large historical photographs. This was the first hotel-casino to introduce the cheap shrimp cocktail to Las Vegas, and its 99-cent wonder is a perennial winner in the Las Vegas Review-Journal's annual Best of Las Vegas survey. A piano player entertains the crowds eating the crunchy crustacean cocktails in the Deli. ⊠ *1 Fremont St., Downtown,* ☎ *702/385–1906,* WEB *www. goldengatecasino.net.*

**Golden Nugget Hotel and Casino.** The Golden Nugget is the classiest joint downtown. The white marble walls, gold-plated slots, and etched-glass windows all stand in stark contrast to the many dark and rustic hotels that surround Fremont Street. The Golden Nugget is also the largest hotel-casino downtown, encompassing 2½ city blocks (including the big parking garage). And it has the biggest and best pool downtown, a concrete courtyard surrounded by the hotel towers, always crowded with sunbathers and swimmers. The most amazing thing about the Golden Nugget, though, is the display of gold nuggets just off the lobby. Here you'll find the world's largest nugget, the 61-pound "Hand of Faith," along with several dozen other stunning specimens of the precious metal. ⊠ *129 E. Fremont St., Downtown,* ☎ *702/385–7111 or 800/634–3454,* WEB *www.goldennugget.com.*

**Lady Luck Casino and Hotel.** The Lady Luck started out as Honest John's newsstand in 1964. It's grown a bit since then. The high-rise casino now includes 40,000 square feet of casino space designed specifically for tourists looking to lay their money down. A large neon arch beckons one and all. The prime-rib specials in the coffee shop are locally famous, as is the funbook handed out free to all out-of-town visitors; one of the coupons is good for a free three-minute long-distance phone call from a 1950s English phone booth. ⊠ *206 N. 3rd St., Downtown,* ☎ *702/477–3000 or 800/634–6580,* WEB *www.ladylucklv.com.*

**Las Vegas Academy of International Studies, Visual and Performing Arts.** This historic structure, the oldest permanent school building in Las Vegas, was built as a high school in 1930 for $350,000. It's a state historical landmark, the only example of 1930s art deco architecture in the city. ⊠ *315 S. 7th St., Downtown,* ☎ *702/799–7800.*

**Las Vegas Club Hotel and Casino.** Established in the early 1900s, the Las Vegas Club is a sports-theme casino and hotel. There's not much in the way of entertainment here, but value seekers are sure to appreciate the low-price meals and drinks. It was expanded in the mid-'90s and is now a bit of a maze, covering half a city block. The Las Vegas Club also houses a large private collection of sports memorabilia, some of which is displayed throughout the property. ⊠ *18 E. Fremont St., Downtown,* ☎ *702/385–1664 or 800/634–6532,* WEB *www.playatlvc.com.*

☺ **Las Vegas Natural History Museum.** The museum has displays of mammals of places from Alaska to Africa, and has rooms full of sharks (including live ones, swimming in a 3,000-gallon reef tank), birds, dinosaur fossils, and hands-on exhibits. Here kids have a chance to walk past a 35-foot Tyrannosaurus rex that lowers its head and roars, see the ichthyosaur Shonisaurus, Nevada's state fossil, and tour the Wild Nevada Gallery, where they can see, smell, and even touch Nevada wildlife. The big gift shop is full of games, puzzles, books, clothes, and animals. ⊠ *900 Las Vegas Blvd. N, Downtown,* ☎ *702/384–3466.* ☞ *$6 for adults, $3 children 3–11.* ◔ *Daily 9–4.*

☺ **Lied Discovery Children's Museum.** One of the largest children's museums in the nation at roughly 25,000 square feet, the Lied (pronounced *leed*) contains more than 100 hands-on exhibits covering the sciences, arts, and humanities. Children can pilot a space shuttle, perform on stage, or stand in a giant bubble. In the Desert Discovery area for children age five and under, youngsters are entertained and educated with a number of hands-on interactive displays, including Boulder Mountain, where children don hard hats and mine soft sculpture boulders in geometric shapes. Also in Desert Discovery is the Baby Oasis, a safe haven for tots who aren't yet walking that has colorful and stimulating props and toys, including a mirrored pull-up bar and a crawling structure of gently inclined ramps that encourage large-muscle development. ⊠ *833 Las Vegas Blvd. N, Downtown,* ☎ *702/ 382–3445,* WEB *www.ldcm.org.* ☞ *$6 for adults, $5 children 1–17.* ◔ *Tues.–Sun. 10–5.*

★ **Main Street Station Casino, Brewery & Hotel.** Downtown's largest and best buffet can be found here, along with the only microbrewery downtown (the Triple 7 Brew Pub, with live entertainment every weekend night). The hotel has a fabulous collection of antiques, artifacts, and collectibles. There are self-guided tours of the collection, which includes Buffalo Bill Cody's private rail car; a fireplace from Scotland's Prestwick Castle; lamps that graced the streets of 18th-century Brussels; and beautiful statues, chandeliers, and woodwork from American mansions of long ago. There's even a piece of the Berlin Wall—in the men's room off the lobby. ⊠ *200 N. Main St., Downtown,* ☎ *702/387–1896 or 800/713–8933,* WEB *www.mainstreetcasino.com.*

☺ **Nevada State Museum and Historical Society.** Regional history, from the time of the Spanish exploration to the building of Las Vegas after World War II, is the subject of this museum, which also covers the archaeology and anthropology of southern Nevada. It's near the lake in Lorenzi Park, an open space dotted with ponds and home to plants and animals native to the region. ⊠ *700 E. Twin Lakes Dr., Downtown, (2 mi west of the corner of Fremont and Main Sts.),* ☎ *702/486– 5205.* ☞ *$2.* ◔ *Daily 9–5.*

☺ **Old Las Vegas Mormon Fort.** Southern Nevada's oldest historical site was built by the Mormons in 1855 as an agricultural mission to give refuge to travelers along the Salt Lake–Los Angeles trail, many of whom were bound for the California gold fields. Left to the Native Americans after the gold rush, the adobe fort was later revitalized by a miner and his partners. In 1895 it was turned into a resort, and the city's first swimming pool was constructed by damming Las Vegas Creek. Today the restored fort contains more than half the original bricks. Antiques and artifacts help re-create a turn-of-the-20th-century Mormon living room. ⊠ *Washington Ave. and Las Vegas Blvd. N, at Cashman Field (enter through parking lot B), Downtown,* ☎ *702/486–3511,* WEB *www.state.nv.us.* ☞ *$2.* ◔ *Daily 8:30–4:30.*

**Plaza Hotel and Casino.** Jackie Gaughan is a Las Vegas legend. He spent time in Nevada during World War II, first in Las Vegas and later in Tonopah, where he trained gunners for the Air Corps' B-17 bombers. He and his wife Roberta (Bertie) and their two sons, the late Jackie Jr. and Michael (who became a casino mogul himself), settled here for good in 1951. He bought a 3% interest in the old downtown Boulder Club on Fremont Street, where the Horseshoe now stands. A short time later he bought a 3% interest in the Flamingo Hotel on the Strip. In 1961, he opened the Las Vegas Club and in 1963 he bought the Cortez. He purchased the Union Plaza Hotel & Casino in 1971 and the Gold Spike Hotel & Casino in 1983. The Plaza sits at the end of Fremont Street, looming over the Fremont Street Experience. It's a sleeper, but it does have low table minimums and great nickel machines, live lounge entertainment, excellent snack-bar food at rock-bottom prices, and a hall of mirrors lining the south staircase. Also here is the largest downtown showroom (one of only three), a second-floor pool deck, and the Center Stage Restaurant, which sits in a dome looking right down the throat of Glitter Gulch. ⊠ *1 Main St., Downtown,* ☎ *702/386–2110 or 800/ 634–6575,* WEB *www.plazahotelcasino.com.*

**Vegas Vic.** The famous Las Vegas icon known as Vegas Vic is about the same age as the average Las Vegas visitor. The original version of this well-known landmark was unveiled in 1947, but was replaced by a newer version in 1951. Now Vegas Vic, a 50-foot-tall neon cowboy, stands outside the Pioneer Club, waving to visitors. Vegas Vic's neon sidekick, Sassy Sally, went up across the street in 1980.

# 3 CASINOS

In a town with over one hundred hotel-casinos, all pushing basically the same product, each has to outsell the next. Some joints discount the product more than others. Some use loss leaders to attract customers into the store. Some emphasize service, while others tout exclusivity. Gimmicks, glitz, flesh, and gluttony are all employed in the merchandising. Part of the fun of Las Vegas is to surrender to your temptations. Chances are you'll only remain seduced for a few days, and win or lose, you'll take home very fond memories.

By Deke
Castleman

Updated by
Mike
Weatherford

**C**ONVENTIONAL WISDOM NOTWITHSTANDING, you *can* win in the casinos and many people do. But, as explained in Chapter 9, the odds are riding against you. And that's just for starters. The dazzling lights, the free beer and cocktails, the play money, the absence of windows and clocks, even the oxygen—and, lately, seductive aromas—pumped into the air are all calculated to overwhelm you with a sense of holiday impetuousness that keeps you reaching into your pocket or purse for the green.

Tens of millions of people who *don't* know the odds of, or the strategies for, casino games come to Las Vegas every year, and some of them even win now and then. But let's face it: most people go home with a lighter wallet. Las Vegas casinos make a fortune by taking a big bite out of millions of bankrolls. With table games they keep on average 15% of the cash a player gives for chips; with the slot machines they hold around 25%.

So walk into the casino knowing that the house always has the edge. But who knows, you could beat the odds and walk away a winner. Spend a little time beforehand memorizing the game rules, studying casino etiquette, and taking one of the free gambling lessons offered at most casinos. Then you can join the tables with the all the aplomb of James Bond.

## Casino Etiquette

### Getting In and Around

Casinos can be confusing places for the first-time visitor. They tend to be large, open rooms full of people who seem to know exactly what they're doing, while you wander around lost. Cameras hung from the ceiling watch your movements, and all the security guards, pit bosses, and dealers seem to be doing the same. Worst of all, there are no signs, announcements, or tour guides to inform newcomers of the rules of behavior. So we'll do that right here.

All players must be at least 21 years of age with no exceptions. If you're playing a slot with a child by your side, a security guard will quickly appear (dispatched by casino surveillance) and ask you to leave. But you can walk through the casino with your youngster in tow; as long as you're on the move, you're OK.

Your personal electronic items are also frowned upon in the casino. No electronics, including cell phones, can be used while seated at a casino game. The thick walls of most large casinos block cell phone reception anyhow so you'll have to walk outside to get a dial tone. In the sports book of the casino, pagers and cell phones cannot be used at all.

Casinos are traditionally camera shy, but no longer as stringent about no-photography rules that for years protected players; management feared they would get up and leave if a camera was pointed their way. Gambling is now more accepted as a mainstream pastime, and it's hard to separate the gaming floor from the public right-of-way in many a casino. Moreover, few casinos want to come off as less friendly than the Four Queens, Excalibur, and Harrah's casinos that now allow photos. When in doubt, ask a security guard.

Smokers on the other hand find casinos a welcome relief. Those who are annoyed by cigarette or cigar smoke will need to find a non-smoking table or slots area. The casinos' smoke permeates clothing quickly so don't count on re-wearing too many outfits.

The security of your person and pocketbook shouldn't be forgotten in the bustle of the casino. While the casino tries to protect its patrons with omnipresent security cameras and guards, the crowds and distractions overwhelm their vigilance. You probably won't be mugged inside a casino, but theft or short-changing can easily happen. Do not leave purses on a table or hanging off the back of a chair. Instead, keep the purse in your lap. Casino chips should not be left on the table under the dealer's protection while you take a quick bathroom break. Recount any chips and cash that casino personnel hand over to you immediately—once you leave the table or cage, you cannot get a mistake corrected. Finally, do not hesitate to request a security guard to escort you to the casino parking lot late at night, especially in downtown Las Vegas.

## Joining The Games

Almost all casinos offer craps, blackjack, slots, video poker, and roulette. The major casinos will, in addition, have live poker, sports betting, baccarat, keno, and an ever-growing list of table games. Stick to video poker, slots, and roulette if you're nervous about the arcane rules and want a relaxing visit.

Table games, especially blackjack and craps, offer the novice the greatest challenges. However, these games remain two of the most popular in Las Vegas. Free daily lessons at most Strip casinos will warm the tables for blackjack or craps. The beginner's course will let you belly up to the tables with confidence. Don't hesitate to ask any question you like at the table. If a dealer doesn't answer, or is rude, walk away to another table—or another casino. At some of the smaller and less crowded gambling houses, dealers will take time to orient players to new games. If you're a newcomer to the tables, avoid the larger houses, especially at peak hours, because the personnel may be too busy to help you.

Before you sit down at a table, be sure to look at the little placard that announces the betting minimum and maximum. Most casinos offer a range of betting minimums, but the low minimum tables tend to be packed. For example, blackjack tables have minimums of $1 to $500 and maximums up to $10,000. Minimums in casinos on the Strip are generally higher than those of downtown casinos.

Consider also the timing of your casino visit. Las Vegas wakes up around lunchtime, then peaks between 11 PM and midnight. If you arrive at a busy hour, tables may be scarce at the minimums you desire. Weekends are also the busiest time of the week for Vegas as half of California drives in for a quick roll.

## Comps and Tipping

Within a few minutes of joining any table, you'll be offered your first casino comp, or complimentary gift: "drinks, anyone?" The cocktail waitress will smilingly offer free alcohol and other liquids as long as you keep playing. Comps go way beyond free booze to include free rooms, shows, meals, gifts, limos, and airfares. It all depends on your rating, the casino's estimate of how much you bet and for how long. The rating determines how much in comps you'll receive. Comps include stuffing your mailbox with outstanding coupons to entice you to return even if you only bet a little. Smaller casinos may even give you coupons just for walking onto their property. To get on the comps gravy train, get a player's card, either from the pit boss or the player's club. Make sure that all of your gambling is rated, or recorded by the casino. Slot machines have small slots for the player's card, but at table games you'll have to make sure the pit boss receives your card. After about 30 minutes of play you can try to ask politely for a buffet comp, a relatively easy comp to earn. Perhaps he sniffs at your request—but then again you might have a free meal.

Tipping the dealers and cocktail waitresses is also a key element of casino etiquette. Dealers are paid minimum wage at the casinos, and they expect to be tipped when you are winning. It's neither mandatory nor necessary, however, it's only up to your own discretion. Some dealers will "suggest" a tip of 10% of your net win, but this is very generous on your part. Slipping a dealer or change person a chip is like any other tip: a small gratuity for services rendered. This small generosity usually relaxes the dealer, and thus the game, considerably. At most casinos, dealers pool their tips and then split them evenly. So be aware that no matter how much you toke a good dealer, he or she will receive only a percentage. Cocktail waitresses expect $1 for each drink brought to you.

## Las Vegas Lingo

Before you start gambling, you'll want to learn some key words in the local language.

**Bankroll.** The amount of cash an individual has to gamble with.

**Black chip.** $100 casino chip, usually black.

**Buy-in.** The amount of cash with which a player enters a game.

**Cage.** The casino cashier station where you can exchange your chips for cash.

**Check.** Another name for a casino chip.

**Comp.** A gift from the casino of a complimentary drink, room, dinner, or show; a freebie.

**Eye.** The overhead video surveillance system and its human monitors in a casino. All videotapes are kept for seven days in Nevada.

**Full-pay video poker.** A video poker game that, if you know perfect strategy, gives you an edge over the casino. Perfect video poker strategy is very difficult to memorize and the casino's counting on player errors.

**Green chip.** $25 casino chip, usually green.

**Grind joint.** A gambling house that promotes low table minimums and slot denominations. You won't find too many high rollers at one.

**High roller.** A casino customer who plays with a bankroll of $5,000 or more. Some grind joints consider a $1,000 bankroll to be high-roller action; some premium joints require a $10,000 bankroll.

**Hold.** The house profit from all the wagers; what the casino wins.

**Live poker.** Traditional poker games such as seven-card stud that are played against other individuals and not the casino.

**Low roller.** A typical tourist making 25¢ slot machine bets or $1 and $2 table-game bets.

**Marker.** A casino IOU. Players sign markers and get chips at the tables; they then pay off the markers with chips or cash.

**Pit.** A group of tables forming a closed circle on the casino floor. The pit bosses and dealers stand in the middle and serve the customers who sit on the outside. Visitors can't walk into the middle of the pit.

**Pit boss.** The person who supervises the action on the gaming tables. The pit boss's domain, the pit, is an area surrounded by tables that is off-limits to the general public.

**Player's card.** A card with a magnetic stripe on it used to track a gambler's activities in a casino. A player's card makes it easy for the casino to rate you and therefore give you comps.

**Rating.** Tracking a gambler's average bet, length of time played, and net loss. Getting rated helps you get comps.

**RFB.** The cream of comps—room, food, and beverage, courtesy of the casino. All you have to do is play (depending on the casino) $75–$250 a hand for four hours a day.

**Red Chip.** $5 casino chip, usually red.

**Shill.** A person employed by the casino to sit at the tables and play games during the less busy hours—with the casino's money. Shills are only used in live poker games.

**Sports Book.** The casino area for sports betting. Cell phones and pagers are prohibited in sports book.

**Sweating the money.** Pit boss nervousness and anger toward a winning player.

**Table Games.** All games of chance such as blackjack and craps played against the casino with the help of a dealer.

**Toke.** A tip (short for token, or token of your esteem). This may be the word you'll hear most often; many of the folks you encounter will be expecting a toke.

## How Not to Go Broke

You should decide before leaving on your vacation how much money you will spend on gambling. This is your gambling bankroll. Gambling newbies will be shocked at how quickly the bankroll disappears at the table. As a rule of thumb, a $1,000 bankroll for a weekend trip of gambling will let you bet $5 to $10 a hand at blackjack or play 25¢ slots. That's it if you hope to get in five hours of gambling. If you bet $25 a hand at blackjack with the $1,000 bankroll you will most likely run out of money within an hour. ATM or credit card cash withdrawals carry hefty surcharges and should be avoided at all times. A cash advance also leads to you gambling with money you don't have and its devastating consequences.

If you want to shrink the casino's edge over you, take the time to read up on the game strategy in Chapter 9. Then, when you have some idea of the basics, attend the free gambling lessons provided at most major casinos. Even if you think you know the rules, these lessons will give you an opportunity to play the game at an actual session and learn the etiquette using practice chips instead of your own cash. Call ahead and get the exact schedule of these free lessons. Most gift shops will also sell you a small plastic card of a rough strategy for the various games. You can have one in hand as you play your game of choice.

# THE CASINOS

This guide progresses as most Las Vegas vacations do, starting with the casinos on the Strip, or Las Vegas Boulevard, then continuing to the growing ranks of major off-Strip and "locals" casinos (those frequented by area residents). After that come the downtown casinos on and near Fremont Street, then the casinos on the "Boulder Strip" and the "Rancho Strip." The final journey is to the farthest-out casinos in the fast-growing suburb of Henderson. The listings in each area are arranged in alphabetical order. These descriptions are intended to help you find the casinos that will most appeal to you. If you'd like to save time by sleeping where you gamble, Chapter 5 has details on the hotels in which most of these casinos are found. All the casinos have restaurants and most have all-you-can-eat buffets so you can also eat where you sleep and gamble.

## The Strip

The Strip casinos, all along Las Vegas Boulevard, are packed in so tight you'll see nothing driving by but one frenetic neon sign on top of another. Strip casinos run the gamut in size and style, from the overwhelming spectacle of the MGM Grand to the small pit at Slots–A–Fun, and from low-roller heaven at Circus Circus to high-roller tension at Bellagio. In general Strip casinos are big and ritzy, with high playing minimums and few comps to give to visitors. Keep in mind, though, that Las Vegas casinos, whether premium or shabby, welcome all comers, no matter what they're wearing. When it comes right down to it, the casinos really care about only one aspect of your attire: that it include a wallet or purse from which you can easily remove your cash.

**Aladdin Resort and Casino.** If the Aladdin casino seems a bit cramped, it's partly because it is a new resort that has risen from the ashes of its original namesake, demolished on the same site in 1997. The casino's financial struggles make it easy to criticize design departures from the other "megaresorts" that, in hindsight, seem like mistakes. The casino comes off as small and generally underwhelming, and its entrances are hard to find—concealed, some would say—behind the camouflage of an elevated sidewalk along the Strip and the labyrinthine Desert Passage mall from behind. Given recent political turmoil, you can't blame the Aladdin for downplaying its Middle Eastern theme in favor of one that vaguely touches upon the Arabia of myth. The bars are adorned with figures from Scheherazade's tales: atop the Lamp Bar is a 36-foot-long Aladdin's lamp, and the Roc Bar lounge towers over the casino on a second level, guarded by the giant bird from Sinbad the Sailor. Things perk up once you head upstairs. Not only does the elevated lounge offer an unusual setting for lounge bands, but there's also an entirely separate casino on the second floor: the London Club is a more sophisticated high-roller salon, operated by London Clubs International, a British company. Table and machine limits are high, but you will feel very James Bond in an environment much like the 007 movies, complete with dealers in tuxes. Parking at the Aladdin involves a wearying walk through the shopping mall, so use the valets if possible. ✉ *3667 Las Vegas Blvd. S, Center Strip,* ☎ *702/785–5555 or 877/333–9474.*

**Bally's Las Vegas.** Bally's owns a huge chunk of one of the most popular intersections in the world—it's across the street from the Flamingo, Caesars Palace, and the Bellagio—and it accommodates a perpetually large convention crowd of older players. Despite the prime location, Bally's threatened to become a dormitory annex to flashier sister property Paris, to which it is connected (via a tunnel that replaced the showroom where Dean Martin and Frank Sinatra once performed), but parent company Park Place Entertainment took steps in late 2002 and 2003 to freshen up Bally's, adding a tequila bar and retro-theme lounge off the casino floor. The 67,000-square-foot casino proper is laid out in an old-fashioned rectangle that offers a good, organized contrast to the busy, heavily themed Paris. Comps earned at Bally's are good at Paris; plus Park Place Entertainment now has a Las Vegas–wide Park Place Connection Card (which will eventually be good at all its properties nationwide) for its "cash back" slot club. The monorail that once connected Bally's to the MGM was taken out of service in early 2003, to be incorporated into a larger monorail with a target opening date of January 2004. If you're trying to park at Bally's, use the Paris garage for a one-minute walk to the casino. ✉ *3645 Las Vegas Blvd. S, Center Strip,* ☎ *800/634–3434.*

**Barbary Coast Hotel and Casino.** The Barbary Coast casino is modeled after late 19th-century San Francisco saloons, with Victorian chandeliers and lamps, tasteful stained-glass signs (including the largest stained-glass mural in the world), and cocktail waitresses who wear garters on their thighs. The Coast is known as a "sweat shop" among blackjack and craps players, meaning the bosses take it personally when you win, but casino table minimums are frequently lower than its larger neighbors. The video poker is playable (the pay schedules are not prohibitive) and the slot club is pretty good, with decent, if not great, cash back and benefits. This joint with 680 machines is usually fairly crowded, and it now seems almost unusually small compared to its surrounding neighbors: Caesars Palace, the Flamingo, and Bally's. ✉ *3595 Las Vegas Blvd. S, Center Strip,* ☎ *888/227–2279.*

**Bellagio Las Vegas.** Bellagio is the most opulent and expensive casino ever built anywhere on Earth. It's roomy, luxurious, and filled with a big money international elite surrounded by gawking tourists. Under its hushed orange canopies you can easily spot a high-roller betting $5,000 a hand as if it were pennies. Yet 5¢ slots are tucked in the back corners somewhere for low rollers and excellent blackjack games are offered for serious players. The outstanding and large live poker room sees some serious piles of chips in the pot, but you're better off playing video poker almost anywhere else. The race and sports book is super high-tech; each seductive leather seat is equipped with its own TV monitor. With good games and posh surroundings, the Bellagio scoffs at even middle-market comp seekers. Parents take note: those under 18 are unwelcome everywhere within Bellagio, but especially in the casino. There's a free monorail to take the footsore to the Monte Carlo. ✉ *3600 Las Vegas Blvd. S, Center Strip,* ☎ *702/693–7111.*

**Caesars Palace.** At 129,000 square feet, Caesars is the never-ending casino. Two sprawling wings in a gentle horseshoe shape change character from one end of the property to the other. A gradual remodeling brought most of the casino space into alignment with the faux–ancient Roman theme of the adjacent Forum Shoppes mall, but spared enough of the original south casino to remind people of its 1966 splendor. The old wing—low ceiling, high stakes—is still where you find the more *serious* older gamblers. The newer Olympic Casino wing, with its high ceiling, soaring marble columns, graceful rooftop arches, and lower limits, embraces the middle market with 5¢ slots. Adjacent to the mall, it underwent even more remodeling in 2002 to direct traffic to the 4,000-seat Colosseum where Celine Dion performs. There's a new food court near the Colosseum steps and an outdoor plaza and live entertainment area on top of a new underground parking garage at the south end. The huge race and sports book with its megadisplay must be seen to be believed. The slot club is connected to all Park Place Entertainment properties on the Strip. Wear your walking shoes and prepare to get lost in this Roman empire which, with its various staircases, was not designed for gamblers with mobility problems. You can even get your picture taken with Caesar, Cleopatra, and the centurion guard. ⊠ *3570 Las Vegas Blvd. S, Center Strip,* ☎ *877/427–7243.*

**Circus Circus.** Only in Las Vegas would you find a 125-foot neon sign of a clown sucking a lollipop next to a statue of a nude dancer. And only in Las Vegas could you find Circus Circus, the tent-shape pink casino with live circus acts performing over the gamblers' heads. The aging Circus Circus is low-roller and poor-service central, with nickel slots galore amid its 101,000 square feet of casino floor and 2,200 gaming machines. The two must-see attractions here are the slot carousel—20 slots sit on a revolving platform, and players ride in circles as they operate the machines—and the merry-go-round bar, which sits atop the carousel on the midway, with actual carousel horses. Those under-21 can whoop it up in a glittering arcade of carnival games and circus acts upstairs. As part of the Mandalay Resort Group, Circus Circus offers the One Club comp card, good at all of its sister properties in Las Vegas. ⊠ *2880 Las Vegas Blvd. S, North Strip,* ☎ *877/224–7287.*

**Excalibur Hotel and Casino.** This giant medieval-theme casino is in one continuous room, and the ringing of the Merlin slot machines can become overpowering at times. At first glance it's a Camelot for low-rollers with $3 blackjack tables and plenty of 5¢ slot machines, but the lousy rules beef up the house's edge way above its Strip rivals. The tables are among those to embrace a controversial 6-to-5 rule, lowering the payoff for a "natural" in single-deck blackjack. The Excalibur is known for a readily available funbook with some good coupons, and there's usually a free-pull promotion going on. A good perch to watch the action is the King's Pavilion, a beautiful circular bar in the middle of the casino. As part of the Mandalay Resort Group, the One Club comp card is good at all of its sister properties in Las Vegas. There's also a free monorail between this casino and Mandalay Bay and Luxor. ⊠ *3850 Las Vegas Blvd. S, South Strip,* ☎ *800/937–7777.*

**Flamingo Las Vegas.** This is where modern Las Vegas began, when Bugsy Siegel imported Miami luxury to the desert. Bugsy, of course, wasn't able to hang around long enough to experience the impact of his vision and would no longer recognize any of his original construction, which has been demolished or folded into the larger property. Unlike many strip casinos, it's a quick stroll from the sidewalk into the 77,000-square-foot casino, which has been gradually remodeled in an attempt to expand its appeal beyond the older crowd with which it has long been associated. More than 70 tables offer reasonable minimums for the moderate-stakes gambler. There are more than 2,000 machine games as well. The Irish-theme casino annex next door—the two-story O'Sheas Casino—is the place for low rollers, low-limit poker players, and small-time racing and sports bettors. ⊠ *3555 Las Vegas Blvd. S, Center Strip,* ☎ *800/732–2111.*

**Harrah's Las Vegas Casino & Hotel.** Carnival music from outside of the Mardi Gras–theme Harrah's will get your heart pumping from far down the sidewalk. The slots are mere feet from the sidewalk, so step inside for a quick look while you're strolling by. Dealers tend to be friendly in this festive purple, green, and gold casino. But be prepared to get lost trying to navigate the sprawling, seemingly endless floor of the 86,654-square-foot casino. There are 70 tables with 13 varieties of games. Harrah's Total Gold is a nationwide player's club: you can play at any of Harrah's 26 casinos around the United States using a single account number. Sign up for their comp program for generous coupons from the chain. ⊠ *3475 Las Vegas Blvd. S, Center Strip,* ☎ *800/634–6765.*

**Imperial Palace Hotel and Casino.** A blue pagoda-style building with an Asian theme, this house of dragons does a booming business with tour groups. Plan on spending a few minutes finding your way around its 75,000 square feet of gaming space (the fact that there are few signs adds to the sport). Except for the 2002 addition of a youthful bar called Tequila Joe's, the Imperial Palace joins the Riviera as the only sizeable Strip properties to still look exactly as they did in the '80s, without any significant facelifts or improvements. However this aging dowager of the Strip is a budget-minded alternative to its hifalutin' neighbors. It has a reputation for generously doling out the comps, so try for a free buffet; just don't expect gourmet food. Table minimums entice low rollers, but the rules generally hurt the player. Perhaps because it's by itself on an upper floor, the race and sports book equipped with 230 individual TV screens is an old favorite on the Strip. The late 2002 death of owner Ralph Engelstad created uncertainty as to whether this faded property—which coasts to a large degree on the appeal of its prime location—would perk up or continue its slow fade. ⊠ *3535 Las Vegas Blvd. S, Center Strip,* ☎ *800/634–6441.*

**Luxor Resort & Casino.** This magnificent bronze-tint pyramid is arguably the most unusual casino in the world, inside and out. Luxor's casino is not only huge, it's also round, so it will take some time to get your bearings. (Orient yourself by looking for periphery landmarks such as the coffee shop, sports book, and lounge.) Comps are tough to come by but, as a Mandalay Resort Group property, Luxor easily transfers your points to its sister properties. You'll find surprisingly fresh air and a muted noise level as a solid middle class and black-clad chic crowd gawk at this eighth wonder of the world. Cool your heels on the free tram to Mandalay Bay and Excalibur. ⊠ *3900 Las Vegas Blvd. S, South Strip,* ☎ *888/777–0188.*

 ★ **Mandalay Bay Resort & Casino.** Pagodas and gardens rise out of the vast floors of this Asian-theme newcomer to the ranks of luxury high-roller casinos. Drool at the hordes of fabulous beautiful people and millionaires crowding the tables of this very hip casino, which feels more casual and lively than pretentious counterparts such as the Bellagio or Venetian. Low rollers will be able to find $5 tables on weekdays, but by sunset will have to hop on the monorail to the Luxor or Excalibur to find blackjack tables with less than a $10 or $25 limit. Slot players, however, won't have to search the dark corners to find nickel or quarter machines. The comp program links Mandalay Bay with its sister properties around Las Vegas; play here and then try for freebies at other casinos. While its wide-open spaces could terrify an agoraphobe, Mandalay Bay is very well organized and its pleasant walkways make wheelchair navigation a breeze. For a break from the action, sit amid the virtual vegetation, rock waterfalls, and lily pond of the Coral Reef Lounge, one of the largest lounges in town. ⊠ *3950 Las Vegas Blvd. S, South Strip,* ☎ *877/632–7000.*

**MGM Grand Hotel and Casino.** The MGM seems to be in a constant state of reinvention since it first opened with an ill-fated budget family appeal in late 1993. It still tries (perhaps a little too hard) to be something for everyone, but changes in 2002–03 reflect a deepening focus on the business/convention market and a clientele that's either well-heeled or traveling on an expense account. New additions such as the Zuri lounge—a tony martini bar draped in hanging fabric—are gradually replacing the original motif of lions and vintage movie photos. But don't worry, kids, there's still a lion habitat on the casino's west perimeter. The biggest of the Las Vegas casinos, the MGM has 3,500 slot machines and 165 table games with high minimums (blackjack and roulette starting at $10 on weekend nights) and tough comp requirements for its crowd of older high-rollers. The casino is so big and so sprawling that few will notice the loss of a Wheel of Fortune-theme slot area in 2002 to make way for yet another nightclub, Tabu. Plan on spending at least an hour going from one end to the other. The Strip entrance is slot heavy, with a live music lounge and elevated bandstand towering over players. The table games and separate high-roller casino fall in the middle of the long hike to the "restaurant row" on the east end. It's another good hike from the parking lot to the casino. However, those in a wheelchair will appreciate the spacious isles and well-spaced slot machines. Search the retail corridor between the hotel and garage for the monorail, which at press time was set to join a more expansive system in 2004. ⊠ *3799 Las Vegas Blvd. S, South Strip,* ☎ *800/929–1111.*

★ **Mirage Hotel and Casino.** In many ways the ultimate carpet joint, the Mirage rang in the modern era of Las Vegas and has held up impressively to competition both from outside and within its own corporate family. The casino has high minimums (such as $500 slots and a plush private pit where the minimum bet is $1,000), ionospheric maximums, intense security, and the most professionally trained staff in the casino business. Blackjack at the Mirage has some of the best rules of any Strip casino, while single-zero roulette offers the gambler a strong game. The poker room has a stellar reputation for good action, low and high. The decor is rain-forest rustic: pits are distinguished by separate thatch roofs. There's even a wonderfully lush tropical garden in the middle of the casino to clean your lungs with fresh air. The cumulative effect is entirely energizing for a casino. And don't miss the display of the white tigers of Siegfried and Roy near the south exit on the Caesars Palace side. If your feet are tired there's a complimentary slow-moving tram to Treasure Island next door. ⊠ *3400 Las Vegas Blvd. S, Center Strip,* ☎ *800/627–6667.*

**Monte Carlo Resort and Casino.** Modeled after the opulent Place du Casino in Monaco, the Las Vegas version of Monte Carlo replicates its sophistication and opulence with a bright and graciously laid-out casino. The theme elements are unobtrusive and take a background role, however, rather than trying to steal the show as they do at some of the other places. Unpretentious, with a simple flow, the casino is well-organized, considering that it has 2,100 machines and 95 tables quietly serving the mid-level players drawn by the hotel's mid-price room rates. The single-zero roulette wheels are a nice plus here. Points on the One Club card are transferrable to other Mandalay Resorts Group properties. A free monorail hidden in the back of the casino can quickly whisk you several blocks to the Bellagio. ⊠ *3770 Las Vegas Blvd. S, South Strip,* ☎ *800/311–8999.*

**New Frontier Hotel and Gambling Hall.** It's hard to get too excited about a casino when its owner (Phil Ruffin) has been openly trying to sell it for more than two years. Until the day comes when the New Frontier is imploded to make way for a planned San Francisco-theme resort, it remains a dingy Western-theme joint for low-rollers. With 10x craps odds and double-deck blackjack cutting the house advantage way down, a beginning player can easily earn comps. A bingo room, rare for the Strip, occupies a former restaurant on the West side of the property. Beginning live poker lessons are given every day but Sunday. ✉ *3120 Las Vegas Blvd. S, North Strip,* ☎ *800/634–6966.*

**New York–New York Hotel and Casino.** The Big Apple theme runs rampant through this casino both outside and in. The casino, like Manhattan itself, is crowded and cramped. The main casino pit has a vague Broadway feel with its noise, overwhelming neon signs, and confusing layout. The tables and video poker have moderate minimums, but the rules are slightly less inviting than a stick-up on the subway. But try and find the roller coaster ride that departs from the second-floor arcade for an unforgettable upside-down view of the Strip. ✉ *3790 Las Vegas Blvd. S, South Strip,* ☎ *702/740–6969.*

**Paris Las Vegas.** The casino is all decked out in Gallic regalia, including three massive legs of the 50-story Eiffel Tower replica jutting through the roof and resting on the floor. Game rules are poor for the player—blackjack players will frown at the 6-to-5 payoff for a natural—minimums high, and comps tough to get, but the Park Place Connection card transfers points and comps to other properties. The main casino floor conveys a dreamlike feeling under its artificial sky, and the attention to French detail, down to fancy floral wash basins in the Provençal-style bathrooms, adds up to a charming yet classy casino. There's even a cobblestone walkway to Bally's, with kiosks selling French pastries and a mime on the loose. As all the dealers say, bon chance at this French beauty of a casino. ✉ *3655 Las Vegas Blvd. S, Center Strip,* ☎ *800/634–6753.*

**Riviera Hotel and Casino.** This vaguely French-theme casino is getting a little run down and dumpy, suffering from lack of new investment in recent years. There's been little follow-up to its last interesting addition, a separate slot area on the north side of the building, known as Nickel Town and serviced by a budget snack bar. The main casino is of the low-ceiling, smoke-filled variety (it was used as a '70s setting for the movie *Casino*). It does, however, boast a big race and sports book, a convenient fast-food court, nearly 90 table games, betting minimums of mostly $5 and $10, and more than 1,500 slot and video-poker machines. What was once the open LeBistro lounge is now a cabaret for ticketed acts, so there's less energy—or distraction, depending on how one felt about the music—in the casino. ✉ *2901 Las Vegas Blvd. S, North Strip,* ☎ *800/634–6753.*

**Sahara Hotel and Casino.** This middle-market casino has a clean and unobtrusive Arabian theme. Some of the peripheral changes by bargain-minded 1990s owner Bill Bennett—the buffet, the Steve Wyrick magic theater—were dubious, but the casino proper has undeniably benefitted from a lighter, brighter look. The smartest move has been its low-minimum blackjack tables. Instead of trying to keep up with the South Strip, the Sahara went the opposite direction and became the only place on the Strip to find primarily $1 tables: A dozen of them were nearly full on a typical weekend night, and only one $10 table among them. Full-pay video poker and very generous slot payouts make this casino a good destination for the gambler minimizing the house edge. The friendly player's club and frequent gambling promotions enhance its popularity. An open lounge with live bands and a big square "Cheers"-style bar near the small sports book add to the friendly feel. Bennett died in late 2002, leaving the Sahara's future course in question. ✉ *2535 Las Vegas Blvd. S, North Strip,* ☎ *702/737–2111.*

**Slots–A–Fun.** A fun little joint to go slumming without feeling like you're in a slum. As you leave Circus Circus, you'll be handed a sheet of coupons for free popcorn, 50¢ hot dogs, 99¢ shrimp cocktails, free pulls of a slot machine, and a free gift (usually a key chain). Redeem them at this noisy, smoky, 17,700-square-foot casino next door, where you will find 586 slots and 22 tables offering plenty of $1 and $2 blackjack. ⊠ 2880 Las Vegas Blvd. S, North Strip, ☎ 702/734–0410.

**Stardust Hotel and Casino.** The Stardust has one of the best neon facades on the Strip, but the casino, which dates back to the 1950s and has been expanded umpteen times, retains the dim ambience of an old-time sawdust joint. Still, because of its size and sprawling layout, the Stardust never feels overly crowded or claustrophobic. It's a good place to play $2 craps, $5 blackjack, and low-limit poker. The slot club offers excellent perks (especially constant free-room offers). The sports book is nationally famous for the "Stardust line," which is usually the first odds posted for upcoming games; for that reason, radio sports talk shows emanate from the Stardust each day. ⊠ 3000 Las Vegas Blvd. S, North Strip, ☎ 800/634–6757.

**Stratosphere Casino Hotel & Tower.** Good games and a gradual remodeling of the original, unappealing World's Fair theme have made the Stratosphere's 80,000-square-foot casino worth a second look if you were underwhelmed or passed it by on the way to the tower during your original visit. The off-the-beaten-track location forces the casino managers to offer often noticeably better odds at the games. You'll find signs advertising 98% RETURN ON DOLLAR SLOTS and 100% RETURN ON QUARTER VIDEO POKER. (And no, they can't claim it if it's not true). Full-pay video poker, 100x odds at the crap tables, and a single-zero roulette wheel or two give the gambler a good shot at breaking even. The slot club offers frequent promotions, including comps to meals at the top of the tower, with its unparalleled view. Parking at the Stratosphere is easy and unsnarled by heavy traffic. Walking here from other casinos, however, will wear out your feet. ⊠ 2000 Las Vegas Blvd. S, North Strip, ☎ 800/998–6937.

**Treasure Island Las Vegas (TI).** Head to Treasure Island for first-class service in a more laid-back atmosphere than its bigger sibling the Mirage. TI has nixed the juvenile pirate motif in an effort to focus on a more adult, less family-oriented, audience. Even the popular pyrotechnic pirate show in Buccaneer Bay has been revised to include flashy dance numbers. However, the crowds—ferocious any time of the night and day—are especially troublesome when one of the six pirate performances ends. At those times the population of the casino reaches critical mass, and it's best to try and sip on a comped drink until the throngs disperse. The table limits are high but expect to earn comps much faster than at the very similar Mirage and Bellagio. A free tram can take you next door to the Mirage. ⊠ 3300 Las Vegas Blvd. S, Center Strip, ☎ 800/944–7444.

**Tropicana Resort and Casino.** The Tropicana's background is one of the lushest in town, having had more than 40 years to fill in. Its luxuriant 5-acre water park has swim-up blackjack: yes, you can actually sit in the pool and play 21. Stuff some cash in your swimsuit pocket and when you reach the table, put it into the Trop's money dryer. If you wind up blowing your soggy bankroll, just return to your breaststroke. Indoors, the casino doesn't do as good a job competing with its South Strip neighbors. Its crowded, confusing layout speaks to piecemeal additions and the days when the casinos *wanted* you to wander around lost and confused. But there's an almost quaint nostalgia in the '70s-style crystal chandeliers and the stained-glass dome that runs the length of the main pit. Cardsharps may still want to play here since the blackjack rules shrink the house edge greatly; table minimums usually range $5–$25. The casino has excellent perks for points accumulated by members of its players club—during the summer it's particularly generous with "Les Folies Bergere" tickets for new sign-ups—and the Casino Hall of Fame displays the largest collection of Nevada casino memorabilia in existence. ⊠ *3801 Las Vegas Blvd. S, South Strip,* ☎ *800/634-4000.*

**Venetian Resort-Hotel-Casino.** Walking from the hotel lobby into the casino is one of the great experiences in Las Vegas: overhead, reproductions of famous frescoes, highlighted by 24-karat-gold frames, adorn the ceiling; underfoot, the geometric design of the flat-marble floor provides an M. C. Escher-like optical illusion of climbing stairs. But the pretty pink-and-gold icing of the Venetian is the only plus a gambler will find. The underwhelming gaming area reflects management's focus on the hotel operation and convention industry; you almost get the idea the gaming is there only because people expect it to be. Don't look for an Italian hospitality with comps—the Venetian can be very tight. The table-game minimums tend to be high—blackjack starting at $15 on an average weekend night—and with very poor rules for the player. At least there's an open lounge with live music at one end of the casino and a food court not too far from that. A high-limit slot area is nestled into a subdued corner, and the player's club employs an ultra-high-tech tracking system that enables you to comp yourself using your slot club points at any machine in the casino. ⊠ *3355 Las Vegas Blvd. S, Center Strip,* ☎ *702/733–5000.*

**Westward Ho Motel and Casino.** The Westward has something few Strip casinos can offer: parking close to the casino. It also has plenty of low-limit blackjack tables, and the progressive video poker machines are among the best on the Strip. Pit bosses practically throw the buffet comps at players. The casino snack bar has good cheap sandwiches and huge servings of strawberry shortcake if you'd rather pay. ⊠ *2900 Las Vegas Blvd. S, North Strip,* ☎ *800/634–6803.*

## Beyond the Strip

**Arizona Charlie's Hotel and Casino West.** It's smoky and generic, more like the tribal casinos spreading across the country than the theme palaces of the Strip, but like most casinos that cater to area residents, Charlie's tries to attract players by offering the best slot club benefits for its 1,600 machines and the best casino coupons that it can—without giving away the store. The video poker provides the best schedules available, and the slot club is so straightforward that a printed flyer indicates the number of points that anything in the joint costs. The bingo parlor runs 24 hours a day. Service seems indifferent although the table games have low minimums and average rules. Promotions are continuous; there are three or four good ones almost every day. The buffet is among the cheapest in town (and not bad to boot); play on a double-points day for an hour or so, and you'll earn enough points to get it comped. ⊠ *740 S. Decatur Blvd., West Side, take W. Charleston from the corner of Charleston and Las Vegas Blvd. about 2 mi, then go right on Decatur Blvd. for ½ mi; the casino is on the left,* ☎ *800/342–2695.*

**The Cannery.** A new casino rang in 2003 in a "new" area of town where it has little competition. The Cannery opened north of downtown, near the Las Vegas Motor Speedway, to tap into a fast-growing residential population. It's small compared to the Station Casinos, with 201 hotel rooms and no movie theaters or child care. The payout schedules on the 1,278 gaming machines didn't overly excite slot buffs in the early going either. The casino, however, offers a bright, snappy theme of California in the 1940s and is full of blown-up reproductions of the colorful fruit labels of vintage canning companies. Four attractive restaurants and an unusual indoor/outdoor entertainment venue geared to festivals help justify an out-of-the-way visit. ⊠ *4336 Losee Rd., North Las Vegas, exit I–15 at Craig Rd. and go west, using the Cannery's "smokestack" sign as your guide; the casino is on the south side of Craig Rd., at Losee Rd.,* ☏ *702/399–4774.*

**Gold Coast Hotel and Casino.** Whenever you're at the airport and you see people losing money in the slots, think of the Gold Coast: this casino west of the Strip and west of I–15 was built on airport slot losses. From the mid-1980s, it has charted the course for a whole niche of "locals casinos" focused on the Las Vegas valley's ever-swelling population. Perhaps because of its head start, the Gold Coast retains the loyalty of residents. It has some of the loosest slots in town, as well as a favorite slot club. It also offers a poker room, a bingo parlor, a race and sports book, and a 72-lane bowling center. Most of the gaming space was remodeled top to bottom to step up for competition with the Palms in 2001. The most significant change is an expanded buffet divided into different ethnic cuisines. Like Palace Station, the friendly Gold Coast has low minimums and sizable crowds at times. ⊠ *4000 W. Flamingo Rd., West Side,* ☏ *888/402–6278.*

★ **Hard Rock Hotel and Casino.** Owner Peter Morton made his fortune on a trendy international chain of Hard Rock Cafes (and T-shirts advertising the same), with its rock-and-roll memorabilia and cutting-edge concerts. Slots have guitar-neck handles, blackjack layouts are customized with rock-related art, crap tables are adorned with Grateful Dead lyrics, and rock music pervades the place. It's terribly hip with those under 35—actor Ben Affleck and other young Hollywood stars drop their cash at these tables. There's a fun pickup bar in the middle that's designed for eyeballing the miniskirts walking by. But looking is a lot more fun than playing here. The dealers at these very poor games are young and good looking, with a hyperattitude and a concern for carding those under 30. The Hard Rock also has a pool with one of Las Vegas's two swim-up blackjack tables. ⊠ *4455 Paradise Rd., Paradise Road,* ☏ *800/675–3267.*

**Las Vegas Hilton.** Under a chandelier the size of an 18-wheeler, the Hilton's main pit runs down the middle of this conservatively attired casino. The sports "super book" is one of Las Vegas's largest and most elegant (with 46 video screens). Because the Hilton is next door to the Las Vegas Convention Center, many delegates stay here, and they pack the casino at all hours along with some older high rollers. Video poker fans can find excellent games with outstanding cash paybacks. The slot club has been integrated with the Park Place network, but goes a step beyond when it comes to show discounts for weeknight headliners in its big theater. The Hilton also has a smaller SpaceQuest Casino, which fronts the Star Trek: The Experience attraction; it's the most high-theme and high-tech casino in town and has a far-out space bar. ⊠ *3000 Paradise Rd., Paradise Road,* ☏ *800/732–7117.*

**Orleans Hotel and Casino.** Orleans is a big barn of a casino designed for the locals market and is outrageously popular with residents. There's a roomy pit under a high ceiling, scads of full-pay video-poker units among its 3,000 machines, five comfortable bars (and revealing cocktail-waitress uniforms), and hot lounge entertainment. Lots of locals like to leave their children at the Kid's Tyme child-care center, the 70-lane bowling alley, the 18-theater multiplex, or the big arcade and take advantage of the frequent double- and triple-points slot club promotions, cash drawings, and car giveaways. The 23-table poker room is popular, too. A much-needed parking garage came on line in 2002, which will be handy for the sports arena built on the north side of the property, scheduled to open in May 2003. ✉ *4500 W. Tropicana Ave., West Side,* ☎ *800/675–3267.*

**Palace Station Hotel and Casino.** This friendly casino with solid food deals at a variety of restaurants is the one that launched Station Casinos as a company that would dominate the locals market. Ironically, the newer properties have siphoned away some of the interest, but the railroad-theme Palace Station has bounced back with a facelift and attractions such as an Irish-theme pub and a comedy club. The knowledgeable gambler will be interested in 10x odds and good blackjack rules. There are 2,200 video and slot machines, 50 tables, a 600-seat bingo room (the casino got its start as a place called the Bingo Palace), a poker room and two keno lounges. The Boarding Pass slot club reciprocates with the other properties and lets you march to the head of restaurant and buffet lines. ✉ *2411 W. Sahara Ave., West Side,* ☎ *800/ 634–3101.*

★ **The Palms.** Striated shadows across the ceiling bring to mind palm fronds in this contempo-California style casino. The Palms has mostly succeeded in its bold plan to be a locals casino on the West Side—with a food court, movie theater, and easy garage parking—and hip competition for the Hard Rock Hotel on Paradise Road, which houses trendy nightclubs and restaurants. While a subtly retro design hearkens back to the Sands of the 1950s, the born-in-2001 Palms is also clean and well-ventilated, with slot sections sprinkled comfortably along its length. If you're feeling lucky, get the fortune teller to read your tarot cards and pick a number for you. Palms does take big bets but the game rules are average. Experts, however, consider the slot club to be among the best in town. A complimentary shuttle bus whisks you to Caesars Palace on the Strip. ✉ *4321 W. Flamingo Rd., West Side,* ☎ *866/725–6773.*

**Rampart Casino at JW Marriott Las Vegas.** If the casino seems tiny compared to the Suncoast next door, it's because gambling was originally planned to be only an amenity of a luxurious, upscale resort (which opened as the Regent Las Vegas) that devoted equal attention to golfers, spa aficionados, and older visitors who wanted an "alternative" to Las Vegas. That idea never caught fire, but the casino remains compact, not cluttered. A gorgeous back-lit apricot-color dome decorated with a palm-tree design rises above the pit. Most minimums start at $5 at tables outfitted with plush chairs of outstanding comfort. The roulette wheels are single zero. The sports book is without a doubt the best part: small but elegant, with comfortable couches and picture windows overlooking the lush grounds. The slot club gives you points for anything you buy on the property (including a buffet and a newspaper). This is an excellent place to stop on your way to or from Red Rock Canyon. ✉ *221 N. Rampart Blvd., Summerlin,* ☎ *877/869–8777.*

★ **Rio All-Suite Hotel and Casino.** The Brazilian theme of this popular off-Strip hotel originally captured the fancy of locals, but the hotel just kept growing and growing into a sprawling resort now geared more to visitors. The Masquerade Village packs tables and machines underneath a free attraction called the "Masquerade Show in the Sky." Parade floats packed with dancing showgirls circle an overhead, suspended monorail track as dozens of specialty performers sing, dance, mime, and stilt-walk below. It all happens several times each day; call ahead for the exact schedule. The Village segues into the older, more traditional casino to the west; in all, there are 1,710 machines and 70 tables throughout the 120,000 square feet of casino space. The player's club at Rio is part of the Harrah's Total Awards Program, which enables you to earn Rio comps at Harrah's locations around the country. With garages on both sides, remembering where you parked the car may be the biggest challenge of the evening. ⊠ *3700 W. Flamingo Rd., West Side,* ☎ *800/752–9746.*

★ **Suncoast Hotel and Casino.** The newest addition to the Coast Resorts family takes everything that locals love about the Gold Coast and the Orleans, and puts them into an elevated setting—literally, given its hilltop perch, and metaphorically in terms of overall niceness—near the affluent Summerlin area of northwest Las Vegas. The Suncoast has a 16-screen movie theater and a parking garage on its west end, and a 400-seat showroom and a surface lot to the east. In between lie 2,300 gaming machines and 50 table games, all neatly laid out. A 150-seat race and sports book rivals its companion properties' popularity on weekends. ⊠ *9090 Alta Dr., Summerlin,* ☎ *702/636–7111.*

# Downtown

Fremont Street is the foundation of Las Vegas, and, to some degree, still the place to come for low table minimums, food bargains, a motley street life, and the concentrated explosion of neon lights that made it famous to begin with. However, historic Glitter Gulch has been pummeled from both sides in recent years. The Strip's megaresorts have stolen the dazzle and luster, while the explosion of so-called locals casinos have come in with more inviting casino atmospheres and food bargains that make many of the downtown properties look faded and second-rate by comparison.

But there's hope for downtown yet. Plans were afoot in early 2003 to update the Fremont Street Experience light show, the 2-million-bulb display under the 100-foot-high awning that encloses four blocks between Main and 4th streets on Fremont Street. Live bands and sidewalk entertainers make for some fun evenings along the pedestrian mall that runs under the canopy. The most recent investment downtown is the Neonopolis shopping center, at Fremont Street and Las Vegas Boulevard, offering restaurants, shops and 12 movie screens. More significant than any of these upgrades, however, may be the announced sale in December 2002 of four downtown properties by longtime owner Jackie Gaughan: the Las Vegas Club, Plaza, Gold Spike, and Western were to be sold to a start-up called Barrick Gaming, which also has an option for the El Cortez. The impact of the sale isn't likely to be apparent before 2004, but significant investment in the hotels obviously could alter the descriptions of those that follow. Fitzgeralds and the Lady Luck also changed hands since 2001, but neither sale resulted in immediate physical improvements.

In the meantime, downtown forges on with 25¢ craps, 50¢ roulette, $2–$3 blackjack, and even 1¢ video poker to accommodate Las Vegas's hordes of beginning and low-stakes players, tinhorns, slummers, and, of course, locals. Soak in the atmosphere and enjoy the neon mascots, Vegas Vic and Vegas Vicky, who still preside over Glitter Gulch. But after dark exercise great care on the sidewalks and parking lots around the downtown area.

★ **Binion's Horseshoe Hotel and Casino.** The Horseshoe is historically where serious gamblers come to play; the 21 tables are always packed and a single pit holds eight craps tables, all crowded. Behind the hotel, by the parking garage, is a 15-foot statue of Horseshoe founder Benny Binion, wearing a Stetson and sitting on a horse. A former bootlegger, Binion came to Vegas from Texas in the 1940s and built a joint boasting the highest table limits in the world at that time. No entertainment, no fancy hotel rooms—just good cheap food and gambling. In time, the Horseshoe acquired the Mint hotel next door, expanding both its casino floor space and room count while turning a music lounge into the only serious race book downtown. In more recent days, the casino has suffered from a news-making feud in the Binion family and weathered financial setbacks. But blackjack players—especially those perturbed by the Strip's embrace of the 6-to-5 payoff for a natural—will still be cheered by the number of tables with single-deck games and old-fashioned rules, albeit with mostly $10 minimums. People who have difficulty with tobacco fumes might want to select other casinos. This is the home of the annual World Series of Poker in April and May; the final event has a $10,000 buy-in and a $1-million first prize. ⊠ *128 E. Fremont St., Downtown,* ☎ *800/937–6537.*

**California Hotel and Casino.** Though the name is California, the motif is Hawaiian: all the dealers wear Hawaiian shirts, the carpet has tropical flowers, the snack bars serve Hawaiian dishes, and many of the customers are in fact islanders. Plane loads of Hawaiian tourists on package tours stay at the hotel and enjoy the Polynesian coffee shop menu and casual and uncrowded casino, which offers lots of $3 tables and 5¢ slots. The tourists have made a good choice, too, because the California—part of the Boyd Group that owns the Stardust and Sam's Town—serves up good slots, video poker, and blackjack games. ⊠ *12 E. Ogden Ave., Downtown,* ☎ *800/634–6255.*

**El Cortez Hotel.** The oldest standing casino in Las Vegas, the Cortez opened for business on Fremont Street in 1941, when cowboys still rode horses up and down the street. The smelly, old, wood-paneled casino seems little changed from 60 years ago with locals and desperados cramming the tables. The El Cortez still has great blackjack games, including single-deck blackjack with $3 minimums shrinking the house edge to nothing. Perhaps in an attempt to reduce the "character" quotient, the coffee shop no longer boasts the rock-bottom deals it once was known for. However, Roberta's fine-dining room remains a cherished, not-so-well-kept secret among long-timers. Be careful walking to the El Cortez from Fremont Street after dark. ⊠ *600 E. Fremont St., Downtown,* ☎ *800/634–6703.*

**Fitzgeralds Hotel and Casino.** If you don't trust the luck of the Irish, pick up the Fitzgeralds funbook which always includes a good free souvenir and $3–$4 worth of gambling coupons. This two-story casino comes off as a bit cheesy in most aspects, but does offer a high-tech slot club: you can use your club card to pay for rooms and meals and check your point balance on-line. Fitzgeralds makes up for its generosity though with lousy rules on its table games. There's an outdoor balcony right off the second-floor casino, with lounge chairs and tables, a great place for watching the street life below and the Fremont Street Experience above. ⊠ *301 E. Fremont St., Downtown,* ☎ *800/ 634–6045.*

**Four Queens Hotel and Casino.** If the carnival barkers don't get your attention first, you'll know you've found this casino when you walk along Fremont Street and come upon four painted playing cards in the pavement—four queens, in fact. The casino floor conveys a hint of a New Orleans theme and comes off as a little lighter and brighter than some of the downtown hotels of similar age. There are plenty of blackjack tables with mostly $5 minimums, going as low as $3 but seldom higher than $10. An area that once was a music lounge now is a "Nickel Palace." The Four Queens is also known for frequent free-money promotions: walk in, take a free pull on a slot machine, and get a coupon for two free dollar-slot tokens, or pay $21 for 50 spins on the machine of your choice, with a jacket or stuffed animal guaranteed even if you don't win. ✉ *202 E. Fremont St., Downtown,* ☎ *800/634-6045.*

**Fremont Hotel and Casino.** In the heart of Glitter Gulch and adding immeasurably to the light show with its block-long neon facade, the Fremont has been a landmark since it opened in 1956. It has become the least interesting member of its Boyd Group family, however, thanks to crowded aisles, a low ceiling, and a generic atmosphere. Blackjack minimums follow suit: mostly $5 and $10, with few tables for either the low-roller or the big shot. The hotel does have one of the oldest and most respected race and sports books, which attracts a lot of gamblers, especially during football season. The Fremont also has a keno progressive that often rises into positive territory—rare for keno. Table game rules are OK while the Players Gold Club is pretty generous. ✉ *200 E. Fremont St., Downtown,* ☎ *800/634-6182.*

**Gold Spike Hotel and Casino.** This small and odorous gambling hall, one block north of Fremont Street, looks like the place where the dream dies in Las Vegas. It's here you find the hard-core, the desperate, the addicted—in short, the downtown fringe. Once famous for its penny slots, the Gold Spike no longer even has that distinction; it switched to "no coin" games that you see in other casinos now as well, which do allow one-cent bets but only if you start with a dollar bill. You can also try your luck on one of the four blackjack tables, all with a $2 minimum. ✉ *400 E. Ogden Ave., Downtown,* ☎ *800/634-6703.*

**Golden Gate Hotel and Casino.** The first structure to house Las Vegas's most historic hotel was built in 1906. Opened as the Hotel Nevada, it was sold to a group of San Francisco investors in 1955; the famous shrimp cocktail, which started a Vegas tradition, dates from then. The Golden Gate's casino is small and crowded, but offers an authenticity that might be just the antidote to the faux-European sameness of the Strip. Ceiling fans beat back the smoke over the tables, where low rollers play $3–$5 blackjack in a fairly relaxed atmosphere. The crowning touch is the piano player who serenades the deli diners; the sound of tinkling ivories wafts into the pit, making it the only place in town where you can shoot craps to live Scott Joplin or George Gershwin. ✉ *1 Fremont St., Downtown,* ☎ *800/426-1906.*

★ **Golden Nugget Hotel and Casino.** This is the only downtown hotel still elegant enough to draw four-star ratings and compete with the Strip on most any level of gaming or dining. Don't worry, though, there's still plenty of downtown gaudiness, including gold-plated elevators, pay phones, and slot machines—and the world's largest gold nugget. The games, however, cater to its wealthier and older gamblers. You can find a couple of $5 blackjack tables, but $10 and $25 minimums dominate. But all is not lost for those with little to lose. The slot club now recognizes nickel and quarter players, so low rollers can now partake in the good comps here. The relaxed politeness of the entire staff adds to the coziness, although even the President doesn't have this many security guards patrolling his home. One anomaly in the high-roller casino is the race and sports book, which is little more than a tiny lounge next to the music lounge. ✉ *129 E. Fremont St., Downtown,* ☎ *800/ 634-3403.*

**Lady Luck Casino and Hotel.** The Lady Luck, at 3rd and Ogden streets across from the Gold Spike, is a bit off the beaten track, but folks are drawn to the rare casino where you can see daylight, thanks to big picture windows that make it the lightest and airiest downtown. There's a small sports book and a lounge that may have the distinction of being the smallest stage for live entertainment in all of Las Vegas. A change of ownership in 2002 left the future course uncertain, but may put an end to the holding pattern of indecision the casino seems stuck in. ⊠ *206 N. 3rd St., Downtown,* ☎ *800/523–9582.*

**Las Vegas Club Hotel and Casino.** This casino has been around since day one and has been owned for nearly 50 years by downtown juice-men Jackie Gaughan and Mel Exber. It's a typical Glitter Gulch joint, except for the high ceilings, which give it a roomy and airy feeling, and a pervasive sports theme; don't expect a sports version of a Hard Rock Cafe, but the memorabilia all over the walls was innovative for its day. Low limits—mostly $5 tables and quarter machines—and easy comps make this a good choice for budget-minded action. The Las Vegas Club somewhat coasts on the coattails of a reputation it enjoyed for years as a blackjack paradise. It's still known for offbeat games and rules, such as a "suited blackjack" paying two-to-one. You can watch some of the action from a balcony overlooking the casino annex, which includes a small race book equipped with individual TV monitors. ⊠ *18 E. Fremont St., Downtown,* ☎ *800/634–6532.*

**Main Street Station Casino, Brewery & Hotel.** Possibly the classiest casino in Las Vegas, Main Street Station is chock full of antiques, stained glass, bronze bas-reliefs, marble, and wood wood wood. It's a pint-size property, connected to the California, a Boyd Group sister property, by an overhead pedestrian bridge. This place is worth a visit for the aesthetics alone, but as long as you're here, there are plenty of machines (live and electronic) to risk your money on. Games are good with 20x odds on craps and good blackjack rules. ⊠ *200 N. Main St., Downtown,* ☎ *800/465–0711.*

**Plaza Hotel and Casino.** Back in the 1920s, when cowboys rode their horses on Fremont Street and miners came to town to buy grub, the corner of Main and Fremont streets was anchored by the railroad depot. It still is, but today that station has a 1,000-room hotel and giant casino around it. A swanky joint when it capped off Fremont Street in 1971, the Plaza now smells of damp air conditioning and is frozen in the early '70s, with better days reflected in everything from the retro signage to the chandeliers. The one-man-band entertainer from the nearby stage will keep you chuckling as you play in this smoky low-roller casino. You'll find lots of low-minimum ($2) table games nearby. ⊠ *1 Main St., Downtown,* ☎ *800/634–6575.*

# Boulder Strip

The Boulder Strip suddenly emerged in 1995 as a destination of its own, competing with downtown and the more famous Strip along Las Vegas Boulevard South. If you're driving to Vegas, the Boulder Strip has some of the nicest facilities at the lowest prices in town, but you'll certainly need a car to get out there.

**Arizona Charlie's East.** Headline-grabbing investor Carl Icahn first bought the original westside Arizona Charlie's (not to mention the Stratosphere), then doubled his investment by acquiring this sputtering Boulder Strip casino, renaming it and turning it into a twin of the first Charlie's. The two-story casino has the advantage of being roomier with higher ceilings than the westside original, and early returns were good enough to warrant a $5 million expansion in 2002. There's a 24-hour bingo room and a 50-seat race and sports book. The Ultimate Rewards Club offers both cash back and comps, and a high-tech tracking system. ⊠ *4575 Boulder Hwy., Boulder Strip,* ☎ *702/951–9000.*

**Boulder Station Hotel and Casino.** Boulder Station is an east-side clone of the popular west-side locals casino, Palace Station. The rich wood, stone, even brick floors; the central luxurious pit framed by big stained-glass murals; the plentiful video-poker machines backed by a good slot club that can be used at all Station properties; and the fast-food counters outside the fine restaurants (serving the same food at half the price) all improve on Palace Station's already successful formula. Kids' Quest, a giant indoor play area just off a small satellite pit, makes this the only casino in Las Vegas where parents can play blackjack and watch their children romp at the same time. This is the ultimate indoor playground, 8,000 square feet of fun things to keep youngsters from six weeks to 12 years old happily occupied for hours (there is an hourly fee and a time limit). Boulder Station also has a state-of-the-art 11-plex movie theater. ⊠ *4111 Boulder Hwy., Boulder Strip,* ☎ *800/683–7777.*

**Castaways Hotel, Casino, and Bowling Center.** The Castaways is the renamed Showboat that was revamped with a Mediterranean seaside resort theme. While it renovates the property in a hurry, the management is trying to stay competitive with aggressive food bargains, a lounge with better-than-average acts, and lots of slot promotions and special events. To some degree, however, the Castaways will always be most famous for housing the country's largest bowling alley, and the fanciest (and brightest and airiest) bingo hall in town. ⊠ *2800 Fremont St., Boulder Strip,* ☎ *800/634–3484.*

★ **Sam's Town Hotel and Gambling Hall.** The Boulder Strip really began in earnest with Sam's Town. It's a sprawling off-Strip destination for everything imaginable, including an 18-screen movie theater complex and expanded child-care facilities. Sam's motif is touted to be "contemporary western," but sequential remodeling has toned down, if not eliminated completely, most of the red carpet and velvet wallpaper of its cowboy past. The casino is built around a 25,000-square-foot indoor park with animatronic howling wolves, restaurants, and a waterfall under a glass, greenhouse-style atrium. The two-story casino has row after row of 25¢ video-poker machines, a hardwood floor under the pit, and a multi-purpose entertainment venue called Sam's Town Live! It also has low-limit table games like 25¢ roulette and $5 blackjack all under large HDTV screens showing every sporting event. For the mid-stakes bettor the great games and OK comps make Sam's Town a recommended watering hole. If you're driving to Hoover Dam (Boulder Highway is much more picturesque than the freeway), you might stop in on your way. ⊠ *5111 Boulder Hwy., Boulder Strip,* ☎ *800/634–6371.*

## Rancho Strip

In 1990 the Santa Fe opened in the far northwest part of town, one of the fastest-growing areas of the valley. It "owned" the whole northwest for nearly five years, until the Fiesta opened a couple of miles closer to downtown. The Fiesta was so successful that Texas Station opened directly across the street less than a year later. The competition was particularly intense in the video poker, blackjack, and buffet departments until Station Casinos bought the Fiesta and Santa Fe in 2000. Now Rancho Strip is Station's Strip, but the winners, ultimately, are those of us who patronize the places. A car is mandatory to getting to the Rancho Strip area.

**Fiesta Hotel and Casino.** Fiesta was a little locals joint with a big, well-deserved reputation, which is probably why Station Casinos bought it. The Fiesta is a popular sports betting venue, thanks to the drive-up betting window complete with pneumatic tubes and teller call buttons. It has also achieved a reputation among local experts and pros for having the best video poker, a distinction its rivals have aggressively challenged. The bingo hall is mind-bogglingly big. Overall, the table game rules are poor for the player although comps are doled out to all comers. The Fiesta's Festival Buffet is a solid bargain, with its gigantic barbecue fire pit, Mongolian grill, and specialty nights. ⊠ *2400 N. Rancho, Rancho Strip,* ☎ *800/731–7333.*

**Santa Fe Station Hotel and Casino.** Santa Fe offers a 60-lane bowling alley, a 17,000-square-foot ice-skating rink, a 700-seat bingo hall, and a children's nursery. The big casino—2,000 slot and video-poker machines—generally rams and jams and has one of the largest no-smoking sections in Las Vegas. ⊠ *4949 N. Rancho, Rancho Strip,* ☎ *702/ 658–4900.*

★ **Texas Station Gambling Hall & Hotel.** Texas Station is longhorn territory, with Texas-shape brick sidewalks, Lone Star carpeting design, and a revolving mirrored disco ball that looks like an armadillo. Texas Station's Market Street Buffet is one of the best in Las Vegas, with a Texas chili bar and cooked-to-order fajitas. The casino and race and sports book are huge, with video poker galore and all the usual table games. The player's club is one of the best in town: play at Texas Station and redeem your points at any of the Station casinos. Games overall are only OK for the older clientele. A 16-theater multiplex fills the parking lots nightly, and there's a huge indoor playground called Kids' Quest for children from six weeks to 12 years old. ⊠ *2101 Texas Star La., Rancho Strip,* ☎ *800/654–8804.*

# Henderson

Henderson was founded in 1940 as a company town for Basic Magnesium, Inc., a giant production plant built to process magnesium mined in huge quantities from a site in central Nevada for the war effort. The site for the factory was selected for its proximity to the unlimited electricity supplied by Hoover Dam; a town to house 10,000 workers was built alongside the magnesium plant. Since then, the magnesium plant has been subdivided into smaller industrial and chemical factories, but Henderson—like its next-door neighbor Las Vegas—has become one of the fastest-growing communities in the country, thanks to the economic boom in southern Nevada over the past decade. Now a vast bedroom community of Vegas, Henderson has overtaken Reno as the second-largest city in Nevada. It has a small downtown, a fine local museum, and several major locals casinos.

★ **Green Valley Ranch Resort.** Under the iron scrollwork of this pleasant green and tan Mission-style casino locals are feted in grand style. The Stations company opened Green Valley for its big bettors with high limits, excellent service, and hipper than hip bars and nightclubs. Check out Whisky Bar, which starts indoors and extends into the pool area and a garden with acres of vineyards, waterfalls, and fountains. Slots players accustomed to the jingle of coins will be disappointed in the paper payouts of the Green Valley machines. A few full-pay video poker machines lurk in the distant corners here. Comps can be tough to come by but certainly easier than the major strip casinos. Because this is a Station casino, the player's card transfers to its other properties. If you're seeking hopping nightlife without the traffic of the Strip, stop by Green Valley. The well-organized parking attendants make finding space stress-free. ⊠ *2300 Paseo Verde Pkwy., Henderson,* ☎ *888/ 319–4661.*

★  **Sunset Station Hotel and Casino.** The casino has a Spanish-Mediter-
   ranean theme, with ceramic tiles, brick facades, fountains, and wrought-
   iron balconies. Its size is about standard for a neighborhood joint: 80,000
   square feet, with 3,000 slot and video-poker machines, and 50 table
   games. The video poker is decent, not great, but the slot club is a good
   one. The middle market Sunset Station is almost always packed with
   local players, patrons of the excellent buffet and microbrewery, and
   residents dropping their children at Kids' Quest, the casino's giant indoor play area, on their way to the movies, or going to a show at the
   rockin' lounge. (Kids' Quest is for children from six weeks to 12 years
   old; there is an hourly fee and a time limit.) ⊠ *1301 Sunset Rd., Henderson,* ☎ *702/547–7777.*

# 4 WHERE TO EAT

For decades, Vegas dining logic said that bargain buffets, giveaway bacon-and-eggs breakfasts, and cheap steak dinners would attract players whose losses in the casino would more than make up for the hotel's losses in the dining rooms. Change was a long time in coming, but Las Vegas now is finding itself (with some surprise, it seems) increasingly hailed as one of the best restaurant cities in the country—even in the world. You can still save a bundle on prime rib, but in an increasing number of restaurants you might think you're in New York, San Francisco, New Orleans, or Paris.

Updated by
Heidi Knapp
Rinella

AS VEGAS HAS—HOWEVER IMPROBABLY—BECOME AMERICA'S
hottest restaurant market. During the past several years the number of restaurants in the city has nearly doubled to more than 1,000.
On average, a new dining establishment opens every week. Each new
megaresort brings its own multiple dining options, with celebrity chefs
adding clones of famous signature restaurants and newborn establishments to the mix. And while bargain buffets and coffee shops still
abound, the arrival of the superchefs has left its mark on the steak houses
and buffets—many of the latter of which have gone upscale. Away from
the Strip, the unprecedented population growth in the city's newly minted
suburbs has brought with it a separate and continuous wave of new
restaurants, both familiar chains and independent spots opened by local
entrepreneurs.

Spurred on by Wolfgang Puck, who tested the desert waters with a
local Spago nearly a decade ago, a flood of newer restaurants has rad-
ically changed the experience of eating in Las Vegas. Status-conscious
hotel-casinos now compete for star chefs and create lavish, built-to-
order spaces for well-known restaurant tenants. These new establishments rival the upscale restaurants of the country's dining capitals
in quality and service.

Among the big-name restaurants you'll find in Las Vegas are five Puck
outposts spread among four different hotels (Caesars Palace, Mandalay
Bay, the Venetian, and MGM Grand). Other hotels have followed
suit. The Bellagio has a branch of New York City's famed Osteria del
Circo, along with Jean-Georges Vongerichten's Prime steak house,
and Todd English's Olives, an offshoot of the Boston landmark. MGM
Grand houses Mark Miller's Coyote Cafe. The Venetian has Valentino
from Los Angeles überchef Piero Selvaggio. Mandalay Bay offers Charlie Palmer's Aureole (from New York); China Grill (also from New York);
Red Square (from Miami Beach); and Border Grill, an L.A. import run
by famed TV chefs, the Too Hot Tamales, Mary Sue Milliken and Susan
Feniger. The valley's newest hotels—The Palms just off the Strip and
Green Valley Ranch in Henderson—have made even more contribu-
tions to restaurant quality and diversity in Las Vegas. Little Buddha
at the Palms is an offshoot of Paris' famed Buddha Bar.

The restaurant explosion has been partially geared toward satisfying
high rollers, who are fed for free as a reward for their often-astro-
nomical bets at the blackjack and baccarat tables, but the city's new
reputation as a culinary capital is also drawing attention from those
who simply enjoy fine dining. Las Vegas's tendency to do everything
to an extreme creates the possibility that too many spectacular restaurants will starve each other, but there's no sign of that yet. While Sin
City's reputation as being recession-proof may be a bit overstated, the
city knows how to continually re-invent itself to ensure that the annual average of 37 million visitors—many of them with fat expense
accounts—keep coming.

But even low rollers with thin wallets have plenty of dining options in
Las Vegas. Despite the influx of upscale restaurants, you can still find
a complete steak dinner for only $4.95 (Ellis Island), a 99¢ shrimp cock-
tail (Golden Gate), and $2.49 breakfast specials (Arizona Charlie's).
And of course, the ever-popular buffet is found in nearly every casino
in town.

But crowds at the hotels, long lines at the buffets, and the jangling noise
of slot machines prompt some to seek refuge away from the casinos.
If you venture into the residential areas, you'll find a steadily increas-

ing variety of restaurants that satisfy every pocketbook. Rosemary's, Andre's, Wild Sage Cafe, Bonjour Casual French, the Tillerman, and other off-Strip dining rooms satisfy the craving for a civilized meal. And mid-price family eateries (such as Tenaya Creek Restaurant & Brewery, Memphis Championship Barbecue, India Oven, Dona Maria, and Billy Bob's Steak House) offer reliable quality at reasonable prices.

## Buffets

Today, the top three buffets in town are generally considered the Bellagio ($24.95 to $31.95 at dinner, $14.95 at lunch), Paris's Le Village Buffet ($18.95 to $21.95 at dinner, $11.95 at lunch), and the Aladdin's Spice Market Buffet ($19.99 at dinner, $13.99 at lunch).

But nearly every resort of any size presents its own version of the classic buffet. One of the lowest-priced is at Circus Circus ($8.99 at dinner, $6.99 at lunch), where the buffet serves an estimated 10,000 daily. Regular prices at Caesars Palace are $16.99 for dinner and $11.99 at lunch, but the venerable resort has instituted options including the $20 Champagne dinner Sunday through Thursday. Even the refined Four Seasons has a buffet, on Saturday and Sunday mornings in its Verandah restaurant ($22).

The locals casinos have followed suit; one example is the buffet at the Suncoast, where the breakfast buffet ($4.95) is considered among the best in town. Another is Sam's Town, with its Firelight Buffet ($10.99 at dinner, $6.99 at lunch), which offers steak and fillet nights ($12.99), and a Thursday and Friday seafood and fish fry ($15.99).

Oh, and don't forget the Sunday brunch buffets. Bally's Sterling Brunch ($52.95) is still considered the best in the valley, and it's pretty much alone in the firmament since the closure of MGM Grand's Brown Derby. Other great brunch bets are Paris ($21.95), especially if you like crepes, and Caesars Palace ($16.99). There's a gospel brunch at House of Blues at Mandalay Bay ($37), jazz brunch Friday through Sunday at Commander's Palace adjacent to the Aladdin ($35, or à la carte), and margarita brunches at Garduno's at the Fiesta ($11.99) and the Palms ($11.99).

Expect long lines at peak times, especially at the best buffets. You'll want to remember to tip; the suggested minimum is $1 per person, depending on service. And here's a tip for you: if you're kind of tricky and very hungry, you can go toward the end of a buffet serving period (the end of the breakfast hour, say) at some buffets and hang around as they start to put out selections for the next meal, saving a few bucks in the process.

## Costs

Restaurants, both in and out of hotels, are listed below according to cuisine. A tip of 15%–20% is common practice in Las Vegas restaurants, and in some circumstances you might want to slip the maître d' $5 or $10 for a special table.

| CATEGORY | COST |
| --- | --- |
| $$$$ | over $35 |
| $$$ | $28–$35 |
| $$ | $19–$27 |
| $ | $10–$18 |
| ¢ | under $10 |

*Prices are per person for a main course at dinner.*

## What to Wear

The dining dress code, like nearly every other social protocol in Las Vegas, is permissive: As long as you wear your wallet, you'll be welcome most anywhere. While the well-heeled new resorts have inspired more people to dress to impress, you'll still see flip-flops and cutoffs in the buffet line and cowboy hats in the steak house.

We mention dress only when men are required to wear a jacket or a jacket and tie.

# The Strip

## American

**$$–$$$**  ✕ **Nobhill.** San Francisco cuisine is the star here (but you already knew that), and so is celebrated chef Michael Mina. The menu's emphasis is on seasonal regional favorites such as Gilroy garlic soup, fillet of beef Wellington with lobster cream spinach and tarragon oil, or sautéed Monterey Bay abalone. The mashed-potato cart is included with dinner, and you can bet the bread's good. ✉ *MGM Grand Hotel and Casino, 3799 Las Vegas Blvd. S, South Strip,* ☎ *702/891–3110. AE, D, DC, MC, V. No lunch.*

## American/Casual

**¢–$$**  ✕ **Grand Lux Café.** The Venetian's 24-hour operation is no diner or coffee shop. A member of the same family as the Cheesecake Factory, Grand Lux is an attractive, expansive space in contemporary colors. The menu's all over the place, including such items as Asian nachos, Madeira chicken, and Mongolian steak. And whatever you do, be sure to leave room for dessert. ✉ *The Venetian Resort-Hotel-Casino, 3355 Las Vegas Blvd. S, Center Strip,* ☎ *702/414–3888. AE, D, DC, MC, V.*

**¢–$**  ✕ **NASCAR Cafe.** The Carzilla—a model of a vastly overgrown racing car that's suspended over the bar—in the center of the place sets the mood, and there is auto racing (and sometimes other sports) on TVs all over the restaurant. The menu is sprinkled with auto-racing references, too, and contains such items as the NASCAR Burger and Collision Chicken. Points Leader Chicken Pasta is linguine with Alfredo sauce and chicken, sugar snap peas, mushrooms, and chunks of ripe tomato. Portions are big, just like Carzilla. Even if you're not a racing fan, it's a fun place to get a quick meal. ✉ *Sahara Hotel and Casino, 2535 Las Vegas Blvd. S, North Strip,* ☎ *702/734–7223. AE, D, DC, MC, V.*

**¢–$**  ✕ **Roxy's Diner.** Be ready to be entertained at this playful replica of a 1950s-era diner, where you can dig into mammoth hot-fudge sundaes, sizable burgers, fried catfish, old-fashioned thick milk shakes, blue-plate specials that include meat loaf and chicken-fried steak, and other inexpensive American classics. This joint is always jumping. ✉ *Stratosphere Casino Hotel Tower, 2000 Las Vegas Blvd. S, North Strip,* ☎ *702/380–7777. AE, D, DC, MC, V.*

## Brazilian

**$$–$$$**  ✕ **Samba Brazilian Steakhouse.** The Mirage's Samba Brazilian Steakhouse presents a lively, colorful, *rodizio* dinner—a parade of rotisserie-style roasted meats, chicken, and fish cooked on skewers and carved table-side, all you can eat. À la carte entrées range from roasted herb-crusted halibut to Australian lobster tail. For dessert, try the coconut crème brûlée or chocolate mousse cake. The sparkling open kitchen adds to the room's excitement. ✉ *Mirage Hotel and Casino, 3400 Las Vegas Blvd. S, Center Strip,* ☎ *702/791–7111. Reservations essential. AE, D, DC, MC, V. No lunch.*

## Buffets

**$–$$$**  ✕ **The Buffet at Bellagio.** In keeping with the resort, this is one of the ★  most beautifully decorated buffet rooms in town. For cozier dining, it is divided into many alcoves, one of which replicates an outdoor café with umbrellas. But the design isn't the main attraction here; even the

most discerning foodie should find something to like with selections
that include Kobe beef (yes, Kobe beef), roast sirloin of elk, tandoori
game hen, steamed clams and mussels, acorn squash ravioli, and white
miso soup. The requisite king-crab legs are present as well, and there's
quite an array of elaborate pastries—and an in-restaurant bar. ⊠ *Bellagio Las Vegas, 3600 Las Vegas Blvd. S, Center Strip,* ☎ *702/693–
7111. AE, D, DC, MC, V.*

$$ ✕ **Le Village Buffet.** Let the other buffets touch on various international
★ foods; Paris Las Vegas owns the world's foremost cuisine and shows
it to advantage at Le Village Buffet. The buffet stations are themed to
the regions of France; accordingly, you may find chicken sauté *chas-
seur* (in a brown sauce of mushrooms, shallots, and white wine) and
roasted duck with green peppercorns in Brittany, seafood bouillabaisse
in Provence, veal *Marengo* (in olive oil with tomotoes, onions, olives,
garlic, and white wine) in Burgundy, smoked salmon salad with fresh
dill in Normandy, and braised lamb with Riesling and curry in Alsace.
Brittany offers dessert crepes, too, while bananas Foster and French
bread pudding are served up at the Le Flambe station. ⊠ *Paris Las
Vegas, 3655 Las Vegas Blvd. S, Center Strip,* ☎ *702/946–7000. AE,
D, DC, MC, V.*

$–$$ ✕ **Spice Market Buffet.** This buffet in the traffic-challenged Aladdin Resort & Casino is one of the best in town—and one of the best values.
It's probably the only one with a Middle Eastern station (in keeping
with the Aladdin's theme), where you'll find such delights as skewered
lamb, basmati rice with lentils and raisins, and tandoori chicken. The
Italian station offers stromboli, pizza, chicken scallopini, and macaroni
with Gorgonzola cream, while the Asian one has super pot stickers, fried
rice, and spring rolls. ⊠ *Aladdin Resort & Casino, 3667 Las Vegas Blvd.
S, Center Strip,* ☎ *702/785–5555. AE, D, DC, MC, V.*

## Cajun/Creole

¢–$$ ✕ **House of Blues.** Like the Houses of Blues in other tourist-friendly
cities, this one is a gaudy, stylized version of a Delta shack with a de-
liberately ramshackle look (making it easy to find in the tropical-
theme hotel). The HOB compound has a concert hall and the requisite
gift shop. Cold beer goes well with just about everything on the menu,
from the smoked pork or mesquite-grilled chicken sandwiches to the
center-cut pork chop in bourbon sauce or crawfish and shrimp étouf-
fée. ⊠ *Mandalay Bay Resort & Casino, 3950 Las Vegas Blvd. S,
South Strip,* ☎ *702/632–7777. AE, D, DC, MC, V.*

## Caribbean

$$–$$$$ ✕ **Ortanique.** Chef Cindy Hutson, who became known for her "cuisine of the sun" at her signature Ortanique in Miami, shines a little
light on Las Vegas in the walkway between Paris and Bally's. The menu
melds flavors from South America, the West Indies, and Asia in such
appetizers as jerked, seared foie gras, and West Indian curried crab cakes
with papaya coulis and tropical fruit salsa. Entrées include Rasta Pasta,
which is penne pasta topped with sun-dried tomatoes, shiitake mushrooms, and tropically seasoned chicken, all in a cream sauce, and is-
land-spiced, seared ahi tuna with horseradish mashed potatoes. ⊠ *Paris
Las Vegas, 3655 Las Vegas Blvd. S, Center Strip,* ☎ *702/946–4346.
AE, D, DC, MC, V.*

$$–$$$$ ✕ **rumjungle.** This Mandalay Bay establishment is so hugely popular
as a dance club frequented by the see-and-be-seen set that some locals
are surprised to learn it even serves food in the evening hours. That's
not exactly how it was intended. The intensely themed interior—all
waterfalls and fiery displays—was designed with the Brazilian rodizio
"fire pit" in mind; a popular choice is the prix-fixe dinner of pork, lamb,
chicken, fish, and vegetables served on skewers. Individual entrées in-

clude many Caribbean-theme dishes. ⊠ *Mandalay Bay Resort & Casino, 3950 Las Vegas Blvd. S, South Strip,* ☎ *702/632–7777. AE, D, DC, MC, V. No lunch.*

## Chinese

**$$–$$$$** ✕ **Empress Court.** This venerable upscale Chinese eatery entered a new era when was it relocated to a spot overlooking Caesars' Garden of the Gods swimming pool and the extensive gardens that surround it. Thai, Malaysian, and Indonesian specialties are part of the program, and seafood plays a starring role. Accordingly, some of the sea creatures can be found swimming in the restaurant's tanks until they're ordered. Offerings include abalone and shark-fin soup, Peking duck, and sautéed scallops with macadamia nuts. ⊠ *Caesars Palace, 3570 Las Vegas Blvd. S, Center Strip,* ☎ *702/731–7110. Reservations essential. Jacket and tie. AE, D, DC, MC, V. Closed Tues.–Wed. No lunch.*

**$$–$$$$** ✕ **Royal Star.** Seafood-oriented dishes are the center of attention in this simple, emerald-toned dining room with lacquered black furniture. Dim sum is the star at lunchtime, when rolling carts offer a quick but quality feast of pan-fried scallion cakes, barbecue-pork puffed pastries, shrimp-stuffed eggplant, and more. The evening menu ranges from lobster or crab fresh from the tank to regional specials such as spicy garlic scallops and Six Hour Spare Ribs served over a bed of sautéed spinach. And yes, for the less adventurous there are well-executed versions of familiar dishes such as *kung pao* chicken and orange beef. ⊠ *Venetian Resort-Hotel-Casino, 3355 Las Vegas Blvd. S, Center Strip,* ☎ *702/ 414–1888. AE, D, DC, MC, V.*

**$–$$$$** ✕ **Peking Market.** An 800-gallon tropical aquarium, pastoral murals, and oversize tables accent this Chinese restaurant that serves such dishes as moo goo gai pan; orange-peel beef; and, for dessert, fried banana fritters with whipped cream. The Market's attentive staff speaks Vietnamese, Thai, and several Chinese dialects to serve the specific needs of its Asian customers. Off-the-menu orders are also welcome. ⊠ *Flamingo Las Vegas, 3555 Las Vegas Blvd. S, Center Strip,* ☎ *702/ 733–3111. AE, D, DC, MC, V. No lunch.*

**¢–$** ✕ **P. F. Chang's China Bistro.** "Americanized" versions of Chinese classics are served at this high-energy eatery. Chinese sculptures and murals are offset by high-tech lighting fixtures and a modern, earth-tone color scheme. The 60-item menu ranges from basic sweet-and-sour pork and barbecued spareribs to more adventurous lemon-pepper shrimp and Chang's spicy chicken. Vegetarians will find plenty of noodle, rice, and vegetable dishes at this East-meets-West hot spot. ⊠ *Aladdin Resort and Casino, 3667 Las Vegas Blvd. S, Center Strip,* ☎ *702/785– 5555. Reservations not accepted;* ⊠ *4165 S. Paradise Rd., Paradise Road,* ☎ *702/792–2207;* ⊠ *1095 S. Rampart Blvd., Northwest Las Vegas,* ☎ *702/968–8885. AE, MC, V.*

## Contemporary

**$$–$$$$** ✕ **Postrio.** In many ways, this location in the Venetian's retail mall is the most elegant of Wolfgang Puck's Las Vegas rooms. Like most Puck places there's an "outdoor" sidewalk café in front of a formal dining room, which is trimmed in rich burgundy and accented with jeweled stained-glass pieces, curved to resemble film strips in a slightly Gaudí-like effect. The menu includes the familiar Puck pizzas, but also offerings such as a lobster club sandwich. The emphasis at dinner is on seafood: choose from dishes such as seared black bass with sautéed winter greens and warm lentil vinaigrette. ⊠ *Venetian Resort-Hotel-Casino, 3355 Las Vegas Blvd. S, Center Strip,* ☎ *702/796–1110. AE, D, DC, MC, V.*

**$$–$$$$** ✕ **Red Square.** This Soviet-chic restaurant is one of several China Grill– group eateries in Mandalay Bay that manage to tastefully combine theatrical interior design, such as a bar made of ice, with fine dining. There are 100 varieties of vodka, and a walk-in vodka freezer (in which frequent patrons can rent their own space). For starters, consider the variety of caviars, a crab-stuffed Portobello mushroom, or tuna and smoked salmon tartare. Entrées include potato-crusted snapper, lobster and black-truffle fettuccine, and Roquefort-crusted filet mignon. For dessert try the warm chocolate cake or crème brûlée. ⊠ *Mandalay Bay Resort & Casino, 3950 Las Vegas Blvd. S, South Strip,* ☎ *702/632–7777. Reservations essential. AE, D, DC, MC, V. No lunch.*

$$–$$$ ✕ **Pinot Brasserie.** James Beard Foundation Award–winning chef Joachim Splichal and his wife and partner Christine have duplicated their acclaimed Los Angeles Pinot restaurant—an urban-casual bistro featuring Franco-Californian cuisine. The storefront facade imported from France allows passersby to glimpse diners at their tables and cooks at work. Seafood includes oysters on the half shell (imported from wherever they are the freshest), scallop tartare, Pacific shrimp and Dungeness crab. Other offerings include sweetbreads, lamb, venison, and poultry. ⊠ *Venetian Resort-Hotel-Casino, 3355 Las Vegas Blvd. S, Center Strip,* ☎ *702/735–8888. AE, D, DC, MC, V.*

$–$$ ✕ **Wolfgang Puck Cafe.** An open-air venue inside the MGM Grand Hotel, this casual eatery is literally two steps off the casino floor. (You may have to speak up to be heard above the sounds of the slot machines and sports book.) It offers a leaner version of the basic Spago patio menu of gourmet pizzas, pasta, salads, and meat loaf. ⊠ *MGM Grand Hotel and Casino, 3799 Las Vegas Blvd. S, South Strip,* ☎ *702/891–1111. Reservations not accepted. AE, DC, MC, V.*

## Continental

$$–$$$ ✕ **Pietro's.** Customers here face the difficult choice of which creations to try: pâté en croûte with lingonberry sauce, coquilles St. Jacques, and Nova Scotia smoked salmon are among the appetizers. Breast of capon Kiev with wild rice and roast duckling à l'orange or Montmorency (flamed with Bing cherries) are among the favored entrées, many of which are prepared tableside by Pietro himself. Among the desserts is Crespelle Flambe au Cointreau, a lovely light crepe in a buttery orange-flavored sauce, flamed tableside. Pietro's dining room is intimate (only 40 seats), service is exquisite, and tables are adorned with fresh flowers. ⊠ *Tropicana Resort and Casino, 3801 Las Vegas Blvd. S, South Strip,* ☎ *702/739–2222. Reservations essential. AE, D, DC, MC, V. Closed Mon. and Tues. No lunch.*

## French

$$–$$$ ✕ **Mon Ami Gabi.** This French steak house has the highest-profile location at Paris Las Vegas and, indeed, one of the highest in town; it's the rare restaurant with sidewalk dining on the Strip. For those who prefer a less lively atmosphere, a glassed-in atrium just off the street conveys an outdoor feel, and there are still-quieter dining rooms inside, adorned with chandeliers dramatically suspended three stories above. The specialty of the house is steak frites, offered four different ways: classic, au poivre, Bordelaise, and Roquefort. There are fish and poultry dishes as well. ⊠ *Paris Las Vegas, 3655 Las Vegas Blvd. S, Center Strip,* ☎ *702/946–7000. Reservations essential. AE, D, DC, MC, V.*

## Italian

$$–$$$$ ✕ **Onda.** You enter this ristorante through a piano bar opening onto the casino. Beyond the lounge, with its arched, stained-glass ceiling and marble floor, is the restaurant, tucked behind one-way glass. The menu offers seafood choices such as garlic-crusted sea bass and lobster *Milanese* (breaded and pan-fried) as well as traditional pasta dishes such as lasagna, fettuccine Alfredo, and angel-hair pasta with shrimp, gar-

lic, white wine, tomatoes, and bread crumbs. There's roasted chicken and chicken cacciatore, too. ⊠ *Mirage Hotel and Casino, 3400 Las Vegas Blvd. S, Center Strip,* ☎ *702/791–7111. Reservations essential. AE, D, DC, MC, V. No lunch.*

$$–$$$$ ✕ **Osteria del Circo.** With its view of the lake, this is one of Bellagio's prime dining spots. The colorful Circo, with its velveteen harlequin-patterned seats and whimsically decorated chandeliers, serves home-style Tuscan food. Among the appetizers are prosciutto with seasonal fruit and the Tuscan fish soup made with lobster, prawns, calamari, monkfish, clams, and mussels. The homemade pastas include ravioli with spinach and sheep's milk ricotta in butter-sage or fresh tomato sauce. Caviars by the ounce are offered for dinner, and the extensive wine cellar has selections from every wine-producing region of the world. ⊠ *Bellagio Las Vegas, 3600 Las Vegas Blvd. S, Center Strip,* ☎ *702/ 693–8150. AE, D, DC, MC, V.*

$$–$$$$ ✕ **Terrazza.** This dazzling Italian eatery in Caesars' spectacular Palace Tower has great views of the 4-acre Garden of the Gods pool; you also can dine alfresco on a terrace adjacent to the pool area. Terrazza offers excellent Caesar salads, designer pizzas, mushroom ravioli, lamb, veal chops, and steaks. Imported Italian beers and mineral waters are available. ⊠ *Caesars Palace, 3570 Las Vegas Blvd. S, Center Strip,* ☎ *702/731–7110. Reservations essential. AE, D, DC, MC, V. No lunch.*

$$–$$$$ ✕ **Trattoria del Lupo.** Wolfgang Puck's first Italian eatery is set in a rustic-looking dining room with a bar and wine room, an exhibition pizza and antipasto station, and a 20-foot communal table. Imaginative traditional and contemporary dishes include grilled vegetables with roasted peppers and marinated artichokes, various pizzas, spinach-and-ricotta cannelloni, saffron risotto with sizzling shrimp and garlic, and grilled Sicilian-style swordfish with raisins and pine nuts. For dessert, try the tiramisu cappuccino. ⊠ *Mandalay Bay Resort & Casino, 3950 Las Vegas Blvd. S, South Strip,* ☎ *702/740–5522. Reservations essential. AE, D, DC, MC, V. No lunch.*

$$–$$$$ ✕ **Valentino and P. S. Italian Grill.** The Italian Grill, the busy front room of this dual restaurant on the Venetian's convention-friendly "restaurant row," has a casual, urban vibe. Choose either appetizer or entrée portions of pasta, or heartier fare such as a New York steak in Tuscan barbecue sauce or pork chops marinated in apple cider. The dining-room menu offers four meat and four seafood dishes, among them possibly Maine scallops with a tomato-horseradish sauce and fresh oregano pesto or roasted chicken breast wrapped in smoked bacon with red-wine sauce, polenta, and spinach. ⊠ *Venetian Resort-Hotel-Casino, 3355 Las Vegas Blvd. S, Center Strip,* ☎ *702/414–3000. AE, D, DC, MC, V. Valentino: No lunch.*

$$–$$$$ ✕ **Zeffirino.** Everything—from the tile work to many of the employees—comes straight from Italy, and all who enter here feel Italian, at least for the day. Seafood dominates the menu, which includes sautéed lobster, red snapper, and swordfish steak with herbs. Some dishes, such as the seafood symphony, bring the chef from the kitchen to layer assorted seafood and pasta in heated olive oil tableside. The pasta with pesto is said to have been a favorite of Pope John Paul II when he dined at the original Zeffirino in Genoa (Italy, not Nevada). Desserts include *crema caramella*, tiramisu, and *torta al cioccolato Milanese.* ⊠ *Grand Canal Shops at the Venetian Resort-Hotel-Casino, 3355 Las Vegas Blvd. S, Center Strip,* ☎ *702/414–1000. AE, D, MC, V.*

$–$$$ ✕ **Market City Caffe.** Recipes passed down through generations are the centerpiece of this lively restaurant owned and operated by a family with successful eateries in southern California. The menu includes such hearty selections as pizzas (such as pizza gamberetto, with shrimp, goat cheese, fresh tomatoes, and pesto), salads (such as insalata di calamari, with calamari, diced tomatoes, capers, and mixed greens), and pastas (such as spaghetti *alla puttanesca*, with a tomato-anchovy sauce). ☒ *Monte Carlo Resort and Casino, 3770 Las Vegas Blvd. S, South Strip,* ☎ *702/730–7967. AE, D, DC, MC, V.*

$–$$ ✕ **Bertolini's.** Tables at this sidewalk café inside the Forum Shops at Caesars are set up in the piazza surrounding the Fountain of the Gods. The outside section is noisy; if you want to talk, take a table in the dark, clubby interior, where booths line the black-and-yellow antiqued walls. An open kitchen turns out soups, salads, wood-fired pizzas, and even wood-fired pastas (!), that include roasted chicken cannelloni and rigatoni *al forno* (oven-baked). And if you'd rather avoid the traffic (both vehicular and pedestrian) of the Strip, there's a slightly more sedate outpost out in the suburbs. ☒ *The Forum Shops at Caesars, 3500 Las Vegas Blvd. S, Center Strip,* ☎ *702/735–4663;* ☒ *9500 W. Sahara Ave., West Side,* ☎ *702/869–1540. Reservations not accepted. AE, DC, MC, V.*

$–$$ ✕ **Il Fornaio.** Cross the Central Park footbridge inside the wonderfully quirky New York–New York Hotel and Casino and you'll come to Il Fornaio, a cheery and bright Italian café. You can dine "outdoors" on the patio by the pond and watch the world go by, or opt for a table inside. An exhibition kitchen prepares fresh fish, wood-oven pizzas, spinach linguine with shrimp, and gnocchi with sausage, onions, mushrooms, tomato cream sauce, and Parmesan. Very good breads (including ciabatta) are baked twice daily, and you can buy loaves to go. ☒ *New York–New York Hotel and Casino, 3790 Las Vegas Blvd. S, South Strip,* ☎ *702/650–6500;* ☒ *Green Valley Ranch Resort, 2197 Paseo Verde Pkwy., Henderson,* ☎ *702/614–5283. AE, MC, V.*

## Japanese

$–$$$$ ✕ **Hamada of Japan.** No matter what type of Japanese food you're in
★ the mood for, you'll find it here. Hamada of Japan has a teppan room, which offers entrées of the sort found in Japanese steak houses; a sushi bar (which offers a dish called "sushi for beginners"); and a dining room, with a menu that includes teriyaki and tempura dishes, among others. There's a bit of overlap between menus, so if you're seated in the teppan room, you still can order sushi. ☒ *The Flamingo, 3555 Las Vegas Blvd. S, Center Strip,* ☎ *702/733–3455;* ☒ *The Luxor, 3900 Las Vegas Blvd. S, South Strip,* ☎ *702/262–4548;* ☒ *Polo Towers, 3745 Las Vegas Blvd. S, South Strip,* ☎ *702/736–1984;* ☒ *Stratosphere Casino Hotel & Tower, 2000 Las Vegas Blvd. S, North Strip,* ☎ *702/380–7777. No lunch;* ☒ *365 E. Flamingo Rd., Paradise Road,* ☎ *702/733–3005;* ☒ *Rio All-Suite Resort, 3700 W. Flamingo Rd., West Side,* ☎ *702/252– 7777;* ☒ *JW Marriott Las Vegas, 221 N. Rampart Blvd., Summerlin,* ☎ *702/869–7710; AE, D, DC, MC, V. No lunch.*

$–$$$$ ✕ **Mizuno's Japanese Steak House.** Lobster, steak, and chicken entrées are sliced, diced, and grilled at your teppan table by chefs who wield flashy knives and are possessed of witty tongues. Quality teriyaki and seafood dishes are other pluses at this fun Japanese restaurant. ☒ *Tropicana Resort and Casino, 3801 Las Vegas Blvd. S, South Strip,* ☎ *702/739–2713. AE, DC, MC, V. No lunch.*

## Mediterranean

$$–$$$$ ✕ **Olives.** Chef/owner Todd English combines the best features of his
★ Boston-area Olives and Figs restaurants in his Las Vegas eatery. The patio overlooking the Bellagio's spectacular lake is perfect for alfresco dining. Among the fare are appetizers of beef carpaccio on crispy Roquefort polenta, Portabello picatta, and venison bruschetta. Entrées include crispy-skinned duck breast on pumpkin *agrodolce* (with a sweet-sour pumpkin sauce) and a signature butternut squash tortelli. The chocolate Falling Cake is tantalizing. ☒ *Bellagio Las Vegas, 3600*

*Las Vegas Blvd. S, Center Strip,* ☎ *702/693–8181. Reservations essential. AE, D, DC, MC, V.*

## Pan-Asian

**$$–$$$**   ✕ **China Grill.** Postmodern architecture and appointments set the stage for Asian dishes with a contemporary accent in this Mandalay Bay restaurant. Start with appetizers such as tempura sashimi or broccoli rabe dumplings. The selection of entrées leans toward seafood, with options such as barbecued salmon, but there also are such fusion offerings as green tea–spiced roasted lamb rack with pear jam and roasted vegetables. ✉ *Mandalay Bay Resort & Casino, 3950 Las Vegas Blvd. S, South Strip,* ☎ *702/632–7777. Reservations essential. AE, D, DC, MC, V.*

**$–$$$**   ✕ **Chinois.** Yet another Wolfgang Puck creation, Chinois has a Pacific Rim flair. The menu changes daily, but there's a good balance of classic Chinese dishes and more innovative offerings, such as sweet curried beef satays or a tartare trio for starters, or sweet and sour sesame chicken or basil shrimp for entrées. And there's plenty of sushi. ✉ *The Forum Shops at Caesars, 3500 Las Vegas Blvd. S, Center Strip,* ☎ *702/ 737–9700. AE, D, DC, MC, V.*

## Southwestern

**$$–$$$$**   ✕ **Star Canyon.** "New Texas" fare is transplanted to the Las Vegas Strip in an understated room cleverly accented with Lone Star State miscellany. An open grill tempts with the scents of chilis and barbecue. The menu goes far beyond fajitas and ribs, however, with familiar ingredients used in pleasing new combinations: consider Hudson Valley foie gras with mole sauce and corn pudding, or crabmeat-stuffed halibut on a cumin-tinged three-bean melange. A wine list with selections from all over the world includes a number of Texas bottles. ✉ *Venetian Resort-Hotel-Casino, 3355 Las Vegas Blvd. S, Center Strip,* ☎ *702/733–5000. AE, D, DC, MC, V.*

**$–$$$**   ✕ **Border Grill.** The hosts of TV's "Too Hot Tamales," Mary Sue Mil-
★   liken and Susan Feniger, have developed quite a following at their Las Vegas location at Mandalay Bay. Appetizers include green-corn tamales, ceviche, and plantain empanadas; for lunch try the turkey tostada or grilled skirt steak; and for dinner the sautéed rock shrimp, stacked enchilada Manchego or chicken chilaquiles. Oaxacan mocha cake and Key lime pie are among the desserts. ✉ *Mandalay Bay Resort & Casino, 3950 Las Vegas Blvd. S, South Strip,* ☎ *702/632–7394. AE, D, DC, MC, V.*

**$**   ✕ **Coyote Café and Miller's Grill Room.** Mark Miller has transplanted his self-named "gourmet Southwestern" food to Las Vegas from the original Coyote Café in Santa Fe. The café out front offers an excellent alternative to the crowded buffets and coffee shops for breakfast through dinner. Breakfast is a treat—you walk right in, sit right down, and are offered six choices, including *huevos rancheros,* quiche, and fruit and yogurt. Miller's Grill Room, adjacent to the café, offers an imaginative dinner menu. Appetizers such as Southwestern Painted Soup, a cheese-and-salsa-based soup "painted" with a topping of chipotle cream, and tamales complement entrées such as Howlin' Chile Relleno and the Cowboy Rib Chop. ✉ *MGM Grand Hotel and Casino, 3799 Las Vegas Blvd. S, South Strip,* ☎ *702/891–7349. Reservations essential. AE, D, DC, MC, V.*

## Steak

**$$–$$$$**   ✕ **Bally's Steakhouse.** The dining room of this traditional steak house has a mirrored food-and-wine display, large fireplace, and comfortable furnishings. The menu includes sausage-filled mushrooms baked with garlic, spinach, and fontina cheese; Scottish smoked salmon with bagel chips and horseradish crème fraîche; and jumbo pancetta-wrapped sea scallops with fresh-basil relish. Try the aged prime rib or the mesquite-grilled 20-ounce bone-in rib eye with garlic-herb butter. Be sure your dessert pocket is not full—among the magnificently presented sweets is a signature banana cream pie. ⊠ *Bally's Casino Resort, 3645 Las Vegas Blvd. S, Center Strip,* ☎ *702/967–4661. AE, D, DC, MC, V. No lunch.*

**$$–$$$$** ✕ **Luxor Steakhouse.** This attractive restaurant, with its classic cherrywood bar and walls, is divided into several rooms and alcoves to afford intimate dining. Whole stuffed artichokes and hearty Portobello mushrooms filled with seafood, spinach, and Gorgonzola are among the favorite appetizers. Succulent entrée selections include the thinly-sliced Chicken Breast Giza, filled with couscous and spinach and served with pistachio nuts and sun-dried tomatoes. And the steaks, of course, are super-aged prime beef in the usual cuts, including filet mignon, porterhouse, and rib eye. ⊠ *Luxor Hotel-Casino, 3900 Las Vegas Blvd. S, South Strip,* ☎ *702/262–4778. AE, D, DC, MC, V. No lunch.*

**$$–$$$$** ✕ **Prime.** Even among celebrity chefs, Jean-Georges Vongerichten has
★ established a "can't touch this" reputation. Prime—with its gorgeous view of the fountains—has become a place to see and be seen at the Bellagio. In a velvet-draped, gold and burgundy room, eight cuts of beef are presented with a choice of seven mustards and six sauces, from the classic (béarnaise) to the more adventurous (tamarind). Diners can also get a taste of a few signature Vongerichten dishes, such as garlic soup with frogs' legs. ⊠ *Bellagio Las Vegas, 3600 Las Vegas Blvd. S, Center Strip,* ☎ *702/693–7223. Reservations essential. AE, D, DC, MC, V. No lunch.*

**$$–$$$$** ✕ **Smith & Wollensky.** The legendary New York restaurant has been replicated on the Strip. With hardwood floors and no plush surfaces to soak up the ricocheting sound, it's a raucous place, but that's part of the fun. This is one of the few places where you can still get Beef Wellington—and a good one, at that; other specialties include Maryland crab cakes, prime steaks, lamb and veal chops, and the famed crackling pork shank with applesauce. Wollensky's Grill, a lively, more casual gathering spot that's open until 3 AM, serves the same menu, as well as sandwiches and pizzas. ⊠ *3767 Las Vegas Blvd. S, South Strip,* ☎ *702/862–4100. AE, DC, MC, V. Lunch in grill only.*

**$$** ✕ **Steak House.** Believe it or not, many local residents think this steak house set within the craziness of Circus Circus is among the best in town. It's totally unlike the rest of Circus Circus; wood paneling and antique brass furnishings adorn a dark, quiet room reminiscent of 1890s San Francisco. A ton of beef—aged 21 days—is displayed in a glassed-in area at one side; the cooking takes place over an open-hearth mesquite grill. Steaks, chops, chicken, and seafood make up the menu, and all entrées are accompanied by soup or salad, fresh bread, and a giant baked potato. ⊠ *Circus Circus, 2880 Las Vegas Blvd. S, North Strip,* ☎ *702/734–0410. Reservations essential. AE, D, DC, MC, V. No lunch.*

# Downtown

## American/Casual

**¢–$$** ✕ **Carson Street Cafe.** The Golden Nugget is widely considered one of the gems of Downtown, and the Carson Street Cafe does it proud. The restaurant has a stylish Southern plantation feel and plays host to downtown's movers and shakers during weekday breakfast and lunch hours. Among the breakfast selections are eggs Benedict and the Vegas Experience—banana bread with walnut-cinnamon cream cheese, bananas, kiwi, and strawberries. Old familiars on the lunch and dinner menus include rainbow trout, Southern fried chicken, and slabs of baby-back ribs. ✉ *Golden Nugget Hotel and Casino, 129 E. Fremont St., Downtown,* ☎ *702/385–7111. AE, D, DC, MC, V.*

¢–$   ✕ **Jillian's.** Jillian's puts the fun in the downtown Neonopolis entertainment complex, with its bowling alley, pool room, and video games, and it's a great spot for watching the goings-on in the eclectic complex outside. The food's more serious, and includes everything from the Authentic Ybor City Cuban Sandwich to pot roast, meat loaf, and barbecued ribs. Jumpin' Jack's Jambalaya is about as spicy as they come, but the bar offers plenty to put out the fire. For dessert, consider some Southern bread pudding with Southern Comfort-spiked New Orleans sauce. ✉ *Neonopolis, 450 Fremont St., Downtown,* ☎ *702/759–0450. AE, D, MC, V.*

## Chinese

$–$$$$   ✕ **Lillie Langtry's.** This restaurant turns out fine Chinese food, but steaks have a starring role as well. The Cantonese dishes include old familiars such as moo goo gai pan and moo shu pork, plus spicier choices such as Szechuan shrimp. The black-pepper steak is a must for charcoal aficionados, and the lemon chicken is a classic. But if you'd rather, you can always go with a 22-ounce porterhouse or a 28-ounce rib eye. Don't miss the dragon-eye fruit for dessert. ✉ *Golden Nugget Hotel and Casino, 129 E. Fremont St., Downtown,* ☎ *702/385–7111. Reservations essential. AE, D, DC, MC, V. Closed Mon. and Tues. No lunch.*

## Contemporary

$$–$$$$   ✕ **Second Street Grille.** Although you'll find steaks, Chinese roast duck, and Mongolian rack of lamb on the menu, seafood is the specialty here. Daily specials are flown in fresh from Hawaii. For starters try the *ahi* sashimi or seared sea scallops. For an entrée opt for the cedar-grilled salmon, sautéed soft-shell crab, or whole Thai snapper. The room is dark and intimate; the service is professional but not pretentious; and, best of all, Second Street Grille is relatively unknown in the Las Vegas fine-dining firmament, so you can usually count on same-day reservations. ✉ *Fremont Hotel and Casino, 200 E. Fremont St., Downtown,* ☎ *702/385–3232. Reservations essential. AE, D, DC, MC, V. Closed Tues. and Wed. No lunch.*

## French

$$–$$$$   ✕ **Andre's French Restaurant.** Cynics predicted an early demise for Andre
   ★        Rochat's venture when in 1980 he opened a classic French restaurant in an ivy-covered 1930s-era home blocks from the bright lights of downtown's famous Glitter Gulch. That was in 1980, and Las Vegans and visiting conventioneers are still savoring his oven-roasted rack of lamb with mustard and herb sauce, filet mignon in green-peppercorn sauce, and amazing soufflés. You'll also find more updated creations; the selections change daily. A second location at the Monte Carlo serves French food that's just as fine, but in a more spectacular room. ✉ *401 S. 6th St., Downtown,* ☎ *702/385–5016;* ✉ *Monte Carlo Resort and Casino, 3770 Las Vegas Blvd. S, South Strip,* ☎ *702/798–7151. Reservations essential. AE, DC, MC, V. No lunch.*

## Italian

$$–$$$$   ✕ **Stefano's.** Tiles from Salerno, graceful hand-blown chandeliers from Venice, and colorful murals produce an island of serenity, and singing waiters (how can you not like a place where the waiters sing "Volare" and "Pepino the Italian Mouse"?) keep things lighthearted in this ristorante named for Las Vegas legend Steve Wynn. The menu includes such standards as prosciutto with melon or mozzarella marinara as well as updated creations such as pappardella carbonara, lobster tail Milanese, and scampi Bella Anna. ✉ *Golden Nugget Hotel and Casino, 129 E. Fremont St., Downtown,* ☎ *702/385–7111.*

*Reservations essential. AE, D, DC, MC, V. Closed Tues. and Wed. No lunch.*

**$–$$** ✕ **Chicago Joe's.** Tucked away in a quiet section of downtown Las Vegas, this modest brick house with lace curtains and faded framed photographs offers a welcome respite from the glitzy casino hustle. Chicago Joe's has been drawing informed tourists and Vegas locals for more than two decades. The marinara sauce, which tops generous portions of pasta, veal, and chicken, has just the right amount of bite. Order "The Works" on any lunchtime sandwich (rib eye, sausage, or meatball) and savor a mound of sautéed green peppers, mushrooms, and onions. Extra napkins are essential. ⊠ *820 S. 4th St., Downtown,* ☎ *702/382–5637. AE, D, DC, MC, V. Closed Sun.*

### Mexican

**¢–$** ✕ **Dona Maria.** You'll forget you're in Las Vegas after a few minutes
★ in one of these relaxed and unpretentious cantinas. Stop in at the downtown location on a Wednesday night and you might see a crowd gathered for the fútbol game on satellite-provided Mexican TV. All of the combinations and specials are good, but the best play here is to order the enchilada-style tamale (with red or green sauce), for which Dona Maria is justly renowned. You also won't go wrong with the queso fundido con chorizo—Mexican-style sports-bar food. ⊠ *910 Las Vegas Blvd. S, Downtown,* ☎ *702/786–6358;* ⊠ *3205 N. Tenaya Way, Northwest Las Vegas,* ☎ *702/656–1600. AE, D, DC, MC, V.*

**¢** ✕ **El Sombrero.** In Las Vegas, where buildings that have been around for just a couple of decades are routinely flattened (sometimes on TV), a restaurant that's been in existence since 1950 is rare indeed. But that's the case with El Sombrero, a small spot downtown. It's not fancy, but the crowds packing in at lunch and dinner—including lots of Mexican expatriates—attest to a deft hand with classics such as enchiladas, tacos, burritos, and the like. The guacamole's homemade, and the pesole is among the best in town. The delicate air-filled sopaipillas make the perfect dessert after a meal of Mexican classics. ⊠ *807 S. Main St., Downtown,* ☎ *702/382–9234. AE, MC, V. Closed Sun.*

### Steak

**$–$$$** ✕ **Pullman Grille.** It may be close to one end of downtown Las Vegas'
★ Glitter Gulch, but Main Street Station is a quiet island of Victorian elegance, and that old-world feel is magnified in the Pullman Grille. There's even a Pullman car right there in the restaurant; you can retreat to it for a cigar and a port after dinner if you'd like. Dinner leans heavily to steaks, but owing to the Hawaiian clientele of the hotel-casino there are a lot of Asian offerings, too, including a sashimi appetizer of sea-breeze-fresh ahi tuna. Other choices include a seafood medley casserole and succulent lamb chops. ⊠ *Main Street Station, 200 N. Main St., Downtown,* ☎ *702/387–1896. Reservations essential. AE, D, DC, MC, V. Closed Mon. and Tues. No lunch.*

# Paradise Road

### American

**$$–$$$** ✕ **Lawry's The Prime Rib.** In a city famous for low-priced prime rib
★ specials, Lawry's is an upscale, art deco–style palace dedicated to the pursuit of excellence in the guise of slow-roasted, aged prime rib. The dining room, with hardwood floors and plush banquettes, is staffed by waitresses in 1930s-style uniforms and by white-clad carvers, who roll gleaming domed silvery carts up to your table. Atlantic lobster tails and a daily fresh-fish entrée are available for those who don't eat meat. ⊠ *4043 Howard Hughes Pkwy., Paradise Road,* ☎ *702/893–2223. Reservations essential. AE, MC, V. No lunch.*

## American/Casual

**$–$$** ✕ **Gordon Biersch Brewing Co.** This Palo Alto import is popular with both singles and the power-lunch crowd. Glassed-off brewing kettles are the design centerpiece as well as the main attraction at the square center bar, which offers specialty brews such as Marzen and Hefeweizen. The menu has one of the city's most creative selections of appetizers, including chili- and ginger-glazed chicken wings and crispy artichoke hearts tossed with Parmesan. Entrées range from pasta and wood-oven pizza to pan-seared ahi tuna and old-fashioned meat loaf with beer-mustard gravy. ⌧ *3987 Paradise Rd., Paradise Road,* ☎ *702/312–5247. AE, D, DC, MC, V.*

**¢–$** ✕ **Mr. Lucky's 24/7.** The hippest casino coffee shop in Las Vegas is inside the Hard Rock Hotel, where banks of slot machines bear the likenesses of Jimi Hendrix and Sid Vicious. Clean, modern lines; light-wood floors; and vintage rock-and-roll posters highlight this bubbly, circular café. Menu items range from vegetable omelets and entrée salads to pizza and pasta. More filling options include burgers and fries, steak, grilled salmon, and baby-back ribs. The garlic mashed potatoes are superb. It's open 24 hours, seven days a week—hence the numbers in the name. Beware: the music is loud. ⌧ *Hard Rock Hotel and Casino, 4455 Paradise Rd., Paradise Road,* ☎ *702/693–5000. Reservations not accepted. AE, D, DC, MC, V.*

## Brazilian

**$–$$** ✕ **Yolie's.** If you like rodizio served in the fashion of a *churrascaria* (a Brazilian "house of meat"), then this is the place for you. The fixed price of $26.95 ($14.95 at lunch) gets you bread, soup, sides, and all-you-can-eat slices of turkey, lamb, brisket, chicken, sausage, and steak, all grilled over a mesquite-fired, glass-enclosed rotisserie that you can see from the dining room. It's a fun place to eat. ⌧ *3900 Paradise Rd., Paradise Road,* ☎ *702/794–0700. Reservations essential. AE, D, DC, MC, V. No lunch weekends.*

## Caribbean

**$** ✕ **Bahama Breeze.** No worries, mon; Bahama Breeze is a casual spot with tropical flavors and flair—a bit of Jamaica, a bit of Cuba, a lot of fun. Signature dishes include the satisfying coconut curry chicken, with raisins, cashews, and pineapple; and jerk chicken pasta, with asparagus and mushrooms in an herb cream sauce; as well as such classics as ropa vieja, steak churrasco, conch chowder, and black beans and rice. Starters are tropically flavored, too, such as the tostones con pollo, in which crispy plantains are topped with chicken and cheese, or Jamaican grilled chicken wings. And watch out for those tropical drinks. ⌧ *375 Hughes Center Dr., Paradise Road,* ☎ *702/731–3252. Reservations not accepted. AE, D, DC, MC, V. No lunch.*

## Eclectic

**¢–$** ✕ **Hamburger Mary's.** A bun choice called You're White Bread might be your first clue that things are different at Mary's; another is a pizza named for Las Vegas' popular Mayor Oscar Goodman, with gin-sautéed mushrooms in honor of Hizzoner's favorite brew. There are other choices, but burgers are the thing; the Blueboy Burger features bacon and blue-cheese dressing. Finish things up with the Hawaiian sweetbread pudding with Captain's Morgan spiced-rum sauce, or tiramisu with macadamia nuts. ⌧ *4503 Paradise Rd., Paradise Road,* ☎ *702/735–4400. AE, D, MC, V.*

## Indian

**$–$$** ✕ **Gandhi India's Cuisine.** If you're tired of all of the steak and prime-rib specials offered in town, try this alternative. Gandhi offers dishes from major regions of India; large *thali* platters range from milder North

Indian tandoori dishes to spicier versions favored in the country's southern regions. A vegetarian thali includes *samosas* (vegetable fritters), *alu Gobi* (cauliflower and baked potatoes), and *mattar panner* (peas with homemade cottage cheese). Colorful Indian fabrics decorate this airy eatery; there's a small loft for more intimate dining. A buffet lunch is served weekdays. ⊠ *4080 Paradise Rd., Paradise Road,* ☎ *702/734–0094. Reservations essential. AE, D, DC, MC, V.*

$ ✕ **Shalimar Fine Indian Cuisine.** Las Vegan Wayne Newton is reportedly a frequent visitor to this sedate restaurant just minutes from the Strip. White tablecloths, hanging brass lamps, and taped Indian music provide a comfortable spot for excellent North Indian cuisine. House specialties include eight lamb dishes that can be prepared mild, wild hot, crazy hot, and one-way ticket to the moon, plus marinated seafood and chicken tandoori dishes cooked over a mesquite grill. The weekday luncheon buffet includes 25 different dishes. ⊠ *3900 S. Paradise Rd., Paradise Road,* ☎ *702/796–0302. AE, D, DC, MC, V. No lunch weekends.*

## Italian

$–$$ ✕ **Buca di Beppo.** Want to really have fun while dining out? Get together a big group of friends and head to Buca di Beppo. While a lot of restaurants aren't particularly welcoming to large groups, Buca di Beppo revels in them. Maybe you can sit in the Pope's room, with the bust of the pontiff on a turntable in the center of the table. Dishes are served family-style—and how; a small Caesar salad can easily serve four. Try the rigatoni Positano, with chicken, eggplant, marinara sauce, and fresh mozzarella; the chicken cacciatore, also billed as "7 pounds of love"; or a Neapolitan-style pizza. ⊠ *412 E. Flamingo Rd., Paradise Road,* ☎ *702/866–2867;* ⊠ *7690 W. Lake Mead Blvd., Northwest Las Vegas,* ☎ *702/363–6524. AE, D, DC, MC, V. No lunch weekdays.*

## Japanese

$$–$$$$ ✕ **Nobu.** Chef Nobu Matsuhisa has replicated the decor and menu of
★ his Manhattan Nobu (in the trendy TriBeCa neighborhood) in this sparkling restaurant with bamboo pillars, a seaweed wall, and wooden birch trees. Imaginative specialties include spicy sashimi, caramelized sweet miso–marinated black cod, red-bean and green-tea ice cream, mochi balls, and a bento box with warm chocolate soufflé. ⊠ *Hard Rock Hotel and Casino, 4455 Paradise Rd., Paradise Road,* ☎ *702/ 693–5000. AE, D, DC, MC, V. No lunch.*

## Mexican

$–$$ ✕ **Cozymel's Mexican Grill.** This Dallas-based chain spotlights fresh seafood like the Yucatan Especial seafood medley, which is shrimp and scallops tossed in a creamy sauce with poblano peppers, spinach, and mushrooms. More familiar Mexican dishes (fajitas, enchiladas, and oversize tacos) are available, along with vegetarian dishes and flavored margaritas to get you into the beach-party spirit. The festive room is decorated with fishing nets and indoor palms for a south-of-the-border fishing resort feel. ⊠ *355 Hughes Center Dr., Paradise Road,* ☎ *702/732–4833. AE, D, DC, MC, V.*

¢–$ ✕ **Pink Taco.** Nothing inside the Hard Rock Hotel is boring, and that goes for this over-the-top take on a Mexican cantina. The food is serviceable but takes a decided backseat to the party atmosphere, which includes a huge four-sided bar, patio doors that open onto the hotel's elaborate pool area, and waitresses in soccer jerseys that are low-cut from every direction. The eyebrow-raising name refers, of course, to the grilled salmon taco, one of six special tacos on the menu. Alternatives include the chicken tostada salad and achiote grilled chicken breast. ⊠ *Hard Rock Hotel and Casino, 4455 Paradise Rd., Paradise Road,* ☎ *702/693–5000. AE, D, DC, MC, V.*

## Seafood

**$–$$$**  ✕ **McCormick & Schmick's.** This Portland-based spot has old-tavern
★     charm (complete with stained glass) and offers a huge menu of appe-
tizers, oysters on the half shell, salads, lunch sandwiches, and imagi-
natively prepared fresh fish dishes (the selection changes daily). Popular
choices are Oregon Dungeness crab cakes with red-pepper aïoli,
Louisiana catfish with chipotle pepper sauce, Mexican yellowtail tuna
with pepper balsamic vinaigrette, and Alaskan troll king salmon with
pinot noir sauce roasted on a cedar plank. If the weather's pleasant,
you can dine on the patio. ⊠ *335 Hughes Center Dr., Paradise Road,*
☎ *702/836–9000. AE, D, DC, MC, V.*

## Southwestern

**¢–$**  ✕ **Z' Tejas Grill.** This Austin, Texas–based chain first conquered Las
Vegas with a location on the Paradise Road convention corridor, then
added a gorgeous building in the fast-growing Peccole Ranch area in
the far west end of town. Both locations offer signature dishes such as
catfish beignets, Voodoo Tuna (blackened tuna with spicy soy mustard),
ancho-rubbed pork tenderloin, and jerk chicken salad. The Peccole Ranch
location serves Southwestern-style Sunday brunch. ⊠ *3824 Paradise
Rd., Paradise Road,* ☎ *702/732–1660;* ⊠ *9560 W. Sahara Ave., West
Side,* ☎ *702/638–0610. AE, D, DC, MC, V.*

# Greater Las Vegas

## American

**$–$$$**  ✕ **The Broiler.** Station Casinos has emerged as one of the front-run-
ning off-Strip casino organizations; its resorts serve as neighborhood
casino outposts of the original Palace Station. Branches of the Broiler,
its good, inexpensive steak and seafood house, are found at both
Palace and Boulder Stations. Both locations have excellent soups,
breads, and a salad bar, which set the stage for medium-price mesquite-
grilled steaks, veal, and chicken. ⊠ *Boulder Station Hotel and Casino,
4111 Boulder Hwy., Boulder Strip,* ☎ *702/432–7777;* ⊠ *Palace Station Hotel and Casino, 2411 W. Sahara Ave., West Side,* ☎ *702/367–
2411. AE, D, MC, V.*

**¢–$$**  ✕ **Tenaya Creek Restaurant & Brewery.** Tenaya Creek is a brew pub
with a contemporary design, and one that happens to have super cus-
tomer service. The menu's contemporary, too—a far cry from the old
bar food. It has starters such as stacked Ahi tuna tartare, buffalo moz-
zarella and tomatoes, or Red Rock Salad, a chopped salad with avo-
cado, bacon, blue cheese, scallions, and lettuce. Entrées include grilled
Hawaiian escolar on horseradish mashed potatoes, a petite filet mignon
with a pinot noir sauce, and a bone-in rib eye. At dessert time, remember
that the bananas Foster is made with Frangelico. ⊠ *3101 N. Tenaya
Way, Northwest Las Vegas,* ☎ *702/362–7335. AE, D, DC, MC, V.*

## American/Casual

**¢–$**  ✕ **5 & Diner.** Meals at this bright and cheerful eatery with multiple lo-
cations around town include soup or salad, vegetable, and choice of
potato—starting at $5.29. Thick milk shakes, baked homemade meat
loaf with rich brown gravy, big hamburgers, spaghetti with garlic
bread, chicken-fried steaks, and roast beef are menu mainstays. The
quality is surprisingly good, and the atmosphere is friendly. It's open
from 6 AM until the wee hours. ⊠ *6840 W. Sahara Ave., West Side,* ☎
*702/368–7903;* ⊠ *1825 E. Flamingo Rd., University District,* ☎ *702/
892–3510;* ⊠ *1900 N. Buffalo Dr., Northwest Las Vegas,* ☎ *702/804–
8044. Reservations not accepted;* ⊠ *8820 S. Eastern Ave., East Las
Vegas,* ☎ *702/966–2650;* ⊠ *375 N. Stephanie St., Henderson,* ☎
*702/940–2050. AE, MC, V.*

¢–$ ✕ **Mimi's Cafe.** Mimi's may sound French—a Frenchwoman was the
★ inspiration behind the name of this growing California-based chain—
and the decor may look French, but the menu is wide-ranging American. For starters, consider a Thai chicken wrap, Cajun popcorn
shrimp, or spinach-and-artichoke dip. Entrée choices include barbecued meat loaf, penne with pine nuts and feta, and turkey breast with
corn-bread dressing. And don't pass the dessert case without peeking
or you might miss the warm chocolate praline bars or New Orleans
bread pudding. ✉ *1121 S. Fort Apache Rd., Northwest Las Vegas,*
☎ *702/341–0365;* ✉ *596 N. Stephanie St., Henderson,* ☎ *702/458–
0726. AE, D, MC, V.*

¢–$ ✕ **Smitty's Famous Fish & Chicken.** Smitty's serves just what the name
specifies and most of it's fried, but what a way to indulge your tastes
when you're feeling a little sinful. You can get something as simple as
a chicken breast with fries or as extensive as two pieces of fish, two
pieces of chicken, six medium shrimp *and* oysters, for that super-size
appetite. Fish varieties include red snapper, salmon, catfish, and whit-
ing, and sides run a Southern-style gamut. Have some hush puppies
while you're at it, and finish up with a piece of peach cobbler. Smitty's
is a casual kind of place, and with such an eclectic clientele that you
can be assured you'll always be one of the crowd. ✉ *4760 W. Sahara
Ave., West Side,* ☎ *702/822–6900. MC, V.*

¢ ✕ **L&L Hawaiian Barbecue.** This isn't barbecue as most mainlanders
think of it, but L&L is authentic nonetheless and reflects the growing
Hawaiian population in Henderson and other parts of the valley. One
specialty is the Loco Moco, which is fried eggs on hamburger patties
topped with gravy and accompanied by macaroni salad and rice. The
plate lunch is the thing here, and comes in various permutations, with
macaroni salad and rice. The chicken *katsu* (thinly-cut, breaded, and
fried) is crisp; the barbecue sauce is island-sweet; and of course there's
Spam on the menu. For filling food at a bargain price, L&L is it. ✉
*687 N. Stephanie St., Henderson,* ☎ *702/433–0240. MC, V.*

## Barbecue

¢–$ ✕ **Buckingham Smokehouse Bar-B-Q.** You can smell the barbecue—
actually the smoking wood that's used to cook these down-home fa-
vorites—the minute you walk in the door, sometimes even before.
Buckingham advertises that its beef brisket and pork loin are smoked
for 18 hours, and the proof is in the flavor. The baby back ribs are Buckingham's signature piece, but there are plenty of other, less expensive
choices, such as the smoked ham, smoked salmon fillet, hot link,
pulled pork, and even a hickory-smoked Philly sandwich. For a zesty
change of pace, consider the horseradish cole slaw; the sweet-potato
french fries are a sweet taste on the side. And for dessert you might
want to try a slice of apple pie or pecan pie—maybe à la mode. ✉ *2341
N. Rainbow Blvd., Northwest Las Vegas,* ☎ *702/638–7799 or 702/
638–8699. AE, D, MC, V.*

¢–$ ✕ **H&H B-B-Q.** Barbecue's in the name and barbecue's the game, but
H&H also has Southern specialties. The barbecue's done on an open
pit right out by the parking lot; among the dishes prepared indoors
are smothered pork chops or chicken, liver and onions, fried chicken
or pork chops, catfish or snapper. Portions are huge: order a pork plate
and you'll get a pile of big, meaty ribs with that fine smoky flavor. Get
a vegetable plate if you're feeling guilty; if not, try the banana pudding, peach cobbler, or one of the homemade cakes. ✉ *910 N. Martin Luther King Blvd., West Side,* ☎ *702/646–4856. AE, D, MC, V.*

¢–$ ✕ **Memphis Championship Barbecue.** Barbecue the old-fashioned way:
that's what fans are looking for, and that's what Memphis Championship Barbecue delivers. The owner/founder hails from Murphysboro,

Illinois, which apparently is a well-kept secret as a barbecue stronghold, and cooks Memphis-style; hence the name. If you've got a big appetite—or a big family—try Mama Faye's Down Home Supper Dinner for four; you won't go away hungry. Other choices include smoked hot links, barbecued pork shoulder, and catfish. Oh, and on the side, treat yourself to some fried dill pickles. ⊠ *2250 E. Warm Springs Rd., East Side,* ☎ *702/260–6909;* ⊠ *4379 Las Vegas Blvd. N, North Las Vegas,* ☎ *702/644–0000;* ⊠ *Santa Fe Station, 4949 N. Rancho Dr., Las Vegas,* ☎ *702/396–6223. AE, D, MC, V.*

## Buffets

$–$$  ✕ **Carnival World Buffet.** This was one of the first Las Vegas buffets with separate theme areas; the buffets-within-a-buffet here serve up fresh Mexican, Italian, Chinese, Japanese, American, and other ethnic specialties under one large and colorful roof. The centerpiece is the Mongolian barbecue, where you choose your own meats and veggies to be stir-fried before your eyes on one of two sizzling-hot grills. Hamburgers and french fries, fish and chips, barbecue, sushi, salads, desserts, and more are also available. ⊠ *Rio All-Suite Hotel and Casino, 3700 W. Flamingo Rd., West Side,* ☎ *702/252–7777. AE, D, DC, MC, V.*

¢–$  ✕ **Feast Around the World.** The buffet at Green Valley Ranch Resort has a name similar to those at some of Station Casinos' other properties, and the options are somewhat similar, but there's no mistaking that the company has improved its offerings with each new casino. A huge display of fresh produce and the use of natural stone and carefully designed lighting lend a decidedly upscale touch to the entrance hall. Specialty stations include a Mongolian grill, Italian, Mexican, and American, plus a good-size salad bar and a belt-busting selection of pastries. ⊠ *Green Valley Ranch, 2300 Paseo Verde Pkwy., Henderson,* ☎ *702/614–5283. AE, D, DC, MC, V.*

## Chinese

¢–$  ✕ **Cathay House.** Cathay House is a bit of a rarity in Las Vegas—a restaurant that has the feel of a mom-and-pop spot, but with a sophisticated atmosphere and a menu that combines the best of both worlds. Among appetizers are the classic soups plus sizzling rice soup, curry puffs, and Hawaiian-style skewered beef and chicken; house entrée specialties include strawberry chicken and sautéed crystal shrimp. ⊠ *5300 W. Spring Mountain Rd., West Side,* ☎ *702/876–3838. AE, D, MC, V.*

## Contemporary

$$–$$$  ✕ **Rosemary's.** Husband-and-wife chefs Michael and Wendy Jordan, ★  who made their reputation in Las Vegas with a West Side location that caters to locals, recently added a just-off-the-Strip spot at the Rio. The menu's American regional: among the signature dishes are a starter of veal sweetbreads and wild mushroom–garlic toast, and there are such main courses as rosemary roasted lamb, brick quail, and Texas barbecued shrimp. For dessert, try the chocolate beignets. ⊠ *8125 W. Sahara Ave., West Side,* ☎ *702/869–2251. No lunch weekends;* ⊠ *Rio All-Suite Hotel and Casino, 3700 W. Flamingo Rd., West Side,* ☎ *702/ 362–2033. No lunch. Reservations essential. AE, D, DC, MC, V.*

$–$$  ✕ **Roy's.** Don't worry about fusion confusion here; Roy Yamaguchi practically invented the trend and knows how to do it right. The menu changes daily, but you can expect appetizers such as seared shrimp on a stick with wasabi cocktail sauce or Hawaiian crispy crab cakes in sesame beurre blanc. Entrées might include signature Yamaguchi dishes such as blackened ahi tuna in a spicy hot soy mustard sauce, teriyaki hibachi-grilled salmon with Japanese vegetable salad and citrus ponzu sauce, hoisin-glazed pork, or charred sea scallops. ⊠ *8701 W. Charleston*

*Blvd., West Side,* ☎ *702/838–3620;* ✉ *620 E. Flamingo Rd., Paradise Road,* ☎ *702/691–2053. AE, D, DC, MC, V. No lunch.*

## Eclectic

¢–$  ✕ **J. C. Wooloughan Irish Pub.** What do you get when you build a
★  pub in Ireland, dismantle it, and ship it across the ocean, to be re-constructed in the desert? An Irish pub in a Las Vegas off-Strip re-sort that looks like a wee bit o' the Emerald Isle. J. C. Wooloughan offers Irish beers and beer blends and lots of Irish foods, both familiar and not-so. Cheek-by-jowl with the corned beef and cabbage, you'll find beef and Guinness pie, all-day Irish breakfast, or a Murphy's beef boxty (a sort of stuffed potato omelet). For dessert, the fantastic Aunt Maura's Sticky Toffee Pudding is among the choices. ✉ *JW Marriott Las Vegas, 221 N. Rampart Blvd., Summerlin,* ☎ *702/869–7777. AE, D, MC, V.*

¢  ✕ **Crown & Anchor British Pub.** With its 24-hour service and grave-yard specials, Crown & Anchor is uniquely Las Vegas, but most of the food's British, including the steak and kidney pie; Ploughman's Lunch; bangers and mash; and authentic fish and chips. Sandwiches with American and British flavors are plenty, and the nightly specials make this spot even more of a bargain proposition. There are "draught" beers from all over the world and a "British Shoppe" selling "salad cream," Branston Pickle, and the like. If you still doubt the authenticity, know that the trifle is made with Bird's English custard. The decor's decid-edly British, and special events add to the fun: on New Year's Eve the celebration starts at the English midnight, eight hours before the Las Vegas one. ✉ *1350 E. Tropicana Ave., East Side,* ☎ *702/739–8676. AE, D, MC, V.*

## French

$–$$  ✕ **Bonjour Casual French.** The *hauteur* that French restaurants are fa-
★  mous for is about all that's lacking at Bonjour, which says it's casual and means it. The food at this charming country-French spot is a blend of the classic and the innovative. Among the appetizer offerings are a warm Roquefort-and-pear Napoleon and onion soup gratinée; entrée choices include crusted salmon with spinach, pine nuts, and tar-ragon sauce, and vegetable ravioli with wild mushrooms and arti-chokes. A tarte Tatin is a fine finish. ✉ *8878 S. Eastern Ave., South Las Vegas,* ☎ *702/270–2102. AE, D, DC, MC, V. Closed Mon.*

$–$$  ✕ **Pamplemousse.** The late singer—and restaurant regular—Bobby Dar-rin chose the name, which means grapefruit in French, on a whim. The dominant color here is burgundy, orchestral music is played over the stereo system, and the food is classic French. Because the entrées change daily, there is no printed menu; instead, the waiter recites the bill of fare. Specialties of the house include roast duckling with cran-berry and Chambord sauce and Norwegian salmon with curry sauce. This room is small and popular with the convention trade, so be sure to make reservations as far in advance as possible. ✉ *400 E. Sahara Ave., East Side,* ☎ *702/733–2066. Reservations essential. AE, D, DC, MC, V. Closed Mon. No lunch.*

## Indian

$  ✕ **India Oven.** There are a number of super Indian restaurants in Las Vegas, but India Oven stands tall among them. The inside is plain, the outside even plainer. But the location—sort of diagonal from the Sa-hara Hotel and Casino—makes India Oven easy for tourists to find, and its food makes it a favorite among locals—especially Indians, who make up a large part of the clientele. The menu is typically wide-rang-ing Indian, with tandoori meats and nan bread prepared in the tan-door oven; other specialties include lamb korma with cashews, almonds, and raisins, and chicken vindaloo. ✉ *226 W. Sahara Ave., West Side,* ☎ *702/366–0222. AE, D, MC, V.*

## Italian

**$–$$$$** ✕ **Venetian.** You can't miss this landmark Italian restaurant, which opened in 1955 as the first pizza place in Las Vegas: murals of Venice grace the exterior and interior walls. Culinary traditions here include a jumbo bowl of pork neck bones in a wine marinade served as an appetizer (use the bib!), and Venetian greens on a bed of pasta. You can't go wrong with any dishes that have a "p" in the name: think pasta, Parmigiana, eggplant, pizzaiola, scallopini, peppers. The selection of homemade bread is outstanding. ✉ *3713 W. Sahara Ave., West Side,* ☎ *702/876–4190. Reservations essential. AE, D, DC, MC, V.*

**$$–$$$** ✕ **Antonio's.** Inlaid marble floors, a blue-sky dome, and murals depicting Italian scenes decorate this quiet restaurant, which has an open kitchen. The long menu offers well-prepared northern and southern Italian cuisine with old favorites such as cioppino, eggplant Parmesan, osso buco Milanese, and spaghetti con aragosta. If it's available, order the five-onion soup—and you can ask the waiter for the recipe. Desserts include tiramisu. ✉ *Rio All-Suite Hotel and Casino, 3700 W. Flamingo Rd., West Side,* ☎ *702/252–7737. Reservations essential. AE, DC, MC, V. No lunch.*

**$–$$$** ✕ **Ferraro's Restaurant & Lounge.** Gino Ferraro's dependable Italian cuisine has been a favorite of Las Vegans since 1985. The dining room of this casual restaurant is trimmed with black lacquer and pink neon accents. Family recipes are featured, fresh breads and pastas are made on the premises, the wine list is extraordinary, the osso buco is *magnifico,* and Rosalba's tiramisu is *fantastico.* The service is good and prices are moderate, too. ✉ *5900 W. Flamingo Rd., West Side,* ☎ *702/ 364–5300. AE, D, DC, MC, V.*

**$–$$** ✕ **Carrabba's Italian Grill.** "Chain" may seem like a dirty word to anyone who's especially fond of mom-and-pop Italian joints, but Texas-based Carrabba's manages to put a different spin on things; that's immediately evident when you see the trees on the roof. Relax and enjoy such delights as bruschetta Carrabba (which pairs tomato and mushroom varieties of bruschetta), Cozze in Bianco (mussels steamed in a lovely white-wine mixture), tagliarini Picchi Pacchiu (with a crushed-tomato sauce), or chicken Bryan (with caprini cheese and sun-dried tomatoes). At dessert time, the tiramisu is equalled only by the Chocolate Dream. ✉ *10160 S. Eastern Ave., Henderson,* ☎ *702/990–0650;* ✉ *8771 W. Charleston Blvd., West Side,* ☎ *702/304–2345. Reservations not accepted. AE, D, MC, V. No lunch.*

**$–$$** ✕ **Spiedini Ristorante.** Gustav Mauler, who had long been chef and restaurant developer for the former Mirage Resorts company, struck out on his own with this stylish Italian restaurant. The menu is a contemporary take on traditional favorites. Starters include a sumptuous antipasto platter and fried, thinly sliced potatoes and zucchini with a creamy Gorgonzola sauce. Entrées encompass hand-crafted pastas, a veal chop stuffed with fontina and sage, osso buco, and a lobster-and-shrimp fra diavolo. Desserts often are deliciously whimsical, as in the case of the pineapple carpaccio with raspberry sorbet. ✉ *JW Marriott Las Vegas, 221 N. Rampart Blvd., Summerlin,* ☎ *702/869–8500. AE, D, DC, MC, V. No lunch.*

## Mediterranean

**$–$$** ✕ **Grape Street Cafe, Wine Bar & Grill.** Grape Street's menu is designed to coordinate nicely with the restaurant's interesting—and not stratospherically priced—wine list. There are salads, sandwiches, pizzas and the like, plus dinner specials such as grilled salmon. Desserts range from austere Stilton and Port to positively decadent dark-chocolate fondue.

Grape Street is brick-lined, candle-lit, and cozy, and there's a patio for pleasant evenings. ⊠ *7501 W. Lake Mead Blvd., Northwest Las Vegas,* ☎ *702/228–9463. AE, D, MC, V. Closed Mon.*

## Mexican

**\$–\$\$** ✕ **Viva Mercado's.** The explosion of new chain restaurants in suburban neighborhoods makes it easy to forget the charms of the first Las Vegas restaurant to bring a chef's touch to Mexican food. You can get enchiladas and burritos here if you want, and bountiful plates of them at that. More rewarding are the daily specials and fish dishes, such as orange roughy cooked four different ways (including with the ultra-hot *salsa de arbol*), or *banderilla de camaron* (shrimp grilled in garlic, lemon, and pico de gallo). Stucco, fake plants, and tile awnings over rows of booths vaguely suggest an outdoor Mexican plaza, though in a mom-and-pop way compared to the many "theme" and "designed" restaurants around here. ⊠ *6182 W. Flamingo Rd., West Side,* ☎ *702/ 871–8826. Reservations essential. AE, MC, V.*

**\$** ✕ **La Barca Mexican Seafood Restaurant.** If you want to eat where Mexicans eat and have no patience for Texas or California twists on Mexican food, this is the place for you. This busy spot inside the otherwise faded Commercial Center doesn't put chips and salsa on the table and the emphasis is on seafood, not gloppy things covered with cheese. Fish and shrimp tacos are the most popular orders, along with the Seven Seas Soup—a mixture of seafood with implied medicinal benefits. The Whaler is a 45-ounce shrimp cocktail that creates an instant party. Mariachi bands enhance the weekend-only atmosphere. ⊠ *953 E. Sahara Ave., East Side,* ☎ *702/657–9700. AE, D, DC, MC, V. Closed Mon.–Thurs.*

**¢–\$** ✕ **Lindo Michoacán.** *Lindo* means pretty; Michoacán is a state in central Mexico. Gavier Baragas, the congenial owner and host of this colorful cantina named for his native state, presents outstanding specialties that he learned to cook while growing up. Many menu items are named for his relatives, including *flautas Mama Chelo* (corn tortillas filled with chicken). Michoacán is known for its carnitas, so don't miss them. Or try the *cabrito birria de chivo* (roasted goat with red mole sauce). Guacamole is made tableside. At dessert time, remember that the flan is a silken wonder. ⊠ *2655 E. Desert Inn Rd., East Side,* ☎ *702/735–6828 or 702/257–6810. AE, D, MC, V.*

**¢–\$** ✕ **SuperMex Restaurant & Cantina.** Here's a superlative case of truth in advertising: The California-based SuperMex, a big barn of a place, has a super menu—32 combination plates, plus seven different kinds of burritos in two sizes, combination burritos, salads, tostadas, appetizers, fajitas, tacos, taquitos, and more. You can even get a chili relleno burrito or an enchilada with a taco or an enchilada and a tamale or . . . you get the picture. "Extras are extra," the menu says, and you can use them to tailor-make your dish to your tastes. There's even a "lite" menu, for those seeking, say, a whole-wheat quesadilla. ⊠ *3460 E. Sunset Rd., Henderson,* ☎ *702/436–5200. AE, MC, V.*

## Pan-Asian

**\$–\$\$** ✕ **Little Buddha.** It may sound like a mixed metaphor—an Asian restaurant in Paris—but France's Buddha Bar has achieved world fame for its food and its music. The associated Little Buddha in Las Vegas continues the mystique. The kitchen produces such Pacific Rim wonders as Hawaiian smoked pot stickers, wok-fried salt and pepper calamari and frog's legs, grilled Asian pork ribs, and curry shrimp in banana leaf. Finish things off with a sweet touch of coconut sticky rice with mango and Florentine crisp or liquid-center chocolate cake with vanilla ice cream. ⊠ *The Palms, 4321 W. Flamingo Rd., West Side,* ☎ *702/942–7777. AE, D, DC, MC, V.*

$-$$   ✕ **Mayflower Cuisinier.** You'll find creative Chinese dishes with Californian, Pan-Asian, and French accents on the menu at this off-Strip eatery. Try the ginger-chicken ravioli, Asian Portobello mushroom burrito, pistachio-encrusted salmon with ginger-caper sauce, or Mongolian lamb chops with creamy cilantro sauce. For dessert, consider a delectable trio of crème brûlées flavored with almond, orange, and pineapple-ginger. ⊠ *4750 W. Sahara Ave., West Side,* ☎ *702/870–8432. AE, D, DC, MC, V.*

## Seafood

$$$-$$$$   ✕ **The Tillerman.** Its location on Flamingo Road, almost 3 mi east of the Strip, makes the Tillerman a quiet refuge from the casinos. The garden setting also does its part: the restaurant is built around a huge ficus tree growing in the center of the room, under a skylight that's open on hot desert nights. Specialities include linguine with clams, mussels, shrimp, scallops, lobster, white wine, and garlic and blackened yellowfin tuna with roasted-red-pepper sauce. Up to a dozen fresh-fish selections are offered each night, and the steaks are always done just right, too. ⊠ *2245 E. Flamingo Rd., East Side,* ☎ *702/731–4036. AE, D, DC, MC, V. No lunch.*

## Southwestern

¢–$$   ✕ **Garduño's Chili Packing Co.** The Garduño family imported their restaurants from Albuquerque, along with ongoing shipments of fresh green chilis from Hatch, New Mexico. The chilis are used in many of the spicier dishes; those with more timid taste buds should sample the milder seafood tacos and fajitas that arrive on sizzling iron skillets. The salsa bar has an impressive array of sauces, the bar an even more impressive selection of tequilas. Meals come with sopaipillas that can be drenched with honey to cool off the chili burn. On Sunday, a margarita brunch is served. ⊠ *Palms, 4321 W. Flamingo Rd., West Side,* ☎ *702/942–7777;* ⊠ *Fiesta Rancho Hotel and Casino, 2400 N. Rancho Dr., Rancho Strip,* ☎ *702/631–7000. AE, D, DC, MC, V.*

## Steak

$$–$$$$   ✕ **Billy Bob's Steak House.** Big food is the name of the game at the Western-theme Billy Bob's Steak House at Sam's Town. The 28-ounce rib eye is Texas-size, the barbecued brisket could feed a rodeo. And then there's dessert: the chocolate eclairs are a foot long, and the chocolate cake could fill up a good chunk of the Grand Canyon. Sharing is recommended. ⊠ *Sam's Town Hotel and Gambling Hall, 5111 Boulder Hwy., Boulder Strip,* ☎ *702/456–7777. AE, D, DC, MC, V. No lunch.*

$$–$$$$   ✕ **Golden Steer.** In a town where restaurants come and go almost as quickly as visitors' cash, the longevity of this steak house, opened in 1962, is itself a recommendation. And while it changed hands a couple of years ago, the tradition continues. Folks still come to this San Francisco–theme restaurant with red leather chairs, polished dark wood, and stained-glass windows for the huge slabs of well-prepared meat. Steak, ribs, and game are particularly popular. Although you wouldn't know it from the outside, the Steer is cavernous. Lots of small, intimate rooms, however, break up the space. ⊠ *308 W. Sahara Ave., West Side,* ☎ *702/384–4470. AE, D, DC, MC, V. No lunch.*

$$–$$$$   ✕ **Sonoma Cellar.** Sonoma Cellar was one of the first upscale restaurants in a locals casino, and it hasn't lost its verve. It's elegant and serene, with a redwood wine cellar and a cigar lounge. The menu includes, in addition to steaks, such classics as oysters Rockefeller, lobster bisque, and clams casino and more updated offerings such as Mediterranean shrimp and mesquite-grilled or pan-seared salmon fillet. The details are there, too; don't miss the pretzel rolls. ⊠ *Sunset Station Hotel and*

*Casino, 1301 W. Sunset Rd., Henderson, ☎ 702/547–7898. AE, D, DC, MC, V. No lunch.*

## Vegetarian

¢ ✕ **The Raw Truth Veggie Cafe and Juice Bar.** The name of this vegetarian café refers to the fact that nothing is cooked at temperatures higher than the 100°F-plus it takes to make flat breads and pizza dough. And yet, reasonable facsimiles of pizza (made of dehydrated sprouted bread and fermented almond cheese) and lasagna take their place alongside the expected salad choices. ⊠ *2381 E. Windmill La., Southwest Las Vegas, ☎ 702/450–9007. AE, D, DC, MC, V.*

¢ ✕ **Wild Oats Community Market.** Wild Oats has all the stuff you'd expect in the small café of a whole foods market—an extensive salad bar, for example, and smoothies and vegetable juices—but a lot of the unexpected as well; for example, somebody's enlightened enough to separate vegan dishes (biryani, stuffed tofu pockets) from regular vegetarian (kung pao tofu, traditional slaw) in the deli. Selections include a Reuben sandwich that combines smoked tomato slices with sauerkraut, Swiss cheese, and Thousand Island dressing. ⊠ *7250 W. Lake Mead Blvd., Northwest Las Vegas, ☎ 702/942–1500; ⊠ 517 N. Stephanie St., Henderson, ☎ 702/458–9427. AE, D, DC, MC, V.*

# 5 WHERE TO STAY

Las Vegas has upward of 130,000 hotel rooms, and it probably offers more choices and types of accommodations than anywhere else, from 95-year-old downtown digs to exclusive hotels with 10,000-square-foot penthouse villas. No matter where your head hits the pillow, though, there's sure to be a casino, coffee shop, buffet, lounge, convenience store, and neon sign within shouting distance.

Updated by
Gregory
Crosby

THE LAS VEGAS STRIP IS A CITY within a city, where vast megaresorts, some of them replicating whole cities of their own (from New York to Paris to Venice), cater to the whims of travelers from around the globe. From the small, one or two story Palms Springs-style hotel-casinos of the 1950s, the typical Vegas resort grew in size and stature, first with the high-rise hotels like the Riviera, then with the "theme" resorts like Caesars Palace, and finally with the huge properties like Mandalay Bay offering every conceivable pleasure, from shopping malls and cinema multiplexes to amusement parks and roller coasters.

Choosing where to stay depends on both your budget and what you want to do. The more upscale and luxurious properties—those with shopping malls, big showroom entertainment, and thrill rides—are clustered around the south end of the Strip, though family-friendly and more inexpensive hotels like the Excalibur can be found here as well. Those wanting to be at the "heart" of the Strip will want to look into the intersection of Flamingo and Las Vegas Boulevard, where the Bellagio, Bally's, Caesars Palace and the Flamingo Las Vegas overlook the constant stream of visitors. North of Treasure Island, smaller and older hotels like the Stardust and the Riviera offer lower room rates and fewer amenities beyond the classic Vegas trio of casino, lounge, and dining. Downtown, the hotels are cheaper and are favored by those with strictly adult pleasures: dice and drinks.

Another consideration in the hotel decision is timing. Las Vegas is now home to 9 of the 10 largest hotels in the United States. If 130,000 hotel and motel rooms seems like a lot, consider that visitor volume on average is nearly 36 million. That means well over a half-million visitors a week—the equivalent of every man, woman, and child living within Seattle's city limits being suddenly transported to Las Vegas. In short, accommodations fill up fast around here, even when no major conventions or events are in town.

When it's time for a big convention, it's not unusual for Las Vegas to sell out completely. Nearly two dozen conventions a year each attract more than 25,000 participants. Combine those with three-day weekends, holidays, large sporting events, and normally crowded weekends, and you can see why it's wise to make your lodging arrangements as far ahead of your visit as possible. On the other hand, things change quickly in Las Vegas. If you arrive at the last minute without accommodations, you'll almost always be able to find a room somewhere in town—though the price might be double or triple what you would have paid with reservations. And if your original room is not to your liking, you can usually upgrade it around checkout time the next day.

| CATEGORY | COST |
| --- | --- |
| $$$$ | over $200 |
| $$$ | $150–$200 |
| $$ | $100–$150 |
| $ | $50–$100 |
| ¢ | under $50 |

*Price categories are assigned based on the range between the least and most expensive standard double rooms in non-holiday high season, based on the European Plan (with no meals), unless otherwise noted. Service charge and 10% tax are extra. In listings, we always name the facilities that are available, but we don't specify whether they cost extra. When pricing accommodations, always ask what's included and what entails an additional charge.*

# The Strip

**$$–$$$$**  🏨 **Aladdin Resort and Casino.** One of the few imploded hotel-casinos to retain its original name, the Aladdin was reborn as one of Las Vegas' modern-day megaresorts. Costing more than $1.3 billion to build, the Aladdin is still themed after the legendary tale from the *Arabian Nights*. The casino has everything from flying horses to a giant version of Aladdin's lamp; the property also includes the Desert Passage mall, a 7,000-seat performing arts center, and a wedding chapel. Rooms are decorated with Arabian flair, but are more geared toward the business world than traveling sheiks. In addition to marble bathrooms and custom furniture, the oversize rooms have high-speed Internet access. ✉ *3667 Las Vegas Blvd. S, Center Strip 89109,* ☎ *702/736–0111 or 877/333–9474,* FAX *702/736–7107,* WEB *www.aladdincasino.com. 2,344 rooms, 223 suites. 21 restaurants, in-room data ports, 2 pools, health club, spa, lounge, casino, nightclub, theater, shops, business services, meeting room. AE, D, DC, MC, V.*

**$$–$$$$**  🏨 **Bally's Las Vegas.** One of the largest resorts on the Strip—with
★    nearly 3,000 rooms, six restaurants, three showrooms, a wedding chapel, and a 40-store mall—it's clear why Bally's calls itself "a city within a city." The hotel also has a huge casino, separate health spas for men and women, and an attractively landscaped outdoor pool. The large rooms are full of bright, overstuffed furniture, and have great views of Vegas's parade of neon. ✉ *3645 Las Vegas Blvd. S, Center Strip 89109,* ☎ *702/ 967–4111 or 888/742–9248,* FAX *702/739–4405,* WEB *www.ballyslv.com. 2,567 rooms, 265 suites. 6 restaurants, in-room data ports, 8 tennis courts, pool, health club, spa, bar, lounge, casino, comedy club, 3 showrooms, shops, concierge, no-smoking rooms. AE, D, DC, MC, V.*

**$$–$$$$**  🏨 **Caesars Palace.** The opulent entrance, fountains, Roman statuary,
★    bas-reliefs, and roaming centurions all add up to the quintessential Las Vegas hotel, the first on the Strip to fully embrace an overarching theme. The Forum Shops at Caesars are among the most extravagant in town and Cleopatra's Barge a one-of-a-kind lounge floating in an indoor pool. The hotel also hosts world-class sporting events and performances by top superstars like Celine Dion, who will be performing here for many years to come. While the Palace Tower's spacious rooms offer everything from vaulted ceilings to whirlpool baths, the smaller rooms at the front of the Forum Tower have a spectacular view of the Strip. ✉ *3570 Las Vegas Blvd. S, Center Strip 89109,* ☎ *702/731–7110 or 800/ 223–7277,* FAX *702/731–6636,* WEB *www.caesarspalace.com. 2,364 rooms and 100 suites. 7 restaurants, in-room data ports, 4 tennis courts, 3 pools, health club, spa, squash, 4 bars, lounge, casino, showroom, theater, shops, concierge, business services, meeting room, no-smoking rooms. AE, D, DC, MC, V.*

**$$–$$$$**  🏨 **Mandalay Bay Resort & Casino.** Upon its opening, Mandalay Bay
★    quickly became one of the city's most popular megaresorts. It's a hip, fun, imaginative joint, with some unique elements: a wave pool with 5-foot swells, a million-gallon walk-through aquarium, and a 12,000-seat arena complex that hosts major sporting contests and superstar concerts. The House of Blues operates not only a restaurant and a 1,800-seat concert hall, but the Foundation Room, an exclusive club on the 34th floor that's open to the public on Monday nights. The fabulous rumjungle restaurant turns into the city's trendiest nightclub after 11 PM. Guest rooms are spacious, with extra large beds and separate tubs and showers. ✉ *3950 Las Vegas Blvd. S, South Strip 89119,* ☎ *702/ 632–7777 or 877/632–7400,* FAX *702/791–7446,* WEB *www.mandalaybay. com. 3,700 rooms. 11 restaurants, in-room data ports, pools, health club, spa, 7 bars, casino, concert hall, nightclub, showroom, shops, meeting room, no-smoking rooms. AE, D, DC, MC, V.*

**$$–$$$$** 🏨 **MGM Grand Hotel and Casino.** The largest hotel in the world has
♻ four emerald-green towers, three of them 30 stories high, set on 112
acres and housing over 5,000 guest rooms, including 733 Hollywood-
inspired suites. Also here are a special-events arena, a complete day-
care facility, a wedding chapel, and a lion habitat. Rooms are of
average size, with a contemporary take on art deco in the decor and
picture windows. Bungalow suites in the Grand Tower have plush fab-
rics, polished wood, and black-and-white Italian marble bathrooms.
The MGM offers airport check-in from 9 AM to 11 PM. ✉ *3799 Las
Vegas Blvd. S, South Strip 89109,* ☎ *702/891–7777 or 800/929–
1111,* FAX *702/891–1030,* WEB *www.mgmgrand.com. 5,004 rooms. 10
restaurants, in-room data ports, 5 pools, health club, spa, 2 lounges,
casino, nightclub, 2 showrooms, shops, business services, meeting
room, no-smoking rooms. AE, D, DC, MC, V.*

**$$–$$$$** 🏨 **Mirage Hotel and Casino.** This $630-million South Seas–theme resort
★ is appropriately named. The property—including a rain forest with
3,000 tropical plants, a habitat for tigers, a 53-foot-long aquarium filled
with tropical fish, seven dolphins in the largest saltwater pool in the world,
and a 50-foot waterfall that becomes an exploding volcano after dark—
seems to have been created by master illusionists Siegfried and Roy, who
reigned in the showroom until an accident forced an indefinite closing
in October 2003. The rooms are immaculate, with botanical colors. Bathrooms, however, tend to be small. Request a room with a view (at check-
in, for no extra charge) and enjoy an eye-popping view of the Strip and
the volcano. ✉ *3400 Las Vegas Blvd. S, Center Strip 89109,* ☎ *702/
791–7111 or 800/627–6667,* FAX *702/791–7446,* WEB *www.themirage.com.
2,825 rooms, 224 suites. 11 restaurants, café, 2 pools, spa, 5 bars,
lounge, casino, showroom, shops, business services, convention center,
meeting room, no-smoking rooms. AE, D, DC, MC, V.*

**$$–$$$$** 🏨 **New York–New York Hotel and Casino.** The resort's facade includes
half-size re-creations of the Statue of Liberty, the Empire State Build-
ing, the Chrysler Building, and the Brooklyn Bridge. Inside, it's no less
thematically realized, with another clever reproduction of a Big Apple
icon everywhere you look. The only detail missing is the NYC attitude:
everyone is more than willing to lend you a hand. The downside is
cramped and crowded public areas, just like Manhattan; a long trek
from the front desk to some of the towers; and noise from the Man-
hattan Express roller coaster that loops around the hotel. But the ac-
commodations are fairly large, some with separate sitting areas and
sofas. ✉ *3790 Las Vegas Blvd. S, 89109, South Strip,* ☎ *702/740–6969
or 800/693–6763,* FAX *702/740–6700,* WEB *www.nynyhotelcasino.com.
2,024 rooms. 10 restaurants, in-room safes, pool, health club, spa, 3
bars, lounge, casino, showroom, shops, business services, meeting
room, no-smoking rooms. AE, D, DC, MC, V.*

**$$–$$$$** 🏨 **Paris Las Vegas.** In addition to reproductions of the Arc de Tri-
★ omphe and the Eiffel Tower, the 2,900-room, $785-million Paris Las
Vegas includes a 200-foot-tall sign resembling a hot-air balloon, an
in-house parfumerie, a patisserie, and a wedding chapel. Fountains
and statues are everywhere. Each spacious room has custom-designed
furniture, rich French fabrics, and separate marble bath tubs and
showers. Request a Strip view and you'll get to see the Bellagio fountains dancing right from your room. Otherwise your room may overlook the pleasant pool area. The fabulous buffet serves dishes from
five different French regions. ✉ *3655 Las Vegas Blvd. S, Center Strip
89109,* ☎ *702/739–4111 or 888/226–5687,* FAX *702/946–4405,* WEB
*www.paris-lv.com. 2,621 rooms, 295 suites. 13 restaurants, in-room
data ports, in-room safes, pool, health club, spa, 7 bars, casino, showroom, shops, business services, meeting room, no-smoking rooms. AE,
D, DC, MC, V.*

**$$–$$$$** ⊡ **Treasure Island Las Vegas (TI).** The resort's facade overlooks Buc-
★    caneer Bay, a marvelously detailed replica of a South Seas pirate vil-
lage, where six times a night you can watch pirates and sailors duke
it out aboard the *Hispaniola* and HMS *Britannia* (the best spot to see
it is from the casino's outdoor Battle Bar). If you want something even
more jaw-dropping, see the Cirque du Soleil production *Mystère*,
which has a permanent home here. The opulent lobby overlooks the
tropical pool and the newly redecorated rooms are modern and invit-
ing, with soft hues, plants in ceramic pots, and marble bathrooms. The
pool area is very pleasant, and at night you can have drinks outdoors
at the "Kahunaville" tropical nightclub. ⊠ *3300 Las Vegas Blvd. S,
Center Strip 89109,* ☎ *702/894–7111 or 800/944–7444,* FAX *702/894–
7414,* WEB *www.treasureislandlasvegas.com. 2,885 rooms. 7 restaurants,
in-room data ports, in-room safes, pool, health club, spa, 4 bars,
casino, nightclub, showroom, meeting room, no-smoking rooms. AE,
D, DC, MC, V.*

**$–$$$** ⊡ **Barbary Coast Hotel and Casino.** The Barbary Coast has one of the
most central locations in Las Vegas, across from Caesars and next-door
to the Flamingo. It's a small, lively hotel with a San Francisco Gold Rush
theme. Victorian-style rooms have brass four-poster beds with canopies,
old-fashioned lamps, lacy curtains, etched mirrors, separate eating areas,
and good rates. The views are of the Strip or the Flamingo. The number of rooms and suites is limited, so it's not always easy to get a reservation. ⊠ *3595 Las Vegas Blvd. S, Center Strip 89109,* ☎ *702/737–7111
or 888/227–2279,* FAX *702/737–6304,* WEB *www.barbarycoastcasino.
com. 188 rooms, 12 suites. 3 restaurants, in-room data ports, lounge, 3
bars, casino, no-smoking rooms. AE, D, DC, MC, V.*

**$–$$$** ⊡ **Flamingo Las Vegas.** The Fabulous Flamingo that opened in 1946,
with everyone from Bugsy Siegel to the janitors dressed in tuxedos, was
a 98-room oasis with palm trees imported from California. The Flamingo
has changed a lot since then: today its six high-rise towers overlook a
15-acre pool area—one of the largest in town—where the original low-
rise bungalows once stood. The Flamingo is pervasively pink, from the
outside neon sign to the lobby carpeting to the in-room pens and vases.
The pool area is one of the largest and prettiest in town. The spacious
rooms in the towers offer expansive views of the Strip. Bonus: the reg-
istration area is near the elevators, so you won't have to carry your lug-
gage through the casino. ⊠ *3555 Las Vegas Blvd. S, Center Strip
89109,* ☎ *702/733–3111 or 800/732–2111,* FAX *702/733–3353,* WEB *www.
flamingolv.com. 3,466 rooms, 176 suites. 8 restaurants, 4 tennis courts,
3 pools, health club, spa, lounge, casino, showroom, shops, business
services, meeting room, no-smoking rooms. AE, D, DC, MC, V.*

**$–$$$** ⊡ **Luxor Resort & Casino.** This 36-story, pyramid-shape hotel-casino is
★    pure Egyptian, Vegas style. Four "inclinators" travel the 39-degree in-
cline of the pyramid to the guest rooms; "hallways" to the rooms overlook the world's largest atrium. Two "step towers," each with almost
1,000 rooms, were later added, making Luxor the second-largest hotel
in Las Vegas. Rooms are large and continue the Egyptian motif, with
scarabs, palms, ankhs, and hieroglyphics incorporated as design elements.
There is a two-level arcade with interactive race cars, small motion sim-
ulators, and state-of-the-art video games. A tram connects Luxor with
its sister casinos, Mandalay Bay and Excalibur. ⊠ *3900 Las Vegas
Blvd. S, South Strip 89119,* ☎ *702/262–4000 or 800/288–1000,* FAX *702/
262–4452,* WEB *www.luxor.com. 4,476 rooms. 6 restaurants, in-room
data ports, 5 pools, health club, spa, 7 bars, casino, showroom, 3 theaters, shops, meeting room, no-smoking rooms. AE, D, MC, V.*

**$–$$$** ⊡ **Monte Carlo Resort and Casino.** Modeled after the opulent Place du
★ ☾  Casino in Monaco, the Las Vegas version of Monte Carlo replicates
its fanciful arches, domes, ornate fountains, marble floors, gas-lit

promenades, and Gothic glass registration area overlooking the lush pool area. But don't expect high glamour here. Underneath the pseudo-Euro veneer are many family-friendly features: a fast-food court; an inexpensive buffet; a high-tech video arcade; and a water park consisting of adults' and children's pools, a hot tub, and a wave pool and "lazy river" combo. The standard-size rooms are packed with cherry wood furniture and Italian marble. Surprisingly good lodging deals are often found here. ⊠ *3770 Las Vegas Blvd. S, South Strip 89109,* ☎ *702/730–7777 or 888/529–4828,* FAX *702/730–7200,* WEB *www.monte-carlo.com. 2,746 rooms, 259 suites. 7 restaurants, in-room data ports, 3 tennis courts, pool, health club, hot tub, spa, lounge, casino, showroom, shops, meeting room, no-smoking rooms. AE, D, DC, MC, V.*

**$–$$** 🏨 **Excalibur Hotel and Casino.** The Arthurian theme is omnipresent at this megaresort, from the casino to the arcade, restaurants, and 20-plus-shop Renaissance Village (complete with strolling performers). At the wedding chapel you can tie the knot with all the trappings of King Arthur and Lady Guinevere. The Excalibur is notable for its good-value accommodations. The standard-size rooms, decorated in bright colors, aren't spectacular, but the occupancy rate is almost always 100%: don't be surprised at long lines to check-in and crowded public areas. The hotel's Web site often posts discounted rates for nights months in advance. Try to get a room that overlooks the Strip, rather than the hotel's back parking lot. ⊠ *3850 Las Vegas Blvd. S, South Strip 89119,* ☎ *702/597–7777 or 877/750–5464,* FAX *702/597–7040,* WEB *www.excaliburcasino.com. 4,008 rooms. 6 restaurants, 2 pools, 9 bars, casino, showroom, shops, meeting rooms, no-smoking rooms. AE, D, DC, MC, V.*

**$–$$** 🏨 **Harrah's Las Vegas Casino & Hotel.** A Holiday Inn when it opened in 1973, the flagship of the large Harrah's casino fleet now has an attractive carnival theme, and there is live entertainment in its outdoor Carnival Court facing the Strip. The rooms are modest, featuring light-wood furniture, brass fitting, blackout drapes and double sound-proofed walls. Harrah's is within easy walking distance of such popular resorts as Caesars Palace, the Mirage, and the Venetian. Popular Vegas singer and entertainer Clint Holmes has a long-standing gig here. ⊠ *3475 Las Vegas Blvd. S, Center Strip 89109,* ☎ *702/369–5000 or 800/427–7247,* FAX *702/369–5008,* WEB *www.harrahs.com. 2,579 rooms, 164 suites. 7 restaurants, in-room data ports, pool, health club, hair salon, spa, lounge, casino, showroom, business services, meeting rooms, no-smoking rooms. AE, D, DC, MC, V.*

**$–$$** 🏨 **Imperial Palace Hotel and Casino.** The Imperial Palace was the first hotel built in Las Vegas around an Asian theme, featuring crystal, jade, and carved wood. In the heart of the Strip, it houses one of Las Vegas's most popular long-running shows, *Legends in Concert,* and one of Las Vegas's most popular tourist attractions, the Imperial Palace Automobile Museum, with over 350 vintage automobiles on display, all of them for sale. The hotel offers two buffets, the only multi-tier sports book in Las Vegas, and its own wedding chapel. Standard-size rooms are without frills, except for their views of Caesars Palace and the Mirage; the hotel's "Luv-Tub" suites feature a canopy king bed and a Roman bathtub for two. ⊠ *3535 Las Vegas Blvd. S, Center Strip 89109,* ☎ *702/731–3311 or 800/634–6441,* FAX *702/735–8578,* WEB *www.imperialpalace.com. 2,412 rooms, 225 suites. 8 restaurants, pool, health club, massage, lounge, casino, showroom, shops, no-smoking rooms. AE, DC, MC, V.*

**$–$$** 🏨 **Stardust Hotel and Casino.** If the interior of the Stardust looks familiar, it's because you've likely seen it in dozens of Hollywood films. ★ Beneath one of the most beautiful neon signs ever to grace the Strip, the 2,500-room Stardust emphasizes slots, low table minimums, and good deals on food. Good room bargains can often be found here, and given its central Strip location between the megaresorts and Downtown, the Stardust is the best option for the budget-minded traveler who wants a nice, no-frills room and easy access to the action. "Mr. Vegas" himself, Wayne Newton, has his own theater here. ⊠ *3000 Las Vegas Blvd. S, North Strip 89109,* ☎ *702/732–6111 or 800/634–6757,* FAX *702/ 732–6257,* WEB *www.stardustlv.com. 2,500 rooms. 6 restaurants, in-room data ports, in-room safes, 2 tennis courts, 2 pools, health club, lounge, casino, showroom, laundry service, meeting room, car rental, no-smoking rooms. AE, DC, MC, V.*

$–$$   🏨 **Tropicana Resort and Casino.** Although the Tropicana positions it-
     ⓒ  self as an adult-oriented hotel, it's a great place for families. The Trop is a beautifully landscaped hotel-casino, with an especially lush 5-acre pool area, including a meandering swimming pool and swim-up bars. Rooms vary in size, depending on whether you're staying in the Paradise Tower (standard size), one of the Garden rooms by the pool (somewhat larger), or in the rear Island Tower (spacious). All have rattan furnishings and some even have a terrace (again, a plus for families). ⊠ *3801 Las Vegas Blvd. S, South Strip 89109,* ☎ *702/739–2222 or 888/826–8767,* FAX *702/739–2448,* WEB *www.tropicanalv.com. 1,708 rooms, 200 suites. 5 restaurants, 3 pools, health club, massage, spa, 3 bars, casino, showroom, business services, meeting room, no-smoking rooms. AE, D, DC, MC, V.*

¢–$$   🏨 **New Frontier Hotel and Gambling Hall.** While the Frontier of today stands on the same property as the original 1942 hotel, it bears no resemblance to the old place. An Old West motif prevails, but the rooms have been upgraded, and you won't find cacti or branding irons on the walls as in the original. The Atrium Tower has minisuites decorated in earth tones, with separate dining areas and views of the Strip or the Frontier garden area; the center of the 14-story tower is open to the sky. These rooms are some of the best lodging deals in town. ⊠ *3120 Las Vegas Blvd. S, North Strip 89109,* ☎ *702/794–8200 or 800/421–7806,* FAX *702/794–8326,* WEB *www.frontierlv.com. 986 rooms, 396 suites. 3 restaurants, 2 tennis courts, pool, lounge, casino, showroom, business services, meeting rooms, no-smoking rooms. AE, D, DC, MC, V.*

¢–$$   🏨 **Stratosphere Casino Hotel and Tower.** This complex includes the tallest observation tower west of the Mississippi (1,149 feet), the world's two highest thrill rides, a shopping mall, a showroom and lounge, and a 97,000-square-foot casino. The accommodations are standard, with dark purple drapes and matching bedspreads and light wood furniture. Due to Stratosphere's out-of-the-way location between the Strip and Downtown, room deals abound. ⊠ *2000 Las Vegas Blvd. S, North Strip 89104,* ☎ *702/380–7777 or 800/998–6937,* FAX *702/739–2448,* WEB *www.stratospherehotel.com. 2,249 rooms, 195 suites. 6 restaurants, pool, health club, spa, lounge, casino, showroom, shops, no-smoking floors. AE, D, DC, MC, V.*

¢–$$   🏨 **Westward Ho.** The largest motel in the world has hundreds of rooms, seven swimming pools, and a casino. Beware, on Saturday night this part of town is gridlocked, and returning to your room by car will take considerable time—unless you learn the shortcut from Industrial Road through the Stardust parking lot. Because of its size, location, and deals, it's often crowded with conventioneers, slot-club members, and tournament players. ⊠ *2900 Las Vegas Blvd. S, North Strip 89109,* ☎ *702/731–2900 or 800/634–6803,* FAX *702/731–6154,* WEB *www.westwardho.com. 662 rooms, 115 apartments. Restaurant, café, 7 pools, casino. AE, D, DC, MC, V.*

¢–$   🏨 **Circus Circus.** Circus Circus lives up to its name. Upstairs in the old
     ⓒ  towers you'll find some of the most garishly appointed guest rooms in Las Vegas: bright red carpets, matching red chairs, and pink walls. The newer tower's rooms are more subdued. The casino attracts so many

visitors that drivers will find it a major achievement just getting into the parking lot. On a Saturday night the stretch of Las Vegas Boulevard leading up to Circus Circus is often gridlocked; the valet parking sign reads FULL and the nearest parking space is halfway to Arizona. (If you spend a few minutes learning the back way in, from Industrial Road, you'll save yourself a lot of grief.) Nonetheless, Circus Circus is a favorite of families: parents can drop the children off at the midway above the casino to play games or watch the circus acts while the adults hit the slots; five-minute circus acts are performed every 20 minutes from 11 AM to midnight. The Adventuredome, a 5-acre theme park with a flume ride, a roller coaster, bumper cars, laser tag, and kiddie rides, is directly behind the hotel. ⊠ *2880 Las Vegas Blvd. S, North Strip 89109,* ☎ *702/734–0410 or 877/224–7287,* FAX *702/734–2268,* WEB *www.circuscircus.com. 3,774 rooms. 8 restaurants, 3 pools, 6 bars, casino, meeting room, no-smoking rooms. AE, D, DC, MC, V.*

¢–$  🏨 **Sahara Hotel and Casino.** The oasis theme, established in 1952 when the Sahara opened for business, still remains 50 years later—an eternity in Las Vegas. Like many of its neighbors, the Sahara began as a small motor hotel and grew by adding towers, towers, and more towers. The Sahara's largest expansion doubled the size of the casino, replaced the facade and sign, and added a parking garage. Another $100-million makeover added the NASCAR Café and thrill-ride Speed. Rooms are large, with king-size beds and views of either the Strip or Paradise Road. Of the many value properties in Las Vegas, the Sahara offers the nicest rooms, along with such bargains as $1 blackjack tables. ⊠ *2535 Las Vegas Blvd. S, North Strip 89101,* ☎ *702/737–2111 or 888/696–2121,* FAX *702/791–2027,* WEB *www.saharavegas.com. 1720 rooms, 75 suites. 5 restaurants, room service, 2 pools, 2 lounges, casino, showroom, business services, car rental, no-smoking rooms. AE, D, DC, MC, V.*

# Beyond the Strip

$$–$$$$  🏨 **Green Valley Ranch Station.** A 10-minute drive from the Strip on I-215, this is the first luxury property created by Station Casinos, who long ago conquered the locals' casino market. The lobby, built to resemble an intimate country club, opens up onto 2 acres of vineyards, a strikingly modern pool with a small, soft-sand beach area. There's also a European day spa with cascading waterfalls. Rooms are spacious, with cherry furniture, plush chairs, and beds with down comforters. The hotel has several excellent restaurants and lounges including Whiskey Sky, a hot spot for the young and the fabulous with king-size mattresses strewn about its outdoor patio area overlooking the pool. ⊠ *2300 Paseo Verde, Henderson 89052,* ☎ *702/617–7777 or 866/ 617–1777,* FAX *702/617–7778,* WEB *www.stationcasinos.com. 201 rooms. 7 restaurants, in-room data ports, in-room safes, minibars, pool, health club, spa, 2 lounges, casino, no-smoking rooms. AE, D, DC, MC, V.*

$$–$$$$  🏨 **Hard Rock Hotel and Casino.** It's impossible to forget you're in the
★  Hard Rock, no matter where you go in this rock-fixated joint: even the hall carpeting is decorated with musical notes. The rooms are large and sparsely furnished; beds have leather headboards, bathrooms have stainless-steel sinks, and the double French doors actually open. The Lagoon pool has a sandy bottom, a water slide, and floating craps tables. One of the hippest hang-outs for twentysomethings is the fun Pink Taco restaurant and bar, packed to the gills on weekend nights. Be prepared for very crowded (but fun) public areas with plenty of opportunities for people-watching. ⊠ *4455 Paradise Rd., Paradise Road 89109,* ☎ *702/693–5000 or 800/693–7625,* FAX *702/693–5010,* WEB *www.hardrockhotel.com. 657 rooms. 7 restaurants, in-room data*

*ports, pool, health club, spa, 3 bars, casino, showroom, no-smoking rooms. AE, D, DC, MC, V.*

**\$\$–\$\$\$\$** ✋ **Hyatt Regency Lake Las Vegas Resort.** It's just 17 mi from the city, but it's a world away on the shores of Lake Las Vegas. Designed to mirror a Moroccan castle, this lovely hideaway is set against the backdrop of hills, a championship golf course, and the sparkling 320-acre lake. Plush rooms continue the Moorish theme with rich earth tones complementing the sweeping views of the lake and desert. There's even a small beach where 8 tons of soft, white sand is trucked in every summer. Free shuttle service to the Strip is provided. ✉ *101 MonteLago Blvd., Henderson 89011,* ☎ *702/567–1234,* FAX *702/567–6067,* WEB *www.lakelasvegas.hyatt.com. 496 rooms, 47 suites. 2 restaurants, room service, in-room data ports, in-room safes, refrigerators, 2 pools, lake, health club, spa, boating, 2 bars, casino, children's programs, concierge floor, meeting rooms, no-smoking rooms. AE, D, DC, MC, V.*

**\$\$–\$\$\$\$** ★ **JW Marriott Las Vegas.** Overlooking two of the city's most popular golf courses and within a few miles of Red Rock Canyon, the JW, formerly the Regent Las Vegas, is a good escape from the hectic Strip. The combination of elegance and comfort will help you unwind. The Aquae Sulis Spa will work all the knots out, and the spacious rooms—with everything from marble bathrooms with separate whirlpool and shower to cordless Internet connections—are designed to soothe. ✉ *221 N. Rampart Blvd., Summerlin 89145,* ☎ *702/869–7777 or 877/869–8777,* FAX *702/869–7325,* WEB *www.jwmarriottlv.com. 541 suites. 9 restaurants, in-room data ports, in-room safes, minibars, refrigerators, pool, health club, spa, 3 lounges, casino, business services, meeting rooms, no-smoking rooms. AE, D, DC, MC, V.*

**\$\$–\$\$\$\$** ✋ **Las Vegas Hilton.** Though the Hilton, which is adjacent to the Las Vegas Convention Center, no longer holds the title of largest hotel in town, it's still a sight to see—best of all by standing at its foot and staring up at the 29-story three-wing tower. The rooms are spacious, with soft colors, large beds, and telephones in the bathrooms; those on the higher floors have great views of the city. The two-story lounge seats 900, there's a wedding chapel, and the sports book is the largest and busiest in town. There's a fabulous pool area next to a spacious recreation deck with lighted tennis courts for night games. ✉ *3000 Paradise Rd., Paradise Road 89109,* ☎ *702/732–5111 or 800/732–7117,* FAX *702/732–5834,* WEB *www.lv-hilton.com. 2,833 rooms, 124 suites. 12 restaurants, in-room data ports, 18-hole golf course, putting green, 6 tennis courts, pool, health club, spa, lounge, casino, showroom, children's programs, business services, meeting room, no smoking rooms. AE, D, DC, MC, V.*

**\$\$–\$\$\$\$** ★ **The Palms.** The first true luxury boutique hotel in Las Vegas, the \$265 million Palms is just off the Strip. Its lounges, clubs, and restaurants attract a younger crowd who keep the public places hopping every weekend night. Rooms are large, opulent, and modern, with some unusual amenities for Las Vegas—such as beds with ultrafirm mattresses, duvets, coffeemakers, and Neutrogena products. Most rooms provide a good view of the city and you don't have to venture far to enjoy the nightlife at the hotel's popular "Rain" nightclub. ✉ *4321 W. Flamingo Rd., West Side 89103,* ☎ *702/942–777 or 866/942–7777,* FAX *702/942–7001,* WEB *www.palms.com. 447 rooms. 7 restaurants, in-room data ports, in-room safes, minibars, pool, health club, hair salon, spa, 4 lounges, casino, cinema, no-smoking rooms. AE, D, DC, MC, V.*

**\$\$–\$\$\$\$** ✉ **Residence Inn by Marriott.** This town house–style all-suite hotel on nicely landscaped grounds is across the street from the convention center and a short cab ride (1¼ mi) from the Strip. The studios and two-bedroom suites all have kitchens. Curbside parking is a plus. A complimentary Continental breakfast is included in the room rate. ✉ *3225 Paradise Rd., Paradise Road 89109,* ☎ *702/796–9300 or 800/ 331–3131,* FAX *702/796–9562,* WEB *www.residenceinn.com. 144 studios, 48 2-bedroom suites. In-room data ports, some kitchens, pool, hot tub, some pets allowed, no-smoking rooms. AE, D, DC, MC, V. CP.*

**$$–$$$$** 🏨 **Rio All-Suite Hotel and Casino.** The Rio was the first all-suite hotel-
★ ☺ casino in Las Vegas. The striking blue-and-red, four-tower hotel is just off the Strip and has a Brazilian theme, complete with a sandy beach beside the pool. While suites here don't have separate bedrooms, they're spacious with extra-large sofas, sitting areas, dining tables, big bathrooms, and floor-to-ceiling windows. The Rio has a large, color-ful casino and an excellent seafood buffet. The VooDoo Lounge is a hip nightspot 52 stories above Las Vegas, with an outdoor patio that offers stunning views of the Strip and the city. ✉ *3700 W. Flamingo Rd., West Side 89109,* ☎ *702/252–7777 or 800/888–1808,* FAX *702/ 253–6090,* WEB *www.playrio.com. 2,554 suites. 14 restaurants, refrig-erators, in-room safes, 4 pools, gym, hair salon, spa, lounge, casino, nightclub, showroom, shops, business services, meeting room, no-smoking rooms. AE, D, DC, MC, V.*

**$–$$$** 🏨 **Crowne Plaza.** This all-suites hotel close to the convention center caters to business travelers and is quiet and intimate. The lobby is ex-pansive, with its glass atrium leading to modern and comfortable rooms with separate sleeping areas and small kitchenettes with cof-feemakers. You'll find two TVs in every suite as well as a sleeper sofa in the living room. There's a small pool and hot tub. ✉ *4255 S. Par-adise Rd., Paradise Road 89109,* ☎ *702/369–4400,* FAX *702/369–3770,* WEB *www.crowneplaza.com. 201 suites. Restaurant, in-room data ports, refrigerators, pool, gym, outdoor hot tub, bar, airport shut-tle, no-smoking rooms. AE, DC, MC, V.*

**$–$$$** 🏨 **Embassy Suites.** A block away from the Hard Rock Hotel, this at-
☺ tractive property has the Embassy Suites' signature atrium. A compli-mentary, cooked-to-order breakfast is served in the airy and expansive space every morning. Every suite has a separate living area; all are well furnished and geared towards business, with a desk and four telephones with voice-mail and Internet connection. There are two TVs and a cof-feemaker in each unit, and a complimentary newspaper is delivered to your door each morning. Neutrogena bath products are a nice touch. Children will enjoy the large pool area and the two resident swans: Elvis and Priscilla. The hotel provides a free shuttle to the Strip. ✉ *4315 Swenson St., Paradise Road 89119,* ☎ *702/795–2800,* FAX *702/795–1520,* WEB *www.embassylasvegas.com. 220 suites. Restaurant, in-room data ports, microwaves, refrigerators, pool, gym, lounge, shop, meet-ing room, airport shuttle, no-smoking rooms. AE, D, DC, MC, V. BP.*

**$–$$$** 🏨 **Embassy Suites Convention Center.** This very attractive, newer Em-bassy suites caters to business and leisure travelers who crave space. Each suite is modern and spacious and comes with separate bedroom and living room with sofa sleeper. There are coffeemakers and Web TV in the suites. In the morning, enjoy your complimentary newspaper over the full breakfast that is included in the room rate. ✉ *3600 Par-adise Rd., Paradise Road 89109,* ☎ *702/893–8000,* FAX *702/893–0378,* WEB *www.eslvcc.com. 286 suites. Restaurant, in-room data ports, kitchens, microwaves, refrigerators, bar, no-smoking rooms. AE, D, DC, MC, V. BP.*

**$–$$** 🏨 **Alexis Park Resort Hotel.** Will businesspeople come to a hotel in Las Vegas that has no neon, no gaming tables, and no slots? The Alexis Park discovered that the answer is yes. Halfway between the conven-tion center and the airport, this is a favorite spot for conventioneers who want as "normal" an experience as possible during their business trip. The individual buildings of the all-suite desert hotel are two-story, white-stucco blocks with red-tile roofs, all set in a water garden. Views are of either a rock pool or a lawn, but neither is anything too special. Rooms are clean and adequate; some have fireplaces. ⊠ *375 E. Harmon Ave., Paradise Road 89109,* ☎ *702/796–3300 or 800/582–2228,* FAX *702/796–0766,* WEB *www.alexispark.com. 500 suites. Restaurant, in-room data ports, minibars, some in-room hot tubs, 3 pools, spa, lounge, meeting room, no-smoking rooms. AE, D, DC, MC, V.*

**$–$$** ⊡ **AmeriSuites.** Close to the Hard Rock, this all-suite hotel is an excellent value if you're looking for a non-gaming property. Quiet and fairly modern, bright rooms have separate living rooms and kitchenettes with coffeemakers. There's a free breakfast buffet. ⊠ *4520 Paradise Rd., Paradise Road 89109,* ☎ *702/369–3366,* FAX *702/369–0009,* WEB *www.amerisuites.com. 202 suites. In-room data ports, microwaves, refrigerators, pool, gym, laundry facilities, meeting room, no-smoking rooms. AE, MC, V. BP.*

**$–$$** ⊡ **DoubleTree Club Hotel.** Close to the airport and popular with pilots and airline personnel, this immaculately maintained hotel is located just off the Airport Connector and I–215 and a few minutes' drive from the Strip. Geared toward the business traveler with easy, ample outdoor parking just outside the hotel's entrance, this is a good place to avoid crowded check-in lines and lengthy walks from parking lots. The rooms are modern and colorfully elegant, and all come with an oversize work desk, two dual-line speaker phones with voice-mail, and coffeemakers. There's also a free shuttle to the strip and to the airport. ⊠ *7250 Pollock Dr., 89119, South Las Vegas,* ☎ *702/948–4000 or 800/222–8733,* FAX *702/948–4100,* WEB *www.doubletree.com. 190 rooms. Café, in-room data ports, pool, gym, lounge, business services, meeting rooms, airport shuttle, no-smoking rooms. AE, D, DC, MC, V.*

**$–$$** ⊡ **Texas Station.** This place and its three sisters—Palace Station, Boulder Station, and Sunset Station—are primarily casinos/entertainment complexes designed for locals, with friendly odds, fast-food joints, expansive buffets, arcades, and large movie theaters. On the northwest side of Vegas, the Texas has all the action and amenities of many Strip properties. Though not lavishly appointed, rooms are large and comfortable, with separate sitting areas and dining tables. The key perk for families is that each Station casino contains a Kids' Quest, a 8,000-square-foot multi-level indoor playground and activity center. A free shuttle provides transportation to the Strip. ⊠ *2101 Texas Star La., Rancho Strip 89036,* ☎ *702/631–1000 or 800/654–8888,* FAX *702/631–8120,* WEB *www.texasstation.com. 200 rooms. 5 restaurants, food court, in-room data ports, pool, bowling, lounge, casino, theaters, airport shuttle, no-smoking rooms. AE, D, DC, MC, V.*

**¢–$** ⊡ **Budget Suites of America.** A nearby alternative to the Westward Ho is this sprawling complex on the corner of Industrial and Stardust roads. Every room here is a minisuite with a living-dining room, a small separate bedroom, and a full kitchenette; the TV is mounted on a swivel between the living room and bedroom. Weekly rates offer a good discount; rooms on the second and third floors are the least expensive and are even cheaper if you bring your own sheets and towels. ⊠ *1500 Stardust Rd., West Side 89109,* ☎ *702/732–1500 or 800/752–1501,* FAX *702/732–2656,* WEB *www.budgetsuites.com. 639 suites. Kitchens, pool, spa, laundry facilities, no-smoking rooms. AE, MC, V.*

**¢–$** ⊡ **Sam's Town Hotel and Gambling Hall.** Pioneer gambler Sam Boyd built a small grubstake into one of the largest casino companies in Nevada. His namesake casino hotel has long been a favorite with locals, thanks to liberal slots, plenty of good, inexpensive food, and such amenities as an 18-screen cinema. The standard rooms, done in muted colors, are built around a nine-story glass-roof atrium filled with tall live trees, cobblestone paths, and a rock waterfall. This busy hotel is on the Boulder Strip, 6 mi from downtown. ⊠ *5111 Boulder Hwy., Boulder Strip 89122,* ☎ *702/456–7777 or 800/634–6371,* FAX *702/454–8014,* WEB *www.samstownlv.com. 646 rooms. 8 restaurants, pool, bowling, lounge, casino, theaters, meeting rooms, no-smoking floors. AE, D, DC, MC, V.*

¢ 🖼 **Motel 6.** Welcome to the largest Motel 6 in the United States, with 877 rooms, a pool, and a big neon sign. Rooms here look like those of any other Motel 6, but when travelers think in terms of cheap accommodations, they think of this chain, so it tends to get booked up fast. ⊠ *195 E. Tropicana Ave., 89109, Paradise Road,* ☎ *702/798–0728,* FAX *702/798–5657,* WEB *www.motel6.com. 607 rooms. Pool, laundry facilities, some pets allowed, no-smoking rooms. AE, D, DC, MC, V.*

## Downtown

$–$$$ 🖼 **Golden Nugget Hotel and Casino.** The best hotel downtown, the
★ Golden Nugget was transformed by Steve Wynn from a simple gambling hall into an elegant joint. Red rugs flow over white marble, leading you to the lobby with faux-marble columns, etched-glass windows, and fresh flowers in gold-plated vases. Almost everything here is gold (or, more accurately, brass-plated)—the telephones, the slots, the elevators. The well-kept rooms are modern and comfortable, though the bathrooms are considerably smaller than at the newer hotels on the Strip. The Nugget has 27 opulent duplex suites, some with a personal room-service waiter. The pool is the biggest one downtown. ⊠ *129 E. Fremont St., Downtown 89101,* ☎ *702/385–7111 or 800/634–3454,* FAX *702/386–8362,* WEB *www.goldennugget.com. 1,805 rooms, 106 suites. 7 restaurants, in-room safes, pool, health club, spa, lounge, casino, showroom, meeting room, no-smoking rooms. AE, D, DC, MC, V.*

$–$$$ 🖼 **Main Street Station Casino, Brewery & Hotel.** Filled with antiques, collectibles, and memorabilia, the elegantly-appointed, Victorian-style Main Street Station is brimming with things to look at, including Theodore Roosevelt's Pullman railroad car, dropped-dome chandeliers from the El Presidente Hotel in Buenos Aires, and a section of the Berlin Wall. Guest rooms, accented in dark wood and gold-frame mirrors, continue the theme. Make sure to get one on the south side of the building, facing Main Street—it's hard to get away from the noise of I–15 on the north side. There's a free shuttle service to the Strip. ⊠ *200 N. Main St., Downtown 89101,* ☎ *702/387–1896 or 800/713–8933,* FAX *702/386–4421,* WEB *www.mainstreetcasino.com. 406 rooms. 4 restaurants, in-room data ports, in-room safes, lounge, casino, meeting rooms. AE, DC, MC, V.*

¢–$$ 🖼 **Lady Luck Casino and Hotel.** The two towers of this hotel are across the street from each other, connected via a glass-enclosed pedestrian bridge on the third-floor level. Lady Luck has small, bright rooms with white walls and half-windows that look out on Ogden Street. The coffeemaker in each room is an added bonus. There are also 115 junior suites and 385 "senior" suites for the Lady's many high rollers. Why are there so many high rollers at the Lady Luck? Because the casino has some of the least demanding criteria for comps in town. ⊠ *206 N. 3rd St., Downtown 89101,* ☎ *702/477–3000 or 800/634–6580,* FAX *702/477–3002,* WEB *www.ladylucklv.com. 792 rooms. 4 restaurants, pool, 2 bars, casino, showroom, shop, no-smoking rooms. AE, D, DC, MC, V.*

¢–$ 🖼 **Binion's Horseshoe Hotel and Casino.** For more than 35 years, Binion's Horseshoe had 80 rooms; in order to get one of these downtown domiciles, you had to know patriarch Benny Binion. But in 1988, Binion's bought the 26-floor, 300-room Mint next door and expanded west. The addition has modern, medium-size rooms that are decorated in light colors. The east-side rooms reflect the Western style of the original Horseshoe: they have Victorian-style wallpaper and brass beds with quilted spreads. The pool is on the roof. The snack bars have down-to-earth food and prices; the deli (by the sports book) and steak house (on the 24th floor, reached by a glass elevator) are enormously popular. ⊠ *128 E. Fremont St., Downtown 89101,* ☎ *702/382–1600 or 800/237–6537,* FAX *702/384–1574,* WEB *www.binions.com. 366 rooms. 4 restaurants, pool, 2 bars, casino, no-smoking rooms. AE, D, DC, MC, V.*

¢–$   🏨 **Four Queens Hotel and Casino.** This prominent downtown hotel has rooms furnished in a contemporary style, with purple pastel curtains and bedspreads, light wood furniture, and impressive views of the Fremont Street Experience, Fitzgeralds, or the Golden Nugget. Its coffee shop is one of the least expensive in the downtown area, and the secluded Hugo's Cellar, a longtime local favorite, is still one of the better restaurants on Fremont. ⊠ *202 E. Fremont St., Downtown 89101,* ☎ *702/385–4011 or 800/634–6045,* FAX *702/383–0631,* WEB *www. fourqueens.com. 690 rooms. 2 restaurants, in-room data ports, in-room safes, casino, no-smoking rooms. AE, D, DC, MC, V.*

¢–$   🏨 **Las Vegas Club Hotel and Casino.** The sports theme prevails everywhere but in the guest rooms. The small rooms have a light-brown finish, the beds have small awnings, and the tiny half windows overlook Fremont and Main streets. The hotel's newer tower houses 186 rooms, two restaurants, and a casino annex. ⊠ *18 E. Fremont St., 89109, Downtown,* ☎ *702/385–1664 or 800/634–6532,* FAX *702/387–6071,* WEB *www.playatlvc.com. 410 rooms. 3 restaurants, in-room data ports, lounge, casino, laundry service, business services, meeting room. AE, DC, MC, V.*

¢–$   🏨 **Plaza Hotel and Casino.** The Plaza anchors Fremont Street and could be seen in the center of nearly every photo of the street before the canopy of the Fremont Street Experience was built. Rooms are almost always available, even during big conventions. Be sure to ask for one overlooking Fremont Street; otherwise you'll have a view of the railroad tracks. Rooms are medium-size, with bright bedspreads. There's a showroom (the largest downtown) and a wedding chapel on the premises. ⊠ *1 Main St., Downtown 89101,* ☎ *702/386–2110 or 800/634–6575,* FAX *702/382–8281,* WEB *www.plazahotelcasino.com. 1,037 rooms. 3 restaurants, 4 tennis courts, pool, gym, hair salon, lounge, casino, showroom, laundry facilities, meeting rooms, no-smoking rooms. AE, D, DC, MC, V.*

¢   🏨 **El Cortez Hotel.** The El Cortez is a slice of historic Las Vegas: it's the only downtown hotel to retain its original 1940s facade. There are two floors of tiny rooms, each of which has twin beds, a small TV, and a narrow window with a view of Fremont Street. Rooms in the tower are newer, larger, and only a little more expensive. ⊠ *600 E. Fremont St., Downtown 89109,* ☎ *702/385–5200 or 800/634–6703,* FAX *702/ 385–1554,* WEB *www.elcortez.net. 299 rooms. 2 restaurants, lounge, casino, meeting room, no-smoking rooms. AE, D, DC, MC, V.*

¢   🏨 **Gold Spike Hotel and Casino.** The hotel is billed as "Las Vegas as it used to be," with penny slots and video poker, 40¢ live keno, and $2 blackjack tables. Small, plain double rooms have twin beds, a nightstand, a TV, and a view of East Ogden Avenue. A suite adds a four-poster bed, couch, and balcony. All rates include breakfast. ⊠ *400 E. Ogden Ave., Downtown 89101,* ☎ *702/384–8444 or 800/634–6703,* FAX *702/384–8768,* WEB *www.goldspikehotelcasino.com. 107 rooms, 3 suites. Coffee shop, lounge, casino, no-smoking rooms. AE, D, DC, MC, V. BP.*

# RV Parks & Campgrounds

Las Vegas is an RVer's oasis. The city offers thousands of hook-ups, some next to casinos, some tucked away in private resorts. Nearby options are more limited if you plan to camp, however. Only a small number of places allow tent camping, but with numerous state and national parks within an hour of the city, it's possible to find a place to pitch the pup tent.

¢ ⚠ **Boulder Lakes.** Located near Sam Boyd Stadium, Boulder Lakes is a good hike from the Strip. But this RV park is more for people looking to spend some serious time in Vegas than those who want to just hang out for a weekend. With monthly rates and numerous perks—including a playground, a clubhouse, three spas, and a ballroom—Boulder Lakes is designed for extended stays. Pets are allowed. ✉ *6201 Boulder Hwy., East Side 89122,* ☎ *702/435–1157,* 🖷 *702/435–1125. 417 sites. Toilets, hook-ups, drinking water, laundry facilities, showers, public telephone, general store, playground, 4 pools.* 🍴 *$22. MC, V.*

¢ ⚠ **Circusland RV Park.** The only RV park right on the Strip, Circusland makes for easy access to Las Vegas's main drag. The only problem: like Circus Circus, the casino it is attached to, Circusland tends to fill up quickly, often running at capacity on weekends and holidays. Pets are allowed. ✉ *500 Circus Circus Dr., North Strip 89109,* ☎ *702/794–3757 or 800/444–2472,* 🖷 *702/792–2280. 399 sites. Toilets, hook-ups, dump station, drinking water, laundry facilities, showers, public telephone, general store, pool.* 🍴 *$19–$35. AE, D, DC, MC, V.*

¢ ⚠ **KOA Las Vegas.** On Boulder Highway, KOA Las Vegas is a good click from the Strip—at least 15 minutes by the surface streets or the expressway. But the trade-off is familiarity and consistency. Like most KOAs across the country, KOA Las Vegas has good, clean facilities that are hard to beat. It's also one of the few places in Vegas that allows tent camping, and there's also a free shuttle to the Strip. Pets are allowed. ✉ *4315 Boulder Hwy., Boulder Strip 89121,* ☎ *702/451–5527 or 800/562–7782,* 🖷 *702/434–8729,* 🖳 *www.koa.com. 40 sites. Toilets, hook-ups, dump station, drinking water, laundry facilities, showers, public telephone, general store, pool.* 🍴 *$25–$33. AE, D, MC, V.*

¢ ⚠ **Oasis Las Vegas RV Resort.** As much a resort as a place to park the mobile kingdom, Oasis Las Vegas is a plush, well-landscaped RV park with 701 sites and lots of amenities—including a pool and its own clubhouse. Just minutes from the Strip—there's even a shuttle that runs from Oasis to the heart of casino row—as well as within walking distance of the Belz Outlet Mall, Oasis is perfectly situated to enjoy the neon without feeling overpowered by it. Just make sure to make your reservations early. Though Oasis Las Vegas is the area's largest RV park, it tends to fill up during holiday weekends and winter months. Pets are allowed. ✉ *2711 W. Windmill Rd., South Las Vegas 89123,* ☎ *702/260–2000 or 800/566–4707,* 🖷 *702/263–5160. 701 sites. Toilets, hook-ups, dump station, drinking water, laundry facilities, showers, public telephones, general store, pool.* 🍴 *$20–$50. AE, D, MC, V.*

¢ ⚠ **Sam's Town RV Park.** There are two separate RV locations, one on Boulder Highway, just to the east of the casino, and one just north on Nellis Boulevard. Both offer the standard amenities, as well as shuttle service to the Strip. The only difference is that the Nellis park allows pets. Given Sam's Town's guaranteed price of $18, these are the cheapest spots in town. ✉ *5111 Boulder Hwy., Boulder Strip 89122,* ☎ *702/456–7777 or 800/634–6371,* 🖷 *702/456–5665. 499 sites. Toilets,*

hook-ups, drinking water, laundry facilities, showers, public telephone.
✉ $18. AE, D, DC, MC, V.

¢ ⚠ **Silverton RV Park.** Like the casino it's named for, the Silverton RV
Park is all about down-home charm. Located just to the southwest of
the Strip, it has telephone and cable hook-ups for every stall. There's a
recreation room, and, when the urge hits, there's a shuttle to the Strip.
Pets are allowed. ✉ 3333 Blue Diamond Rd., 89139, South Las Vegas,
☎ 702/263–7777 or 800/588–7711, FAX 702/897–4208, WEB www.
silvertoncasino.com. 460 sites. Toilets, dump station, drinking water, laundry facilities, showers, general store, pool. ✉ $20. AE, D, DC, MC, V.

# 6 NIGHTLIFE & THE ARTS

With Las Vegas–style revues old and new, traditional headliner rooms and concert halls, umpteen lounges, hi-tech discos, low-tech honky-tonks, comedy clubs, free light-and-water shows, amusement parks, magicians, showgirls, and of course people-watching, the only way to arrive in Las Vegas and not be entertained is in a coffin.

Updated by
Mike
Weatherford

T HE VERY NAME "LAS VEGAS" HAS BEEN synonymous with a certain style of showbiz entertainment ever since Jimmy Durante first headlined at Bugsy Siegel's Fabulous Flamingo Hotel in 1946 and *Minsky Goes to Paris* introduced topless showgirls at the Dunes in 1957. In those days the lounges gave up-and-coming performers a chance to polish their acts on their way to the showrooms; the camaraderie and informality lent an anything-can-happen-here-tonight air to the entertainment. Through the years the Entertainment Capital of the World has weathered a number of changes in its stage presentations, policies, and prices, but one thing has remained consistent for the past 50 years—doing things big with as much attention called to the doing as possible.

Headliners such as Tom Jones, David Copperfield, Wayne Newton, and George Carlin still pack the traditional showrooms. Extravagant revues such as *Folies Bergere,* and *Jubilee!* still stage 12 shows a week, with outrageous sets, costumes, variety acts, and song and dance. But young and exuberant shows such as *Blue Man Group* and Cirque du Soleil's *O* and *Mystère* have modernized the spectacle; while illusionists such as Siegfried and Roy and Lance Burton, who started out as brief breaks for the major action, went on to become stars in their own right. Female and superstar impersonators, "dirty" dancers, comedians—all perpetuate the original style of razzle-dazzle entertainment that Las Vegas has popularized for the world.

Some traditions have changed, however. Certain hotels have eliminated nudity and foul language in the name of family entertainment. Some even encourage parents to bring their children along by offering special prices for youngsters (usually in the summer months). And the dinner show has gone the way of the mink stole, unless you count the utensil-free "medieval style" dining at Excalibur's "Tournament of Kings."

In the not-so-old days, the shows were loss leaders, much as the buffets are today: they were intended to draw patrons who would eventually wind up in the casino. Admission prices to shows were dirt cheap, and the programs were fairly short. Nowadays, it will cost you $60 or more to see Newton or Gladys Knight, and a ticket to the biggest production, *O*, will set you back $93–$150. Yet many of the smaller shows have much lower prices. Bargain-hunters have learned to look to afternoon shows, such as Tropicana magician Rick Thomas or the Flamingo's campy burlesque revue "Bottom's Up," as ways to hold ticket prices under the $20 line.

There are several kinds of shows in Las Vegas. What used to be known as the "big room headliners" are a vanishing breed, and so are the old table-and-booth showrooms where they used to perform. But you can still find a few of the old names, along with a new generation of "resident headliners"—singer Clint Holmes and impressionist Danny Gans—who keep the tradition alive. The big-production spectaculars also remain a Las Vegas trademark, presenting little or no language barrier to the city's large numbers of international tourists. But the classic "feather show"—90 minutes of song, dance, topless showgirls, specialty acts, and special effects—has taken a backseat to the stylized eye candy of Cirque du Soleil, or the avant-garde stunts of the Blue Man Group. Foreign visitors also seem to love magic shows; you don't have to understand English to enjoy them. The same is true for a number of burlesque-derived revues that still rely on the topless showgirl or dancer, whose blatant charms can be appreciated in any language.

The Strip also broke down the walls that used to exist between old-school Las Vegas headliners and contemporary concert attractions. The casinos conformed to the modern concert industry by building two arenas—the MGM Grand Garden and Mandalay Events Center—and music clubs such as the House of Blues at Mandalay Bay. Las Vegas is now a mandatory tour stop for top-name stars of all ages and musical genres. The boldest step to date was taken in March 2003, when Celine Dion opened a three-year commitment to a 4,000-seat venue at Caesars Palace, staying in one place while her fans do the "touring."

The latest Las Vegas converts, however, are the young singles who may not buy a ticket for any conventional show. In the latter half of the '90s, the Strip became a nightlife capital, drawing favorable comparisons to Ibiza, Spain, among "clubbers" worldwide. A wave of large dance clubs, such as the Luxor's Ra and the Hard Rock Hotel's Baby's, was followed by a trendy new batch of cozier "ultra lounges" such as the MGM Grand's Tabú.

## Finding Out What's Going On

Information on shows, including their reservation and seating policies, prices, suitability for children (or age restrictions), and smoking restrictions, is available by calling or visiting the box offices. It's also listed in several local publications. The **Las Vegas Advisor** (✉ 3687 S. Procyon Ave., Las Vegas 89103, ☎ 800/244–2224) is available at its office for $5 per issue or $50 per year; this monthly newsletter is invaluable for its up-to-the-minute information on Las Vegas dining, entertainment, gambling promotions, comps, and news. You can also pick up free copies of *Today in Las Vegas* and *What's On in Las Vegas* at hotels and gift shops.

The **Las Vegas Review-Journal,** the city's morning daily newspaper, publishes a tabloid pullout section each Friday called "Neon." It provides entertainment features and reviews, and showroom and lounge listings with complete time and price information. The "Neon" section is sold separately for a quarter in some news boxes along the resort corridor. The *Review-Journal* maintains a Web site (WEB www.lasvegas.com), where show listings are updated each week. The **Las Vegas Sun,** the city's afternoon daily paper, also maintains a Web site with the latest details (WEB www.vegas.com).

A trio of alternative weekly newspapers are distributed at retail stores and coffee shops around town and maintain comprehensive Web sites. They usually offer more detail on the nightclub scene and music outside the realm of the casinos: **Las Vegas Mercury** (WEB www.lasvegasmercury.com), **Las Vegas Weekly** (WEB www.lasvegasweekly.com), and **Las Vegas City Life** (WEB www.lasvegascitylife.com).

## Getting Tickets

Most hotels have switched over to reserved-seat ticketing through corporate networks such as Ticketmaster. Many Internet-savvy travelers now pick their seats and purchase tickets for some attractions on-line well before their visits. In fact, it's advisable to do so for the hotter shows, such as Gans and the Cirque du Soleil productions.

**Ticketmaster.** Most of the showrooms and concert venues in town are part of Ticketmaster, making it possible for you to buy tickets for many Las Vegas shows at your hometown Ticketmaster outlet or through the company's Web site. Las Vegas's **Tower Records** (✉ 4580 W. Sahara

Ave., West Side) is conveniently located for ticket buyers. ☎ 702/474–4000, WEB *www.ticketmaster.com.*

**unlvtickets.com.** The notable holdout from Ticketmaster is the Thomas and Mack Center on the University of Nevada–Las Vegas (UNLV) campus. The center hosts Runnin' Rebels basketball, concerts, and special events such as *Disney on Ice.* Tickets can be purchased on-line, by phone, or at the arena itself. ☎ 888/388–3267 or 702/739–3267, WEB *www. unlvtickets.com.*

**Allstate Ticketing and Tours.** Allstate operates box offices all over town, most prominently in casinos without a show of their own. It sells tickets for almost every casino show except the two Cirque du Soleil productions. It's important to know that Allstate works on a system in which producers pay commissions for each ticket sold, which may prejudice a ticket broker's enthusiasm about a particular show. The lesser shows sometimes offer the highest commissions. ☎ 800/634–6787, WEB *www.showtickets.com.*

CLOSED OR IN-HOUSE TICKETING

Other shows have reserved seats but "closed" or "in-house" ticketing networks operating more on a first-come, first-served basis or which restrict advance purchases. On weekends it can be tough getting in to see the top names and production revues. Your chances of getting a seat are usually better when you're staying—and gambling—at the hotel. If you plan on spending a fair amount of time at the tables or slots, call VIP Services or a slot host and find out what their requirements are for getting a comp, tickets that have been withheld, or a line pass (that allows you to go straight to the VIP entrance without having to wait in line with the hoi polloi). Then be sure to have your play "rated" by the pit boss when you gamble, in order to qualify for the privileges.

MAÎTRE D' SEATING

Computerized ticketing and customer preference for reserved seats have all but eliminated the once-frightening realm of maître d's (who assigned the seats at the door) and captains (who show you to your seats). The Imperial Palace's "Legends in Concert" remains the only show in a mid- to large-size room that still operates on the fabled system, though it should come as no surprise that sometimes a little cash can upgrade seating even in rooms with assigned seating. To ensure a good seat, arrive early and discreetly toke the maître d' (with bills or chips the denomination of which he can readily see); $5 is usually sufficient.

## Venues

In addition to the hotel showrooms and theaters, Las Vegas has four large multi-purpose arenas for both concerts and sports, and several smaller performance venues.

**Aladdin Theatre for the Performing Arts.** This 7,000-seat concert hall was spared the wrecking ball when the old Aladdin was destroyed; the new Aladdin was built to surround it. Since Las Vegas does not have its own municipal theater, the Aladdin often hosts touring companies for Broadway musicals such as *Les Misèrables.* ✉ *Aladdin Resort and Casino, 3667 Las Vegas Blvd. S, Center Strip,* ☎ *702/785–5555.*

**Mandalay Bay Events Center.** With a capacity of 8,000 to 11,000, this venue is slightly smaller than the city's other two large arenas, the MGM Grand Garden and the Thomas and Mack Center. ✉ *Mandalay Bay Resort & Casino, 3950 Las Vegas Blvd. S, South Strip,* ☎ *702/632–7777.*

**MGM Grand Garden.** This arena tends to get the biggest concert names, from Bruce Springsteen to Britney Spears. But to secure the acts with adult appeal, such as Cher and Jimmy Buffett, the MGM has a reputation for outbidding the rival arenas, then passing the costs along to fans in the form of triple-digit ticket prices. It holds from 12,000 to 15,200 people. ✉ *MGM Grand Hotel and Casino, 3799 Las Vegas Blvd. S, South Strip*, ☎ 702/891–7777.

**Sam Boyd Stadium.** An outdoor football stadium, it still hosts the occasional concert that has the ability to pull in 30,000 or more people. But the UNLV-operated stadium has been busier lately with motorcycle and "Bigfoot truck" exhibitions. ✉ *Off Boulder Hwy. on Russell Rd., East Las Vegas*, ☎ 702/739–3267.

**Thomas and Mack Center.** On campus at UNLV, the center has come to rely on more sporting events such as the National Finals Rodeo since the MGM Grand and Mandalay Bay both built their own concert and sporting arenas. It holds anywhere from 7,000 to 18,000 people. There's now a smaller "field house" that connects to the main arena: the **Cox Pavilion** has hosted concerts for 2,000 to 4,000 people. ✉ *Tropicana Ave. at Swenson St., University District*, ☎ 702/739–3267.

**UNLV Performing Arts Center.** Like the Thomas and Mack Center, this complex is also on the UNLV campus but tends to stage more genteel events. It is divided into the the 400-seat **Judy Bayley Theatre**, which hosts ballet and plays, and the 1,800-seat **Artemus Ham Concert Hall.** ✉ *4505 S. Maryland Pkwy., University District* ☎ 702/895–2787.

Two nightclub/concert hall hybrids divide up most of the market for one-night concert attractions that aren't big enough for an arena, or ones who accepted a lofty paycheck to play a cozier room for their well-heeled fans. Each holds about 1,800. **The Joint** (✉ 4455 Paradise Rd., Paradise Road, ☎ 702/693–5000) is inside the Hard Rock Hotel and ★ Casino. The **House of Blues** (✉ 3950 Las Vegas Blvd. S, South Strip, ☎ 702/632–7600), at Mandalay Bay, is the seventh entry in this chain of successful music clubs.

For those who venture off the Strip, the Station Casinos family caters more to locals, with mid-level concert acts at reasonable prices. **The Railhead** (✉ 4111 Boulder Hwy., Boulder Strip, ☎ 702/432–7777) is in Boulder Station. **Club Madrid** (✉ 1301 E. Sunset Rd., Henderson, ☎ 702/547–7777) is in Sunset Station. These small showrooms have hosted everyone from Toby Keith to Keith Sweat, and from Merle Haggard to Jerry Vale. The Railhead got some competition with the arrival at Sam's Town Casino of **Sam's Town Live!** (✉ 5111 Boulder Hwy., Boulder Strip, ☎ 888/464–2468), a smartly designed concert and convention hall with retractable seating.

# NIGHTLIFE

## Bars & Lounges

### The Strip

The lounges of the Las Vegas casino-hotels were once places where such headliners as Frank, Dean, and the gang would go after their shows, taking a seat in the audience to laugh at the comedy antics of Shecky Greene or Don Rickles or to enjoy the music of Louis Prima and Keely Smith. Now the lounges have been mostly reduced to small bars within the casino, where bands play Top 40 hits in front of small crowds of people pie-eyed from the slots. Virtually every casino has such a spot; all you need to do is buy a drink or two and you can listen to the music all night long. A few lounges—the Las Vegas Hilton and Treasure Island among them—have computerized lighting and larger dance floors, making them as much a small dance club or live music club. Some of the nicest are at Paris Las Vegas, the Tropicana, the Stratosphere, Mandalay Bay, and the Orleans.

The turn of the 21st century, however, brought an explosion of hybrid nightspots aiming for the middle ground between dance club and conversational lounge.

**Caramel.** The owners of the Bellagio's dance club, Light, opened Caramel as a warm-up, wind-down, or distinct alternative to the larger club. The sweet name is backed up by martinis served in signature chocolate and caramel-coated chilled glasses. ⊠ *Bellagio Las Vegas, 3600 Las Vegas Blvd. S, Center Strip,* ☎ *702/693–7111.*

**Carnaval Court.** Harrah's has the rare outdoor lounge to take advantage of the Strip's parade of street life. Misters cool the scene in the summertime, and performing "flair bartenders" juggle bottles to the awe of customers. ⊠ *Harrah's Las Vegas Casino & Hotel, 3475 Las Vegas Blvd. S, Center Strip,* ☎ *702/369–5000.*

**Coyote Ugly.** This noisy joint brings the 2000 movie's title nightspot to life with choreographed routines, courtesy of barmaids in tight clothes who break into bar-top dances intended to make Hooter's look like a church picnic. ⊠ *New York–New York Hotel & Casino, 3790 Las Vegas Blvd. S, South Strip,* ☎ *702/7401–6969.*

**Drai's.** Closer to a full-bore dance club than a lounge is the wild scene inside Drai's, once the tony restaurant's tables are cleared away after evening dining hours. ⊠ *Barbary Coast Hotel and Casino, 3595 Las Vegas Blvd. S, Center Strip,* ☎ *702/737–0555.*

★ **Fontana Lounge.** Inside the Bellagio, this bar is styled like a 1940s-era supper club and offers a spectacular view of the dancing water shows outside. ⊠ *Bellagio Las Vegas, 3600 Las Vegas Blvd. S, Center Strip,* ☎ *702/693–7111.*

★ **Ghostbar.** Perched on the penthouse level of the Palms, Ghostbar has a glassed-in view of the city and an outdoor deck cantilevered over the side of the building, with a Plexiglas platform that allows revelers to look down 450 feet below. ⊠ *Palms, 4321 W. Flamingo Rd., West Side,* ☎ *702/942–7777.*

**Mist.** The partners behind the Bellagio's Caramel room opened this more casual counterpart, intended as a place to relax and watch sports on big-screen TVs. ⊠ *Treasure Island Las Vegas, 3300 Las Vegas Blvd. S, Center Strip,* ☎ *702/894–7111.*

**Shadow.** Caesars Palace converted one of its traditional lounges into Shadow, thus named because of the seemingly naked women dancing behind scrims in silhouette. ⊠ *Caesars Palace, 3570 Las Vegas Blvd. S, Center Strip,* ☎ *702/731–7990.*

**Tabú.** Tabú combines the high-tech touches of a big dance club with the coziness of a lounge. A former Cirque du Soleil lighting designer created "murals" of light that change depending on the perspective of the viewer. Square tables double as "canvases" for projected images and as makeshift dance floors once the music steps up a notch or two around midnight. ⊠ *MGM Grand Hotel and Casino, 3799 Las Vegas Blvd. S, South Strip,* ☎ *702/891–1111.*

**V Bar.** This small hot spot inside the Venetian was launched by the founders of New York's Lotus and Los Angeles' Sunset Room and started the "cool bar" trend in Las Vegas, but as competition heated up around the Strip, the V Bar responded by relaxing the dress code (on weeknights, at least) and going for more of a casual, Los Angeles rock 'n' roll vibe. ⊠ *Venetian Resort-Hotel-Casino, 3355 Las Vegas Blvd. S, Center Strip,* ☎ *702/733–5000.*

**Venus Lounge and Tiki Bar.** The retro design of this spot in the Venetian's retail mall will appeal to "Cocktail Nation" nostalgists, though the club has since repositioned itself to have a more mainstream appeal. ⊠ *Venetian Resort-Hotel-Casino, 3355 Las Vegas Blvd. S, Center Strip,* ☎ *702/414–4870.*

## Away from the Strip

Outside the realm of the big casinos, the Las Vegas bar scene is dominated by so-called "video poker taverns," named for the 15 video poker machines they are legally allowed to have. Most are generic, but there are exceptions.

**Double Down Saloon.** For the boho crowd, there's this deliberately downscale bar, with a jukebox blasting everything from Patsy Cline to classic punk. Fans of the place include filmmaker Tim Burton. (Don't bother checking it out before midnight, though.) ⊠ *4640 Paradise Rd., Paradise Road,* ☎ *702/791–5775.*

**Gordon Biersch Brewing Co.** Also a full-scale restaurant, this brewpub caters to Las Vegas's new breed of white-collar workers. ⊠ *3987 Paradise Rd., Paradise Road,* ☎ *702/312–5247.*

**J. C. Wooloughan Irish Pub.** In order to create the proper environment for serving Guinness, Bass, and Harp, the entire exterior of the pub was constructed in Dublin, then shipped to Las Vegas. The crowd is yuppie-leaning after work, then gets more casual and more diverse as the evening wears on. There is live music (usually Celtic rock bands) Wednesday through Saturday nights, but the bands are treated more as incidental additions than as the main attraction. ⊠ *JW Marriott Las Vegas, 221 N. Rampart Blvd., Summerlin,* ☎ *702/869–7777.*

# Comedy Clubs

Even when Las Vegas wasn't the hippest place to catch a musical act, it was always up-to-the-minute in the comedy department. From Shecky Greene to Chris Rock, virtually every famous comedian has worked a Las Vegas showroom or lounge. While the franchised comedy club boom of the 1980s went bust in most cities, the Strip still has five comedy clubs, all with multiple-act formats featuring the best names on the circuit. Cover charges are in the $18 range, but two-for-one coupons are easy to come by in freebie magazines and various coupon packages.

**Catch A Rising Star.** A former restaurant on the second-floor Attractions level of the Excalibur now houses a spacious 450-seat, budget-minded comedy club with two performers each night. ⊠ *Excalibur Hotel and Casino, 3850 Las Vegas Blvd. S, South Strip,* ☎ *702/597–7600.* ☉ *Nightly 7:30 and 10.*

**Comedy Stop.** There are two shows each night at this 400-seat club. Three comedians perform during each show. The price of admission includes two drinks. ⊠ *Tropicana Resort and Casino, 3801 Las Vegas Blvd. S, South Strip,* ☎ *702/739–2714.* ☉ *Nightly 8 and 10:30.*

**An Evening at the Improv.** This 300-seat showroom is in the old bingo hall on the second floor of Harrah's. The Improv is dark on Monday night, and drinks are not included in the admission price. ⊠ *Harrah's*

*Las Vegas Casino & Hotel, 3475 Las Vegas Blvd. S, Center Strip,* ☎ *702/369–5111.* ☉ *Tues.–Sun. night 8:30 and 10:30.*

**Laugh Trax.** This 300-seat club at the locals-friendly Palace Station undercuts the price of its Strip competitors but only books two comedians for each program. Weekends, however, often include a singer-guitarist as a change-of-pace host. ✉ *Palace Station Hotel and Casino, 2411 W. Sahara Ave., West Side,* ☎ *888/464–2468.* ☉ *Tues.–Sat. night 7:30 and 10.*

**Riviera Comedy Club.** There are two shows each night of the week at this cozy 375-seat club. ✉ *Riviera Hotel and Casino, 2901 Las Vegas Blvd. S, North Strip,* ☎ *702/794–9433.* ☉ *Nightly 8 and 10.*

## Dance Clubs

Dance clubs have been the Strip's biggest entertainment innovation of the past few years. Hotels, tired of watching their guests hop a cab to off-Strip nightspots, built fantasy-theme dance palaces that only establishments with unrestricted budgets could create. Cover charges have correspondingly crept into the $10 to $20 range—and don't be surprised to find that, even in these "enlightened times," men will pay more than women to get in. While that level of capital investment gives these clubs a longevity their New York counterparts don't enjoy, dance clubs are still a fickle, fleeting enterprise by nature.

Each club sets its own dress code standard, but all clubs enforce a fairly rigorous one: no T-shirts, ball caps, or tennis shoes, and no logos that could be affiliated with gangs. Prepare for frustration, depending on the whim of the doorman, if you try to argue for the validity of designer tennis shoes or pullovers without a collar. How much you paid for them doesn't seem to matter.

**Baby's.** The concept of an "underground" club is literal at the Hard Rock Hotel, which buried at least part of this dance-club as a space-saving technique on a crowded site. An antechamber with a low ceiling, stone walls, and a tiny dance floor gives way to the main room, where a sloping seating area gradually rises to curve around the dance floor at second-story level. Video walls and servers dressed in black leather to match the black-upholstered booths from the 1950s create a futuristic *noir*. Guest big-city DJs play house, trip-hop, and drum and bass dance music. Thursday's "Can You Feel It?" is the signature night for locals and informed clubbers. The club is open Thursday through Saturday from 10:30 PM. ✉ *Hard Rock Hotel and Casino, 4455 Las Vegas Blvd. S, Paradise Road,* ☎ *702/693–5000.*

**The Beach.** Life is one nonstop fraternity bash at this two-story club designed to look like a South-of-the-Border party barn. Still known for a less-restrictive dress code than those imposed by the hotels, the Beach has lately jumped in on the trend of theme "parties" and promotions that vary by the night or according to whatever big events happen to be in town. It's open nightly, but hours vary, especially on weeknights. ✉ *365 Convention Center Dr., Paradise Road,* ☎ *702/731–1925,* WEB *www.beachlv.com.*

**Bikinis.** Since Las Vegas is a city where innovation is followed by imitation, the Rio swiped pages from both the Beach and Coyote Ugly to create this "year-round indoor beach bash" in late 2002. The 14,000 square-foot club augments its theme with water tanks, Jacuzzis, and "exhibition showers." ✉ *Rio All Suite Hotel and Casino, 3700 W. Flamingo Rd., West Side,* ☎ *702/777–7777.*

**C2K.** The Venetian's "megaclub" is a leased-out, separately run operation with an opera-house design. Decorated in black and chrome accented with purple, the club spans three levels and is capable of holding nearly 3,000 people. The intense nightclub competition of recent years has relegated C2K to more of a room-for-rent than a continuous operation; independent promoters book the room for themed public "parties" often tied in to such special events as boxing matches. ✉ *Venetian Resort-Hotel-Casino, 3355 Las Vegas Blvd. S, Center Strip,* ☏ *702/933–4255.*

**Club Rio.** This pioneering dance club inside a casino offers all the essentials: wraparound video screens, a big stage, and a large dance floor. To combat the loss of novelty as newer clubs open in other casino-hotels, Club Rio has embraced Latin pop and house music to make Thursday's Latin La-Beat-Oh its signature night. If the dance floor gets too hot, overhead misters cool everyone down. It's open Wednesday through Sunday from 10:30 PM. ✉ *Rio All-Suite Hotel and Casino, 3700 W. Flamingo Ave., West Side,* ☏ *702/252–7727.*

**Curve.** The Aladdin pulled victory from the jaws of defeat when it turned part of the underutilized London Club on the second floor of the casino into a busy nightspot. It's a large club with the feel of a small one, thanks to separate rooms featuring different music and an outdoor balcony with a view of the Strip for those in need of a little fresh air. ✉ *Aladdin Resort and Casino, 3667 Las Vegas Blvd. S, South Strip,* ☏ *702/785–5525,* WEB *curvelasvegas.com.*

**Light.** Nightclub entrepreneurs Keith and Chris Barish, along with operating partner Andrew Sasson, were charged with bringing Bellagio a nightclub that would match the upscale (pricey) image and celebrity appeal of the larger hotel. This 600-capacity room at the Bellagio emphasized the exclusivity of its 40 reserved tables and expensive "bottle service" in the early going, but it is also open to those of average means. It's open nightly from 9:30 PM. ✉ *Bellagio Las Vegas, 3600 Las Vegas Blvd. S, Center Strip,* ☏ *702/693–8300,* WEB *www.lightlv.com.*

★ **Ra.** Luxor's $20-million hot spot is still the most fancifully designed of Las Vegas clubs, with a theme park–style interior inspired by the "Egyptian-deco" futurism of the sci-fi movie *Stargate.* Live bands sometimes take to the center stage; dancers gyrate in cages. The club spotlights visiting DJs from other cities and its signature night is Wednesday's "Pleasuredome." Collared shirts for men are required. It's open Wednesday through Saturday from 10:30 PM. ✉ *Luxor Resort & Casino, 3900 Las Vegas Blvd. S, South Strip,* ☏ *702/262–4949,* WEB *www.rathenightclub.com.*

**Rain in the Desert.** This club by Michael Morton and Scott DeGraff got tons of free publicity in 2002–03 as a major setting for MTV's *The Real World.* The round, 1,500-capacity nightclub and concert house is equipped with dancing waters, video projections on a 40-foot water curtain, and occasional blasts of fire. Perhaps because the Palms shares ownership with the Sacramento Kings, the club even includes "skyboxes" for rent. Thursday is the signature night, "Drenched." In the summer, the action expands to the adjacent pool area for Skin, a "pool lounge" with the same management. ✉ *Palms, 4321 W. Flamingo Rd., West Side,* ☏ *702/938–9999,* WEB *www.rainatthepalms.com.*

**rumjungle.** This Mandalay Bay version of a Brazilian paradise drew Disney-style lines from the day it opened. The "fire wall" out front beckons club goers into a wild 20,000-square-foot room with waterfalls, dancing girls on platforms above the 85-foot-long bar, giant conga drums, and even aerialists attached to trapezelike harnesses. The

## Close-Up

# GETTING HITCHED IN VEGAS

**W**HEN WIDE-OPEN GAMBLING was legalized in 1931, Nevada also adopted liberal divorce and marriage laws as part of the strategy to attract tourists. The rules haven't changed in seven decades: a divorce can still be obtained after only six weeks of residency and a wedding can be arranged without a blood test or a waiting period; once you have a license, a justice of the peace can unite you in marital bliss in five minutes.

Weddings are big business here, to the tune of more than $4 million in marriage licenses alone. To be among the 123,000-plus couples who tie the knot in Las Vegas every year, simply appear at the **Clark County Marriage License Bureau** (⊠ 200 S. 3rd St., Downtown, ☎ 702/455-4415) with $50, some identification, and your beloved. It's open between 8 AM and midnight from Monday through Thursday and 24 hours Friday, Saturday, and holidays. New Year's Eve and Valentine's Day are the most popular wedding dates. Even celebrities (including Jon Bon Jovi, Bette Midler, Joan Collins, Michael Jordan, and Richard Gere) have found it handy to pop into a chapel for a quick ceremony.

For a no-frills, justice-of-the-peace nuptial ceremony, visit the **Commissioner of Civil Marriages** (⊠ 309 S. 3rd St., Downtown), where a surrogate-J.P. deputy commissioner will unite you in holy matrimony for $35. For a more traditional ambience—flowers, organ music, photos—head to one of Vegas's renowned wedding chapels, where the average nuptials cost $200 to $700 (though you can spend a lot more or a bit less); hotel chapels tend to cost more.

The **Candlelight Wedding Chapel** (⊠ 2855 Las Vegas Blvd. S, North Strip, ☎ 702/735-4179 or 800/962-1818, WEB www.nos.net/candlelight) opened its doors in 1967; it's small, elegant, and churchlike.

Weddings are reasonably priced; the most expensive package comes in at $500. The **Little Church of the West** (⊠ 4617 Las Vegas Blvd. S, South Strip, ☎ 702/739-7971 or 800/821-2452) is listed on the National Register of Historic Places; the cedar and redwood chapel is one of the most famous chapels in Vegas, sitting on an acre of land at the south end of the Strip. The **Little White Chapel** (⊠ 1301 Las Vegas Blvd. S, North Strip, ☎ 702/382-3546 or 800/545-8111, WEB www.littlewhitechapel.com), one mi north of the Sahara hotel, is where you can get married in a pink Cadillac while an Elvis impersonator croons. The world-renowned chapel is one of only two chapels that offer drive-through weddings (the other is A Special Memory).

Weddings at **Star Trek: The Experience** (⊠ 3000 S. Paradise Blvd., North Strip, ☎ 702/697-8750 or 800/774-1500, WEB www.startrekexp.com) are held on the bridge of the Enterprise-D from Star Trek: The Next Generation; costumed characters, from Federation officers to Klingon warriors, bear witness to the proceedings.

The **Venetian** (⊠ 3355 Las Vegas Blvd. S, Center Strip, ☎ 702/414-4280 or 800/883-6423, WEB www.venetian.com) offers weddings in a recreation of St. Mark's Square, on a replica of the Rialto Bridge or on the Venetian's canal in a gold-and-white gondola. The gondolier sings and passersby applaud loudly, dimming the lines between a real wedding in Venice and this fanciful interpretation.

The **Viva Las Vegas Wedding Chapel** (⊠ 1205 Las Vegas Blvd. S, North Strip, ☎ 702/384-0771 or 800/574-4450, WEB www.vivalasvegasweddings.com) offers a wide variety of theme weddings, from Elvis's Blue Hawaii to Egyptian to Fairy Tale. Ever dream of a wedding themed for Charo? Here's where you'll find it.

house, hip-hop, and Latin music keep the dance floor hoppin'. It's open Thursday through Saturday from 11 PM. ⌧ *Mandalay Bay Resort & Casino, 3950 Las Vegas Blvd. S, South Strip,* ☎ *702/632–7408.*

**Studio 54.** This tri-level, 22,000-square-foot dance club inside the MGM Grand Hotel and Casino took over the area where a cheesy lion's mouth once welcomed you, leaving the steel beams in place for a stark industrial look. The club can sustain itself on weekends with MGM traffic alone, so Tuesday became the signature night with EDEN: "Erotically Delicious Entertainers Night." It's open from 10 PM Tuesday through Saturday. ⌧ *MGM Grand Hotel and Casino, 3799 Las Vegas Blvd. S, South Strip,* ☎ *702/891–1111.*

**Utopia.** This was the first truly progressive Las Vegas club that could hold its reputation against the hippest nightclubs in London or Ibiza. Management turned the non-hotel location from a negative into a positive by offering a looser "rave" atmosphere with trance and techno music from cutting-edge DJs. A rooftop patio with the view of the Strip almost becomes a second club. ⌧ *3765 Las Vegas Blvd. S, South Strip,* ☎ *702/392–7979,* WEB *www.clubutopia.net.* ☉ *Wed.–Sat. 10 PM–6 AM.*

**Whiskey Bar.** Rande Gerber, the entrepreneur better known to some as "Mr. Cindy Crawford," banked on the popularity of his "Whiskey"-named clubs in other cities to lure celebrities and club-hoppers to Green Valley Ranch, a suburban casino several miles from the Strip. The club appeals to a slightly older demographic and sets the dance floor off in a separate room. ⌧ *Green Valley Ranch Resort, 2197 Paseo Verde Pkwy., Henderson,* ☎ *702/614–5283.* ☉ *Nightly, from 5 PM.*

# Live Music

### Country & Western

**Dylan's Dance Hall & Saloon.** Once known as Rockabilly's, this Boulder Highway honky-tonk is the spiritual heart of Las Vegas country music. It's open Thursday through Saturday from 7:30 PM. ⌧ *4660 Boulder Hwy., Boulder Strip,* ☎ *702/451–4006.*

**Gilley's Dancehall Saloon & Barbecue.** This institution, which Mickey moved from Texas to Las Vegas, has less live music than deejayed line dancing, but it's country's home on the Strip. The club is open Thursday through Saturday from 6 PM for dancing, but the restaurant is open nightly for dinner. ⌧ *New Frontier Hotel and Gambling Hall, 3120 Las Vegas Blvd. S, South Strip,* ☎ *702/794–8434.*

### Jazz

**Jazzed Cafe and Vinoteca.** Away from the Strip, the best bet is this fun room that's decorated as a bold piece of living pop art. It seats about 40 for dinner but stays open past the dinner hour as a cozy spot for live music. ⌧ *8615 W. Sahara Ave., West Las Vegas,* ☎ *702/233–2859.*

**Las Vegas Jazz Society.** Call for information on concerts in parks and municipal library theaters. ☎ *702/455–7340.*

### Rock

**Huntridge Theatre.** Before the arrival of the Hard Rock Hotel and House of Blues, a former movie theater built in 1945 gave Las Vegas locals a chance to see early career performances by the likes of Courtney Love, Beck, and Smashing Pumpkins. ⌧ *1208 E. Charleston Ave., East Side,* ☎ *702/678–6800,* WEB *www.thehuntridge.com.*

**Junkyard Live.** A fashionably downscale spot hosts local bands in all genres, with jam sessions on Monday, Wednesday, and Thursday.

✉ *2327 S. Eastern Ave., East Las Vegas,* ☎ *702/440–8812,* WEB *www. junkyardlive.com.*

## Afternoon Shows

Las Vegas has become a wider-reaching and more family-friendly destination. But at the same time, evening show prices have broken into the triple-digits. These factors are sometimes at odds with one another and help explain a host of afternoon shows that hold their ticket prices under the $20 mark. The following are the most proven and popular.

***Bottom's Up.*** Comedian Breck Wall has been a fixture on the Strip since 1964, when his Dallas-based comedy troupe first offered Las Vegas a campy hour of blackout sketches and burlesque humor that may have inspired TV's "Laugh-In." (Wall says Rowan & Martin used to catch the show when they were working in town.) No joke is too old or raunchy for the only daytime topless show. ✉ *Flamingo Las Vegas, 3555 Las Vegas Blvd. S, Center Strip,* ☎ *702/733–3333.* ✆ *$12.95.* ☉ *Mon.– Sat. 2* PM *and 4* PM.

☽ ***The Illusionary Magic of Rick Thomas.*** If you want your children to see a Las Vegas-style magic show without paying showroom prices, Rick Thomas's well-paced revue offers an overview of the basic stage illusions and even throws in a white tiger. ✉ *Tropicana Resort and Casino, 3801 Las Vegas Blvd. S, South Strip,* ☎ *702/739–2222.* ✆ *$16.95– $21.95.* ☉ *Sat.–Thurs. 2* PM *and 4* PM.

★ ☽ ***Mac King.*** This comic magician keeps the payroll small; the only "exotic animal" is a goldfish that pops out of his mouth at an unexpected moment. King stands apart from the other magic shows on the Strip by offering a one-man hour of low-key, self-deprecating humor and the kind of "close-up" magic that often requires more skill than the the "cabinet tricks" of the larger shows. ✉ *Harrah's Las Vegas Casino & Hotel, 3475 Las Vegas Blvd. S, Center Strip,* ☎ *702/369–5111.* ✆ *$16.45.* ☉ *Tues.–Sat. 1* PM *and 3* PM.

## Evening Revues

☽ ***American Superstars.*** This upstart impersonator show made "Legends in Concert" pick up its energy level by challenging it with rollicking tributes to pop stars such as Ricky Martin and Christina Aguilera. Both shows are better for the competition. ✉ *Stratosphere Casino Hotel & Tower, 2000 Las Vegas Blvd. S, North Strip,* ☎ *702/380–7711.* ✆ *$30.* ☉ *Sun.–Tues. 7* PM. *Wed. and Fri.–Sat. 7* PM *and 10* PM.

★ ***Blue Man Group: Live at Luxor.*** A perhaps unlikely success story on the Strip is a striking example of how far Las Vegas has come in shedding its old image. The New York–based troupe launched its fourth and largest production at the Luxor just before it became ready for prime-time in a series of high-profile computer processor commercials. Three men in utilitarian uniforms, their heads bald and gleaming from cobalt blue greasepaint, prowl the stage committing twisted "science projects" that are alternately highbrow and juvenile. A civil-engineering lesson might be followed by marshmallow spitting. A seven-piece band plays angular spaghetti Western music to complement the Blue Men's signature percussion instruments made from PVC pipe. ✉ *Luxor Resort & Casino, 3900 Las Vegas Blvd. S, South Strip,* ☎ *702/ 262–4400,* WEB *www.blueman.com.* ✆ *$65–$100.* ☉ *Nightly 7 and 10.*

***Crazy Girls.*** An Americanized, low-rent version of the Crazy Horse Cabaret in Paris offers a topless club experience within the safe confines of the hotel. The basic formula is still a chorus line of topless women who lip-sync songs and gyrate to taped music. ⊠ *Riviera Hotel and Casino, 2901 Las Vegas Blvd. S, North Strip,* ☎ *702/794–9433.* ⊠ *$25–$35;* ☽ *Wed.–Mon. 9 PM.*

**An Evening at La Cage.** This durable female impersonator show has been guided for more than a decade by Frank Marino, whose dead-on take on Joan Rivers provides the live voice to introduce lip-synch musical tributes. ⊠ *Riviera Hotel and Casino, 2901 Las Vegas Blvd. S, North Strip,* ☎ *702/794–9433.* ⊠ *$29.95.* ☽ *Wed.–Mon. 7:30 PM and 9:30 PM.*

**Folies Bergere.** The singing male host of this classic French topless revue tells audiences the Folies is the oldest show in America that's still running. It has been at the Tropicana since 1959, and its survival is almost a miracle, considering the city's zeal for imploding its past. The painted flats and dance segments such as the "Can-Can" show their age compared to newer, hi-tech competition, but the hotel preserves the show with some degree of pride, replacing segments now and then with fresh costumes and more current (recorded) music. It would, perhaps, benefit from a cheekier attitude. But there's an argument for playing it straight, now that the Strip has only two classic revues complete with singers, dancers, a juggler, and, of course, showgirls parading around in feathers. Only the late show is topless. ⊠ *Tropicana Resort and Casino, 3801 Las Vegas Blvd. S, South Strip,* ☎ *702/739–2411.* ⊠ *$45–$55.* ☽ *Fri.–Wed. 7:30 PM and 10 PM.*

**Jubilee!** Donn Arden, who produced shows in Las Vegas from 1952 until his death in 1994, put together this spectacular stage tribute to Hollywood in 1981 for the old MGM Grand Hotel, now Bally's. *Jubilee!* has been updated in places since then, but it remains your last chance to experience the scope of Arden's over-the-top vision and to sample the "class" (or kitsch) Vegas of old. A cast of 80 or more performs in a theater with 1,100 seats, but the gargantuan sets and props steal the show: the sinking of the *Titanic* is re-created, and when Samson destroys the temple the wreckage goes up in flames. Showgirls parade about in the largest spectacle of feathers and bare breasts you've ever seen. ⊠ *Bally's Las Vegas, 3645 Las Vegas Blvd. S, Center Strip,* ☎ *702/739–4567.* ⊠ *$50–$66.* ☽ *Sat.–Thurs. 7:30 PM and 10 PM.*

**La Femme.** The MGM Grand Hotel wooed Paris' Crazy Horse Cabaret to Las Vegas by offering to remodel a lounge into a near-spitting image of the French institution. After years of hosting knockoffs such as "Crazy Girls," Las Vegas finally has the original girlie show, a classy affair in which symmetrically matched, naturally endowed women are expertly choreographed and "painted in light" for a succession of humorous or erotically mimed vignettes. ⊠ *MGM Grand Hotel and Casino, 3799 Las Vegas Blvd. S, South Strip,* ☎ *702/891–7777.* ⊠ *$49.* ☽ *Wed.–Mon. 8:30 PM and 10:30 PM.*

☽ **Lance Burton: Master Magician.** The eponymous Lance Burton Theater is an opulent 1,200-seat opera house that makes a splendid long-term home for a nice guy from Kentucky who worked his way up the ranks from specialty act to star. He's a charmer with the ladies, and works youngsters into the show like no other act on the Strip. Unfortunately, the small magic—the sleight of hand and close-up tricks that earned him the prestigious Gold Medal from the International Brotherhood of Magicians—is lost from way up in the balcony. Still, the major illusions, such as making cars disappear, are downright stunning. ⊠ *Monte Carlo Resort and Casino, 3770 Las Vegas Blvd. S, South Strip,* ☎ *702/730–7777.* ⊠ *$55–$60.* ☽ *Tues.–Sat. 7 PM and 10 PM, Sun. 7 PM.*

○ ***Legends in Concert.*** The durable *Legends* rotates impersonations of Madonna, Liberace, Tom Jones, and others, with the Elvis Presley finale the only non-variable rule. There's no lip-synching and always a live band. ⊠ *Imperial Palace Hotel and Casino, 3535 Las Vegas Blvd. S, Center Strip,* ☎ *702/794–3261.* 🎟 *$35.* ⊙ *Mon.–Sat. 7:30 PM and 10:30 PM.*

★ ○ ***Mamma Mia!*** The musical phenomenon parked on the Strip for an open-ended, "sit-down" run in early 2003. The show is such a hit that its producers didn't feel the Las Vegas edition would drain business from the other four North American companies. The '70s pop hits of ABBA are woven into a traditional musical comedy about a bride-to-be who uses her wedding to deduce which of her mother's past suitors is her father. Mandalay Bay gambled that this show's reputation for dancing-in-the-aisles fun would deliver the success that a previous legitimate musical, *Chicago,* failed to. ⊠ *Mandalay Bay Resort & Casino, 3950 Las Vegas Blvd. S, South Strip,* ☎ *702/632–7580.* 🎟 *$65–$85.* ⊙ *Wed., Thurs., and Sun. 7 PM; Fri. 8 PM; Mon. and Sat. 7 and 10:30 PM.*

***Michael Flatley's Lord of the Dance.*** The "apostrophe s" in the title is the key to a show that many believe is falsely advertised. The touring version was created as a vehicle to showcase the athletic Irish folk dancing of PBS darling Flatley, but he no longer performs in any of the companies. Instead, a young and energetic cast is enlisted for a Celtic tale of good and evil staged to New Age-y music. The silly costumes and basic plot are often more like professional wrestling than an artsy dance showcase. The show ended a four-year run at New York–New York in mid-2002, but reopened by year's end at the Showroom at the Venetian, where it seems more crowded with less room onstage for the dancers. ⊠ *Venetian Resort-Hotel-Casino, 3355 Las Vegas Blvd. S, Center Strip,* ☎ *702/948–3007.* 🎟 *$75.* ⊙ *Tues.–Sun. 8 and 10:15 PM.*

***Midnight Fantasy.*** This is the most "innocent" and tamest of the mid-size topless shows. Though it has energetic choreography and eye-catching costumes, it plays more like a theme-park revue, to no complaints from the mainstream couples—heavy on room guests from Mandalay Resorts hotels—who support this Luxor show. ⊠ *Luxor Resort & Casino, 3900 Las Vegas Blvd. S, South Strip,* ☎ *702/262–4400.* 🎟 *$29.95.* ⊙ *Tues., Thurs., and Sat. 8:30 PM and 10:30 PM, Wed. and Fri. 10:30 PM, Sun. 8:30 PM.*

★ ○ ***Mystère.*** This New Age circus performed by Cirque du Soleil is the premier family show in town and is a uniquely memorable experience bound to please all ages. From the moment you enter the big top, you are intimately involved with this show. "Flounes" (clowns) mingle and fool with the audience as it's seated, and roving "devils" make trouble even before the show begins. The music is rousing and haunting, the acrobatics chilling, and the dance numbers inspiring. The usual circus-type distractions are kept to a minimum, and there are no animals. The opening of Cirque du Soleil's newer show, *O,* threatened to make this one seem less special, but so far that hasn't been the case. *Mystère* keeps the audience closer to the action and the human achievements more in the spotlight. ⊠ *Treasure Island Las Vegas, 3300 Las Vegas Blvd. S, Center Strip,* ☎ *702/894–7722.* 🎟 *$88.* ⊙ *Wed.–Sun. 7:30 PM and 10:30 PM.*

★ ***A New Day.*** Las Vegas was built on star power, but Celine Dion pioneers a new concept for Las Vegas entertainment by promising to stay put for three years, letting fans "tour" to see her in the 4,000-seat Colosseum built for her in front of Caesars Palace. Since she doesn't have to take the show on the road, she can surround herself with 50 dancers in a lavish revue directed by Franco Dragone, cocreator of *O* and *Mystère*. In the early going, Dragone's flourishes tended to compete with the star, and it sometimes became a game of "Where's Waldo?" to find her on a 120-foot-wide stage that's too big by a third. But the show's still innovative and undeniably spectacular in places, such as the moment when the singer and several costars fly five stories above the stage. ☒ *Caesars Palace, 3570 Las Vegas Blvd. S, Center Strip,* ☎ *702/474-4000.* ▣ *$87.50–$200.*

★ **O.** Cirque du Soleil's *O* is the most expensive show in history—in Las Vegas or anywhere else. More than $70 million was spent on the theater at Bellagio, and on the liquid stage that takes over as the real star of the show. *O* is the pronunciation of *eau,* French for water, and water is everywhere—1.5 million gallons of it, 12 million pounds of it, contained by a "stage" that, thanks to hydraulic lifts, can change shape. The intense and nonstop action by the show's acrobats, aerial gymnasts and trapeze artists, synchronized swimmers, divers, and contortionists takes place above, within, and even on the surface of the water. True to Cirque tradition, the costumes, music, sets, and timing greatly enhance the overwhelming spectacle. So much is going on, in fact, that at the end of the show you're exhausted from trying to see everything. ☒ *Bellagio Las Vegas, 3600 Las Vegas Blvd. S, Center Strip,* ☎ *702/693-7111.* ▣ *$93–$121.* ⊙ *Fri.–Tues. 7:30 PM and 10:30 PM.*

**The Second City.** Shoehorning itself onto a Strip filled with stand-up comedy clubs, Chicago's ensemble comedy institution is a breath of fresh air. It has the class and polish of a theatrical revue but isn't afraid to go for the cheap or lowbrow when there's a good laugh to be had. Five performers present favorite sketches from Second City's 40-year archives and also pull audience members into improvisational games in Bugsy's Celebrity Theatre. ☒ *Flamingo Las Vegas, 3555 Las Vegas Blvd. S, Center Strip,* ☎ *702/733-3333.* ▣ *$27.95.* ⊙ *Tues. and Thurs.–Sun. 8 PM and 10:30 PM, Wed. and Fri. 8 PM.*

**Siegfried and Roy at the Mirage.** This extravaganza by Roy Horn and Siegfried Fischbacher has been a fixture in Las Vegas since the 1960s, with a robotic fire-breathing dragon, Michael Jackson music, lasers, disappearing elephants and motorcycles, and the two stars levitating each other and their signature lions and white tigers. But the show was closed indefinitely in October 2003 after one of the animals attacked Roy Horn during a performance. Roy is expected to recover and even perform again—nobody yet knows just what the show will be. Stay tuned. ☒ *Mirage Hotel and Casino, 3400 Las Vegas Blvd. S, Center Strip,* ☎ *702/792-7777.*

**Skintight.** This "equal opportunity" topless show includes a dynamic male front man, Darryl Ross, and male dancers along with women in the chorus. ☒ *Harrah's Las Vegas Casino & Hotel, 3475 Las Vegas Blvd. S, Center Strip,* ☎ *702/369-5111.* ▣ *$39.95.* ⊙ *Mon.–Wed. 10:30 PM, Fri. 10 PM and midnight, Sat. 10:30 PM, Sun. 7:30 PM and 10:30 PM.*

**Splash.** The original incarnation of *Splash* was known for its high-energy staging, loud rock and roll, and nonstop specialty acts. But the show was eclipsed by such spectaculars as *O* and *Mystère* and has struggled to bring back the excitement. The name is a bit of a misnomer now, since the water is frozen; the trademark tank was removed in 1999 to shift the focus to ice-skating. Some of the skating adagios are impressive, but the classical music is jarring when interspersed with

Michael Jackson and Madonna tributes held over from previous versions. *Splash* used to be live MTV. Now it's just for channel surfers. ⊠ *Riviera Hotel and Casino, 2901 Las Vegas Blvd. S, North Strip,* ☎ *702/794–9301.* ⌨ *$51.50–$65.* ⊘ *Sat.–Thurs. 7:30 PM and 10:30 PM.*

☾ **Steve Wyrick.** This Texas magician designed a show to match the Sahara's middle-market focus; a production-heavy spectacle with the feel of a theme park stunt show. The giant sets and props help make up for the star's underwhelming, albeit amiable, stage personality. ⊠ *Sahara Hotel and Casino, 2535 Las Vegas Blvd. S, North Strip,* ☎ *702/737–2111.* ⌨ *$45.95–49.95.* ⊘ *Wed.–Sat. 7 PM and 10 PM, Sun.–Mon. 7 PM.*

☾ **Tournament of Kings.** One of Las Vegas's most unusual big shows takes place in a dirt-floor arena, with the audience eating a basic dinner (warning: no utensils) and cheering fast horses, jousting, and swordplay. It's a wonderful family show—especially for families with pre-adolescents, who get to make a lot of noise. ⊠ *Excalibur Hotel and Casino, 3850 Las Vegas Blvd. S, South Strip,* ☎ *702/597–7600.* ⌨ *$39.95.* ⊘ *Nightly 6 and 8:30.*

# Showrooms

## Resident Headliners

The turn of the new century took Las Vegas back to one of the traditions from its past. The success of impressionist Danny Gans opened the doors to a wave of "resident headliners" who live in Las Vegas and perform on a year-round schedule comparable to the revues (as opposed to visiting headliners such as the Moody Blues, Huey Lewis, or Tom Jones, who stay anywhere from three nights to two weeks).

Clint Holmes, Rita Rudner, and even a certain fellow named Wayne Newton, all bet that show goers were tired of special effects and ready to re-embrace the "down front" performing tradition that put Las Vegas on the map.

★ **Clint Holmes (Harrah's).** Harrah's wagered that Danny Gans lightning would strike twice when it backed a relative unknown, and strong word-of-mouth brought Clint Holmes deserved acceptance. The singer has only one distant hit single to his name: the uncharacteristic "Playground in My Mind" from 1973. But his endearing persona and his jazzy way with a baby-boomer pop standard (he prefers 1970s-era material to the Sinatra classics) allow him to pull off the seemingly impossible task of becoming a new-generation crooner who isn't a retro throwback to the swing era. ⊠ *Harrah's Las Vegas Casino & Hotel, 3475 Las Vegas Blvd. S, Center Strip,* ☎ *702/369–5111.* ⌨ *$60.* ⊘ *Mon.–Sat.*

★ **Danny Gans: Man of Many Voices (Mirage).** The impressionist (and former baseball player) pulled off a near miracle in Las Vegas, coming in from the trade show and convention circuit as a "no name" and becoming one of the hottest tickets in town. This talented impressionist leaves 'em standing and cheering every night, after performing upwards of 60 characters—everyone from Gerald Ford and Kermit the Frog to Dean Martin and Homer Simpson. Gans is also a singer, dancer, musician, and comedian, and fronts a live band that provides musical mimicry. With a show that plays more like a one-man theatrical revue than a nightclub act, Gans lacks spontaneity but pushes emotional buttons. ⊠ *Mirage Hotel and Casino, 3400 Las Vegas Blvd. S, Center Strip,* ☎ *702/791–7111.* ⌨ *$80–$100.* ⊘ *Tues.–Thurs. and Sat.–Sun. 8 PM.*

★ **Penn & Teller (Rio).** After years of doing at least a third of their shows in Las Vegas, eccentric comic magicians Penn & Teller finally signed a 2002 contract for a two-year residency in the Rio's gorgeous Samba Theatre, a 1,500-seat auditorium with opulent chandeliers and original artwork in the lobby. Penn & Teller are still an acquired taste for many, but the duo has become almost mainstream for the new Las Vegas. Their magic is unusual and genuinely baffling, and their comedy alternately provocative and thoughtful. ⌧ *Rio All Suite Hotel and Casino, 3700 W. Flamingo Rd., West Side,* ☎ *702/777–7776.* ⌨ *$71.50.* ⊘ *Wed.–Mon. 9 PM.*

★ **Rita Rudner (New York–New York).** It's rare to be a female comedian in Las Vegas and rarer still to offer a "clean" act that's still insightful in its look at domestic life and female obsessions. The folding chairs in the so-called Cabaret Theatre are nothing to write home about, but Rita gets the job done for an intimate evening of soft-spoken wit. ⌧ *New York–New York Hotel & Casino, 3790 Las Vegas Blvd. S, South Strip,* ☎ *702/740–6815.* ⌨ *$46.* ⊘ *Mon. and Wed.–Thurs. 8 PM, Fri. 9 PM, Sat. 7 PM and 9 PM.*

**The Scintas (Rio).** This Buffalo, New York, quartet of three siblings and a drummer possesses a warm charm that helps sell routines that hearken back to the era of the "show band," where every member sported double-threat comic and musical duties. The Scintas lay on the schtick pretty thick, but have a loyal, mostly older fan base for an act that can perhaps be described as Wayne Newton meets the Smothers Brothers. ⌧ *Rio All-Suite Hotel and Casino, 3700 W. Flamingo Rd., West Side,* ☎ *702/252–7776.* ⌨ *$45.* ⊘ *Mon. and Fri.–Sun. 8 PM, Tues. 8 PM and 10:30 PM.*

**Wayne Newton (Stardust).** The years have punished his voice, but Mr. Las Vegas, the Midnight Idol, the King of the Strip remains the epitome of the Las Vegas headliner. A homegrown phenomenon, he has been performing here since his teens. On stage Newton gives it the Al Jolson treatment, working and sweating his way through a leisurely two hours—singing, telling jokes, and playing the guitar, violin, and trumpet. Whatever one thinks of his diminished vocal ability or the cornpone, no one would dispute the fact that he knows how to entertain his audience. Seeing him in this appropriately aged showroom (which once housed the *Lido de Paris*) is as much a part of the experience of visiting Las Vegas as gambling and a trip to Hoover Dam. ⌧ *Stardust Hotel and Casino, 3000 Las Vegas Blvd. S, North Strip,* ☎ *702/732–6325.* ⌨ *$55.* ⊘ *Sat.–Thurs. 9 PM.*

## Headliners Showrooms

Who would have thought the day would come when the traditional headliner room was an endangered species on the Strip? Part of it's due to the previously mentioned effect of the concert industry shifting the action to venues such as the House of Blues. A few rooms do still host a rotating roster of names, but much of the action has shifted to the locals scene away from the Strip proper, with one-night concerts or weekend engagements replacing extended stays.

**Hilton Theater.** Once famous as the home base for Elvis Presley, this large showroom with a balcony has since been converted to theater seating. Four acts were signed as "anchor" tenants in 2003 to make sure there would always be a headliner in the room: Sheena Easton, Engelbert Humperdinck, the Smothers Brothers, and a Beatles tribute act, The Fab Four. Concert acts ranging from Wynonna Judd to Jamie Foxx come in to share the room for late shows on weekends. ⌧ *Las Vegas Hilton, 3000 Paradise Rd., Paradise Road,* ☎ *702/732–5755.*

**Hollywood Theatre.** Tom Jones, Paul Anka, and Carrot Top are among those who make regular visits to this contemporary update of the classic showroom at the MGM Grand, which eliminates the long tables to improve sight lines but keeps the booths. The sound system in the 650-seat venue is among the best in town. ⊠ *MGM Grand Hotel and Casino, 3799 Las Vegas Blvd. S, South Strip,* ☎ *702/891–7777.*

**Les Théâtre des Arts.** This beautiful theater, originally built for a failed stage musical, picked up the slack for headliners once corporate owner Park Place Entertainment decided to close the Circus Maximus at sister property Caesars Palace. The 1,200-seat auditorium hosts an array of acts, from Tony Bennett and Julio Iglesias to Earth, Wind & Fire and comedian Jay Mohr. ⊠ *Paris Las Vegas, 3655 Las Vegas Blvd. S, Center Strip,* ☎ *702/946–4567.*

**Orleans Showroom.** Theater seating and a super-wide stage (designed to lure TV production) highlight this 800-seat room slightly west of the Strip at the Orleans, which has proven popular with both locals and tourists. Frequent headliners include Neil Sedaka and Debbie Reynolds. ⊠ *Orleans Hotel and Casino, 4500 W. Tropicana Ave., West Side,* ☎ *702/365–7075.*

**Suncoast Showroom.** The Suncoast is a locals-oriented casino from the Gaughan family that built the Gold Coast and Orleans. While the latter are only a couple of miles away from the Strip, the Suncoast is a determined drive 15 mi or so west of the tourist corridor in Summerlin. A handsome 400-seat showroom with a classic old-Vegas feel was a risk that paid off, drawing strong local support for acts ranging from Tower of Power to Bobby Rydell. ⊠ *Suncoast Hotel and Casino, 9090 Alta Dr., Northwest Las Vegas,* ☎ *702/365–7075.*

**Theatre Ballroom.** The Golden Nugget once closed its upstairs cabaret, leaving downtown short on entertainment, but the cozy 400-seat room reopened in late 2000 and new tiered seating was added in early 2003, creating a classy downtown venue for both solo acts and revues such as *"Spirit of the Dance."* ⊠ *Golden Nugget Hotel and Casino, 129 Fremont St., Downtown,* ☎ *702/796–9999.*

## Strip Clubs

Strip clubs have become a cottage industry in Las Vegas, their rise paralleling the growth of the convention industry as well as their general boom nationwide. Zoning still restricts most clubs to industrial areas off the Strip, but the "upscale" trend within has caused most of them to institute cover charges of $5 to $20. The real money is made on the "table dances" continuously solicited inside. Most of them cost $20 per song.

Newer clubs seem to succeed by sacrificing their liquor license in exchange for full nudity. Let your own preferences be your guide, but remember that the Palomino Club in North Las Vegas is the only place where you can have both. Otherwise, the choice is between booze and g-strings or soft drinks and full nudity.

In 2002, two "supersize" clubs, Jaguar's and Sapphire, mirrored the grand-scale optimism of the Strip's megaresorts, putting Las Vegas' historic "Sin City" reputation to a serious test.

**Club Paradise.** Its location—directly across the street from the Hard Rock Hotel—has been a plus for this place. It was also one of the first local clubs to embrace the "gentleman's club" boom of the 1990s. Once a run-down place called the Pussycat Lounge, it renovated, changed its name, suited its bouncers in tuxedos, and put computerized lighting over the stage. ✉ *4416 Paradise Rd., Paradise Road,* ☎ *702/734–7990.*

**Jaguar's Gentlemen's Cabaret.** The Las Vegas topless club reached new heights of ambition in 2002 with the opening of this two-story, 25,000-square-foot building that claims to host 200 dancers on even an average night. A stylish interior intensifies the general "upscale" trend for these clubs. ✉ *1531 Las Vegas Blvd. S, Downtown,* ☎ *702/ 385–8987.*

**Olympic Gardens.** Right on the northern edge of the Strip, this is one of the busiest, most easily located jiggle joints in town. It was the first to install several "pod" stages to take the place of the single stage found in older clubs. ✉ *1531 Las Vegas Blvd. S, Downtown,* ☎ *702/ 385–8987.*

**Palomino Club.** One of the oldest strip clubs in the area, it is grandfathered into North Las Vegas zoning codes, which means it's allowed to have both a full bar and full nudity. The Palomino combines the generations by keeping its old "burlesque" stage downstairs, while upstairs the dancers perform on mini-platforms and solicit private dances. ✉ *1848 Las Vegas Blvd. N, North Las Vegas,* ☎ *702/642–2984.*

**Sapphire.** The owners of this club claimed to spend $26 million in late 2002 for the bragging rights of proclaiming themselves the "largest adult entertainment complex in the world." A defunct athletic club was remodeled to dedicate 40,000 square feet to topless dancing, complete with 13 second-floor "skyboxes." Dancers descend a ramp to a clear, elevated main stage that towers over the floor. ✉ *3025 S. Industrial Rd., West Side,* ☎ *702/796–6000,* WEB *www. sapphirelasvegas.com.*

# THE ARTS

While known more for theatrical spectacles than serious theater, Las Vegas does have a lively cultural scene. The groups listed below offer full seasons of productions each year. The **Allied Arts Council** (✉ 3750 S. Maryland Pkwy., East Side, ☎ 702/731–5419) can provide a detailed schedule of local theater, dance, music, and fine-arts exhibits.

## Ballet

**Nevada Ballet Theatre.** The city's longest-running fine-arts organization (this being Las Vegas, it only dates from 1973) stages three to five productions each year, anchored by an annual December presentation of *The Nutcracker.* Bruce Steivel is artistic director for the troupe, and most performances are held in UNLV's Judy Bayley Theatre. ✉ *4505 S. Maryland Pkwy., University District,* ☎ *888/388–3267 or 702/ 739–3267,* WEB *www.nevadaballet.com.*

## Classical Music

**Las Vegas Philharmonic.** Formed in 1998, the Philharmonic is conducted by Hal Weller, formerly of the Flagstaff Symphony Orchestra. The Philharmonic performs at Artemus Ham Hall on the UNLV campus. ✉ *4505 S. Maryland Pkwy., University District,* ☎ *702/258–5438 for schedule information; 888/388–3267 or 702/739–3267 for tickets.*

## Film

The second half of the 1990s saw an explosion of new multiplex construction in Las Vegas—there are 20 theaters and more than 150 screens in town, a surprising number of them attached to casinos. For the first time ever, there's even an eight-theater multiplex on the Strip. Several theaters are conveniently located.

**Boulder Cinemas** The 11-screen facility is at the Boulder Station. ⊠ *Boulder Station Hotel and Casino, 4111 Boulder Hwy., Boulder Strip,* ☎ *702/221–2283.*

**Brenden Theatres at the Palms.** The Palms took a run at the nearby Orleans by opening its own theater with 14 screens, each with stadium seating featuring rocking-chair-style seats with arm rests that can be raised to convert them into love seats. ⊠ *Palms, 4321 W. Flamingo Rd., West Side,* ☎ *702/507–4849.*

**Century 12.** The most popular theater in Las Vegas addressed its only real shortcoming when the Orleans built a parking garage in 2002. ⊠ *Orleans Hotel and Casino, 4500 W. Tropicana Ave., East Side,* ☎ *702/365–7111.*

**Century 18 Sam's Town.** Just down the road from the Boulder Station, Sam's Town has high-back seats, with alternating rows of rockers and love seats with movable arm rests. ⊠ *5111 Boulder Hwy. Boulder Strip,* ☎ *702/547–7469.*

🐾 **Crown Theatres Neonopolis.** A 14-screen theater is a major component of the struggling, $100-million Neonopolis downtown revival project. The theater does its part, with convenient underground parking, wall-to-wall screens and digital sound, with six out of 14 screens THX-certified. ⊠ *Neonopolis, First St. and Las Vegas Blvd. S, Downtown,* ☎ *702/383–9600.*

🐾 **Luxor IMAX Theatre.** Luxor has multiple daily screenings of movies created for the giant screens of the 70mm IMAX process. Films available in this format usually have appealing scientific or natural-history subjects, such as travel on a space shuttle or explorations of the Grand Canyon, but lately have expanded into more purely entertaining attractions such as the Disney films *The Lion King* and *Beauty and the Beast.* ⊠ *Luxor Resort & Casino, 3900 Las Vegas Blvd. S, South Strip,* ☎ *702/262–4000.*

**Showcase 8.** The only movie theater on the Strip is in the Showcase Mall, next to the MGM Grand. It's a great break from the slots for nearby hotel guests but the hidden parking garage is a real challenge for those who for some reason might choose to visit by car. ⊠ *3785 Las Vegas. Blvd. S, South Strip,* ☎ *702/225–4828.*

## Theater

Away from the Strip, a booming community theater scene caters to the area's many new residents, retirees in particular, who are looking for a low-cost alternative to the pricey shows. With the exception of UNLV, Las Vegas Little Theatre, and Nevada Theater Company, most don't have their own performance spaces and instead rent municipal auditoriums for their productions.

**Jade Productions.** This seniors-oriented group focuses almost exclusively on revues themed around Broadway composers or stars. ☎ *702/263–6385,* WEB *www.jadepro.com.*

**Las Vegas Little Theatre.** The focus here is on familiar titles such as Neil Simon comedies or light musicals such as *Nunsense.* ⊠ *3850 Schiff Dr., West Side,* ☎ *702/362–7996.*

**Nevada Theater Company.** This company has come on strong in recent years, moving into a former video store with more adventurous efforts such as *Psycho Beach Party.* ✉ *2928 Lake East Dr., The Lakes,* ☎ *702/873–0191.*

**University of Nevada–Las Vegas Theater Department.** UNLV brings in outside professionals and holds community-wide auditions for a full season of productions each academic year. Most performances are held in the Judy Bayley Theatre on campus. ✉ *4505 S. Maryland Pkwy., University District,* ☎ *702/647–7469 for schedule information; 888/388–3267 or 702/739–3267 for tickets.*

# 7 SPORTS & THE OUTDOORS

What makes Las Vegas a hot spot for outdoor recreation and fitness activities? More than 300 sunny days a year; a flat valley for jogging, walking, and biking surrounded by mountains for hiking, bouldering, and climbing; a fantastic collection of world-class golf courses and tennis courts; swimming in hotel pools; and boating and fishing in one of the world's great lakes. When casino hopping gets old, just step outside. A big world awaits.

THE PLAYFUL SPIRIT OF LAS VEGAS, epitomized in its casinos, is also very much alive in its sports. With more than 50 golf courses (roughly half public or semiprivate), Las Vegas hosts several prestigious tournaments that include a $1-million stop on the PGA tour. Many boxing superstars—Muhammad Ali, Sugar Ray Leonard, Thomas Hearns, George Foreman, Mike Tyson, and Evander Holyfield—have faced each other in a Las Vegas ring. Las Vegas also hosts the 51s triple-A minor-league baseball team and the Runnin' Rebels college basketball team. The Las Vegas Motor Speedway is one of the largest Indy-style racetracks in the country; every March, the Las Vegas 400, a NASCAR Winston Cup race, attracts more than 120,000 spectators to the largest sporting event held in Nevada.

*Updated by Heidi Knapp Rinella*

Most locals-oriented casinos now have world-class bowling alleys. And in how many other cities in the world can you go horseback riding in the desert in the morning, and alpine skiing in the afternoon?

## Participant Sports and Fitness

### Ballooning

Several hot-air balloon companies can take you up, up, and away in their beautiful balloons. The balloon season runs from October through April, depending on the local thermals, though some companies fly year-round. The flights start just before sunrise or sunset, when the air is stillest (you have to get up very early in the morning in the summer so as not to land too long after the sun rises). Most balloon businesses ask for reservations (held by a credit card number) a week in advance. The Las Vegas Balloon Classic, which takes place in October, attracts more than 100 balloons from all across the West.

**The Little White Chapel in the Sky.** This outfit does hot-air-balloon weddings in a 12-passenger basket (the largest basket in town). You have to plan on a three-day window for getting married, since wind conditions are so variable. A wedding package starts at $650 for the couple, with the cost rising (so to speak) from there: $150 per additional guest; $250 for photography or videotaping; and more for flowers, cake, and music. ⊠ *1301 Las Vegas Blvd. S, Downtown,* ☎ *702/382–5943.*

**Nevada High.** Champagne is included in the cost ($125 per person) of your one-hour flight with this company that emphasizes safety. They also offer instruction in flying hot-air balloons, in their balloons or yours. ☎ *702/873–8393.*

### Biking

Because the summer heat is intense, the best times to bike in this area are fall and spring. The winter is often warm enough to brave the outdoors on two wheels, but during the summer, unless you get up at first light, it's too bloody hot. Wherever you ride, whatever the season, carry lots of water.

Las Vegas Valley has a handful of good, long rides. One popular trip is the jaunt out to Red Rock Canyon on West Charleston Boulevard; it's 11 mi from the Rainbow Boulevard intersection to the Red Rock Visitors Center. The road has a good shoulder, or dedicated bike paths, the whole way. Once there, you can continue around Red Rock Canyon's moderately difficult 13-mi scenic loop (the road is one-way).

Another good ride is between the entrance to Red Rock Canyon and the city park in the small settlement of Blue Diamond, just under 8 mi south on Highway 159. The road has good shoulders and long gentle grades with flat recuperation stretches.

A third possibility is a ride out on Boulder Highway through Henderson. It's best to start east of Tropicana Avenue; there's a shoulder the whole way. If you turn around before climbing up and over Railroad Pass, the round trip is a little less than 40 mi.

Mountain biking is limited primarily to Mt. Charleston and the Bristlecone Trail, accessible at the top of the Lee Canyon ski area parking lot. It's a 6-mi loop and climbs 1,400 feet. Another popular mountain-biking locale is Cottonwood Valley. To get there, take the Blue Diamond exit off I–15 south of Las Vegas, head west for 6 mi, and turn off at the sign. You drive another ½ mi to the PACK-IN PACK-OUT sign, then ride on a 14-mi loop. Any bike store in town can give you a map to the place.

**Escape the City Streets.** A conveniently-located store that rents bikes, Escape is on West Charleston Boulevard almost halfway between downtown and Red Rock Canyon. Most folks drive to the store, park there, rent their bikes, and pedal out the rest of the way to Red Rock and back (30 mi round-trip). Bike rentals range from $28 to $50, with both hybrid bikes (fat slick tires) and mountain bikes available. For a fee, Escape will also deliver bikes to your hotel or motel and pick them up again ($12 each way). Tours are available. ✉ *8221 W. Charleston Blvd., West Side,* ☎ *702/838–6966.*

**Las Vegas Scooters.** If you don't want to pedal, rent a scooter. Rentals are available by the hour, half-day, or full day. ✉ *3735 Las Vegas Blvd. S, South Strip,* ☎ *702/736–8633.*

## Boating

★ **Lake Mead National Recreation Area.** All water sports in the Las Vegas area are centered on Lake Mead. The entrance fee of $5 per vehicle is good for five days, and there are lake use fees of $10 per vessel. ☎ 702/293–8907, WEB *www.nps.gov/lame.*

OUTFITTERS & INFORMATION

**Get It Wet.** You can rent personal watercraft such as small motorboats (complete with water-skiing equipment), Jet Skis, and inner tubes here. ✉ *661 W. Lake Mead Dr., Henderson,* ☎ *702/558–7547.*

**Lake Mead Resort and Marina** A variety of motorboats (and water-ski equipment) are available for rent by the hour or day. ✉ *322 Lakeshore Rd., Boulder City,* ☎ *702/293–3484.*

## Bowling

Bowling (and movie theaters) have gone from a novelty to something that locals almost expect at an off-Strip casino. Several casinos have bowling facilities that are open 24 hours a day. And as most facilities were built since the mid-'90s, they include the most up-to-date equipment (automatic scoring, video score screens, and the like), shoe rental, a pro shop, a snack shop, a bar and lounge, and cocktail service. At most places the prices are the same all the time, though at one or two the prices rise a nickel or dime a game on weekends. It's a good idea to call for public bowling hours before you go, since bowling leagues are a major rage in Las Vegas, and the alleys can be closed to the public for hours at a time, especially on weekday evenings.

**The Castaways Hotel & Bowling Center.** With 106 lanes, this is the world's largest bowling alley. (Although given its size, it is surprisingly quiet.) Its pseudo-tropics atmosphere is a charming throwback to another era. ✉ *2800 E. Fremont St., Boulder Strip,* ☎ *702/385–9153.*

**Orleans.** The Orleans is in a working-class neighborhood, and its 70-lane bowling center sees lots of traffic, but its not-far-off-the-Strip location also makes it a popular spot for visitors. ⊠ *4500 W. Tropicana Rd., West Side,* ☎ *702/365–7111.*

**Santa Fe Station.** Santa Fe Station is a locals casino, but it's one of the area's most polished, and that's reflected in its bowling center. The 60-lane bowling facility has the Frameworx scoring system, which has an instant-replay function. ⊠ *4949 N. Rancho Dr., Rancho Strip,* ☎ *702/658–4995.*

**The Suncoast.** Reflecting its upscale Summerlin neighborhood, the bowling center at the Suncoast, with 64 lanes, is designed to provide every high-tech toy for bowlers. ⊠ *9090 Alta Dr., Northwest Las Vegas,* ☎ *702/636–7400.*

★ **Texas Station.** This 60 lane-alley was the first to declare itself a nightclub hybrid, adding fancy lights and a booming sound system for a "cosmic bowling" concept that's since been initiated at the Gold Coast and Suncoast as well. It draws a youngish crowd, so if you like to party while you bowl, this one is for you. ⊠ *2101 Texas Star La., Rancho Strip,* ☎ *702/631–1000.*

## Fishing

**Floyd Lamb State Park.** Tule Lake is a good place to catch rainbow trout (summer) and catfish (winter). The park is open 8 AM–7 PM in summer, until 5 in winter. ⊠ *9200 Tule Springs Rd., North Las Vegas,* ☎ *702/486–5413.*

**Lake Mead.** Fish for largemouth and striped bass, channel catfish, crappie, bluegill, and various types of trout. The lake is stocked with a half-million rainbow trout regularly, and at least a million fish are harvested every year. You can fish here 24 hours a day, year-round (except for posted closings). If you plan to catch and keep trout, be mindful that a trout stamp is required. Nevada nonresident licenses are $12 a day or $51 for the year. ⊠ *Write to 601 Nevada Hwy., Boulder City 89005,* ☎ *702/293–8907 or 702/293–8990.*

**Lorenzi Park.** A good spot to cast your line in Las Vegas itself is the pond at Lorenzi Park, which is stocked with rainbow trout in the winter and channel catfish during the spring and summer; the park is open 7 AM–11 PM. ⊠ *3333 Washington Ave., West Side,* ☎ *702/229–6297.*

### OUTFITTERS & INFORMATION

**Blue Lake Bait and Tackle.** Sure you're going fishing, but you can't snag 'em with patience alone. Stop here for bait and lures sure to entice the elusive denizens of Lake Mead. ⊠ *5485 E. Lake Mead Blvd., Las Vegas,* ☎ *702/452–8299.*

**Las Vegas Fly Fishing Club.** Desert fishermen are a special breed. Contact the Las Vegas Fly Fishing Club for more information on fishing in the Las Vegas area. ⊠ *Box 27958, Las Vegas, NV 89126-1958,* ☎ *702/451–9296.*

**Sandy Cove Bait Store.** You'll know you're getting close to the lake when you reach the Sandy Cove and see rods, reels, bait, and other fishing supplies in the middle of all that desert sand. ⊠ *5225 E. Lake Mead Blvd., East Side,* ☎ *702/459–2080.*

## Golf

With an average of 315 days of sunshine a year and year-round access, Las Vegas's top sports recreation is golf. It's no accident that there are over 50 golf courses in the Las Vegas area and more opening every year. The peak season is from October through May. In May through October only mad dogs and Englishmen are out in the noonday sun, and early-morning starting times are most heavily in demand.

Reservations for tee times can be made up to a week in advance (one or two days are sufficient at some courses, and a select few allow reservations up to three months in advance). Starting times for same-day play are possible, but you're given the first available time. All courses have pros, pro shops, practice facilities, club rentals, and clubhouses. Watch out for the hustlers who hang around the resort courses looking for an easy mark.

The legendary Desert Inn Golf Course isn't scheduled to re-open until fall 2004, as part of the Wynn Las Vegas hotel-casino project. But don't despair; the Strip still has an 18-hole course—the two-year-old Bali Hai Golf Club, just south of Mandalay Bay. There are many courses in the city and on its outskirts, and more scattered around Summerlin, Henderson, Boulder City, Primm, and Lake Las Vegas. Most hotel concierges will help you reserve tee times.

★ **Angel Park.** The municipal course is an intensely popular Arnold Palmer–designed layout. There are four courses here: two 18-hole courses, an 18-hole natural grass putting course, and a par-3 lighted course. The latter, the 12-hole Cloud Nine, replicates a dozen of the world's most famous par-3 holes; nine holes are lighted for night play (hence the name). Call two months prior to set up your tee times, as this place fills up fast. Fees range from $135 to $160. ⊠ *100 S. Rampart Blvd., West Side,* ☎ *702/254–4653.*

**Bali Hai Golf Club.** Inspired by the South Pacific, the 18-hole Bali Hai, with its 2,500 palm trees and 7 acres of water, is reminiscent of a tropical island. The entrance is a mere 10-minute walk from Mandalay Bay—making it the only course within easy walking distance of the Strip. The clubhouse comes complete with a pro shop, restaurant, and a bevy of tropical plants to round out the tropical-paradise theme. Hefty greens fees begin at $250 mid-week, going up to $295 on weekends; ask about twilight specials that start at $150. ⊠ *5150 Las Vegas Blvd. S, South Strip,* ☎ *702/450–8000.*

**Black Mountain Golf and Country Club.** With two large lakes and spectacular desert landscaping, the 40-year-old, 27-hole Black Mountain is a good place for beginners. Fees range from $30 to $100. ⊠ *500 Greenway Rd., Henderson,* ☎ *702/565–7933.*

**Calloway Golf Center.** The 42-acre golf training facility offers instruction, a 110-station driving range, and a 9-hole par-3 course. At Calloway, fees go from $25 to $45. ⊠ *6730 Las Vegas Blvd. S, South Strip,* ☎ *702/896–4100.*

**Craig Ranch.** This 50-year-old public course is short (6,000 yards, par 70) and narrow, with 7,000 trees. It's also the most inexpensive course in Las Vegas, a mere $19 to walk 18 holes ($28 to ride). ⊠ *628 W. Craig Rd., North Las Vegas,* ☎ *702/642–9700.*

**Desert Pines Golf Club.** This 18-hole traditional course has many trees and a good deal of water. Fees range from $90 to $135. ⊠ *315 E. Bonanza Rd., East Side,* ☎ *702/366–1616.*

**Desert Rose Golf Course.** Joe Lee and Dick Wilson, who also designed the Doral, originally designed this 40-year-old municipal course, which was re-designed in the mid-'80s by Jim Colbert. It has a driving range, three putting and chipping greens, a restaurant, and a snack bar. Non-Nevada residents pay $69; or you could take advantage of the twilight rate of $49 offered four hours before sunset. ⊠ *5483 Clubhouse Dr., East Side,* ☎ *702/431–4653.*

**Las Vegas Golf Club.** Established in 1949, this is the oldest golf course in Las Vegas. It's a mature course with lots of trees (though little water). Many local tournaments are sponsored by this popular club, one of three Las Vegas municipal courses. The championship layout is 6,630 yards, par 72. There's a lighted driving range, putting green, restaurant, and snack bar. Non-residents pay upwards of $69 for 18 holes. ⊠ *4300 Las Vegas Dr., West Side,* ☎ *702/646–3003.*

**Painted Desert Golf Course.** The eighth hole at this 18-hole course designed by architect Jay Morrish is challenging. Fees range from $80 to $100. ⊠ *5555 Painted Mirage Rd., Northwest Las Vegas,* ☎ *702/ 645–2568.*

**Reflection Bay Golf Club.** Fifteen miles from the Strip and minutes from the Hyatt resort, the Jack Nicklaus–designed Reflection Bay has a beautiful location fronting Lake Las Vegas, with 10 mi of lakefront beach. La Chandele Restaurant in the elegant clubhouse has a large patio overlooking the lake. If you're staying at the Hyatt Lake Las Vegas Resort or the Ritz-Carlton, Lake Las Vegas, you may reserve your tee times up to three months in advance and get discounted fees. Regular fees are $250. ⊠ *75 MonteLago Blvd., Henderson,* ☎ *702/740–4653.*

**Shadow Creek Golf Club.** This $52-million club is owned by MGM Mirage. One of the most exclusive golf courses in the country, it is a stomping ground for high-caliber celebrities and high rollers. Contrary to popular belief, mere mortals *can* get one of 6 to 12 daily tee times here—if they're staying at any of the MGM Mirage resorts. A round of 18 holes costs $500 and includes a personal caddie and round-trip limo transfers. Check with your concierge at the following hotels: MGM Grand, New York–New York, the Mirage, Golden Nugget, Bellagio, and Treasure Island. ⊠ *3 Shadow Creek Dr., North Las Vegas,* ☎ *702/791–7111.*

**TPC/The Tournament Players Club at the Canyons.** The PGA manages this 18-hole championship lay-out complete with elevation changes, steep ravines, and a canyon lake. Fees range from $130 to $240. ⊠ *9851 Canyon Dr., Summerlin,* ☎ *702/256–2000.*

## Health Clubs

Most big hotels have health clubs, and most charge hefty admission fees, even for guests. **Bally's, Caesars, Flamingo, Harrah's, Imperial Palace,** and the **Riviera** have separate facilities for men and women; the **Las Vegas Hilton, Luxor, Mandalay Bay, MGM Grand, Monte Carlo,** and **Tropicana** are coed. All of the above are open to the public; hotel guests and nonguests pay the same fee, generally $10–$25 per day. The health club at the Bellagio is for hotel guests only, and even then the daily fee is $25.

**Las Vegas Athletic Club.** There are four facilities around the city. Each offers large and clean workout areas and plenty of equipment, along with racquetball courts, indoor pools, big Jacuzzis, coed steam rooms, saunas, Nautilus and free weights, aerobics classes, tanning, massage, and snack bars. The fee is $15 per day or $35 per week. ⊠ *1070 E. Sahara Ave., East Side,* ☎ *702/733–1919;* ⊠ *5090 S. Maryland Pkwy., East Side,* ☎ *702/795–2582;* ⊠ *3830 E. Flamingo Rd., East Side,* ☎ *702/451–2526;* ⊠ *5200 W. Sahara Ave., West Side,* ☎ *702/364–5822.*

## Hiking & Walking

You do a lot of walking in Las Vegas. The distance from one end of the Strip to the other looks deceptively short on a map, but it's 4 mi from Stratosphere at the north end to Mandalay Bay at the south end. Though the terrain is perfectly flat, often you're not wearing proper footwear, or the sun is more ferocious than you think, or the wind is whipping harder than you realize, and usually the distances are farther than you bargained for. Fatigue, overheating, and blisters are common on the Strip. Be prepared for walking more than you're used to during your Las Vegas visit: train a little before you arrive, bring comfortable walking shoes (and moleskin), and either carry water and snacks, or remember to buy them along the way.

For dyed-in-the-wool hikers and climbers, Las Vegas is a year-round draw. Within an hour of the city center are literally hundreds of trails, paths, and bouldering routes around Red Rock Canyon, Lake Mead National Recreation Area, Valley of Fire State Park, and Mt. Charleston Wilderness Area. Where you wind up hiking, bushwhacking, bouldering, and/or climbing usually depends on the season.

The best books on hiking in the area are *Hiking Las Vegas* and *Hiking Southern Nevada,* both by local mountain man Branch Whitney and both published by local publishing company Huntington Press (☎ 800/244–2224 WEB www.huntingtonpress.com.). Each book contains 60 trails located within 60 minutes of the Las Vegas Strip; there are hikes for everyone from rank beginners to mountain goats.

★ **Mt. Charleston.** In summer, hikers escape the heat by traveling 45 minutes up to Mt. Charleston where the U.S. Forest Service maintains more than 50 mi of marked hiking trails for all abilities. Trails range from ¼-mi long (the Robber's Roost and Bristlecone Loop trails) to the extremely strenuous 10-mi North Loop Trail, which reaches the Mt. Charleston summit at 11,918 feet; the elevation gain is 3,500 feet. There are also plenty of intermediate trails, along with marathon two-, three-, four-, and five-peak routes only for hikers who are highly advanced (and in peak physical condition). The Mt. Charleston Wilderness Area is part of the Toiyabe National Forest; for information, contact the U. S. Forest Service (✉ 2881 S. Valley View Blvd., Suite 16, Las Vegas, NV 89103, ☎ 702/873–8800, WEB www.fs.fed.us).

🐾 **Red Rock Canyon Recreation Area.** In winter, when downhill and cross-country skiing are the outdoor activities of choice on Mt. Charleston, hikers head to Red Rock, which encompasses 197,000 acres of Bureau of Land Management recreation lands. Like Mt. Charleston hiking, Red Rock Canyon hiking runs the gamut from short discovery trails for children to all-day routes up the sandstone to various mountain peaks. Note that there are only 35 mi of maintained trails at Red Rock, and it's extremely easy to get lost; search-and-rescue teams, including helicopters, are dispatched regularly to find lost hikers. People are also hurt or killed occasionally in falls. It's imperative to know where you're going (and how to get back!) and what you're doing before you set out to conquer the Aztec sandstone of Red Rock Canyon. Make sure someone else knows where you're going, and when you're expected to return, as well. For guided group hikes in Red Rock Canyon, contact the Southern Nevada chapter of the **Sierra Club** (☎ 702/392–7136). ✉ *W. Charleston Blvd., West Side,* ☎ *702/363–1922,* WEB *www.redrockcanyon.blm.gov.*

## Horseback Riding

★ 🐾 **Bonnie Springs Ranch.** A little past Red Rock Canyon (18 mi from the Strip), Bonnie Springs offers one-hour guided rides at the base of the Spring Mountains, within the canyon. The rides cover 3–4 mi round-trip and cost $25. The ranch also offers a four-hour excursion to see wild horses for $130, including meal; and a sunset ride for $135, including meal. Note that no children under 6 are allowed. ✉ *1 Bonnie Springs Ranch Rd., West Side,* ☎ *702/875–4191.* ⊙ *Rides set out at*

*9, 10:15, 11:30, 12:45, 2, and 3:15. Two rides are added during the summer months at 4:30 PM and 5:45 PM.*

**Sagebrush Ranch.** Sagebrush offers one- and two-hour guided rides as well as breakfast and dinner trail rides. The one-hour ride is $25, the two-hour ride is $50. The breakfast ride includes a big hot meal cooked and served around a campfire ($99); dinner is an all-you-can-eat steak feast ($139). The ranch caters to families, and riding helmets are provided. The rides head up into the Spring Mountains, where the landscape looks like something straight out of a John Wayne movie. ⊠ *12000 West Ann Rd., North Las Vegas,* ☎ *702/645–9422.*

## Jogging

You can spot many joggers at dusk on the wide sidewalks south of the Mandalay Bay, running parallel to the airport and the Bali Hai golf course. However, it gets noisy on the boulevard and somewhat polluted. A little calmer are the jogging trails that run around the Las Vegas Hilton. The most pleasant time to hit the streets of Las Vegas, especially in the hot months, is early in the morning. You can also jog at Red Rock Canyon: the 2-mi Moenkopi Loop begins and ends at the Visitors Center; the Willow Springs Trail is a 3-mi circuit.

**University of Nevada–Las Vegas.** Your best bet for jogging in Las Vegas is UNLV's regulation track (Bill Cosby's favorite hangout when in town), from which you can see the Strip in the distance as you run without inhaling exhaust fumes. ⊠ *4505 S. Maryland Pkwy., University District,* ☎ *702/739–3011.*

## Racquetball

Several places in Las Vegas have racquetball courts that are open to the public for a fee.

**Las Vegas Athletic Club.** There are courts at this and four other locations; the fee is $15 per day for non-members or you can pay a weekly fee of $35 if you plan to play more than once. This Athletic Club is open 24 hours a day and the other three are open 7 AM to 8 PM. ⊠ *1070 E. Sahara Ave., East Side,* ☎ *702/733–1919.*

**YMCA.** The local branch issues daily passes for its facilities including a jogging track. Passes are $10. ⊠ *4141 Meadows La., West Side,* ☎ *702/877–7200.*

## Rafting

Black Canyon, just below Hoover Dam, is the place for river running near Las Vegas. You can launch a raft here on the Colorado River year-round. The 11-mi run to Willow Beach on the Arizona side is reminiscent of rafting the Grand Canyon, with its vertical canyon walls, bighorn sheep on the slopes, and feeder streams and waterfalls coming off the bluffs. The water flows at roughly 5 mph, but some rapids, eddies, and whirlpools can cause difficulties, as can head winds, especially for inexperienced rafters.

**U.S. Bureau of Reclamation.** If you want to go rafting in Black Canyon on your own, you must apply for a $5 permit. Permits are issued immediately. The bureau will also send a list of guides and outfitters. Launches take place every morning at 8:30 AM and 10 AM. ⊠ *Box 60400, Boulder City, NV 89006,* ☎ *702/293–8204.*

## Rock Climbing

★ **Red Rock Canyon Recreation Area.** The best places to climb in the area are among the Calico Hills in Red Rock Canyon. This is a year-round international rock-climbing destination, with more than 1,500 known routes up the sandstone-limestone escarpment (Todd Swain's *Red*

*Rocks Select* details many of them). There is a $5 per vehicle entrance fee to the park. ⊠ *W. Charleston Blvd., West Side,* ☎ *702/515–5138,* WEB *www.redrockcanyon.blm.gov.*

OUTFITTERS & INFORMATION

**Desert Rocks Sports.** Indoor and outdoor equipment are available, and the knowledgeable salespeople will happily advise you on routes. ⊠ *8201 W. Charleston Blvd., West Side,* ☎ *702/254–1143.*

**Powerhouse Climbing Center.** Beginner to advanced rock climbers hone their climbing skills indoors on these simulated rock walls. ⊠ *8201 W. Charleston Blvd., West Side,* ☎ *702/254–5604.*

★ **Sky's the Limit.** Half-day ($180) and full-day ($280) private lessons or private guided hikes are available; Sky's the Limit also has two-day classes ($260). All equipment is provided. Sky's the Limit also has the largest indoor climbing facility in the state. ☎ *702/363–4533.*

## Swimming

Most hotels and motels have outdoor pools that are open from about mid-March through October. While hotel pools used to be an afterthought, they've been getting better and better in recent years. The pool at the Flamingo, for example, is actually a series of pools connected by water slides, and Mandalay Bay's pool has a beach. Other cool pools are at the Hard Rock Hotel, the Palms, Caesars Palace, the Tropicana, Bellagio, the Mirage, and the MGM Grand. For lake swimming, make the 30-mi drive to Lake Mead.

**Public Pools.** There are several in town; two are conveniently located for visitors. **Baker Swimming Pool** (⊠ 1100 E. St. Louis Ave., East Side, ☎ 702/229–6395) is open June through August. The **Municipal Pool** (⊠ 430 E. Bonanza Rd., Downtown, ☎ 702/229–6309), built in the late '90s, is open year-round and is a reasonable walk from Fremont Street hotels.

**YMCA.** The Y is across the street from the large Meadows Mall and has a full-size indoor pool with separate children's pool. It reciprocates with YMCA memberships in other cities. ⊠ *4141 Meadows La., West Side,* ☎ *702/877–7200.*

## Tennis

Las Vegas has an abundance of tennis courts, many of them lighted for evening play. The Flamingo, New Frontier, MGM Grand, and Riviera have tennis courts where the public is welcome, though hotel guests take priority. At the New Frontier, there is no charge for hotel guests.

**Bally's Casino Resort.** Eight courts are open to the public for a $10–$15 (per hour, per person) court fee. ⊠ *3645 Las Vegas Blvd. S, Center Strip,* ☎ *702/739–4111.*

**Sunset Park.** Court rentals are $3 per person per hour during the day, $5 per person per hour at night. Racket stringing, sales, and other supplies also are available. ⊠ *2601 E. Sunset Rd., East Side,* ☎ *702/455–8200 or 702/260–9803.*

# Spectator Sports

## Baseball

★ **Las Vegas 51s.** The triple-A Pacific Coast League team used to be the Las Vegas Stars. But when the parent team switched from the San Diego Padres to the Los Angeles Dodgers, the team adopted a more distinctive and publicity-generating name, taken from nearby Area 51, rumored home of UFO and mysterious military activity. The 51s play at

Cashman Field (✉ 850 Las Vegas Blvd. N, Downtown), the field where professional baseball made its Las Vegas debut in 1983. ☏ 702/386–7200.

## Basketball

**Runnin' Rebels.** The hottest tickets in town during the school year were once the basketball games of the former NCAA champions at the University of Nevada–Las Vegas. But since head coach Jerry Tarkanian was fired in the early 1990s, the Rebels—and their ticket sales—have cooled off considerably. Charlie Spoonhour coached the 2002–03 season. Games take place at the **Thomas and Mack Center** (✉ 4505 S. Maryland Pkwy., University District) on the UNLV campus. ☏ 702/739–3267.

## Bowling

**Castaways Invitational Bowling Tournament.** The Professional Bowling Association's oldest competition takes place in Las Vegas at the **Castaways Hotel and Casino** every January.

## Boxing

Championship boxing came to Las Vegas in 1960, when Benny Paret took the welterweight title from Don Jordan at the Las Vegas Convention Center. Since then most of boxing's superstars have fought here. A title match draws the well-heeled and the well-known from all fields—and brings out the high roller in everyone. Spectators willingly fork over $200 to $1,500 a seat to watch two guys pummel each other, then hang around the casinos laying down chips for the rest of the evening, sometimes for the rest of the week. Major fights are usually held at Mandalay Bay, Caesars Palace, the MGM Grand or the Thomas and Mack Center. To learn about upcoming boxing events, look for the fight odds posted in the race and sports book of any casino.

**Caesars Palace.** For the most comprehensive fight listings, check Caesars' Web site ᴡᴇʙ *www.caesarspalace.com.*

## Football

**Las Vegas Gladiators.** The Gladiators, an arena football team, play home games at the **Thomas and Mack Center** (✉ 4505 S. Maryland Pkwy., University District). ☏ 702/739–3267.

**Runnin' Rebels.** Spectator interest couldn't have been lower for UNLV's Division 1A, Mountain West Conference football team during the years when the men's basketball team was a national power. But spectator interest shifted somewhat to the football Rebels when John Robinson came on board as coach. Home games are held at **Sam Boyd Stadium** (✉ 7000 E. Russell Rd., East Side). ☏ 702/739–3267.

## Golf

★ **Las Vegas Invitational.** October brings this annual golf tournament, with top PGA golfers competing for high stakes. Now that the Desert Inn is closed, the tournament is held at the Tournament Players Club at Summerlin, Southern Highlands and Tournament Players Club at the Canyons. ☏ 702/242–3000.

## Rodeo

★ **National Finals of Rodeo.** When the rodeo comes to town in December, the casinos showcase country stars and the fans sport Western gear. The NFR, said to be the Super Bowl of professional rodeo, offers more than $2 million in prize money. It is held at the Thomas and Mack Center on the UNLV campus. ☏ 702/895–3011.

# 8 SHOPPING

Like most other experiences in Las Vegas, shopping here scales the heights and plumbs the depths. The square footage in the Forum Shops at Caesars is the most valuable retail real estate in the country; bring two credit cards to buy any one thing. On the other hand, all the Elvis clocks and gambling-chip toilet seats you never wanted to see are available in a hundred tacky gift shops.

**S**HOPPING IN LAS VEGAS IS SO FUN and so rich in world-class options rivaling New York, London, or Rome, that you'll start to think those darn casinos only get in the way of your shopping safaris. Choices run the gamut from Elvis memorabilia, such as a piece of his pillowcase, to the jewelry from Cartier and Yves St. Laurent.

Revised and updated by Lenore Greiner

Strip shopping malls take their themes to extremes: you can stroll along a Venice canal at the Venetian or traverse North African trade routes at the Aladdin. Most Strip hotels offer expensive dresses, swimsuits, jewelry, and menswear; almost all have shops offering logo merchandise for the hotel or its latest show. Inside the casinos the gifts are elegant and expensive. Outside, all the Elvis clocks and gambling-chip toilet seats you never wanted to see are available in the tacky gift shops. Beyond the Strip, Vegas shopping encompasses such extremes as a couture ball gown in a vintage store and, in a Western store, a fine pair of Tony Lamas leftover from the town's cowboy days. Shoppers looking for more practical items can head for neighborhood malls, supermarkets, shopping centers, and specialty stores. And to avoid the stratospheric prices on the Strip, shoppers not averse to driving a bit can find the same high-ticket items at lower prices at the town's factory outlet malls.

## Shopping Neighborhoods

### South Strip

The south end of the Strip, from the famous and much-photographed WELCOME TO LAS VEGAS sign to the always traffic-filled Tropicana Avenue, offers fewer chances to max out your credit card than the Strip's center. However, like slot machines and free drinks, places to spend your money can be found just about anywhere in Vegas—if you know where to look. On the east side of this section of the Strip you'll find gas stations, tourist centers, fast-food restaurants, and a few incidental motels and casinos. Prime examples of Vegas's theme and upscale resorts, **Mandalay Bay** and **Luxor,** inhabit the west side. At the intersection of Tropicana Avenue and Las Vegas Boulevard, informally known as the Four Corners, four major hotels are visual juxtapositions of old and new Vegas. The **Excalibur** and **Tropicana** refuse to yield to the encroachment of the newer, slicker properties; they face, respectively, **New York–New York,** with its big-city spires and mini Brooklyn Bridge, and the **MGM Grand,** with its emerald-green building and brass lion. North of the MGM Grand, the **Showcase Mall** offers sweet temptations.

The hotels occupying the south end of the Strip offer the typical upscale shops found in most of the major hotels, albeit with different themes and ambiences. You can easily spend outrageous sums on clothes, jewelry, luggage, and other luxury items. Mandalay Bay has stores, expensive restaurants, an art gallery, and a gourmet coffee shop. A must-see store is the **Bali Trading Company;** reminiscent of a market you might find on a South Seas island, it offers an assortment of unusual gifts. As long as you're at Mandalay Bay, don't miss the chance to see the **House of Blues.** The outside of the restaurant and bar is made up of eye-popping "garbage" art: everything from bottle caps to mirror shards has been used to create its eclectic exterior. Buy music, books, hot sauce, and T-shirts at the souvenir shop. **Mandalay Place,** a mall with 36 stores and four restaurants, will form a skybridge between Mandalay Bay and Luxor. As this book went to press, the opening was scheduled for late 2003. A free tram runs between Mandalay Bay, Luxor, and Excalibur.

Talking camels greet you at the entrance of the **Giza Galleria** at Luxor. The galleria shops are worth a look-see, especially the **Treasure Chamber,** where you can purchase real Egyptian artifacts, and the **Cairo Bazaar,** designed to look like an open market with canvas-covered carts of merchandise. Upstairs from the Luxor casino is a faux mini-city with the inevitable souvenir shops. A walkway takes you from the Mideast to the medieval—the Excalibur. While most of the retail offerings here aren't too noteworthy, it's worth a trip to the castle to visit **Merlin's Mystic Shoppe.** This store, just after the indoor walkway to the Luxor, has the benign (key chains) and the bizarre (a toilet-brush holder in the shape of a skull).

The Tropicana offers very little shopping fun. New York–New York does not measure up to its namesake, but does have some places to shop and eat in **SoHo Village** and on the second floor mezzanine. The MGM Grand's cavernous **Studio Walk** includes more places to eat than places to shop, but more stores can be found at the lower-level **Star Lane Shops.**

## Center Strip

The best shopping on the Strip can be found in its mid-section, from Harmon Avenue to Spring Mountain Road. Here are some of the most extravagant shopping experiences in the world. Where else on earth can you explore exotic North African bazaars, stroll through a Parisian shopping lane, cross the street to visit the elegant boutiques of international designers, then traverse the short distance to ancient Rome?

Occupying corners of the intersection of Flamingo Road and Las Vegas Boulevard, **Bellagio** and **Caesars Palace** create a shopper's dream of shoes, handbags, evening wear, jewelry, art, and more—all within a two-block radius. Not many Strip hotels can compete with the posh **Via Bellagio** promenade. Shoppers at Bellagio enjoy a nearly child-free spending spree: no children under the age of 18, except those of registered hotel guests, are allowed on the property. Caesars rules the retail market with the **Forum Shops at Caesars** and **The Appian Way** that include everything from lingerie to linguine.

Just south of this power duo, the battle for your gold card continues. The 13 shops of **Le Boulevard** at **Paris Las Vegas** mimic a Continental shopping excursion. However, Paris's next-door neighbor, the **Desert Passage at the Aladdin,** presents an exotic experience, almost beating out the changing-sky ceiling and animatronic shows at the Forum Shops at Caesars. The Desert Passage, with over 130 retail shops and 11 restaurants, reconstructs the ancient trade routes through Spain, North Africa, India, a port on the Arabian Sea, and a mysterious Lost City.

Across the Strip and just north of the **Monte Carlo Resort Hotel and Casino** stands a convenient **CVS Pharmacy** that's open 24 hours like the rest of the Strip. Here, you can develop photos or buy a show ticket as well as fill a prescription.

A mile north of the Flamingo Road intersection, on the corner of Sands Avenue and Las Vegas Boulevard, are the sumptuous **Grand Canal Shoppes** at the **Venetian.** The usual assortment of stores can be found just south at **Harrah's,** but the hotel also has a nice outdoor mall with a Ghirardelli's chocolate store, a liquor store (one of the few on the Strip), a deli, and lots of places to sit. Concerts and other events are held on the covered stage.

Across the street from the Venetian, the **Mirage** and **Treasure Island (TI)** have a smattering of shops. Visiting TI is more fun; not only do you get to see a pirate battle, but the shops have names such as **The Candy Reef, Damsels,** and **Captain Kids.** On the corner of Spring Mountain Road and the Strip is the **Fashion Show Mall.** The two-story building contains 250 retail shops, including eight department stores.

## North Strip

The Fashion Show Mall marks the end of serious mall shopping, but lots of little places along the last stretch of the Strip offer cheap and varied Las Vegas souvenirs such as key chains, shot glasses, and magnets. For one-stop souvenir shopping, go to **Bonanza,** the "World's Largest Gift Shop," at the corner of Sahara Avenue. As for hotel shops, other than the regular logo gift stores and newspaper stands, choices are limited. **Circus Circus** has a 40,000-square-foot promenade with the usual eateries and souvenir shops.

Shopping opportunities grow sparse between Sahara Avenue and downtown Las Vegas. Past the Stratosphere Hotel you'll end up among Vegas's seedier establishments: small motels, pawn shops, bail bond offices, and adult video stores. The older, stand-alone wedding chapels also populate this end of Las Vegas Boulevard. If you're close by and need film, money, or a quick meal, **Walgreens, Wells Fargo,** and fast food establishments are located just before Charleston Boulevard.

## Paradise Road

The **Deep Space 9 Promenade** in the **Las Vegas Hilton's** *Star Trek Experience* has a collection of Star Trek souvenir shops, including the **Admiral Collection** where you can buy actual props from the Star Trek television shows. Pick up a Vulcan lute or the same phaser Captain Kirk screamed into. High-rollers take note—Klingon warrior uniforms cost only $12,000.

## Downtown

The **Fremont Street Experience** is a four-block downtown pedestrian mall covered by a spectacular canopy featuring 2.1 million lights. Do a little shopping in hotel-casinos that line the street, or browse the kiosks scattered throughout the outdoor mall for trinkets, jewelry, T-shirts, and more. Depending on your beverage preferences, you can get gourmet coffee or a half-yard of beer (the beer is cheaper and it's served in a tall hard-plastic glass that makes a nifty souvenir). For a one-of-a-kind shopping experience, visit Fremont Street during the nightly light-and-sound shows. The shows begin at 6 PM and continue every hour on the hour until midnight. But don't expect to chat while you browse—the accompanying music reaches near-deafening volume.

## Maryland Parkway

Travel in either direction on any of the major streets that intersect Las Vegas Boulevard and you'll find a number of neighborhood strip malls with grocery, department, and specialty stores. However, a mile east of the Strip is a shopping destination popular with locals: Maryland Parkway. The best shopping areas are at the intersections of Maryland Parkway with Flamingo Road and with Tropicana Avenue, where there are numerous strip malls and lots and lots of stores, including national chains such as **Big & Tall, Best Buy, Marshalls, Target,** and **Tower Records.** There is also a diverse group of businesses across from the **University of Nevada–Las Vegas** campus, on Maryland Parkway between Flamingo Road and Tropicana Avenue. Most of these places appeal to young college students: you can pick up vintage fashions at **Buffalo Exchange,** buy gourmet coffee, grab a burger or taco, rent a video, make copies, drink beer, and even get a tattoo. One of Nevada's largest malls, **Boulevard Mall,** is at the corner of Maryland Parkway and Desert Inn Road.

## Chinatown Plaza

On Spring Mountain Boulevard (about 2 mi west of the Fashion Show Mall), just off Valley View Boulevard, the two-story **Chinatown Plaza** shopping center is made up of restaurants, Asian food markets, gift shops, art stores, jewelers, and florists. Check out the **Snack House** for Asian delectables and unusual drink concoctions.

## Sunset Road & Green Valley Parkway, Henderson

Henderson is one of the fastest-growing cities in Nevada. Minutes away from the Strip, it offers big-time shopping in a small-town atmosphere. In the last three years the popularity of the area around the intersection of Sunset Road and Green Valley Parkway has resulted in the addition of two hotels, three restaurants, and a bank. To get to this trendy little spot, go south on Las Vegas Boulevard until you reach Sunset Road. Turn east and travel about 5 mi. Several shopping centers line either side of the street; stop and shop if you want, or keep driving until you reach Green Valley Parkway. Before the stoplight, on the left side, is a small shopping center with an **Albertson's** grocery store as well as an assortment of eating establishments and shops, including **Alligator Soup,** a gift and card shop. After the stoplight, on the right side of the street, is **Green Valley Plaza.** It has numerous stores, including **Agave,** which has hand-blown glass and other unique gifts; and **Natural Clothing Co.,** which sells imported clothing and jewelry. You'll also find **Trader Joe's,** a huge gourmet foods store, an inexpensive all-you-can-eat Chinese food buffet, and a discount shop where greeting cards are half the regular price.

On the left side of Sunset Road is **Town Center.** This complex includes a movie theater, several restaurants, a pet store, ice-cream parlors, and a grocery store. The front center of the complex has an outdoor seating area; in the summer, outdoor concerts, and other events are held here. A fountain with dancing spigots of water entertains tired shoppers. Several fast-food chains dot both sides of Sunset Road. The street officially ends at the next stoplight, but if you travel through it you'll enter a series of business complexes. Turn left at the first "street" and then right at the stoplight to find **Ethel M. Chocolates Factory,** Henderson's most popular store.

## Sunset Road & Stephanie Street, Henderson

In Henderson, the corner of Sunset Road and Stephanie Street offers scads of shopping options in a fairly new area. On North Stephanie Street, you'll find lots of fast-food places and chain restaurants, but you can also get fresh bread and meats at **Wild Oats,** an upscale gourmet grocery. There's a nice **Barnes and Noble** bookstore sharing space with a **Starbucks.** And you'll find many national chain stores such as **Petco, Ross Dress for Less, Old Navy, Circuit City,** and **Target. Galleria At Sunset,** a two-story mall with more than 130 stores, occupies the northeast corner of Sunset Road and Stephanie Street. Across the street from the mall is a favorite locals hotel-casino, Sunset Station, which has a movie theater, child care, and several eateries. If you continue east, you'll see delis, casinos, boutiques, pawn shops, clothing stores, and Highway 95 (take the highway north to return to the Strip). For a more unusual shopping experience, head for **Ron Lee's World of Clowns** (south on Stephanie Street to Warm Springs Road, turn left).

# Malls & Department Stores

★ **Appian Way at Caesars.** Not to be confused with The Forum Shops at Caesars, these marble halls are centered around an exact replica of Michelangelo's David in Carrera marble. The upscale shops include **Cartier; Cottura,** the only Italian ceramics purveyor in town, with a grand selection of colorful ware; and **Cuzzens** for fine menswear. ⊠ *Caesars Palace, 3570 Las Vegas Blvd. S, Center Strip,* ☎ *702/896–5599,* WEB *www.caesars.com.*

**Belz Factory Outlet World.** Just a few miles away from the Strip's most exclusive and expensive shopping areas is one of the country's largest discount malls. About 3 mi south of Tropicana Avenue on Las Vegas Boulevard South, you'll find 580,000 square feet of shopping choices. There are 155 different stores offering clothing, jewelry, toys, shoes, beauty products, housewares, accessories, sportswear, souvenirs, and much more at discount prices. You'll find **Jones New York** and **London Fog,** to name just a few. Belz has two food courts and a full-size carousel. **Off 5th Saks Fifth Avenue** occupies the majority of space at **Annex One,** a small separate building on Belz's south side. ⊠ *7400 Las Vegas Blvd. S, South Las Vegas,* ☎ *702/896–5599,* WEB *www.belz.com.*

**Boulevard Mall.** You'll see places to shop all along Maryland Parkway, but this one, with 150 stores, has the greatest single concentration of retailers. Less expensive than its counterparts on the Strip, the mall is anchored by **Macy's, Sears, Dillards, Marshalls,** and **JCPenney** department stores. The food court offers mostly fast-food choices; for more leisurely meals away from the mall's hustle and bustle try **Applebee's** or the **International House of Pancakes,** both in separate buildings in the mall's parking lot. Stroller rentals are available; they're dispensed from automatic machines for $3. ⊠ *3528 Maryland Pkwy., East Side,* ☎ *702/732–8949,* WEB *www.blvdmall.com.*

★ **Desert Passage at the Aladdin.** Inspired by the ancient trade routes through Spain, North Africa, and India, the 475,000-square-foot Desert Passage has more than 130 retail stores and 14 restaurants. The circular shopping center surrounds the 7,000-seat Aladdin Theatre of the Arts. Kiosks look like just-opened tents; watch belly dancers and other performers as you peruse the many fine shops. Be sure to watch the storm clouds gather every hour (and half hour Friday–Sunday) at the Merchant's Harbor. A gentle desert thunderstorm washes in and then passes quickly through the port as you sip espresso at the **Merchant's Harbor Coffee House** (sorry, no hookahs). The entrance to the **Endangered Species** store is guarded by a life-size stuffed gorilla. If you prefer your stuffed animals a bit more tame, you can create your own teddy bear at the **Build-A-Bear Workshop.** Other offerings include **bebe, Jhane Barnes, Tommy Bahama,** and **Eddie Bauer.** Desert Passage competes easily with the Forum Shops for upscale clothing boutiques: **Ann Taylor Loft, Hugo/Hugo Boss, Betsy Johnson,** and **White House/Black Market.** Head over to **Sephora** for a make-over. Jewelry lovers have 16 fine stores to choose from, including **Clio Blue Paris, Joli-Joli,** and **Gioia: The Art of Jewels.** For home accessories, check out **Chiasso, Illuminations, Sur La Table,** and **McGrail's of Erin.** Among the restaurants, the **Commander's Palace** is a branch of the Louisiana landmark in Sin City and the **Oyster Bay Seafood and Wine Bar** serves fresh oysters, fried calamari, and fish & chips. Las Vegas is one of only two U.S. cities that can claim the **Blue Note Jazz Club.** ⊠ *3663 Las Vegas Blvd. S, Center Strip,* ☎ *702/866–0703 or 888/800–8284,* WEB *www.desertpassage.com.*

★ **Fashion Outlets Las Vegas.** This outlet mall is definitely worth a shopping safari to nearby Primm, about half an hour west on I–15. Here, you'll find many of the same superstars as on the Strip with prices as much as 75% less. And you often don't see these stores represented at an outlet mall: **Burberry's, Williams Sonoma Marketplace, St. John,** and **Versace Company Store. Last Call from Neiman Marcus** stocks designer as well as their private labels. And there are the usual outlet mall suspects: **DKNY, Banana Republic, Polo Ralph Lauren,** and the **Gap.** A shuttle service runs daily from the MGM Grand and New York–New York, costing $13 each way. Call 702/874–1400 for reservations. ✉ *32100 Las Vegas Blvd. S, Primm,* ☎ *702/874–1400.*

★ **Fashion Show Mall.** After a dramatic expansion, this mall now totals 2 million square feet of retail space, outdistancing every other mall on the Strip. Next to the New Frontier, the Fashion Show is hard to miss due to its new signature architectural element: The Cloud is a 400-foot-long steel shade structure upon which images are projected. The well-maintained mall includes a new 11,000-square-foot food court and the Great Hall, a fashion show venue with an 80-foot-long retractable catwalk. Not everything is overpriced—the two-story building contains 300 shops, anchored by eight department stores: **Neiman Marcus, Saks Fifth Avenue, Macy's, Robinsons–May, Bloomingdale's Home, Nordstrom, Lord & Taylor,** and **Dillards.** You'll find a lot of the same offerings at the casino malls such as **Louis Vuitton** and some different fare, such as a great shoe store, **Stiletto. Waldenbooks,** the only bookstore on the Strip, is also here. Stroller rentals are $5. ✉ *3200 Las Vegas Blvd. S, North Strip,* ☎ *702/369–8382,* WEB *www.thefashionshow.com.*

★ **Forum Shops at Caesars.** This shopping extravaganza resembles an ancient Roman streetscape, replete with immense columns and arches, two central piazzas with fountains, and a cloud-filled ceiling displaying a sky that changes from sunrise to sunset over the course of three hours (perhaps inspiring shoppers to step up their pace of acquisition when it looks as if time is running out). The Festival Fountain (in the west wing of the mall) puts on its own show every hour on the hour daily starting at 10 AM: a robotic, pie-eyed Bacchus hosts a party for friends Apollo, Venus, and Mars, complete with lasers, music, and sound effects; at the end, the god of wine and merriment delivers a sales pitch for the mall. The "Atlantis" show (in the east wing) is even more amazing: Atlas, king of Atlantis, can't seem to pick between his son, Gadrius, and his daughter, Alia, to assume the throne; for eight minutes, the royal family struggles for control of the doomed kingdom amid flame and smoke. If you can tear yourself away from the animatronic wizardry, you'll find both familiar and unusual shops. The upscale and excellent include clothiers **Christian Dior, Gianni Versace, Gucci,** and **Bernini** and jewelers **Bulgari, Judith Leiber** (for jewel-like handbags), and **M. J. Christensen.** Shoppers will also find the **Planet Hollywood Superstore, Virgin Megastore,** and **Nike Town.** There's also a wide array of restaurants such as **Caviarteria, La Salsa, Spago,** and **Chinois.** You can glide into the Forum from the Strip on a moving sidewalk. The mall is open late (until 11 Sun.–Thurs., until midnight Fri.–Sat.). ✉ *Caesars Palace, 3500 Las Vegas Blvd. S, Center Strip,* ☎ *702/893–4800,* WEB *www.caesars.com.*

**Galleria at Sunset.** This 140-store mall in Henderson, on the northeast corner of Sunset Road and Stephanie Street, sits directly across from the popular locals hotel-casino Sunset Station. Anchored by **Dillard's, Robinsons–May, JCPenney, Galyan's,** and **Mervyn's California** department stores, the two-level shopping complex has vaulted skylights, sparkling fountains, and huge palm trees. The food court has mostly fast-food fare with two exceptions; **Edo Japan** stir-fries to order, and the **Bourbon Street Grill** offers New Orleans–style edibles. Several restaurants can be found on the perimeter of the mall, but **Chevy's**, a Tex-Mex restaurant and bar, and **Red Robin**, a gourmet burger joint, are inside the Galleria. Strollers are available for $4; they must be returned within three hours. ⊠ *1300 W. Sunset Rd., Henderson,* ☎ *702/434–0202,* WEB *www.galleriaatsunset.com.*

★ **Grand Canal Shoppes at the Venetian.** The most elegant shopping complex on the Strip is laid out along walkways bordering indoor re-creations of Venice's Grand Canal and St. Mark's Square. For $12.50 per person, gondolas transport shoppers through the canals. Among the stores, **Bertone, Burberry, Lladró,** and **Pal Zileri** offer luxe shopping. Two must-see stores are **Il Prato,** which sells unique Venetian collectibles such as Carnevale masks, stationery sets, and glass pen and inkwell sets and **Ripa de Monti,** offering luminescent Venetian glass. **Canyon Ranch Living Essentials** has cookbooks, body products, and spa robes from Arizona's famous Canyon Ranch spa. The food court has a **Krispy Kreme** and a **Carnevale Coffee,** as well as a variety of fine dining options, including Wolfgang Puck's **Postrio,** or the northern Italian fare of **Canaletto.** The mall is open late (until 11 Sun.–Thurs., until midnight Fri.–Sat.). ⊠ *The Venetian Resort-Hotel-Casino, 3355 Las Vegas Blvd. S, Center Strip,* ☎ *702/733–5000,* WEB *www.venetian.com.*

**Le Boulevard at Paris Las Vegas.** Petite by Vegas standards, this Parisian shopping lane has many Gallic delights. The **Lenôtre** café is the only place in the United States where the famous Lenôtre chocolates are sold. The café also has fresh French pastries and coffee. **La Boutique by Yokohama de Paris** has Parisian designer wear from Celine, among others, and Fendi watches. **Le Journal** is the place to pick up your jaunty French beret. ⊠ *Paris Las Vegas, 3655 Las Vegas Blvd. S, Center Strip,* ☎ *702/946–7000,* WEB *www.parislasvegas.com.*

**Showcase Mall.** Right next to the MGM Grand, this mall is worth a visit, especially for kids. **M&M's World** is a rollicking, four-story homage to the popular candy. There's logo merchandise from stuffed toys to sheets, and, of course, you can buy any type of M&M candy here. Better yet, create your own custom bag (all blue! only red! plain and peanut together!)—huge dispensers with every color and every type line one wall of the fourth level. There's the flagship store of **Ethel M. Chocolates,** the famous local gourmet chocolatier, and **Everything Coca-Cola,** offering collectibles; gifts; and, of course, Coke. You can sip a Coke float at an old-time soda fountain or buy a vintage Coke vending machine. Steven Spielberg had a hand in creating the high-tech **Gameworks** arcade. There's a multi-screen cinema and the **Grand Canyon Experience,** in case you can't make it to the real natural wonder. ⊠ *3785 Las Vegas Blvd. S, South Strip,* ☎ *702/740–2525.*

★ **Via Bellagio.** Steve Wynn spared no expense to create Bellagio, so be prepared to spare no expense shopping at its exclusive boutiques. Via Bellagio is a long passage lined with elegant stores such as **Yves Saint Laurent Rive Gauche, Prada, Chanel, Giorgio Armani, Gucci, Hermès, Moschino,** and **Tiffany and Co.** Bellagio's upscale restaurants include **Prime, Aqua,** and **Le Cirque.** Dine on the balcony at **Olives,** located right in the promenade, and get the best seat for watching the Fountains of Bellagio (otherwise known as the dancing waters). Here, there's children-free shopping except for the children of hotel guests. ⊠ *Bellagio, 3600 Las Vegas Blvd. S, Center Strip,* ☎ *702/693–7111,* WEB *www.bellagiolasvegas.com.*

# Specialty Shops

## Books

### GENERAL

Las Vegas has a full complement of national bookstore chains, though only the Waldenbooks at the Fashion Show Mall is directly on the Strip.

**Barnes & Noble.** ⊠ *2191 N. Rainbow Blvd., North Las Vegas,* ☎ *702/ 631–1775;* ⊠ *3860 Maryland Pkwy., East Side,* ☎ *702/734–2900;* ⊠ *567 N. Stephanie St., Henderson,* ☎ *702/434–1533.*

**B. Dalton.** ⊠ *Boulevard Mall, 3860 S. Maryland Pkwy., East Side,* ☎ *702/735–0008;* ⊠ *Galleria at Sunset Mall, 1300 W. Sunset Rd., Henderson,* ☎ *702/434–1331.*

**Borders Books and Music.** ⊠ *2190 N. Rainbow Blvd., West Side,* ☎ *702/638–7866;* ⊠ *2323 S. Decatur Blvd., West Side,* ☎ *702/258–0999;* ⊠ *1445 W. Sunset Rd., Henderson,* ☎ *702/433–6222.*

**Readmore Magazine and Book Store.** ⊠ *6154 W. Flamingo Rd., West Side,* ☎ *702/362–3762;* ⊠ *2250 E. Tropicana Ave., University District,* ☎ *702/798–7863.*

**Waldenbooks.** ⊠ *Fashion Show Mall, 3200 Las Vegas Blvd. S, North Strip,* ☎ *702/733–1049.*

### DISCOUNT

Used bookstores are as easy to find in Las Vegas as video-poker machines. If you venture out into the greater metro area, you'll inevitably find one stashed in among the many strip malls and neighborhood shopping centers.

**Albion Book Company.** Albion is a 10-minute drive from the Strip, in the Von's shopping center on the corner of Eastern Ave. and Desert Inn. The majority of space in the voluminous bookstore, which takes in about 6,000 books a month, is devoted to hardcovers on almost every possible topic in fiction and nonfiction. First-edition books and rare finds occupy a corner in the front of the store; mass-market paperbacks can be found in the back. ⊠ *2466 E. Dessert Inn Rd., East Side,* ☎ *702/792–9554.*

**Book Magician.** One of the oldest bookstores in Las Vegas has been in the business for 20 years. With more than 150,000 in-stock titles, it's also one of the largest. The store carries a variety of genres, including a few comics, but its specialties are science fiction and metaphysics. ⊠ *2202 W. Charleston Blvd., #2, West Side,* ☎ *702/384–5838.*

### SPECIAL INTEREST

**Gambler's Book Club.** GBC is the world's largest independent book store specializing in books about 21, craps, poker, roulette, and all the other games, as well as novels about gambling, biographies of crime figures, used books and magazines, and anything else that relates to gambling and Las Vegas. Call for the jam-packed free catalog. ⊠ *630 S. 11th St., Downtown,* ☎ *702/382–7555 or 800/522–1777,* WEB *www. gamblersbook.com.*

**Huntington Press.** This small-press publisher produces some of the best books about gambling and Las Vegas. You can buy books, software, and hand-held games at its offices, just two blocks north of the Rio (less than 1 mi from the Strip). ⊠ *3867 S. Procyon Ave., West Side,* ☎ *702/252–0655,* WEB *www.huntingtonpress.com.*

## Clothing for Children

Though the casino-hotel malls and area shopping centers have the usual children's clothing stores such as **Gap Kids** and **Gymboree,** you can find some great gifts for kids at the shops below.

**Desert Brats.** Little girls will find their inner showgirl in these frothy creations with feathers and sequins. ☒ *Desert Passage at the Aladdin, 3663 Las Vegas Blvd. S, Center Strip,* ☎ *888/800–8284.*

**Harley Davidson Café.** The café's retail store is the spot to outfit kids with a Harley Hog Cap, flight jacket, or Captain American tee. ☒ *3725 Las Vegas Blvd. S, Center Strip,* ☎ *702/740–4555.*

**Les Enfants.** This shop carries t-shirts and gifts. ☒ *Paris Las Vegas, 3655 Las Vegas Blvd. S, Center Strip,* ☎ *702/946–7000.*

## Clothing for Men

You can't walk into the shopping areas of the Strip's hotels without stumbling upon high-end men's clothiers. If the price tags on the Strip are too stratospheric, the outlet malls have brand names for less, such as Tommy Hilfiger, Eddie Bauer, and DKNY.

**ESPN Zone SportsCenter Studio Store.** Increase the cool quotient with official ESPN and ESPN Zone merchandise, including sportswear. ☒ *New York–New York, 3790 Las Vegas Blvd. S, South Strip,* ☎ *702/ 933–3776.*

## Clothing for Women

Vegas' shopping will send the most jaded shopper into ecstasy. Prepare to find the greatest selection of women's wear on the planet at area hotel-casino malls and outlet centers. Your favorite national chain store or designer boutique will have a Vegas outlet. In fact, name a designer and you'll find a signature shop in this town.

**Ann Taylor Loft.** The Loft offers value-price career and casual designs for women with more relaxed lifestyles. ☒ *Desert Passage at the Aladdin, 3663 Las Vegas Blvd. S, Center Strip,* ☎ *702/732–3348.*

**DKNY.** Up to the nano-second fashion from this New York designer collection is worth a test-drive. ☒ *Desert Passage at the Aladdin, 3663 Las Vegas Blvd. S, Center Strip,* ☎ *702/732–3348.*

**Last Call from Neiman Marcus.** Irresistible discounts on designer clothing as well as gifts, furniture, and men's clothing. ☒ *Fashion Outlets Las Vegas, 32100 Las Vegas Blvd. S, Primm,* ☎ *702/874–2100.*

**Off 5th Saks Fifth Avenue Outlet.** Don't miss drop-dead low prices on a large selection of upscale casual and formal designerwear. ☒ *Belz Factory Outlet, 7680 Las Vegas Blvd. S, South Las Vegas,* ☎ *702/ 263–7692.*

VINTAGE

★ **The Attic.** No other used-clothing store in the world compares. Thick with incense and booming with club music, the two-story building is filled with an eclectic array of shirts, shoes, pants, hats, jewelry, halter tops, prom dresses, evening wear, and feather boas, as well as furniture and collectors' items. Fans of 1960's and 1970's styles should especially love it. Note that there is a $1 admission fee. ☒ *1018 S. Main St., Downtown,* ☎ *702/388–4088,* FAX *702/388–1047,* WEB *www. theatticlasvegas.com.*

**Buffalo Exchange.** This is a must-stop for the terminally hip. The very extensive array of great vintage clothing at reasonable prices makes for satisfying shopping. You'll also find great recycled discards and, since we all could use the help, lots of suggestions from the friendly staff. ⊠ *4110 S. Maryland Pkwy., East Side,* ☎ *702/791–3960.*

## Food & Drink

**Ethel M. Chocolates Factory and Cactus Garden.** The "M" stands for Mars, the name of the family (headed by Ethel in the early days) that brings you Snickers, Milky Way, Mars Bars, Three Musketeers, and M&Ms. More than 1,000 people come daily to watch the candy-making at this fancy chocolate factory and to taste free samples in the adjoining shop. A 2½-acre cactus garden contains more than 350 species of succulents and desert plants that are very colorful during spring flowering. You'll find nine other Ethel M. stores at casino-hotels and even at the airport. ⊠ *2 Cactus Garden Dr., Henderson,* ☎ *702/458–8864,* WEB *www.ethelm.com.*

★ **M&M's World.** On the Strip about a half block from the MGM Grand, this four-level candy store shares its complex with Gameworks, the Coca-Cola logo shop, and Ethel M's. This popular tourist attraction is usually crowded; it's not easy to maneuver strollers and wheelchairs around the displays. ⊠ *Showcase Mall, 3785 Las Vegas Blvd. S, South Strip,* ☎ *702/458–8864.*

**Rocky Mountain Chocolate Factory.** This chocolate store and ice-cream parlor, in the Belz Factory Outlet, has a nice selection of boxed chocolates and assorted items that make ideal gifts for chocolate lovers. ⊠ *Belz Factory Outlet, 7400 Las Vegas Blvd. S, South Las Vegas,* ☎ *702/ 361–7553.*

**Snack House.** Asian snack foods, dried fruit, and nuts make this Chinatown Plaza shop a popular stop. ⊠ *Chinatown Plaza, 4255 Spring Mountain Blvd., West Side,* ☎ *702/247–9688.*

**Teuscher's Chocolates.** The tempting Swiss chocolates and a coffee bar make for a delightful way to gather energy for more shopping. ⊠ *Desert Passage at the Aladdin, 3663 Las Vegas Blvd. S, Center Strip,* ☎ *702/ 866–6624.*

## Gifts & Souvenirs

★ **Admiral Collection.** Trekkies will salivate over these souvenirs with a Star Trek theme: watches, uniform belt buckles, Klingon black robes, model ships cast in pewter, even a Starfleet Academy diploma. But the exciting offerings are the actual Paramount props for sale dating from the original series that began the Star Trek saga. These very rare collectibles include Dr. McCoy's medical kit for $1,300 or a $5,000 life-size Borg Queen. The only-in-Las-Vegas item has to be the Swarovski crystal evening bag in the shape of a communicator for $1,975! ⊠ *Las Vegas Hilton, 3000 Paradise Rd., Paradise Road,* ☎ *888/697–TREK.*

**African & World Imports.** This small shop tucked inside the Boulevard Mall has a wonderful selection of African art and cultural gift items. You'll also find music, incense, jewelry, and T-shirts. ⊠ *Boulevard Mall, 3680 S. Maryland Pkwy., East Side,* ☎ *702/734–1900.*

**Bali Trading Company.** One of Mandalay Bay's most unusual stores, this is a good place to shop for such gifts as rain sticks and omnariums (semi-enclosed, self-sufficient aquariums), island-style clothing, and South Seas art. ⊠ *Mandalay Bay Resort & Casino, 3950 Las Vegas Blvd. S, South Strip,* ☎ *702/632–6123.*

★ **Bonanza "World's Largest Gift Shop".** Across the street from the Sahara Hotel, Bonanza is the city's best souvenir store. It may not, in fact, be the world's largest, but it's the town's largest. And while it has most of the usual junk, it sells some unusual junk as well. It's so huge that you won't feel trapped, as you might in some of the smaller shops. And it's open until midnight. ⊠ *2460 Las Vegas Blvd. S, North Strip,* ☎ *702/385–7359.*

**Cairo Bazaar.** Designed to look like an open market, this shop in the Luxor's Giza Galleria is filled with canvas-covered carts selling jewelry, scarves, and trinkets. ⊠ *Luxor Hotel-Casino, 3900 Las Vegas Blvd. S, South Strip,* ☎ *702/632–6123.*

**Canyonland.** A big rock fountain gives this place at Belz Factory Outlet an "outdoor" feel. It offers decorative items, including Southwest-style accessories, jade statues, miniature fountains, wind chimes, and cedar trinket boxes. ⊠ *Belz Factory Outlet, 7400 Las Vegas Blvd. S, South Las Vegas,* ☎ *702/361–6682.*

**House of Blues.** Buy music, books, hot sauce, and T-shirts at the souvenir shop in the popular bar/restaurant at the Mandalay Bay hotel. Rest for a bit in the comfortable chairs in the shop's alcove: read a book about the blues or look out the shop's windows into the restaurant. ⊠ *Mandalay Bay Resort & Casino, 3950 Las Vegas Blvd. S, South Strip,* ☎ *702/632–7600.*

**Les Memories.** A Francophile's fantasy, this shop stocks Diptyque candles, Provençal kitchenware, and French-milled soaps. ⊠ *Le Boulevard at Paris, 3655 Las Vegas Blvd. S, Center Strip,* ☎ *702/946–7000 Ext. 64329.*

**McGrail's of Erin.** This one-of-a-kind shop devoted to things Irish is found in an unlikely spot—the Desert Passage at the Aladdin. Buy a bit of the Blarney stone, Celtic jewelry, figurines, and apparel shipped all the way from Ireland. ⊠ *Desert Passage at the Aladdin, 3663 Las Vegas Blvd. S, Center Strip,* ☎ *702/732–8810.*

**Merlin's Mystic Shop.** A life-size figure of Merlin hunched over a selection of crystal figurines sets the tone for this Excalibur gift shop. The eclectic collection includes glow-in-the-dark stickers, 3-D sand pictures, and a skull-shape toilet-brush holder. A palm reader can predict your gambling luck Thursday–Sunday. ⊠ *Excalibur Hotel and Casino, 3850 Las Vegas Blvd. S, South Strip,* ☎ *702/597–7251.*

**Ripa di Monti.** Exquisite Venetian glass creations—everything from magnets and key chains to elaborate vases and figurines—are sold at this store, one of the Grand Canal Shoppes at the Venetian. It's one of Las Vegas's must-see shops. Buy glass-bead necklaces and earrings or a bowl of glass fruit for your dining-room table. ⊠ *Grand Canal Shoppes at the Venetian, 3377 Las Vegas Blvd. S, Center Strip,* ☎ *702/733–1004.*

★ **Treasure Chamber.** Bring home a piece of Egypt (and a lighter wallet). This shop sells real and faux Egyptian artifacts, art, and jewelry in the Luxor's Giza Galleria. Some pieces are over 2,000 years old. ⊠ *Luxor Hotel-Casino, 3900 Las Vegas Blvd. S, South Strip,* ☎ *702/730–5932.*

## Jewelry

Most malls and shopping centers on and off the Strip have jewelry stores, including such national chains as **Ben Bridge, Gordon's, Lundstrom, Whitehall Co.,** and **Zales.** More exclusive jewelers can be found in several of the Strip hotels, most notably Bellagio and the Venetian.

**Agatha.** Chunky, hip, and affordable jewelry—gold and silver bracelets, necklaces, earrings, and even hair clips—is sold here. ⊠ *Grand Canal Shoppes at the Venetian, 3355 Las Vegas Blvd. S, Suite 2010, Center Strip,* ☎ *702/369–0365.*

## Only in Las Vegas

**Dealers Room Casino Clothiers.** If you've caught the gambling spirit and want to go home in a white shirt, black pants, and a big red bow tie, this place will be happy to sell you dealer's duds. ✉ *4465 W. Flamingo Rd., West Side,* ☎ *702/362–7980;* ✉ *3507 S. Maryland Pkwy., East Side,* ☎ *702/732–3932.*

**Elvis-A-Rama Museum Store.** You'll feel ecstatic shopping here if you're an Elvis fan; if not, you might wonder at the decline of our civilization. The store stocks such finds as an Elvis doll (the Army years), an Elvis lunch box, aviator sunglasses, even a swatch of his pillowcase. There are many CDs, videos, and photos; even his old furniture is for sale. ✉ *3401 Industrial Rd., West Side,* ☎ *702/309–7200.*

★  **Gamblers General Store.** There's a big collection of gambling books, such as "Craps for the Clueless," as well as poker chips, green-felt layouts, and slot and video-poker machines. Warning: the highly collectible vintage slots cost $2,000 and up. They'll make sure your state allows the type of slot machine you want before you buy. You can buy used casino card decks here but only after they've been re-sorted and repackaged by guests of the Nevada state penal system. It's eight blocks south of the Plaza Hotel on Main Street. ✉ *800 S. Main St., Downtown,* ☎ *702/382–9903,* WEB *www.gamblersgeneralstore.com.*

**Houdini's Magic Shop.** Magicians are hot in Vegas and it's no surprise that Houdini's corporate headquarters is in town. You'll find seven branches, with its tricks and gags, in almost all the casino-malls. ✉ *Grand Canal Shoppes at the Venetian, 3355 Las Vegas Blvd. S, Center Strip,* ☎ *702/796–0301,* WEB *www.houdini.com.*

**The Liberace Museum Store.** The store stocks the maestro's CDs and videos, jewelry and, in case you're running low, his signature candelabras. ✉ *1775 E. Tropicana Ave., East Side,* ☎ *702/798–5595,* WEB *www.liberace.org.*

**Paul-Son Dice & Card Inc.** Want some authentic casino dice and chips? This store supplies the casinos and also sells retail. The company also designs and produces chips, gaming table layouts, and other tools of the trade—in case you're thinking of going into the business. ✉ *1700 Industrial Rd., West Side,* ☎ *702/384–2425.*

**Ray's Beaver Bag.** This place defies description as Vegas' most bizarre, and not to be missed, shop. As a supplier for pre-1840s mountain man reenactors, it goes beyond moose milk, beeswax candles, black powder, and buffalo jerky. Even if you don't trap or fur trade, poke around the muzzle guns and bear skins and you may find a 1960s Indian trade blanket or a unique 4-foot-long beaded, fringed elk-skin pipe bag made by a Native American craftsman. ✉ *727 Las Vegas Blvd. S, Downtown,* ☎ *702/386–8746.*

**Ron Lee's World of Clowns.** Every kind of clown item known to man is sold at this bizarre shop. They make clown figurines on the premises, and there's a self-guided factory tour. Clown clothing, accessories, and assorted other clown stuff line the walls in the tour area, which is touted as a Clown Museum. There's also a café here, and you'll find a branch at the Desert Passage. ✉ *330 Carousel Pkwy., Henderson,* ☎ *702/434–1700;* ✉ *Desert Passage at the Aladdin, 3663 Las Vegas Blvd. S., Center Strip,* ☎ *702/889–8710,* WEB *www.ronlee.com.*

★  **Serge's Showgirl Wigs.** If you always wished for the sleek tresses of those Vegas dancers (or female impersonators), head here. The largest wig store in the world can transform you into a Rennaisance angel or Priscilla Presley on her wedding day. After checking out Serge's celebrity wall of fame, head for their wig outlet directly across the parking lot. ⊠ *953 E. Sahara Ave., East Side,* ☎ *702/732–1015.*

## Pawn Shops

Las Vegas is a great place to pick up cheap televisions, watches, and cameras pawned by locals feeding video poker habits or visitors who needed a little extra cash to get home.

**Super Pawn.** There are 25 locations around town, but the following locations are the most convenient for those staying on the Strip or downtown. ⊠ *126 S. 1st St., Downtown,* ☎ *702/384–2686;* ⊠ *515 E. St. Louis St., East Side,* ☎ *702/792–2900.*

## Sporting Goods & Clothing

**Nike Town.** This multi-level Nike theme park features booming "Just Do It" videos and giant swoosh symbols amid the latest cool technology in athletic shoes displayed in glass cases. Flashy and crowded, it's full of salespeople running around with 2-way radios. On the second floor, the swoosh info desk has the scoop on local sporting events, bike races, and hiking spots. ⊠ *Forum Shops at Caesars, 3500 Las Vegas Blvd. S, Center Strip,* ☎ *702/650–8888.*

**Saint Andrew's Golf Shop.** In the Callaway Golf Center at the south end of the Strip, this shop is part of a 45-acre state-of-the-art practice, instruction, and learning center. ⊠ *Callaway Golf Center, 6730 Las Vegas Blvd. S, South Strip,* ☎ *702/897–9500.*

## Toys & Games

**Build-A-Bear Workshop.** The store's motto is "Where Best Friends Are Made" . . . if your best friend is a soon-to-be stuffed animal. Choose a furry friend, take it to a stuffing machine (you work the pedals!), and pick out a cloth heart to put inside. An employee sews it up, then it's off for an air bath and brushing. If you don't want your new best friend to go out into the world naked, choose from a variety of tiny clothes, shoes, and accessories. Don't forget to fill out the stats for the birth certificate; all friends go home in a cardboard house. ⊠ *Desert Passage at the Aladdin, 3663 Las Vegas Blvd. S, Center Strip,* ☎ *702/836–0899,* WEB *www.buildabear.com.*

**FAO Schwarz.** No other toy store in Vegas can compare with this one. A two-story wooden Trojan horse, with moving head, whirling gears, and flashing lights, greets delighted shoppers as they enter this toy kingdom. You'll pay a pretty penny for brand-name toys, but you'll also have a lot of fun doling out those dollars. Full sections of the store are devoted to Barbie, Legos, Pokemon, Star Wars, Thomas the Tank Engine, and a multitude of other popular children's playthings. ⊠ *Forum Shops at Caesars, 3500 Las Vegas Blvd. S, Center Strip,* ☎ *702/731–7110.*

## Western Shops

**Shepler's.** Cowboys (and cowgirls) can get their Wranglers and Stetsons here as well as western decor and accessories. ⊠ *4700 W. Sahara Ave., West Side,* ☎ *702/258–2000;* ⊠ *3025 E. Tropicana Ave., East Side,* ☎ *702/898–3000,* WEB *www.sheplers.com.*

# 9 SIDE TRIPS FROM LAS VEGAS

Although Las Vegas is one of the most remote cities in the United States, its surroundings are among its best assets. Stunning mountains of sandstone, in its many hues and shapes, are visible from any west-facing window on the Strip. The largest man-made lake in the Western Hemisphere is a mere 40 mi down the road. And the grandest canyon on the planet is just a hop, skip, and jump by plane or car.

A NY ONE OF THE NATURAL and man-made scenic wonders a short drive away can add a memorable excursion to the unique experience that is Las Vegas. Strike out in any direction and within minutes you can enjoy the solace and serenity only the desert can provide. The most popular side trip is to Hoover Dam, 45 minutes away on the Arizona state line. Or why not fly to the Grand Canyon in an hour, or drive up to Death Valley National Park in three hours?

Updated by
Fred Couzens

# RED ROCK CANYON AREA

*16 mi west of Las Vegas.*

Look west from any vantage point in Las Vegas and your gaze will inevitably be drawn to the Spring Mountains, the big limestone and sandstone wall that hems in one side of the Las Vegas Valley. The centerpiece
★ of this range is **Red Rock Canyon,** with its scenic 13-mi loop road through red-rock formations and unusual high-desert scenery. A 30-minute drive west on West Charleston Boulevard (Highway 159) delivers you to natural vistas every bit as stunning as the unnatural ones found in the city.

The first stops on the one-way loop road are the easy Calico Vistas 1 and 2 trails where even the most amateur rock climber can safely get a feel of the red sandstone and have a "near-professional" experience.
Red Rock's **BLM Visitors Center** exhibits the flora and fauna of the Mojave Desert and the history of the various desert peoples.Farther on, 6½ mi past the vista pullouts, is a turnoff for Willow Springs/Lost Creek. Take this road to reach **Lost Creek Discovery Trail,** an easy ¾-mi loop trail with Native American pictographs and a seasonal waterfall along the trail. There are 20 tables and a great partly-shaded picnicking site next to the rocks, but arrive early to get a table at this popular spot. ⊠ *W. Charleston Blvd.,* ☎ *702/363–1922,* WEB *www. redrockcanyon.blm.gov.* ⊞ *$5 per car.* ☉ *Visitor Center Nov.–Mar., daily 8–4:30; Apr.–Oct. 8–5:30. Loop road Nov.–Feb., daily 6 AM–5 PM; Mar. and Oct., 6 AM–7 PM; Apr.–Sept. 6 AM–8 PM.*

After completing the Red Rock Canyon scenic loop, you'll return to Highway 159. Turn right and go 2½ mi to **Spring Mountain Ranch State Park.** This prime piece of property became a ranch in the 1860s, thanks to the abundant water that percolates down from the Spring Mountains. Past owners have included German actress Vera Krupp and eccentric millionaire Howard Hughes. The red ranch house, white picket fences, long green lawns, and colorful cliffs of the Wilson Range make this a perfect place for a picnic. **Super Summer Theater,** offered from June through August, transforms the sprawling grassy grounds into a playhouse under the stars. A volunteer organization has coordinated this highly successful theater-on-the-lawn since 1976. ⊠ *Hwy. 159,* ☎ *702/875–4141 ranch, 702/594–7529 theater,* WEB *http://parks. nv.gov/smr.htm.* ⊞ *Ranch, $5 per car; theater, prices vary/advanced purchase required.* ☉ *Daily 8 AM–dusk, ranch house 10–4, walking tours of the old ranch at noon, 1, and 2 on weekdays, also 3 on weekends and holidays.*

From Spring Mountain Ranch State Park continue another mile south on Highway 159 to **Bonnie Springs Ranch.** The duck pond, aviary, and animal petting zoo are admission free. The ranch also has a rustic restaurant, a bar, and a 50-unit motel. Equestrians can rent horses from the large stable; one-hour guided trail rides take you past cacti, yucca, and Joshua trees. **Old Nevada,** an Old West theme park at Bonnie Springs

Ranch, includes an opera house, two museums, a cemetery, a stamp mill, several stores, and a wedding chapel. Three times a day the Wild West comes to life here, with fake gunfights and make-believe hangings staged in the street. On weekends, you can ride the stagecoach or hop on a miniature train that chugs its way between the parking lot and the entrance. The stage costs $5, but train rides (10:30–5) are free. ⊠ *1 Bonnie Springs Ranch Rd.,* ☎ *702/875–4191,* FAX *702/875–4424,* WEB *www.bonniesprings.com.* 🎟 *Ranch and petting zoo free, Old Nevada $5 per car weekdays, $7 per car weekends; horseback riding $25.* ☉ *Labor Day–Memorial Day, daily 10:30–5; Memorial Day–Labor Day, 10:30–6.*

# MT. CHARLESTON AREA

*45 mi northwest of Las Vegas on U.S. 95.*

★ For an alpine retreat, head to **Mt. Charleston.** In winter the upper elevations are used for cross-country and downhill skiing; in summer it's a welcome respite from the 115°F desert heat (temperatures are at least 20°F cooler than in the city), as well as a place to hike, picnic, and camp. For camping information, contact the **U.S. Forest Service** (☎ 702/515–5400). For snow reports and wintertime road conditions, call the **Las Vegas Ski and Snowboard Resort** (☎ 702/593–9500).

At the intersection of U.S. 95 and Highway 157, turn left to Kyle Canyon. The first stop on Kyle Canyon Road (about 17 mi up) is the **Mount Charleston Hotel,** built in 1984. The large, lodgelike lobby has a big hearth, bar, and spacious restaurant with a mountain view. ⊠ *2 Kyle Canyon Rd.,* ☎ *702/872–5500 or 800/794–3456,* WEB *www. mtcharlestonhotel.com.*

If you take Highway 157 to its end you'll find the **Mt. Charleston Lodge.** At 7,717 feet above sea level, the lodge overlooks Kyle Canyon; it offers a fireside cocktail lounge, log cabin rentals, and nearby hiking trails. ⊠ *1200 Old Park Rd.,* ☎ *702/872–5408 or 800/955–1314,* FAX *702/872–5403,* WEB *www.mtcharlestonlodge.com.*

From Mt. Charleston Lodge, take Highway 157 down the hill 4 mi to its intersection with Highway 158, then follow Highway 158 for 9 mi and turn left on Highway 156 toward **Las Vegas Ski and Snowboard Resort.** Near the end of the road you'll find two campgrounds (at around 8,500 feet), a trail to a bristlecone pine forest (among the oldest living trees on Earth), and the **Lee Canyon** ski area, with 10 ski trails covering 40 acres. Depending on snowfall, ski season can last from Thanksgiving to Easter, but the 9,000-foot elevation ensures stunning views year-round. ☎ *702/645–2754,* WEB *www.skilasvegas.com.*

# HOOVER DAM & THE LAKE MEAD AREA

Boulder City is an attractive and languid village, full of historic neighborhoods and businesses, parks and greenbelts, and not a single casino. Over the hill from town is the enormous Hoover Dam, which offers a popular tour. Behind it, backed up by mile after mile of rugged desert-canyon country, is incongruous and shimmering Lake Mead, the focal point of water-based recreation for all of southern Nevada and northwestern Arizona. All three are within an hour of Vegas. The breathtaking wonderland known as Valley of Fire, with its fiery red sandstone outcroppings, petrified logs, petroglyphs, and miles of hiking trails, is an hour's drive from Hoover Dam.

# Boulder City

*25 mi southeast of Las Vegas.*

More than 180 bird species have been spotted among the system of nine lagoons at the 200-acre **Bird Viewing Preserve** (✉ 2400 B Moser Dr., Henderson, ☎ 702/566–2939, ⌨ Free, ⏱ Daily 6 AM–3 PM). Four dozen varieties are listed as resident including various ducks, hawks, cormorants, and herons; many species are listed as migrant or winter visitors.

In the early 1930s Boulder City was built by the federal government to house 5,000 construction workers on the Hoover Dam project. A strict moral code was enforced to ensure timely completion of the dam, and to this day, the model city is the only community in Nevada in which gambling is illegal. Note that the two casinos at either end of Boulder City are just outside the city limits. After the dam was completed, the town shrank but was kept alive by the management and maintenance crews of the dam and Lake Mead. Today it is a vibrant little Southwest town.

★ Be sure to stop at the historic **Boulder Dam Hotel,** built in 1932. On the National Register of Historic Places, the 22-room bed-and-breakfast hotel once was a favorite getaway for such notables as Will Rogers, Bette Davis, Shirley Temple, and the legendary Howard Hughes. The **Boulder City Chamber of Commerce** (☎ 702/293–2034, WEB www. boulderchamber.com, ⏱ Weekdays 9–5), on the first floor of the hotel, is a good place to gather information on the Hoover Dam and sights around town. The **Boulder City/Hoover Dam Museum** (☎ 702/ 294–1988, WEB www.bcmha.org, ⏱ Mon.–Sat. 10–5, Sun. 12–5, ⌨ $2) occupies the second floor of the hotel. The museum preserves and displays artifacts relating to the workers and construction of Boulder City and Hoover Dam. ✉ *1305 Arizona St.,* ☎ *702/293–3510,* WEB *www. BoulderDamHotel.com.*

# Hoover Dam

*8 mi from Boulder City via U.S. 93.*

In 1928, Congress authorized $175 million for construction of a dam on the Colorado River for two reasons: flood control and the generation of electricity. Often called one of the seven wonders of the world, ★ the **Hoover Dam** is 727 feet high (the equivalent of a 70-story building) and 660 feet thick at the base (about the length of two football fields). Construction required 4.4 million cubic yards of concrete—enough to build a two-lane highway from San Francisco to New York. Originally referred to as Boulder Dam, the structure was later officially named Hoover Dam in recognition of President Herbert Hoover's role in the project. **The Discovery Tour** allows you to see the power plant generators, the Nevada Intake Tower, the visitors center, the old Exhibit Building, and other vantage points at your own pace. Guide staff give talks every 15 minutes at each stopping point from 9:30 to 4:30. Cameras, pagers, tote bags, and cell phones are subject to X-ray screening. The top of the dam is open to pedestrians during daylight hours only; approved vehicles can cross the dam 24/7. Note: All specified hours are Pacific Time Zone. ✉ *U.S. 93 east of Boulder City,* ☎ *702/293–8000 Bureau of Reclamation,* WEB *www.hooverdam.usbr.gov.* ⌨ *Discovery Tour $10, parking $5.* ⏱ *Daily 9–5. Security, road, and Hoover Dam crossing information: 888/248–1259.*

# Lake Mead

*About 4 mi from Hoover Dam; travel west on U.S. 93 to the intersection with Lakeshore Dr. to reach the Alan Bible Visitors Center.*

★ **Lake Mead,** which is actually the Colorado River backed up behind the Hoover Dam, is the largest man-made reservoir in the country: it covers 229 square mi, and its irregular shoreline extends for 550 mi. You can get information about the lake's history, ecology, and recreational opportunities, as well as about accommodations available along its shore, at the **Alan Bible Visitors Center** (☎ 702/293–8990, ☉ Daily 8:30–4:30). People come to Lake Mead to swim: **Boulder Beach** is the closest to Las Vegas, only a mile or so from the visitors center; **Echo Bay,** roughly 40 mi beyond Boulder Beach, is the best place to swim in the lake because it has better sand and is less crowded than the other beaches. Angling and houseboating are favorite pastimes; various marinas strung along the Nevada shore rent houseboats, along with speedboats, ski boats, and Jet Skis. Divers have a fantastic choice of underwater sights to explore, including the entire town of St. Thomas, a farming community that was inundated in 1937. Other activities abound, such as water-skiing, sailboarding, and snorkeling. WEB *www.nps.gov/lame.* ✉ *$5 per vehicle (good for five days); lake use fees $10 per vessel.* ☉ *Daily.*

At **Lake Mead Cruises** you can board the 300-passenger stern-wheeler that plies the lower portion of the lake; breakfast, cocktail, and dinner and dancing cruises are available. Daily 90-minute sight-seeing cruises and dinner cruises lasting up to three hours are scheduled on weekends. Or you can hop aboard a 57-foot, 50-passenger motorized catamaran that speeds its way (at 40 mph) to the mouth of the Grand Canyon. ✉ *Lake Mead Marina,* ☎ 702/293–6180, FAX 702/293–0343, WEB *www.lakemeadcruises.com.* ✉ *Stern-wheeler, $19–$51; catamaran, $165; reservations strongly recommended.* ☉ *Stern-wheeler tours Nov.–Mar., daily at 10, noon, and 2; Apr.–Oct., daily at 10, noon, 2, and 4.*

**Lake Mead Resort Marina** has boat rentals, a beach, camping facilities, a gift shop, and a floating restaurant. ✉ *322 Lakeshore Rd.,* ☎ 702/293–3484, 800/752–9669, WEB *www.sevencrown.com.*

A drive of about an hour will take you along the north side of the lake, where you'll find three more marinas. When you reach the upper arm of the lake, about a mile past Overton Beach, look for the sign announcing the Valley of Fire. Turn left here, and go about 3 mi to reach the Valley of Fire Visitors Center. At this juncture, it may also be possible to see some of the remnants of St. Thomas, as drought conditions have lowered lake levels dramatically.

# Valley of Fire

*55 mi northeast of Las Vegas.*

The 56,000-acre **Valley of Fire State Park** was dedicated in 1935 as Nevada's first state park. Valley of Fire takes its name from its distinctive coloration, which ranges from lavender to tangerine to bright red, giving the vistas along the park road an otherworldly appearance. The incredible rock formations have been weathered into unusual shapes that suggest beehives, ducks, cobras, even pianos. You'll find petrified logs and the park's most photographed feature—Elephant Rock—just steps off the main road. Mysterious petroglyphs (carvings etched into the rocks) and pictographs (pictures drawn or painted on the rock's surface) are believed to be the work of the Basketmaker and ancestral

Puebloan people who lived along the nearby Muddy River between 300 BC and AD 1150.

The **Valley of Fire Visitors Center** (☉ Daily 8:30–4:30) has displays on the park's history, ecology, archaeology, and recreation, as well as slide shows and films, an art gallery, and information about the 50 campsites within the park. The park is open year-round; the best times to visit, especially during the heat of the summer, are sunrise and sunset, when the light is especially spectacular. ⊠ *Hwy. 169 (Box 515) Overton 89040,* ☎ *702/397–2088,* WEB *www.parks.nv.gov.* ⊡ *$5.* ☉ *Daily.*

| | |
|---|---|
| OFF THE BEATEN PATH | **LOST CITY MUSEUM –** The Moapa Valley has one of the finest collections of ancestral Puebloan artifacts in the American Southwest. Lost City was a major outpost of the ancient culture, which thrived during the early part of the last millennium and disappeared around 1150. The museum's immense collection of artifacts includes baskets, weapons, a restored Basketmaker pit house, and numerous black-and-white photographs of the excavation of Lost City in 1924. To get to the Lost City Museum from Valley of Fire, turn around on the park road and head back to the "T" intersection at the entrance to the Valley of Fire. Turn left and drive roughly 8 mi into Overton. Turn left at the sign for the museum and cross the railroad tracks into the parking lot. ⊠ *721 S. Moapa Valley Blvd. Overton,* ☎ *702/397–2193,* WEB *www.comnett. net/~kolson.* ⊡ *$2.* ☉ *Daily 8:30–4:30.* |

# PRIMM & JEAN, NEVADA

*30 mi south of Las Vegas.*

Las Vegas offers optimum shopping and gawking, but those looking for a less-crowded alternative to the Strip's shops and sights can head out to Primm, Nevada, a 30-minute drive south on I–15 to the California border.

Jean, Nevada, 10 miles shy of Primm heading south, is a good place to catch a view of wide-winged gliders soaring on desert thermals. Two casinos, the Gold Strike and Nevada Landing, flank the highway, and the **Nevada Welcome Center** (☎ 702/874–1360, ☉ Daily 8:30–5) offers information and brochures about the state.

Once you get to Primm, it's shopping for bargains at Fashion Outlets Las Vegas or taking a heart-pounding ride on Desperado, one of the world's tallest and fastest roller coasters. If you're in the mood to gamble or hungry for an inexpensive meal, stop by one of three casinos: Primm Valley Resort, Buffalo Bill's, or Whiskey Pete's. Two challenging Tom Fazio–designed 18-hole championship golf courses are just across the state line in California.

**Fashion Outlets Las Vegas** is a circular building connected to the Primm Valley Resort & Casino. Designed like a cartoon city, complete with car kiosks and streetlights, the 360,000-square-foot mall is anchored by famous-name outlet stores. Take time to see Bonnie and Clyde's shot-up car (yep, the real one) and the last shirt (blood stains and all) worn by Clyde. This mini-museum is up the escalators, just before you enter the casino. Catch a $13 round-trip shuttle at New York–New York or MGM Grand. Shuttles leave six times each day (three times each from MGM and New York–New York); the first shuttle leaves the New York–New York at 9:15 AM and the last leaves the MGM at 3:15 PM. ⊠ *I–15, at Exit 1,* ☎ *702/874–1400, 888/424–6898 for shuttle reservations,* FAX *702/874–1560,* WEB *www.fashionoutletlasvegas.com.* ☉ *Daily 10 AM–8 PM.*

Once you've shopped, you can drop, literally, by riding one of **Buffalo Bill's Rides.** The Desperado roller coaster promises G-forces of 4.0, near-zero gravity, and speeds of 90 mph in less than three minutes—two steep drops add even more thrills. Passengers board inside Buffalo Bill's Casino. Buffalo Bill's also offers the Venture Canyon Log Flume Ride (go splash, then travel the indoor river), the Turbo Drop (a 170-foot drop at 45 mph), a virtual roller coaster, and motion-simulator rides. ✉ *31900 Las Vegas Blvd. S,* ☎ *702/386–7867 or 800/386–7867,* WEB *www.primadonna.com.* ✉ *Rides $3–$6; half-day wristband $22, all-day wristband $30.* ⊙ *Mon. and Thurs. noon–6 PM, Fri. 11 AM–2 AM, Sat. 10 AM–midnight, Sun. 10 AM–7 PM. D, MC, V.*

## Where to Stay

¢–$$ ⊞ **Gold Strike Hotel and Gambling Hall.** The Gold Strike has spacious rooms—with either two queen-size beds or one king and a pull-out sofa—that look out over the untamed Nevada desert. On the inside, the casino has a predictable Old West design, but the weird white-and-orange facade outside is at odds with the brownish desert hues. ✉ *1 Main St., Jean 89019,* ☎ *702/477–5000 or 800/634–1359,* FAX *702/874–1355,* WEB *www.goldstrike-jean.com. 812 rooms. 3 restaurants, pool, lounge, casino, no-smoking rooms. AE, D, DC, MC, V.*

¢–$ ⊞ **Buffalo Bill's Hotel and Casino.** This is one of the three hotel-casinos right at the California border. Owned by the parent company of MGM-Mirage, the trio are a little world all their own, connected by a free monorail. To get people out here from Las Vegas, Bill's has to make it worth their while, and does so with inexpensive rooms and food and coupon funbooks thrown in. Rooms feel like the inside of a cabin, with log wallpaper and rustic furniture, and have great views of the surrounding mountains. Check out the buffalo-shape swimming pool while you're there. ✉ *I–15 at state line, Primm 89019,* ☎ *702/386–7867 or 800/386–7867,* FAX *702/679–5424,* WEB *www.primadonna. com. 1,242 rooms. 4 restaurants, pool, spa, lounge, casino, showroom, cinema, arcade, meeting room. AE, D, DC, MC, V.*

¢–$ ⊞ **Primm Valley Resort & Casino.** Faux ivy, latticework, and the green-and-white interior approximate a country-club theme. Top-notch lounge entertainment complements Buffalo Bill's 6,000-seat Star of the Desert Arena and Whiskey Pete's 700-seat showroom. The outlet mall is accessible from the resort's casino. ✉ *I–15 at state line, Primm 89019,* ☎ *702/386–7867 or 800/386–7867,* FAX *702/679–5424,* WEB *www.primadonna.com. 624 rooms. 3 restaurants, pool, piano bar, casino, convention center. AE, D, DC, MC, V.*

¢ ⊞ **Nevada Landing Hotel and Casino.** Right across I–15 from the Gold Strike (on the westbound side), Nevada Landing closely resembles its neighbor, except it's smaller and has a bright riverboat exterior. Both the Gold Strike and Nevada Landing are owned by Mandalay Resort Group. ✉ *2 Goodsprings Rd., Jean 89019,* ☎ *702/387–5000 or 800/628–6682,* FAX *702/671–1407,* WEB *www.nevadalanding.com. 303 rooms. 3 restaurants, pool, lounge, casino. AE, D, DC, MC, V.*

¢ ⊞ **Whiskey Pete's Casino and Hotel.** It's a noisy, surprisingly busy, state-line hotel-casino, with lounge bands, cheap food, and large, inexpensive rooms with king-size beds. When you're headed for Las Vegas from the west, an overnight stop at Pete's will leave you with just a short drive to those lavish Vegas breakfast buffets. ✉ *I–15 at state line, Primm 89019,* ☎ *702/386–7867 or 800/386–7867,* FAX *702/679–5424,* WEB *www.primadonna.com. 777 rooms. 3 restaurants, pool, arcade, casino, showroom. AE, D, DC, MC, V.*

# LAUGHLIN, NEVADA

*90 mi south of Las Vegas.*

On the way to Laughlin from Las Vegas, stop in at the **Searchlight Museum** (✉ Hwy. 164 at Wendell Way, ☎ 702/455–7955, 💲 Free, ◷ Weekdays 9–5, Sat. 9–1), for the interesting display of artifacts, photos, and "touch-me" tools for young hands. The modern, one-room exhibit area inside the town hall explains the area's rich mining history and extensively describes the lives of its most famous couple, legendary silent screen stars Rex Bell and Clara Bow.

Laughlin is a classic state-line city, separated from Arizona by the Colorado River. Its founder, Don Laughlin, bought an eight-room motel here in 1966 and basically built the town from scratch. By the early 1980s Laughlin's Riverside Hotel-Casino was drawing gamblers and river rats from northwestern Arizona, southeastern California, and even southern Nevada, and his success attracted other casino operators. Today Laughlin is the state's third major resort area, attracting more than 5 million visitors annually. The city fills up, especially in winter, with retired travelers who spend at least part of the winter in Arizona and a younger resort-loving crowd. The big picture windows overlooking the Colorado River lend a bright, airy, and open feeling unique to Laughlin casinos. Take a stroll along the river walk, then make the return trip by water taxi ($3 round trip; $2 one way). Boating, Jet Skis, and plain old wading are other options for enjoying the water.

★ Across the Laughlin Bridge, one-quarter-mile to the north, the **Colorado River Museum** displays rich past of the tri-state region where Nevada, Arizona, and California converge. There are artifacts from the Mohave Indian tribe, models and photographs of steamboats that once plied the river, rock and fossil specimens, and the first telephone switchboard used in neighboring Bullhead City. ✉ *2201 Hwy. 68,* ☎ *928/754–3399,* 🌐 *www.bullheadcity.com/tourism/Hismuseum.asp.* 💲 *$1.* ◷ *Sept.–June, Tues.–Sun. 10 AM–4 PM.*

## Where to Stay & Eat

¢–$ ✕🏨 **Avi Hotel Casino.** The only tribally-owned casino in Nevada is run
★ by the Mohave tribe. The 25,000-square-foot casino houses almost 800 slot and video-poker machines; a new 156-room tower is expected to be open by the end of 2003. The biggest draw, however, is the private white-sand beach; rent a Jet Ski and cruise the Colorado River in style. No trip to Laughlin is complete without a visit to the **Moonshadow Grille,** preferably for the finest Sunday champagne brunch in the tri-state area. ✉ *10000 Aha Macav Pkwy., 89029,* ☎ *702/535–5555 or 800/284–2946,* 🌐 *www.avicasino.com. 456 rooms, 29 spa suites. 5 restaurants, 18-hole golf course, pool, gym, spa, beach, marina, bar, lounge, casino, baby-sitting. AE, D, DC, MC, V.*

¢–$ ✕🏨 **Colorado Belle.** The Mandalay Bay Resort Group owns this Nevada anomaly—a riverboat casino that's actually on a river. The 608-foot replica of a Mississippi paddle wheeler has nautical-theme rooms with views of the Colorado River. Nonsmoking gamblers will appreciate the smoke-free section in the slot machine area. The **Boiler Room Brew Pub** ($–$$), the only micro-brewery in Laughlin pumps out 155,000 gallons of beer each year. ✉ *2100 S. Casino Dr., 89029,* ☎ *702/298–4000, 866/352–3553,* 📠 *702/298–3697,* 🌐 *www.coloradobelle.com. 1,176 rooms. 6 restaurants, in-room data ports, 2 pools, hot tub, casino, dry cleaning, laundry service, no-smoking rooms. AE, D, DC, MC, V.*

¢–$  ✕⊞ **Golden Nugget Laughlin.** A tropical atrium in this miniversion of
★     the Las Vegas Golden Nugget has two cascading waterfalls and more
than 300 different types of plants from around the world. The Deck
($$–$$$) offers the only riverfront dining in town. ⊠ 2300 S. Casino
Dr., 89029, ☎ 702/298–7222 or 800/950–7700, FAX 702/298–7279,
WEB www.gnlaughlin.com. 304 rooms. 4 restaurants, pool, hot tub,
lounge, casino, nightclub, no-smoking rooms. AE, D, DC, MC, V.

¢–$  ✕⊞ **Harrah's.** This is the classiest joint in Laughlin, and it even comes
with a private sand beach. It also has two casinos (one is no-smoking)
and big-name entertainers perform in the Fiesta Showroom and at the
3,000-seat Rio Vista Outdoor Amphitheater. The Range ($–$$$) serves
fine Continental fare. ⊠ 2900 S. Casino Dr., 89029, ☎ 702/298–4600
or 800/427–7247, FAX 702/298–6855, WEB www.harrahs.com. 1,579
rooms. 5 restaurants, some in-room data ports, 2 pools, gym, hair salon,
hot tub, spa, beach, 3 bars, lounge, casino, showroom, meeting rooms,
shops, no-smoking floors. AE, D, DC, MC, V.

¢–$  ✕⊞ **Pioneer Hotel and Gambling Hall.** You can spot this small (by casino
standards) hotel by looking for the neon mascot, River Rick—he's Vegas
Vic's brother. While other casinos stress the new, the Pioneer retains
its laid-back western theme with checker tablecloths and wagon-wheel
light fixtures. Granny's Gourmet Room ($–$$$) serves Continental and
American cuisine. ⊠ 2200 S. Casino Dr., 89029, ☎ 702/298–2442 or
800/634–3469, FAX 702/298–5256, WEB www.pioneerlaughlin.com. 416
rooms. 2 restaurants, pool, hot tub, beach access, lounge, casino. AE,
D, DC, MC, V.

¢–$  ✕⊞ **Riverside Resort.** Town founder Don Laughlin still runs this north-
★     ernmost joint himself. Check out the Loser's Lounge, with its graphic
homage to famous losers, such as the *Hindenburg*, the *Titanic*, and the
like. And don't pass up Don's two free classic car showrooms with more
than 80 rods, roadsters, and tin lizzies. The Gourmet Room restaurant serves Continental and American cuisine. ⊠ 1650 S. Casino Dr.,
89029, ☎ 702/298–2535 or 800/227–3849, FAX 702/298–2614, WEB
www.riversideresort.com. 1,440 rooms. 6 restaurants, 2 pools, hot tub,
bowling, lounge, casino, nightclub, showroom, theater, no-smoking
rooms. AE, D, DC, MC, V.

¢–$  ⊞ **Edgewater Hotel Casino.** Like the Colorado Belle, this 26-story hotel
is a property of the Mandalay Bay Resorts Group. The 60,000-square-
foot casino includes nearly 1,400 machines. ⊠ 2020 S. Casino Dr., 89029,
☎ 702/298–2453 or 800/677–4837, FAX 702/298–8165, WEB www.
edgewater-casino.com. 1,421 rooms. 4 restaurants, pool, hair salon, hot
tub, lounge, casino, no-smoking rooms. AE, D, DC, MC, V.

¢–$  ⊞ **Flamingo Laughlin.** The casino at the largest resort in Laughlin has
1,500 slot and video-poker machines and a sports book. The Flamingo's
3,000-seat outdoor amphitheater, on the bank of the Colorado River,
hosts big-name entertainers. Standard rooms have two double beds or
a queen-size bed. Suites are larger (650–1,000 square feet) and equipped
with coffeemakers, minibars, irons, and ironing boards. ⊠ 1900 S.
Casino Dr., 89029, ☎ 702/298–5111 or 800/352–6464, FAX 702/298–
5116, WEB www.parkplace.com/flamingo/laughlin. 1,824 rooms, 90
suites. 4 restaurants, 3 tennis courts, pool, gym, 2 bars, lounge, casino,
showroom, business center, arcade, no-smoking rooms. AE, D, DC,
MC, V.

¢–$  ⊞ **Ramada Express.** Reserved for adults only, the Gamblers Tower in
this railroad-theme hotel and casino is is a perfect refuge for those seeking a child-free escape. There are also adults-only hours at the pool.
The 53,000-square-foot casino has state-of-the-art slots and a sports
book. A museum focuses on the 1940s, and a miniature train takes
you on a free ride around 27 landscaped acres. ⊠ 2121 S. Casino Dr.,
89029, ☎ 702/298–4200 or 800/243–6846, WEB www.ramadaexpress.

*com. 1,501 rooms. 5 restaurants, pool, hot tub, lounge, casino, no-smoking rooms. AE, D, DC, MC, V.*

¢–$ ⊞ **River Palms Resort Casino.** A large balcony overlooks the table games in the 65,000-square-foot casino. The hotel's south wing, adjacent to the outdoor pool and hot tub, offers a quiet refuge away from the casino. ⊠ *2700 S. Casino Dr., 89029,* ☎ *702/298–2242 or 800/835–7904,* FAX *702/298–2179,* WEB *www.river-palms.com. 1,003 rooms. 4 restaurants, pool, gym, hair salon, hot tub, spa, 5 bars, casino, showroom, meeting rooms, airport shuttle, no-smoking rooms. AE, D, DC, MC, V.*

OFF THE BEATEN PATH

**OATMAN –** Wild burros, descendents from the animals employed in the area's gold mining past, freely roam the streets of modern-day Oatman. The main street is right out of the Old West, and the town served as a backdrop for several films, including *How the West Was Won.* While visiting the gift shops and munching on *churros* (sticks of deep-fried dough), visit the **Oatman Hotel** (⊠ U.S. 66) where Hollywood's Clark Gable and Carole Lombard spent their honeymoon night. A climb up the steep, squeaking staircase leads to their famous room, still adorned with frilly lace. The hotel is on historic Route 66, the "Main Street of America." From the Laughlin Bridge. take Arizona Highway 95 south about 15 mi to Boundary Cone Road. Turn left and go toward the mountains about 11 mi to reach Oatman.

**GOLD ROAD MINE –** Two mi east of Oatman is the Gold Road Mine, an active operation that dates back to 1900. A one-hour tour takes modern-day prospectors underground for a demonstration of drilling equipment and a visit to the "Glory Hole," where the vein structures in the rock are highlighted with a black light to show the gold. ⊠ U.S. 66, ☎ 928/768–1600, WEB goldroadmine.com. ⊠ $12. ☉ Daily 10 AM–5 PM.

## Laughlin A to Z

*To research prices, get advice from other travelers, and book travel arrangements, visit www.fodors.com.*

### AIR TRAVEL
Sun Country flies from 50 cities in 18 states, including Seattle, Portland, Denver, Minneapolis/St. Paul, San Francisco, Phoenix, and Dallas/Ft. Worth. Several hotel-casinos also sponsor charter flights.
➤ AIRLINES: **Allegiant Charters**/(☎ 800/221–1306). **Sun Country Airlines** (☎ 800/359–6786, WEB www.suncountry.com).

### AIRPORTS
➤ CONTACTS: **Laughlin/Bullhead International Airport** (☎ 928/754–2134).

### BUS TRAVEL
Greyhound buses stop at the Airport Chevron at 600 Hwy. 95 in Bullhead City, Arizona. To get to Laughlin, walk to the boat dock across the highway and take a free ride to a Nevada hotel river landing. Individual hotel-casinos also sponsor bus trips from Las Vegas, Los Angeles, and other destinations.
➤ CONTACTS: **Greyhound** (☎ 800/231–2222, WEB www.greyhound.com).

### CAR RENTALS
Avis, Enterprise, and Hertz vehicles are available at the Laughlin/Bullhead International Airport. Other agencies can be found in Bullhead

City; some companies have separate locations in some of the Laughlin hotels. Fuel up in Arizona—all grades of gasoline can be as much as 30–50 ¢ per gallon less in Bullhead City than in Laughlin.

➤ CONTACTS: **Avis-Airport** (☎ 928/754–4686, WEB www.avis.com). **Enterprise-Airport** (☎ 928/754–2700, WEB www.enterprise.com). **Hertz-Airport** (☎ 928/754–4111, WEB www.hertz.com).

### CAR TRAVEL

To get to Laughlin from Las Vegas, take Boulder Hwy. (U.S. 95/93) or I–515 east, then exit where U.S. 95 veers off to the south. Drive for an hour, almost to the California border. There, a left turn onto Hwy. 163 takes you east into Laughlin. ·

### TIME

The state of Nevada is in the Pacific Time Zone, while Arizona is in the Mountain Time Zone. Arizona does not use Daylight Savings Time, however. As a result, during the summer, Nevada and Arizona observe the same hours.

### TRAIN TRAVEL

Amtrak's *Southwest Chief* stops at Needles, California, which is 25 mi south of Laughlin. An Amtrak Thruway bus shuttles passengers to the Ramada Express in Laughlin.

➤ CONTACTS: **Amtrak** (☎ 800/872–7245, WEB www.amtrak.com).

### VISITOR INFORMATION

➤ CONTACTS: **Laughlin Chamber of Commerce** (✉ 1585 S. Casino Dr., 89029, ☎ 702/298–2214 or 800/227–5245, FAX 702/298–5708, WEB www.laughlinchamber.com). **Laughlin Visitors Bureau** (✉ 1555 Casino Dr., 89029, ☎ 702/298–3321 or 800/452–8445, WEB www.visitlaughlin.com).

# LINCOLN COUNTY

Lincoln County, with U.S. 93/Great Basin Highway as its transportation spine, has been long overlooked as a Vegas getaway. No glaring neon or rush-hour freeway traffic here; rather, an occasional dim streetlight in one of the county's four tiny communities breaks up the vast star-studded sky or a sputtering hay-baler negotiates the lonely asphalt ribbon.

Lincoln County encompasses ghost towns and near-ghost towns, national wildlife refuges, large ranches, and abundant water. The five state parks in the area are ideal destinations for just plain relaxing or for more strenuous activities from boating and fishing to hiking and mountain biking.

Plan your trip and make reservations well in advance; the entire county is "tourist-challenged," meaning that it has less than 100 hotel/motel rooms and less than a half-dozen restaurants. Contact the Bureau of Land Management for a map of off-highway travel. And be sure to bring a coat or sweater; it can get chilly since the elevation varies from 3,200 to 6,200 feet.

## Pahranagat Valley

*92 miles from Las Vegas.*

Desert vistas of creosote bushes and towering mountain ranges line the first 65 miles of this drive out of Las Vegas. But after cruising through a narrow volcanic rock pass, the world changes. Underground aquifers turn the landscape from stark to lush.

★ The 5,380-acre **Pahranagat National Wildlife Refuge** is a chain of three lakes, marshes, and meadows that provides a convenient stop on the Pacific Flyway for ducks, herons, egrets, eagles, and numerous other species. The Upper Lake is the most accessible, with campsites, picnic tables, and lots of observation points. ⊠ *Box 510, Alamo 89001,* ☎ *702/725–3417.* ⚏ *Free.* ☉ *Daily.*

Two geological wonders can be seen north of Alamo. **Ash Springs,** formerly a famous spa site, is now fenced and abandoned, but you can still get a glimpse of an active hot springs across from the gas station/convenience store. Early in the morning, when the air is cool, steam rises from the bubbling cauldron. **Crystal Springs,** on the other hand, is a large cool-water spring that fills several ponds before it runs off to the east. This oasis under tall cottonwood trees displays how natural springs can bring the desert to life. It is easily accessible on foot from the junction of highways 375 and 318, less than a half-mile west of U.S. 93.

OFF THE
BEATEN PATH

**AREA 51 –** Known as Dreamland, this is a tiny nub in the northeast corner of the vast 3.5-million-acre Nellis Air Force Base. According to sketchy and unconfirmed media reports, Area 51 is a super-secret military installation where the Air Force has tested top-secret aircraft (such as the U-2 spy plane and the Stealth bomber). Some people also believe that the government stores and does research on UFOs and even collects and studies extraterrestrial beings here. It's illegal to approach the installation; military police have complete authority (including deadly force, if necessary) to prevent intrusions.

Highway 375, a 98-mi road that runs through southeast Nevada from U.S. 93 to U.S. 6, was named the "Extraterrestrial Highway" in 1995. Signs along the road promote the eye-catching label—though they are frequently stolen. A desolate 36 miles from the junction of U.S. 93 is the tiny town of Rachel, about as close as you'll get to Area 51. Today, thanks to its proximity to the secret area (and to the mysterious "Black Box" where the installation's mail was supposedly delivered), Rachel is a pilgrimage site for UFO enthusiasts from around the world. ⊠ *143 mi northeast of Las Vegas, west on Hwy. 375.*

**LITTLE A'LE'INN –** The main gathering spot in Rachel has a UFO theme. ⊠ *Hwy. 375, HCR 61, Box 45, Rachel, NV 89001,* ☎ *775/729–2515,* FAX *775/729–2551,* WEB *www.rachel.dreamlandresort.com.*

## Where to Stay

¢ 🏨 **Alamo Meadow Lane Motel.** Basic prices for basic rooms. Alamo Meadow is the only place to stay on the drive from Vegas to Caliente, and the only dining in town is at Del Pueblo Restaurant across the highway. ⊠ *300 N. Hwy. 93, Alamo 89001,* ☎ *775/725–3371 or 888/740–8009,* FAX *775/725–3372. 15 rooms. Cable TV, pets allowed, no-smoking room. AE, D, MC, V.*

# Caliente

*149 miles from Las Vegas.*

Caliente used to be an important layover stop for water-thirsty steam locomotives making the trek through the steep, narrow canyons surrounding the town. Today, Lincoln County's largest community has 1,100 residents and serves as a hub for visitors striking off in all directions to see the five nearby state parks, the county seat of Pioche, or the ghost town of Delamar. And, as the name implies, it's hot here—not because of oppressive temperatures, but from the hot springs where townsfolk can relax.

The **Caliente Train Depot**, built in 1923, is a classic Mission-style station. Having outlived its usefulness as a depot, it now houses the chamber of commerce, the library, and an art gallery.

Head north on Spring Street to **Company Row.** The railroad company built these 18 homes in 1905 for workers manning this major refueling site for steam locomotives. The historic buildings are still in use today as privately owned homes.

On the south side of town, Highway 317 leads to the magnificent **Rainbow Canyon.** The canyon displays spectacular geologic outcroppings of red, orange, and other colorful hues. Some of the rock faces are marked with ancient petroglyphs. The bank-robbing duo of Butch Cassidy and the Sundance Kid hid out from the law deep inside some of the side canyons. You can also catch a close-up glimpse of a long diesel train winding its way through the chasm on the railroad's mainline. **Kershaw-Ryan State Park,** which is part of Rainbow Canyon, is a destination for picnickers and hikers. ✉ HC 64 Box 3 Caliente 89008, ☎ 775/726–3564, 𝚆𝙴𝙱 www.parks.nv.gov. ⌧ $3 per vehicle. ☯ Daily.

Erosion has shaped the bentonite clay of **Cathedral Gorge State Park** into odd formations; curtains of solidified mud resemble a lunar landscape. Step inside one of the curtains, between the wavy walls of mud, to escape the hot sun, just as the original Native American inhabitants of the area once did. **Miller Point Overlook** is about 2 mi north of the park's entrance. The overlook is a vantage point for viewing part of the ancient lake bed. Eagle View Trail, which starts at the overlook, is one of several park trails that brings hikers closer to the formations. The visitors center for Cathedral Gorge is the regional center for all state parks in Lincoln County. ✉ Box 176 Panaca 89042, ☎ 775/728–4460, 𝚆𝙴𝙱 www.parks.nv.gov. ⌧ $3 per vehicle. ☯ Daily.

OFF THE
BEATEN PATH

**DELAMAR GHOST TOWN –** Some dilapidated buildings and rusted-out equipment are all that remain of this former silver mining town that managed to boast a population of 3,000 around 1900. The so-called "Delamar Dust" inhaled by miners was actually silica dust, and the town earned a reputation as the "Maker of Widows" from the resulting deaths. Four-wheel drive vehicles are recommended for the 16-mi jaunt over the bumpy gravel and rock road that's chopped with several dry washes along the way. ✉ Southerly off U.S. 93, 16 mi west of Caliente, 𝚆𝙴𝙱 www.ghosttowns.com/states/nv/delamar.html. No services.

## Where to Stay & Eat

¢–$ ✕ **Brandin' Iron Restaurant.** This rustic little cafe in the heart of "downtown" prepares some of the best grub found this side of the Colorado River. ✉ 190 Clover St. Caliente 89008, ☎ 775/726–3164. AE, D, MC, V.

¢–$ ✕ **Knotty Pine Restaurant.** As you might expect, the walls are covered with the tongue-and-groove knotty pine, and the fare is standard American. Dig into a stack of the excellent pancakes while listening for the clock that whistles on the hour. There's a railroad mural in the far room. ✉ 690 Front St. Caliente 89008, ☎ 775/726–3137. No credit cards.

¢–$ 🏨 **Caliente Hot Springs Motel.** The rooms may be usual, but what's unusual is the bathhouse with natural hot springs to soothe tightened, car-cramped muscles. The bathhouse is open daily from 8 AM to 10 PM. For those willing to spend a little extra, four rooms have mineral baths inside. Access to the motel is off a side street (look for the directional sign); the motel is set back a distance from the highway and nestled against the mountain to the rear. ✉ 451 N. Spring St. Caliente 89008, ☎ 775/726–3777. 17 rooms. Some pets allowed. AE, D, MC, V.

¢–$ 🏨 **Shady Motel.** The newest, largest, and tallest motel in Lincoln County has twin two-story buildings with ADA-compliant rooms. The two buildings of the modern-looking complex face each other and not the highway, giving customers peace and quiet throughout the night. ✉ *450 Front St. Caliente 89008,* ☎ *775/726–3107. 28 rooms. Some pets allowed, no-smoking rooms. AE, D, MC, V.*

# Pioche

★ *174 mi from Las Vegas.*

A mining town dating back to the 1870s, Pioche once had the reputation of being less law-abiding than such notorious Western towns as Tombstone, Bodie, or Dodge City. According to legend, more than 70 gunfight victims were buried in Boot Hill cemetery before anyone who had died of natural causes found a place there. Relics of the boom-and-bust mining periods—from silver mining in the late 1800s to zinc and lead in the 1940s—are more prevalent on the streets today than gunplay, however. At 6,064 feet, walking around hilly Pioche can take your breath away—literally. Walk slowly and enjoy the sights.

The **Lincoln County Museum** on Main Street houses thousands of rock specimens, photos, and artifacts. The antique X-ray machine, with its long, pointy "arm," looks like something out of a Ray Bradbury novel. ✉ *69 Main St. Pioche 89043,* ☎ *775/962–5207.* ☉ *Mid-April–mid Oct., daily 10–4.* 🎟 *Free.*

The **Million Dollar Courthouse** is so named because that's how much it cost to pay off the building's debt of $16,400 over the course of 66 years. The museum includes restored offices on the first floor while a climb to the second floor reveals a courtroom with original light fixtures, ornate woodwork, and a molded-tin ceiling. Across from the courtroom is the jail with tiny holding cells made of stone and iron. ✉ *Lacour St.,* ☎ *702/962–5182.* 🎟 *Donations.* ☉ *Mid–Apr.–mid Oct., daily 10 AM–4 PM.*

There are several old building along Main Street that you can view from the outside. The **Mountain View Hotel** is a three-story wooden structure built in 1895. Former President Herbert Hoover, himself a mining engineer, stayed here on a visit to the town. Other buildings include the **Old Commercial Building and Fire Hall, Thompson Opera House,** and the **Gem Theater.** On the outskirts of town are the **Glory Holes and Pioche Aerial Tramway,** which hauled ore by gravity from the Treasure Hill mine to the mill in the valley below, and **Boot Hill,** where graves and carved wooden headstones recall the past.

The 65-acre reservoir at **Echo Canyon State Park** is a favorite for fishing and boating. The park has a campground and picnic area. Hikers will encounter abundant wildlife, a wide variety of native plants and the area's unique rock formations. ✉ *12 mi east of Pioche via state routes 322 and 323,* ☎ *775/962–5103,* 🌐 *www.parks.nv.gov.* 🎟 *$3 per vehicle.* ☉ *Daily.*

OFF THE BEATEN PATH

**GREAT BASIN NATIONAL PARK –** One of the newest national parks holds the only active glacier in Nevada. The combination of spectacular limestone-filled Lehman Caves National Monument, the Wheeler Peak Scenic Area, and other federal and private lands makes this a 120 square-mi natural desert-to-alpine wonderland with a "forest" of 5,000 year-old bristlecone pine trees. A jacket and non-skid walking shoes are recommended for cave tours because the inside "weather" is a constant 50°F and 90% humidity. Take U.S. 93 81 mi north to U.S. 6/50 junction, turn right (east) and go 28 mi to Highway 487 turnoff. Turn right (south) and go 5 mi to Baker. ⊠ *NV Hwy. 488 Baker 89311-9702,* ☎ *775/234–7331,* WEB *www.nps.gov/grba.* 🎫 *Free.* ☉ *Visitor center June–Aug. daily 7:30–6, Sept.–May daily 8:30–5; Lehman Cave tours daily.*

## Where to Stay & Eat

¢–$  ✕ **Silver Cafe.** The building dates back to 1907, and the restaurant has been in operation for nearly as long. Owners Sal and Barbi Cammarano serve hearty and plentiful meals at skinny prices. There's a cozy, pot-bellied stove and historic photos on the wall. ⊠ *97 Main St. 89043,* ☎ *775/962–5124. No credit cards.*

¢–$  🏠 **Overland Hotel & Saloon.** This relic from Pioche's past was rebuilt in the 1940s after the original building was destroyed in one of the town's numerous fires. The rooms are quaint, not fancy. You have to climb a long set of creaky stairs to get to them. ⊠ *85 Main St. 89043,* ☎ *775/962–5895,* FAX *775/962–5177. 13 rooms. Air conditioning, some pets allowed, no-smoking rooms. AE, D, MC, V.*

# Lincoln County A to Z

### CAR TRAVEL

Take I–15 north 22 mi from downtown Las Vegas to the U.S. 93 turnoff. Most of the Lincoln County sights, including Caliente and Pioche are along 93.

Given the remoteness of the area and the lack of services, make sure that you have plenty of fuel, water, food, and supplies before leaving any town. A good rule is to keep your gas tank at least half-full at all times. Also, the weather can be tricky in eastern Nevada. Monitor weather reports frequently and check road conditions, especially before leaving U.S. 93.

The Bureau of Land Management publishes a detailed map for off-highway travel in Lincoln County.

➤ CONTACTS: **BLM Caliente Field Station** ⊠ *1400 Front St. Caliente 89008,* ☎ *775/726–8100,* FAX *775/726–8111,* WEB *www.nv.blm.gov/ely.* ☉ *Mon.–Fri. 7:30–4:30. AE, DC, D, MC, V.*

### LODGING

Most Lincoln County motels observe a strict, no-nonsense no-smoking policy that can result in heavy fines ($50–$100 is common) and immediate eviction, no questions asked, if the smell of smoke is detectable or lingers in no-smoking rooms.

### VISITOR INFORMATION

➤ CONTACTS: **Caliente Chamber of Commerce** ⊠ *Caliente Train Depot 89008,* ☎ *775/726–3129,* FAX *775/726–3447.* ☉ *Mon.–Fri. 10–2.* **Greater Lincoln County Chamber of Commerce** WEB *www. lincolncountynevada.com.* **Pahranagat Valley Chamber of Commerce** ⊠ *Box 421 Alamo 89001,* ☎ *775/725–3483.* **Pioche Chamber of Commerce** ⊠ *55 Main St. 89043,* ☎ *775/962–5544.* ☉ *May–early Sept., Mon.–Thurs., 11–3.*

# GRAND CANYON NATIONAL PARK

*240 mi east of Las Vegas; south on U.S. 93 to Kingman, east on I–40 to Williams, north on Hwy. 64.*

Anyone who visits Las Vegas should seriously consider a side trip to the majestic **Grand Canyon National Park.** The twisted and contorted layers of rock, stratified to the lowest depths 1 mi down, reveal a fascinating geological profile. Even the finest photographs fail to deliver a fraction of the impact of a personal glimpse into this vast, beautiful scar on the surface of our planet.

There are two main access points to the canyon: the **South Rim** and the **North Rim,** both within the national park, but the hordes of visitors converge mostly on the South Rim during the summer, for good reason. Here travelers avail themselves of Grand Canyon Village, with most of the lodging and camping, restaurants and stores, and museums in the park, along with the airport, railroad depot, rim roads, scenic overlooks, and trailheads into the canyon. The East or North rims, both of which are less accessible and have fewer, though comparable, tourist services, are less crowded. The geology and vistas of the East Rim closely resemble what you'll see from the South Rim, and the entrance is accessible from both the South Rim and Flagstaff. The North Rim, by contrast, lies 1,000 feet higher than the South Rim and has a more alpine climate, with twice as much annual precipitation. Here, in the deep forests of the Kaibab Plateau, the crowds are thinner, the facilities fewer, and the views even more spectacular. ☎ *928/638–7888,* WEB *www.nps. gov/grca.* ☞ *$20 per car, $10 per individual.* ☉ *South and East Rims, daily; North Rim, mid-May–mid-Oct., daily.*

# South Rim

**Mather Point,** approximately 4 mi north from the south entrance, gives you the first glimpse of the canyon from one of the most impressive and accessible vista points on the rim; from it, you can see nearly a fourth of the Grand Canyon. The **Canyon View Information Plaza,** in Grand Canyon Village at Mather Point, orients you to many facets of the site, and it's an excellent place for gathering information, whether you're interested in escapist treks or group tours. If you'd like a little exercise and great overlooks of the canyon, it's an easy hike from the back of the visitors center to the El Tovar Hotel. Walk through a pretty wooded area for about ½ mi; from there the path runs along the rim for another ½ mi or so.

The **East Rim Drive,** relatively uncluttered by cars and tour buses, also affords some beautiful views of the canyon and the raging river. The 23-mi, 45-minute (one-way) drive along the East Rim takes you past **Lipan Point,** the widest and perhaps most spectacular part of the canyon, and continues to where you'll see partially intact ancient rock dwellings. On East Rim Drive, you'll find **Tusayan Ruin and Museum** (☉ Daily 9–5), which has exhibits about various Native American tribes who have inhabited the region in the past 2,000 years. East Rim Drive ends at the East Rim Entrance Station and the 70-foot **Desert View Watchtower,** which clings precariously to the lip of the chasm.

The **West Rim Drive** runs 8 mi west from Grand Canyon Village. Along this tree-lined, two-lane drive are several scenic overlooks with panoramic views of the inner canyon—all of which are popular sunset destinations. The West Rim Drive terminates at **Hermit's Rest.** Canyon views from here include Hermit's Rapids and the towering cliffs of the Supai and Redwall formations. From March through November, only the free shuttle bus is allowed on West Rim Drive. You can catch it at the West Rim Interchange near Bright Angel Lodge every 10–15 minutes 7:30 AM–sunset. The shuttle stops at all eight canyon overlooks on the 8-mi trip out to Hermits Rest, but only stops at Mohave and Hopi Points on the inbound leg. A complete round-trip takes 80 minutes.

★

## Where to Stay & Eat

$$–$$$$  ✕ ⌂ **El Tovar Hotel.** Built in 1905 of native stone and heavy pine logs, El Tovar is reminiscent of a grand European hunting lodge. For decades

the hotel's restaurant ($–$$$) has served fine food in a classic 19th-century room of hand-hewn logs and beam ceilings. ⊠ *Grand Canyon Village, AZ,* ☎ *303/297–2757 or 888/297–2757; hotel switchboard 928/638–2631,* FAX *303/297–3175,* WEB *www.grandcanyonlodges.com/. 70 rooms, 10 suites. Dining room, room service, bar. AE, D, MC, V.*

**$–$$**  ✕☷ **Bright Angel Lodge.** Built in 1936, this log-and-stone structure a few yards from the canyon rim has rooms in the main lodge or in quaint cabins (some with fireplaces) scattered among the pines. The informal steak house overlooks the abyss. ⊠ *Grand Canyon Village, AZ,* ☎ *303/297–2757 or 888/297–2757; hotel switchboard 928/638–2631,* FAX *303/297–3175,* WEB *www.grandcanyonlodges.com/. 11 rooms with bath, 13 rooms with ½ bath, 6 rooms with shared bath, 42 cabins with bath. Restaurant, coffee shop, hair salon, bar. AE, D, MC, V.*

**$**  ✕☷ **Phantom Ranch.** Talk about roughing it. Popular with hikers and
★   mule riders going to the bottom of the canyon, Phantom Ranch is the only lodging below the canyon's rim. These primitive quarters, built in 1922 along Bright Angel Creek, consist of cabins and dorm spaces. Cabins, which are heated and utilize evaporative cooling during the summer months, are included with the 2-day mule trips, while dormitory-style lodging is available to backpackers. The Canteen has breakfast, sack lunches, and dinners served at two seatings. The early seating serves steak and vegetarian meals while the second seating serves hiker's stew. ⊠ *On the canyon floor, AZ. 11 cabins, two bunks apiece. Restaurant, 2 cafeterias. AE, D, MC, V.*

OFF THE
BEATEN PATH

**HISTORIC ROUTE 66 –** If you are driving to the Grand Canyon from Las Vegas, an easterly diversion at the Andy Devine turnoff in Kingman puts you on the "old highway," known as U.S. Route 66—the longest remaining uninterrupted stretch of the "Main Street of America." Before taking off from Kingman, though, you'll want to start your adventure by exploring the Route 66 Museum and the Mohave Museum of History and Arts—two cultural centers that put into perspective the area's history, including the life of gravelly voiced actor Andy Devine, who grew up in Kingman. Taking I–40 may be 18 miles shorter and 15 minutes quicker, but you'll miss the road made famous by John Steinbeck's novel *The Grapes of Wrath* and the old Hackberry store with an exterior reminiscent of the 1950s and an interior filled with nostalgic goodies, not to mention snacks, pop, and water. Farther down the road are the Peach Springs headquarters for the Hualapai Tribe, one of several Native American tribes living in Northern Arizona, and the Grand Canyon Caverns, limestone caves found more than 200 feet below. Visit the **Powerhouse Visitor Center and Route 66 Museum** (⊠ 120 W. Andy Devine Ave. Kingman AZ 86402, ☎ 928/753–6106, ☏ $3, ☉ Daily, Mar.–Nov. 9–6; Dec.–Feb. 9–5, MC, V) and the **Mohave Museum of History and Arts** (⊠ 400 W. Beale St. Kingman AZ 86401, ☎ 520/753–3195, ☉ Mon.–Fri. 9–5, Sat.–Sun. 1–5)

# North Rim

**Bright Angel Point,** on the North Rim, is one of the most awe-inspiring overlooks on either rim. The trail leading to it begins on the grounds of the Grand Canyon Lodge and proceeds along the crest of a point of rocks that juts into the canyon for several hundred yards. The walk is only 1 mi round-trip, but it's an exciting trek because there are sheer drops just a few feet away on each side of the trail.

For spectacular sunrise views of the eastern canyon and Painted Desert, head to **Point Imperial.** The road to Point Imperial and Cape Royal intersects Highway 67 about 3 mi north of Grand Canyon Lodge. The picture-perfect road winds 8 mi through stands of quaking aspen into a forest of unkempt conifers. When the road forks, continue 3 mi north to the overlook.

## Where to Stay & Eat

$–$$ ✕⌕ **Grand Canyon Lodge.** The 1928 stone structure has comfortable, though not luxurious, rooms and is the only in-park lodging facility on the North Rim. The lounge area, with hardwood floors and high, beam ceilings, has a spectacular view of the canyon through massive plate-glass windows. Surprisingly sophisticated fare is served in the huge dining room ($–$$). ✉ *North Rim, AZ,* ☎ *303/297–2757 or 888/297–2757; hotel switchboard 928/638–2631,* FAX *303/297–3175,* WEB *www.grandcanyonlodges.com/. 40 rooms, 161 cabins. Cafeteria, dining room, bar, shop, laundry facilities, no-smoking rooms. AE, D, MC, V.*

$–$$ ⌕ **Kaibab Lodge.** Rustic cabins with simple furnishings are set in a wooded area just 5 mi from the park's entrance. When you're not out gazing into the abyss, you can sit around a stone fireplace (it can be chilly up here in spring and early fall). The lodge is open mid-May to mid-October. ✉ *Box 2997 Flagstaff AZ 86003,* ☎ *928/638–2389 (reservations for summer), 928/526–0924 (reservations for winter), or 800/525–0924,* WEB *www.canyoneers.com. 29 cabin-style units; limited group quarters available. Restaurant, shop. D, MC, V.*

# Grand Canyon A to Z

*To research prices, get advice from other travelers, and book travel arrangements, visit www.fodors.com.*

### CAR TRAVEL

It's a little less than 300 mi to the South Rim from Las Vegas. Take U. S. 93 to Kingman, Arizona; I–40 east from Kingman to Williams; then Highway 64 and U.S. 180 to the edge of the abyss. The North Rim is about 282 mi from Las Vegas. Take I–15 east to Hurricane, Utah; Highways 59 and 389 to Fredonia; and U.S. 89 and Highway 67 to the North Rim. The North Rim is closed to automobiles after the first heavy snowfall of the season (usually in late October or early November) through mid-May. All North Rim facilities close between October 15 and May 15, though the park itself stays open for day use from October 15 through December 1, if heavy snows don't close the roads before then.

➤ CONTACTS: **North Rim road conditions** ☎ *928/638–7888.*

### LODGING

Lodging reservations at all Grand Canyon National Park facilities are made through a master concessionaire, Xanterra Parks and Resorts. Occasionally, reservations can be made at individual properties on the same day of arrival, but arranging for that once-in-a-lifetime room far in advance is more likely to result in fewer disappointments. Contact Xanterra for dining information as well.

➤ CONTACTS: **Xanterra Parks and Resorts** (✉ 14001 E. Illiff, Suite 600 Aurora CO 80014, ☎ 303/297–2757 or 888/297–2757 (lodging), 928/638–2631 (dining), FAX 303/297–3175, WEB www.grandcanyonlodges.com/.)

### TIME

Hours of operation listed for the Grand Canyon use Arizona time.

The state of Nevada is in the Pacific Time Zone, while Arizona is in the Mountain Time Zone. Arizona does not use Daylight Savings Time, however, and as a result, during the summer, Nevada and Arizona observe the same hours.

### TOURS

Air Vegas, Scenic Airlines, and Grand Canyon Tour Company offer air tours of the Grand Canyon from Las Vegas; each provides ground transportation around the South Rim, stopping at spectacular scenic overlooks and Grand Canyon Village. You can also take a helicopter tour with any of the four Las Vegas–based companies that take you out over Hoover Dam and Lake Mead for a thrilling trip that can last from two to four hours.

➤ AIR TOURS: **Air Vegas** (☎ 702/736–3599 or 800/255–7474, WEB www.airvegas.com). **Grand Canyon Tour Company** (☎ 702/655–6060 or 800/222–9966, WEB www.grandcanyontourcompany.com). **HeliUSA** (☎ 702/736–8787 or 800/359–8727, WEB www.heliusa.net). **Maverick Helicopter Tours** (☎ 702/261–0007 or 888/261–4414, WEB www.maverickhelicopter.com). **Papillon** (☎ 702/736–7243 or 888/635–7272, WEB www.papillon.com). **Scenic Airlines** (☎ 702/638–3300 or 800/634–6801, WEB www.scenic.com). **Sundance Helicopter** (☎ 702/736–0606 or 800/653–1881, WEB www.helicoptour.com).

### VISITOR INFORMATION

➤ CONTACTS: **Grand Canyon Chamber of Commerce** (✉ Box 3007, Grand Canyon, AZ 86023, ☎ 928/638–2901, WEB www.grandcanyonchamber.org). **Grand Canyon National Park Visitors Services** (✉ Box 129, Grand Canyon, AZ 86023, ☎ 928/638–7888 for recorded information, FAX 928/638–7797, WEB www.nps.gov/grca). **Kane County Office of Tourism** (✉ 78 S. 100 E, Kanab, UT 84741, ☎ 435/644–5033 or 800/733–5263, WEB www.kaneutah.com).

# DEATH VALLEY, CALIFORNIA

With more than 3.3 million acres, **Death Valley National Park** is the largest national park outside Alaska. The topography of Death Valley is a mini geology lesson. Two hundred million years ago, seas covered the area, depositing layers of sediment and fossils. Between 35 million and 5 million years ago, faults in the Earth's crust and volcanic activity pushed and folded the ground, causing mountain ranges to rise and the valley floor to drop. The valley was then filled periodically by lakes, which eroded the surrounding rocks into fantastic formations and deposited the salts that now cover the floor of the basin. Today the area has 14 square mi of sand dunes, 200 square mi of crusty salt flats, hills, 11,000-foot mountains, and canyons of many colors. There are more than 1,000 species of plants and trees—21 of which are unique to the valley, such as the yellow Panamint daisy and the blue-flowered Death Valley sage. Distances are deceiving here: some sights appear in clusters, but others require extensive travel. As with any desert travel, especially as the months get hotter, you should always carry plenty of water, sunblock, a hat, a mirror, and other potential lifesaving items—just in case. WEB *www.nps.gov/deva.* ✉ *$10 per vehicle, valid for 7 consecutive days from date of purchase.* ☉ *Daily.*

Lodging facilities at Furnace Creek Ranch and Inn and Stovepipe Wells Village are managed by a master concessionaire, **Xanterra Parks and Resorts.** During the cooler period, October through May, accommodations sell out early, especially over holiday weekends. ✉ *14001 E. Illiff, Suite 600 Aurora CO 80014,* ☎ *303/297–2757 or 888/297–2757,* FAX *303/297–3175,* WEB *www.xanterra.com.*

## Stovepipe Wells Village

Stovepipe Wells Village was the first resort in Death Valley. The tiny town, which dates back to 1926, takes its name from the stovepipe that early prospectors left to indicate that they'd found water. The area contains a motel, a restaurant, a grocery store with unleaded fuel, a landing strip, and campgrounds. Located just minutes away are sand dunes (familiar perhaps from their role in the *Star Wars* films); Devil's Corn Field; Salt Creek, a brackish, salty year-round flow from an underground springs that provides a breeding ground for the endangered pupfish; and colorful Mosaic Canyon.

### Where to Stay & Eat

$ ✕▣ **Stovepipe Wells Village.** An aircraft landing strip is an unusual touch for a motel, as is a heated mineral pool, but the rest is pretty standard. Still, this is the best lodging bargain inside the park, offering pleasant rooms at a reasonable rate, as well as a campground and RV park. The Old West-style Toll Road Restaurant ($) serves steaks, prime rib, and salmon. ⊠ *Hwy. 190, Death Valley National Park 92328,* ☎ *303/297–2757 or 888/297–2757,* FAX *303/297–3175,* WEB *www.xanterra.com. 83 rooms. Restaurant, tennis courts, pool, bar, shop, Internet. AE, D, MC, V.*

## Scotty's Castle Area

*46 mi north of Stovepipe Wells Village; head east on Hwy. 190, then north at signs for castle.*

★ **Scotty's Castle** is an odd apparition rising out of a canyon. This $2.5-million Moorish mansion, begun in 1924 and never completed, is named after Walter Scott, better known as Death Valley Scotty. An ex-cowboy, prospector, and performer in Buffalo Bill's Wild West Show, Scotty always told people the castle was his, financed by gold from a secret mine. That secret mine was, in fact, a Chicago millionaire named Albert Johnson, who was advised by doctors to spend time in a warm, dry climate. The house, which functioned for a while as a hotel—guests included Bette Davis and Norman Rockwell—contains works of art, imported carpets, handmade European furniture, and a tremendous pipe organ. Costumed rangers portray life at the castle in 1939. Fifty-minute tours are conducted frequently, but waits of up to two hours are possible. To avoid delays, try to arrive for the first tour of the day. ☎ 760/786–2392, WEB *www.nps. gov/deva/pphtml/facilities.html.* ⊠ *$8.* ☉ *Grounds daily 7–6, tours daily 9–5.*

The impressive **Ubehebe Crater,** 500 feet deep and ½ mi across, was created as a result of violent underground steam and gas explosions about 3,000 years ago; its volcanic ash spreads out over most of the area, and the cinders are as thick as 150 feet around the crater's rim. You'll get some superb views of the valley from here, and you can take a fairly easy hike around the rim at the west side to Little Hebe Crater, one of a smaller cluster of craters to the south and west.

## Furnace Creek Area

*54 mi south of Scotty's Castle, 25 mi southeast of Stovepipe Wells Village on Hwy. 190.*

Renowned mule teams hauled borax from the **Harmony Borax Works** to the railroad town of Mojave, 165 mi away, and were truly a sight to behold: 20 mules hitched up to two massive wagons, each carrying a load of 10 tons of borax through burning desert. The teams plied the route between 1884 and 1907, when the railroad finally arrived in Zabriskie. The **Borax Museum,** 2 mi south of the borax works, houses original mining machinery and historical displays in a building that once served as a boardinghouse for miners; the adjacent structure is the original mule-team barn. ⊠ *Harmony Borax Works Rd., west off Hwy. 190.* ▧ *Free.* ☉ *Borax works daily, museum weekends.*

Exhibits on the desert, trail maps, and brochures can be found at the **Visitor Center at Furnace Creek.** ⊠ *Hwy. 190,* ☎ *760/786–3200,* W̅E̅B̅ *www.nps.gov/deva.* ☉ *Daily 8–6.*

A mild hike into the spacious **Golden Canyon** landform affords some spectacular views of the glowing yellow and orange rock walls. Farther up the canyon, you'll encounter a colorful formation called Red Cathedral. ⊠ *Badwater Rd., 3 mi south of Furnace Creek; turn left into parking lot.*

The **Artists Palette,** named for the brilliant array of pigments created by volcanic deposits, seems a bit out of place compared to the light and dark brown colors that make up Death Valley's stark landscape. Artists Drive, the approach to the area, heads one-way north off Badwater Road, so if you're visiting Badwater it's more efficient to come here on the way back. The drive winds through foothills composed of colorful sedimentary and volcanic rocks. *8 mi north of Badwater, Badwater Rd. to Artists Dr.; 10 mi south of Furnace Creek, Hwy. 190 to Badwater Rd. to Artists Dr.*

Looking like peaks of whipped chocolate meringue, **Devil's Golf Course** actually is solid mud-color rock salt poking skyward. You don't want to venture off the road because the jagged spires have been known to shred tennis shoes and produce severe scrapes and broken bones should you take a tumble. ⊠ *Badwater Rd., 5 mi north of Badwater, 14 mi south of visitor center at Furnace Creek.*

As you approach **Badwater,** you'll see a shallow pool lying almost lifeless against an expanse of desolate salt flats—a sharp contrast to the expansive canyons and elevation not too far away. Legend has it that one of the early surveyors saw that his mule wouldn't drink from the pool and noted "badwater" on his map. The water contains mostly sodium chloride and is saltier than the sea. Badwater is the lowest spot in the Western Hemisphere—282 feet below sea level—and also one of the hottest. On the rock face behind the road, a marker indicates sea level. ⊠ *Badwater Rd., 19 mi south of visitor center at Furnace Creek.*

**Zabriskie Point** is one of Death Valley National Park's most scenic spots. Not particularly high—only about 710 feet—it overlooks a striking badlands panorama with wrinkled, multicolor hills. Film buffs of a certain vintage may recognize it (or at least its name) from the film *Zabriskie Point.* ⊠ *Hwy. 190, 5 mi south of Furnace Creek.*

From atop **Dante's View,** more than 5,000 feet up in the Black Mountains, you can see most of the valley's 110-mi expanse. The oasis of Furnace Creek is a green spot to the north. The view up and down is equally astounding: the tiny blackish patch far below is Badwater; on the western horizon is Mt. Whitney, the highest spot in the continental United States, at 14,494 feet. ⊠ *Dante's View Rd. off Hwy. 190, 21 mi south of Zabriskie Point.*

**Marta Beckett's Amargosa Opera House** is an unexpected pleasure in an unlikely place. Marta Beckett is an artist and dancer from New York who first saw the town of Amargosa while on tour in 1964. Three years later she impulsively bought a boarded-up theater amid a complex of run-down Spanish colonial buildings and then began performing there in 1968. To make up for the sparse attendance in the early days, Becket painted an audience, turning the walls and the ceiling of the theater into a trompe l'oeil masterpiece. Today the hamlet's population is still in single digits (cats outnumber people here), but it swells when cars, motor homes, and buses roll in to catch the show. Becket often performs her blend of classical ballet, mime, and 19th-century melodrama to sell-out crowds, so advance reservations are strongly encouraged. After the show you can meet her in the adjacent art gallery. ⊠ *Hwy. 127, Death Valley Junction, CA 92328,* ☎ *760/852–4441,* FAX *760/852– 4138,* WEB *www.amargosa-opera-house.com.* 🖾 *$15.* ⊙ *Performances Oct.–May, 8:15 PM. MC, V.*

### Where to Stay & Eat

$–$$$  🏨 **Furnace Creek Ranch.** Originally the crew headquarters for a borax company, the ranch has four two-story buildings with motel-style rooms. The adjacent Furnace Creek golf course, 218 feet below sea level, guarantees you'll play your "lowest" round of golf. The general store sells supplies and gifts, and the visitor center is a short walk away. ⊠ *Hwy 190 (Box 1), Death Valley National Park 92328,* ☎ *760/786– 2345, 303/297–2757 (reservations). 224 rooms. Restaurant, coffee shop, 18-hole golf course, 2 tennis courts, pool, basketball, horseback riding, bar, shop, playground, meeting room. Energy surcharge. AE, DC, MC, V.*

## Panamint Springs Area

*31 mi west of Stovepipe Wells Village on Hwy. 190, 48 miles east of Lone Pine, California on U.S. Hwy. 395.*

Added to the park in 1994, this remote spot is an ideal destination for backcountry enthusiasts, especially those with high-clearance or four-wheel-drive vehicles. To the east and south on Emigrant Canyon Road is Skidoo, the remains of a once-thriving mining town, and Wildrose Charcoal Kilns, which produced fuel for silver ore processing more than 125 years ago. To the west lies Father Crowley Point, a lava-filled landscape that looks out on the colorful Rainbow Canyon. Just outside town is Darwin Falls, a rare water hole in the arid desert.

OFF THE BEATEN PATH    **SHOSHONE MUSEUM –** Displays include numerous artifacts of the region's Tonopah & Tidewater Railroad history as well as a fossilized mammoth discovered nearby. Shoshone, which has a motel, a cafe, a general store, fuel, and an RV park, is 72 mi south of Furnace Creek or 26 mi south of Death Valley Junction on Hwy. 127. ⊠ *Hwy. 127 Shoshone CA 92384,* ☎ *760/852–4414.* ⊙ *Wed.–Sun. 8–4.* 🖾 *Donation.*

### Where to Stay & Eat

$–$$  ✕🏨 **Panamint Springs Resort.** Though inside the park, this privately owned property is not associated with the National Park Service. It overlooks the nearby awesome geological formations as well as the Panamint Valley Sand Dunes. A campground and RV park are available. Summertime barbecues are served outdoors on the porch which has a spectacular view of Panamint Valley. ⊠ *Hwy. 190 (Box 395, Ridgecrest, CA 93556),* ☎ *775/482–7680,* FAX *775/482–7682,* WEB *www.deathvalley. com/reserve/reserve.shtml. 14 rooms, 1 cottage. Restaurant, bar, shop, some pets allowed. MC, V.*

# 10 PLAYING THE GAMES

To a gambler, luck is the ultimate authority. No guardian angel or guiding light; no god or goddess; no religion, science, or philosophy can sway the outcome of a chance event. Gambling is a means by which we strip away our orthodox certainties in order to summon up the deep human instinct to appeal to chance as the ultimate source of control. Strictly speaking, however, casinos don't offer pure games of chance because each gives itself a little edge. It's up to us players to counteract that edge whenever we can. Here's how.

By Deke
Castleman

Revised by Bill
Burton

OVER THE PAST 60 YEARS the name Las Vegas has become synonymous with gambling. Nine out of 10 visitors gamble while they're in town. It is almost perverse to visit Las Vegas and *not* gamble. But while unreasonable expectations can lead to disappointment or, worse still, the loss of a lot of money, the key to having a good time is to approach the casinos with the idea that, contrary to popular opinion, you *can* win or, at the very least, get much more than your money's worth of playing time. Your success depends less on being lucky than on being familiar with the rules of the games, being aware of the concepts *behind* the games, and being conversant with the strategies that enable you to play not only with confidence but also with a fair shot at walking away a winner.

# CASINO STRATEGY

## The House Advantage

The first important concept to understand about gambling in Las Vegas is that the odds for all the games provide an advantage for the casino ("house"), generally known, appropriately enough, as the "house advantage" (or "edge" or "vigorish"). The casino is a business, and wagering is its product. Because the house establishes the rules, procedures, and payoffs on every game, it builds an automatic commission into every bet to ensure a profit margin.

Here's how it works. Let's pretend that I'm the house and you're the customer and we're betting on a series of coin flips. The deal that I make with you is that every time the coin lands heads up, I win and you pay me a dollar. Every time the coin lands tails up, you win—but I only pay you 90¢. The law of averages maintains that out of every 100 coin tosses, heads will win 50 times and tails will win the other 50. If I take a dime out of every one of your winning payoffs, the longer you play, the more dimes will wind up in my pocket. If you started with a $50 bankroll, after 1,000 tosses, *even if you win half of them,* you'd be busted out. (Because it requires two trials—win one, lose one—for the house to make its 10¢ "commission," your "negative expectation," or house edge, in this example is 5%.)

The second important gambling concept is known as "fluctuation" (or "variance"). In plain English, we're talking about "luck." Looking at our coin-toss game through the lens of averages, if you and I flip a coin 1,000 times, it's reasonable to expect that the coin will land heads up and tails up close to 500 times each. However, if we flip the coin only 10 times, it's conceivable that the coin could land heads up only once or twice or as many as eight or even 10 times. Now let's say that we made the same betting deal as above but we limited the number of tosses to 10. This would largely eliminate your 5% disadvantage and leave it up to "the luck of the toss"—in other words, the fluctuation. Thus, a short-term fluctuation in the law of averages eliminates the long-term threat of the negative expectation.

How do these concepts—the house advantage and negative expectation, and the short-term fluctuation—apply to the choices that you make as a casino customer? Your decisions, based on these concepts, will determine not only what you play, but also how you play; how long you play; and, ultimately, how well you play.

# Luck Versus the Edge

The average "bankroll" (cash carried for the sole purpose of gambling) of a Las Vegas visitor who plans to spend some time in the casino is roughly $500. This is a crucial statistic. The amount of your bankroll and your preferred style of "action" (how you risk your bankroll) define your relationship to luck and the house edge.

Basically, the parameters of gambling action are fast and slow. Some people, though they're in the minority, like their action fast and loose and high-risk; these are true "gamblers," in the old-fashioned sense of the word. The extreme version of this type of action is to take the whole $500 bankroll and lay it down on a single play—say, red or black on the roulette table. The odds are not quite even. The green 0 and 00 on the roulette table give the house an advantage of 5.26% (☞ Roulette). Still, even though the odds are less than fair, the immediate result will be the same: double or nothing.

Making one play eliminates both the law of averages and the long-term threat of the house advantage; here you rely solely on the luck of the draw. If you want to go on a roller-coaster ride of luck, with a minute or so of adrenaline-pumping, heart-pounding excitement, lay it all down at once. In a matter of moments, you'll either have twice the money you arrived with or none of it.

A less extreme version of this wild ride is to break your bankroll into two units, and make two bets. Here you can either double your money, lose it all, or break even. Similarly, if you separate your $500 bankroll into five units and make five bets, or 10 units and make 10 bets, your ride lasts a little longer and your outcome is a little less black and white: You can double, bust out, break even, or come out somewhat ahead or behind. Still, the cumulative danger of the house advantage barely comes into play.

Luck can supersede the house advantage, but only in the short run. And though luck accounts for winners big and small—such as the local cocktail waitress who, in January 2000, lined up three Megabucks symbols on the $3 payline to win $35 million, or the $2 dice shooter who parlays a hot hand into a couple of hundred bucks—the lack of luck can obliterate a bankroll faster than a crooked S&L.

Besides, most people who come to Las Vegas like to gamble for as long as they can without running out of money. These people take their $500 bankrolls and split them into 100 units to make $5 bets, 250 units for $2 bets, 500 units for $1 bets, or even 2,000 units for 25¢ bets. This guarantees plenty of time for the law of averages to even out the fluctuations. On the other hand, it puts the house advantage and the negative expectation right back into the game.

So how do you play as long as you like without the certainty of the house advantage grinding your bankroll into dust?

## The Good Bets

The first part of any viable casino strategy is to risk the most money on wagers that present the lowest edge for the house. Blackjack, craps, video poker, and baccarat are the most advantageous to the bettor in this regard. The two types of bets at baccarat have a house advantage of a little more than 1%. The basic line bets at craps, if backed up with full odds, can have a house advantage of as low as 0.5%. Blackjack and video poker, at times, can not only put you even with the house (a true 50-50 proposition) but actually give you a slight long-term advantage.

How can a casino possibly provide you with a 50-50 or even a positive expectation at some of its games? First, because a vast number of suckers make the bad bets (those with a house advantage of 5%–35%, such as roulette, keno, and slots) day in and day out. Second, because the casino knows that very few people are aware of the opportunities to beat the odds. Third, because it takes skill—requiring study and practice—to be in a position to exploit these opportunities the casino presents. However, a mere hour or two spent learning strategies for the beatable games will put you light years ahead of the vast majority of visitors who give the gambling industry an average 12%–15% profit margin.

## Comps, Clubs & Coupons

Not only can you even out the odds to a certain extent, but you can also take advantage of the various attractive incentives casinos offer so that the suckers will stay and play—and, in the long run, lose, due either to house advantage or basic ignorance. These available, profitable, and somewhat prestigious incentives are known as "comps" (short for complimentaries) or "freebies." The most common comps are free parking in downtown parking structures (all you have to do is walk into the casino and validate your ticket at the cashier window) and free cocktails (all you have to do is play at any table or machine). Other comps range from a "line pass" (the right to proceed directly into a showroom or restaurant without having to wait in line) all the way to a penthouse suite complete with private swimming pool, butler, and chef, and round-trip airfare from anywhere in the world. It all depends on how much you're willing to risk: comps are calculated by multiplying your average bet by the amount of time you play by the house advantage.

Say, for example, that you play at a $25-a-hand blackjack table for eight hours. The casino expects you to participate in 60 hands an hour and lose at a rate of 2% (what the casino calculates as its average advantage). Sixty hands an hour times $25 a hand times eight hours times 2% equals $240. Of that anticipated profit, the house is prepared to return 30%–40% to you in complimentaries in order to "reward" you for your action. Thus, under the described circumstances, you'll qualify for $72–$96 worth of comps, whether you win, lose, or break even.

To be eligible for comps, you have to get "rated" as a player. When you sit down to play, have the dealer call over the pit boss—the person who supervises the action on the gaming tables—and tell him that you'd like to have your play rated. The pit boss will fill out a rating card with your name, average bet, and length of play. These data are input into the marketing department computer; based on your "comp equivalency" (for example, the $72–$96 you've qualified for), you'll be provided free food or room or perks. The kings of comps are the "high rollers," those willing to risk a lot of money at high-stakes games.

Slot clubs are another good way to reconcile the house advantage with playing for as long as you like. These clubs, introduced in the late 1980s to give slot and video poker players some high-roller status, are similar to frequent-flier programs offered by the airlines. It costs nothing to sign up for slot clubs and the benefits can be substantial. When you become a member, you're given a plastic card that you insert into the gaming machine you're using; the card tracks your play and you receive points based on the amount of money you risk. Slot-club points can be redeemed for free gifts, food, rooms, invitations to special parties and slot tournaments, VIP status, gift certificates at local stores, and cash. You can join slot clubs at as many casinos as you like, then play at the places that offer the best perks.

Finally, the best bet in any casino is one that is accompanied by a gambling coupon, known as a "lucky buck." These are most often found in hotel "funbooks," small coupon booklets given out free for the asking at casinos; generally all you need is a hotel room key and an out-of-state ID (this prevents locals from taking advantage of the valuable promotions). Most funbooks contain coupons that return 7 to 5, 3 to 2, even 2 to 1 on even-money wagers.

Playing with coupons gives you a decided advantage over the house. In our coin-toss example, you'd wager a dollar of your own and a coupon for another dollar. If you win, I'd pay you $2 (for a return of $3). That extra dollar, though it might not seem like much, would pay my commission on 10 additional coin tosses. Furthermore, because some of the major hotel-casinos and most of the smaller ones distribute free funbooks, you and a partner can collect a dozen of them and then go on a "coupon run." You make even-money bets backed up by coupons, touring a number of casinos while you're at it. Done properly, you could conceivably fill up an entire Las Vegas visit making positive plays with lucky bucks.

# THE GAMES

Each of the casino games has its own rules, etiquette, odds, and strategies. When you've decided on the kind of action you wish to pursue, you can choose a game that best suits your style. Then, if you take the time to learn the basics and fine points thoroughly, you'll be adequately prepared to play with as much of an edge as the game, combined with comps and coupons if possible, provides. In the meantime, good short-term fluctuation can add to your winnings. Some of the casinos offer free lessons to teach you how to play the most popular casino games, including blackjack, craps, roulette, and mini-baccarat. These lessons are a good way to become familiar with the rules of the games and table etiquette.

## Baccarat

The most "glamorous" game in the casino, American baccarat (pronounced *bah*-kuh-rah), is a version of *chemin de fer*, popular in European gambling halls. The Italian word *baccara* means "zero"; this refers to the point value of 10s and picture cards. Most Las Vegas casinos like to surround baccarat with an aura of mystique: the game is played in a separate pit, supervised by personnel in tuxedos; the game's ritual is somewhat esoteric; and the minimum bet is usually $20–$100. Some casinos have forgone the larger baccarat pits in favor of the smaller mini-baccarat tables. Many players prefer mini-baccarat because it is less intimidating and can be played for lower limits. Mini-baccarat is essentially the same game, only it is played in the main blackjack pit, sans tuxedos and ritual, and with $5 minimums.

Up to 15 players can be seated around a baccarat table (six or seven at mini-baccarat). The game is run by four pit personnel. Two dealers sit side by side in the middle of the table; they handle the winning and losing bets and keep track of each player's "commission" (explained below). The "caller" stands in the middle of the other side of the table and dictates the action. A pit boss supervises the game and acts as final judge if any disputes arise.

Baccarat is played with eight decks of cards dealt from a large "shoe" (or card holder). Each player is offered a turn at handling the shoe and dealing the cards. Two two-card hands are dealt: the "player" and the "bank" hands. The player who deals the cards is called the banker,

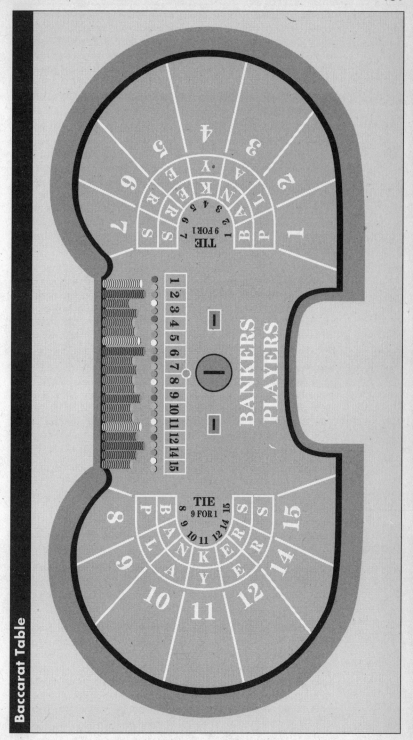

Baccarat Table

though the house, of course, banks both hands. The players bet on which hand, player or banker, will come closest to adding up to 9 (a "natu-ral"). The cards are totaled as follows: Ace through 9 retain face value, while 10s and picture cards are worth zero. If you have a hand adding up to more than 10, the number 10 is subtracted from the total. For example, if one hand contains a 10 and a 4, the hand adds up to 4. If the other holds an ace and 6, it adds up to 7. If a hand has a 7 and 9, it adds up to 6.

Depending on the two hands, the caller either declares a winner and loser (if either hand actually adds up to 8 or 9), or calls for another card for the player hand (if it totals 1, 2, 3, 4, 5, or 10). The bank hand then either stands pat or draws a card, determined by a complex se-ries of rules depending on what the player's total is and dictated by the caller. When one or the other hand is declared a winner, the deal-ers go into action to pay off the winning wagers, collect the losing wa-gers, and add up the commission (usually 5%) that the house collects on the bank hand. Both bets have a house advantage of slightly more than 1%.

The player-dealer (or banker) continues to hold the shoe as long as the bank hand wins. As soon as the player hand wins, the shoe moves coun-terclockwise around the table. Players are not required to deal; they can refuse the shoe and pass it to the next player. Most players bet on the bank hand when they deal, because they "represent" the bank, and to do otherwise would seem as if they were betting "against" them-selves. This isn't really the case, but it seems that way.

Making a bet at baccarat is very simple. All you have to do is place your money in either the bank, player, or tie box on the layout (☞ Bac-carat Table illustration), which appears directly in front of where you sit at the table. If you're betting that the bank hand will win, you put your chips in the bank box; bets for the player hand go in the player box. (Only real suckers bet on the tie, which has a house advantage of 14.4%.)

Because the caller dictates the action, the player responsibilities are min-imal. It's not necessary to know any of the card-drawing rules, even if you're the banker. Playing baccarat is a simple matter of guessing whether the player or banker hand will come closest to 9, and decid-ing how much to bet on the outcome.

# Bingo

Bingo is one of the world's best-known and best-loved games. It's also responsible for raising more money for charities, service organiza-tions, religious institutions, and Native American tribes than any other fund-raiser.

One of the least profitable games for casinos, bingo was originally in-cluded in the roster of games for the same reason that extravaganzas were introduced to the showrooms, cheap steaks and breakfasts ap-peared in the restaurants, and coupons for free souvenirs began to be distributed via funbooks: to attract people into the casino. Simply by offering bingo, casinos can fill large halls with players, who have to pass by the pit and slots on the way in and out, where they'll drop a few bucks on a roulette wheel or in a slot machine.

Bingo is derived from the Italian game lotto but is similar to the orig-inal Chinese game keno. Both use numbered cards, numbered Ping-Pong balls blown from a cage, a caller, and a master board. There, however, the similarities pretty much dissolve. Bingo is played on paper cards marked with a "dauber" or on two-ply cardboard "boards" marked with little round plastic tabs. Bingo cards contain 25 squares. Five horizontal columns are topped with the letters B-I-N-G-O. Under the B are five boxes, with a number in each box between 1 and 15; under the I, five boxes with numbers between 16 and 30; under the N, four boxes numbered between 31 and 45; and a "free" box in the center of the card; under the G, five numbers between 46 and 60; and under the O, five numbers between 61 and 75.

The caller announces the letter and number of each ejected Ping-Pong ball and illuminates them on the master board. For example, if the caller announces "G-58" or "Number 58, under G," the players check their cards under the column topped by the G for the number 58. If it appears, they mark the number with the ink dauber or the plastic tabs. A winning card will have five numbers lined up in a row, either horizontally, vertically, or diagonally. The "free" square is always considered marked, so frequently you'll only need to match four numbers to win a game.

When a player lines up a card with the proper configuration of markings, he or she yells out "Bingo!" A floor person picks up the card and verifies the player's numbers by those on the big board, then declares the player the winner. The caller gives the other players a few moments to determine whether they, too, have won; if there's another winner, the two split the total prize money. Most of the time, however, there's only one winner per game, because great pains are taken to ensure that each card is unique. Prize money can range from $10 on a regular bingo game up to $50,000 for a progressive jackpot.

The variety of patterns for bingo games is vast, from the "no-number" card, where not a single number on the card has been called, to the "coverall" or "black-out," where every number on the card is marked. Configurations such as "inside corner," "outside corner," and shapes such as "diamond," "square," "picture frame," or the letters "L," "X," "T," "H," and "U" are announced by the caller at the start of each game, and the patterns illuminated on secondary boards around the room.

There are almost as many different buy-ins as there are patterns. Cards start at 25¢ and can go up to $500 and higher for special promotions and tournaments. Different-color cards have different buy-in denominations (for example, blue costs $3, green $6, orange $9, etc.); the prize money is determined by the card's worth. "Game packs" or "booklets" consist of a given number of paper cards stapled together and used up in a "session." A quick call to the bingo room can tell you which sessions are played when.

Each game moves fairly quickly. The numbers are called one right after the other, leaving the players just enough time to look for them on their cards. Old bingo hands can play dozens of cards simultaneously, but beginners should limit themselves to a half dozen at most. When you buy in, if it's a paper session (i.e., one played on paper cards), make sure you have a dauber on hand when the game starts; they're for sale at the bingo cashier for $1 or so. By watching, asking your neighbors or a floor person a quick question about something you don't quite understand, and playing, you'll be in the swing of things after the first few games of a session.

Though the pace of bingo can often be blistering, the games start out fairly relaxed—with empty cards and players gearing up for the pattern. Tension mounts as more numbers are called, cards fill up, and players await the magic number or two that will make them winners. Finally, someone yells, "Binnnnnngooooo!" and for a brief moment the tension remains while the other players catch up on the last number or two. Then, as people realize they're not co-winners, the room deflates like a popped balloon. Quickly, the winner is verified and a new game starts the tension building all over again.

## Blackjack

Blackjack is the most popular table game in the casino. It's easy to learn, fun to play, and it involves skill, and therefore presents varying levels of challenge. Blackjack also has one of the lowest house advantages. Furthermore, it's the game of choice when it comes to qualifying for comps: you can play for as long as you like, stand a real chance of breaking even or winning, *and* be treated like visiting royalty while you're at it.

Because blackjack is the only table game in the casino in which players can gain a long-term advantage over the house, it is the only table game in the casino (other than poker) that can be played professionally. And because blackjack can be played professionally, it is the most written-about and discussed casino game. Dozens of how-to books, trade journals, magazines, newsletters, computer programs, videos, theses, and novels are available on every aspect of blackjack, everything from how to add to 21 to when to stand or hit, how to play against a variety of shuffles, and the Level-Two Zen Count. Blackjack pros can spend hours debating whether the two-deck game at the Las Vegas Hilton has a starting house edge of 0.03 or 0.0275 because of the doubling-down-after-splitting option, or whether the Hi-Opt II count system's 88% betting efficiency correlation makes it stronger than the unbalanced count's perfect insurance indicator. Of course, training someone to play blackjack professionally is beyond the scope of this guide. Contact the **Gambler's Book Club** (☎ 702/382–7555) for a catalog of gambling books, software, and videotapes, including the largest selection on blackjack around.

### The Rules
Basically, here's how it works: you play blackjack against a dealer, and whichever one of you comes closest to a card total of 21 without going over is the winner. Number cards are worth their face value, picture cards count as 10, and aces are worth either 1 or 11. (Hands with aces in them are known as "soft" hands. Always count the ace first as an 11; if you also have a 10, your total will be 21, not 11.) If the dealer has a 17 and you have a 16, you lose. If you have an 18 against a dealer's 17, you win (even money). If both you and the dealer have a 17, it's a tie (or "push") and no money changes hands. If you go over a total of 21 (or "bust"), you lose immediately, even if the dealer also busts later in the hand. If your first two cards add up to 21 (a "natural"), you're paid 3 to 2. However, if the dealer also has a natural, it's a push. A natural beats a total of 21 achieved with more than two cards.

You're dealt two cards, either face down or face up, depending on the custom of the particular casino. Two cards go to the dealer—one face down and one face up. Depending on your first two cards and the dealer's up card, you can:

**stand,** or refuse to take another card.

**hit,** or take as many cards as you need until you stand or bust.

**double down,** or double your bet and take one card.

**split** a like pair; if you're dealt two 8s, for example, you can double your bet and play the 8s as if they're two hands.

## Blackjack Table

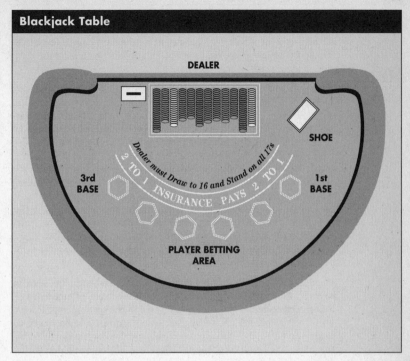

DEALER

SHOE

3rd
BASE

*Dealer must Draw to 16 and Stand on all 17s*

2 TO 1 INSURANCE PAYS 2 TO 1

1st
BASE

PLAYER BETTING
AREA

**buy insurance** if the dealer is showing an ace. Here you're wagering half your initial bet that the dealer does have a natural; if so, you lose your initial bet but are paid 2 to 1 on the insurance (which means the whole thing is a push).

**surrender** half your initial bet if you're holding a bad hand (known as a "stiff") such as a 15 or 16 against a high up card like a 9 or 10.

### Buying In & Playing 21

First you must select a table at which to play. A small sign in the left-hand corner of the "layout" (the diagram printed on the felt tabletop) indicates the table minimum and maximum and often displays the house rules. You can be sure that the $2-minimum tables will be packed, the $5-minimum tables will be crowded, and the $25 tables will have some empty seats. Look carefully before you sit, so as to avoid the embarrassment of parking yourself at a $25 table with $1 chips.

There are generally six or seven betting circles (or squares) on a blackjack layout. When you find an empty space at a table with your chosen minimum, you can join a game in progress between hands. Sometimes you'll have to squeeze in and the other players might not be too eager to make room for you for one reason or another (almost every one of them superstitious). The dealer should help make room for you. If everybody is particularly unfriendly, feel free to leave at any time, but it's to your advantage to spend as much time as possible playing at a crowded table, especially if your intention is to be rated for comps. The more crowded the table, the fewer hands will be played every hour, which reduces your risk. If everybody makes plenty of room for you to be comfortable and the dealer is friendly, you've got it made for hours.

Once you're settled, it's time to "buy in" (convert your cash to casino chips). Place your money on the layout between the betting circles or in the insurance space. If you lay cash *inside* the betting area, the dealer will say something like, "Money plays," and you might wind up betting your whole buy-in amount on the next hand! The dealer should exchange your cash for chips and deposit the bills in the drop slot, using a small plastic "pusher."

Now you can place your wager in the betting circle. You're dealt your two cards. If they're face down, you can pick them up, with one hand, and hold them. If they're face up, don't touch them. If you have a natural, turn them over and the dealer will pay you immediately and take your cards. Otherwise, everyone plays out his or her hand one at a time, from the right side of the table ("first base") to the left ("third base"). If you opt to stand, slide your two cards under your chips, then sit back and relax. If you want to hit, scratch the cards on the layout (seeing this done once will show you how). When you're ready to stand, slide the cards under the chips; if you bust, turn the cards over and the dealer will collect them and your bet. When everyone else has played, the dealer turns over her down (or "hole") card and plays out her hand, then settles up with all the players according to whether they won, lost, or pushed. Then the whole process starts all over again.

Playing blackjack is not only knowing the rules and etiquette, it's also knowing *how* to play. Many people devote a great deal of time to learning strategies, two of which are discussed in the sections that follow. However, if you don't have the time, energy, or inclination to get seriously involved, the following basic rules, which cover more than half the situations you'll face, should allow you to play the game with a modicum of skill and a paucity of humiliation:

1) When your hand is a stiff (a total of 12, 13, 14, 15, or 16) and the dealer shows a 2, 3, 4, 5, or 6, always stand.

2) When your hand is a stiff and the dealer shows a 7, 8, 9, 10, or ace, always hit.

3) When you hold a 17, 18, 19, or 20, always stand.

4) When you hold a 10 or 11 and the dealer shows a 2, 3, 4, 5, 6, 7, 8, or 9, always double down.

5) When you hold a pair of aces or a pair of 8s, always split.

6) Never buy insurance.

### Basic Strategy

Available to anyone with an interest in the game, a system called "basic strategy" consists of a large set of exact decisions for optimum play at blackjack based on a player's hand versus the dealer's up card. These decisions have been developed via computer simulations of hundreds of millions of blackjack hands; they're not open to debate. You must spend several hours memorizing the basic strategy chart and then spend another several hours practicing basic strategy with playing cards. And then you must make the correct play on every hand, regardless of your "hunches" or what the person sitting next to you might recommend.

The accompanying Basic Strategy Chart lists all the possible combinations of blackjack hands against the dealer's up card. Here's how to read it. Say you're dealt a 7 and a 5 and the dealer is showing a 9. First look at the left-hand column, under YOUR HAND for the total, 12. Then follow the line across to the column under the number 9. The "H" stands for hit. So you would hit this hand. Now, suppose you're then dealt a 4. Look back at the left-hand column for the new total, 16. Then follow it across to the number-9 column again. Again you

## Blackjack Basic Strategy Chart

| Your Hand | Dealer's up card | | | | | | | | | |
|---|---|---|---|---|---|---|---|---|---|---|
| | 2 | 3 | 4 | 5 | 6 | 7 | 8 | 9 | 10 | A |
| 5 | H | H | H | H | H | H | H | H | H | H |
| 6 | H | H | H | H | H | H | H | H | H | H |
| 7 | H | H | H | H | H | H | H | H | H | H |
| 8 | H | H | H | H | H | H | H | H | H | H |
| 9 | D | D | D | D | D | H | H | H | H | H |
| 10 | D | D | D | D | D | D | D | D | H | H |
| 11 | D | D | D | D | D | D | D | D | D | D |
| 12 | H | H | S | S | S | H | H | H | H | H |
| 13 | S | S | S | S | S | H | H | H | H | H |
| 14 | S | S | S | S | S | H | H | H | H | H |
| 15 | S | S | S | S | S | H | H | H | H | H |
| 16 | S | S | S | S | S | H | H | H | H | H |
| 17 | S | S | S | S | S | S | S | S | S | S |
| 18 | S | S | S | S | S | S | S | S | S | S |
| 19 | S | S | S | S | S | S | S | S | S | S |
| 20 | S | S | S | S | S | S | S | S | S | S |
| 21 | S | S | S | S | S | S | S | S | S | S |
| A,2 | H | H | D | D | D | H | H | H | H | H |
| A,3 | H | H | D | D | D | H | H | H | H | H |
| A,4 | H | H | D | D | D | H | H | H | H | H |
| A,5 | H | H | D | D | D | H | H | H | H | H |
| A,6 | D | D | D | D | D | H | H | H | H | H |
| A,7 | S | D | D | D | D | S | S | H | H | H |
| A,8 | S | S | S | S | S | S | S | S | S | S |
| A,9 | S | S | S | S | S | S | S | S | S | S |
| A,A | SP | SP | SP | SP | SP | SP | SP | SP | SP | SP |
| 2,2 | H | SP | SP | SP | SP | SP | H | H | H | H |
| 3,3 | H | H | SP | SP | SP | SP | H | H | H | H |
| 4,4 | H | H | H | D | D | H | H | H | H | H |
| 5,5 | D | D | D | D | D | D | D | D | D | H |
| 6,6 | SP | SP | SP | SP | SP | H | H | H | H | H |
| 7,7 | SP | SP | SP | SP | SP | SP | H | H | H | H |
| 8,8 | SP | SP | SP | SP | SP | SP | SP | SP | SP | SP |
| 9,9 | SP | SP | SP | SP | SP | S | SP | SP | S | S |
| 10,10 | S | S | S | S | S | S | S | S | S | S |

have to hit. (Pray for a 5 or less, your only way out of this worst-case blackjack scenario. Most of the time you'll bust.)

Say you're dealt, on the next hand, an ace and a 4 against the dealer's 3; counting the ace as 11, you have a total of 15. Find the A,4 listing in the YOUR HAND column and follow it across to the dealer's 3. According to basic strategy, you should hit. If you get a 6, you've got 21, not 12. If you get a 5, you've got 20; of course you should stand. (If you're in doubt, look up the A,9 listing.) If you get a 9, however, you'll have to count the ace as a 1, for a total of 14; otherwise you'd bust with 23. Now you look up the proper play for 14 against a dealer's 3; you'd stand.

Finally, suppose you're dealt a pair of 7s against a dealer's 7. The chart tells you to split the pair. Here you place both cards face up near your initial bet (don't worry about the exact position; no matter how close you place them, the dealer will *always* rearrange them slightly) and then place a second bet equivalent to the first. Then you play each 7 as its own hand. What if you're dealt a 4 on your first 7 for a total of 11? Some casinos will let you double down after splitting. Ask the dealer if she doesn't volunteer this information. What if you're dealt another 7? Again, some casinos will let you split the new pair and play out three hands.

Rules vary from house to house and city to city. In Las Vegas, some places allow you to surrender; some don't. At some places, dealers stand on soft 17; some places they don't. Basic strategy can get fairly advanced, and there are times when certain variations apply. But for most sets of rules at most Las Vegas joints, basic strategy will put you way ahead of the pikers who swell the casino coffers.

## Card Counting

Card counting is an exacting technique for tracking the cards that have been played during a blackjack round and thereby determining whether the cards remaining to be played are favorable or unfavorable to the player. Card counters designate different plus or minus values for cards that are removed from the deck in play; based on the count, players can make better-informed decisions about playing and betting strategies. *Knock-Out Blackjack—The Easiest Card-Counting System Ever Devised* delivers what it promises in the subtitle: a card-counting system that takes only a few hours to learn and a few more to perfect, without sacrificing any of the power of the most complex and difficult counts. It's available from **Huntington Press** (✉ 3687 S. Procyon Ave., Las Vegas, NV 89103, ☎ 702/252–0655 or 800/244–2224).

Card counting is something the dealers, pit bosses, and video surveillance teams are constantly on the lookout for. In some casinos, if a player is suspected of card counting he will be asked to leave the table ("backed off") or, in some cases, to leave the premises ("barred"). However, some casinos don't sweat card counters too much. Others counter the card counters' edge by using "six-deck shoes"; that is, they combine six decks, which reduces the value of tracking the deck till deep into it. A common misconception is that counters keep track of more than 300 cards in a six-deck shoe; in fact, you're only counting the point totals (2s through 6s are worth +1, 7s and 8s are worth 0, 10s and aces are worth -1). Also, the casinos rarely deal all the way to the bottom of a single deck, two decks, or six decks, because it's easier to figure out what cards are left once you get towards the *bottom* of the pile. Using multideck shoes is just one of myriad countermeasures that casinos employ to foil card counters. Early and unbalanced shuffling, low table limits, and controlled betting spreads are among the many others.

It's a tough business, and only a select few card counters are good enough to consistently win enough money to make a living at it.

## Craps

Craps is a dice game played at a large rectangular table with rounded corners. Up to 12 players can crowd around the table, all standing. The layout (☞ Crap Table illustration) is mounted at the bottom of a surrounding "rail," which prevents the dice from being thrown off the table and provides an opposite wall against which to bounce the dice. It's important, when you're the "shooter," to roll the dice hard enough so that they bounce off the end wall of the table; this ensures a random bounce and shows that you're not trying to control the dice with a "soft roll." The layout grid is duplicated on the right and left side of the table, so players on either end will see exactly the same design. The top of the railing is grooved to hold the bettors' chips; as always, keep a close eye on your stash to prevent victimization by rail thieves.

It can require up to four pit personnel to run an action-packed, fast-paced game of craps. Two dealers handle the bets made on either side of the layout. A "stickman" wields the long wooden "stick," curved at one end, which is used to move the dice around the table; the stickman also calls the number that's rolled and books the proposition bets made in the middle of the layout. The "boxman" sits between the two dealers and oversees the game; he settles any disputes about rules, payoffs, mistakes, etc. A slow craps game is often handled by a single employee, who performs stick, box, and dealer functions. A portable end wall can be placed near the middle of the table so that only one side is functional.

To play, just join in, standing at the table wherever you can find an open space. You can start betting casino chips immediately, but you have to wait your turn to be the shooter. The dice move around the table in a clockwise fashion: the person to your right shoots before you, the one to the left after (the stickman will give you the dice at the appropriate time). If you don't want to roll the bones, motion your refusal to the stickman and he'll skip you.

Playing craps is fairly straightforward; it's betting on it that's complicated. The basic concepts are as follows: if the first roll turns up a 7 or 11, that's called a "natural"—an automatic win. If a 2, 3, or 12 comes up on the first throw (called the "come-out roll"), that's termed "crapping out"—an automatic lose. Each of the numbers 4, 5, 6, 8, 9, or 10 on a first roll is known as a "point": the shooter has to keep rolling the dice until that number comes up again. If a 7 turns up before the number does, that's another loser. When either the point (the original number thrown) or a 7 is rolled, this is known as a "decision"; one is made on average every 3.3 rolls.

But "winning" and "losing" rolls of the dice are entirely relative in this game, because there are two ways you can bet at craps: "for" the shooter or "against" the shooter. Betting "for" means that the shooter will "make his point" (win). Betting "against" means that the shooter will "seven out" (lose). (Either way, you're actually betting against the house, which books all wagers.) If you're betting "for" on the come-out, you place your chips on the layout's "pass line." If a 7 or 11 is rolled, you win even money. If a 2, 3, or 12 (craps) is rolled, you lose your bet. If you're betting "against" on the come-out, you place your chips in the "don't pass bar." A 7 or 11 loses; a 2 or 3 wins (a 12 is a push). A shooter can bet for or against himself or herself, as well as for or against the other players.

**Crap Table**

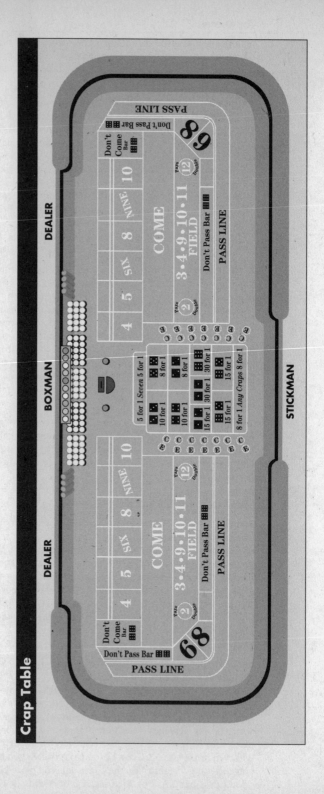

At the same time, you can make roughly two dozen wagers on any single roll of the dice. In addition to the "for" and "against" (pass and don't pass) bets, you can also make the following wagers at craps:

**Come/Don't Come:** After a pass-line point is established, the "come" bet renders every subsequent roll of the dice a come-out roll. When you place your chips in the come box, it's the same as a pass line bet. If a 7 or 11 is rolled, you win even money. If a 2, 3, or 12 is rolled, you've crapped out. If a 4, 5, 6, 8, 9, or 10 is rolled, it becomes another point, and the dealer moves your chips into the corresponding box on the layout. Now if that number comes up before the 7, you win the come bet. The opposite is true for the "don't come" box: 7 and 11 lose; 2, 3, and 12 win; and if the 7 is rolled before the point, you win.

**Odds:** The house allows you to take odds on whether or not the shooter will make his or her point, once it's established. The house pays off these bets at "true odds," rather than withholding a unit or two to its advantage, so these are the best bets in a crap game. Odds on the 6 and 8 pay off at 6 to 5, on the 5 and 9 at 3 to 2, and on the 4 and 10 at 2 to 1. "Back up" your pass line bets with single, double, triple, or up to 100 times odds (depending on the house rules) by placing your chips behind your line bet. For example, if the point is a 10 and your bet is $5, backing up your bet with single odds ($5) returns $25 ($5 + $5 on the line and $5 + $10 single odds); taking triple odds returns $55 ($5 + $5 on the line and $15 + $30). To take the odds on a come bet, toss your chips onto the layout and tell the dealer, "Odds on the come."

**Place:** Instead of waiting for a point to be rolled on the come, you can simply lay your bet on the number of your choice. Drop your chips on the layout in front of you and tell the dealer to "place" your number. The dealer puts your chips on the number; when it's rolled you win. The 6 and 8 pay 7 to 6, the 5 and 9 pay 7 to 5, and the 4 and 10 pay 9 to 5. In other words, if you place $6 on the 8 and it hits, you win $7. Place bets don't pay off at true odds, which is how the house maintains its edge (1.51% on the 6 and 8, 4% on the 5 and 9, and 6.66% on the 4 and 10). You can "call your place bet down" (take it back) at any time; otherwise the place bet will "stay up" until a 7 is rolled.

**Buy:** Buy bets are the same as place bets, except that the house pays off at true odds and takes a 5% commission if it wins. Buy bets have an edge of 4.7%, so you should only buy the 4 and 10 (rather than place them at a 6.6% disadvantage).

**Big 6 and 8:** Place your own chips in these boxes; you win if the 6 or 8 comes up, and lose on the 7. Because they pay off at even money, rather than true odds, the house edge is large—9.09%.

**Field:** This is a "one-roll" bet (a bet that's decided with each roll). Numbers 3, 4, 9, 10, and 11 pay even money, while 2 and 12 pay 2 to 1 (the 12 or "boxcars" pays 3 to 1 in Reno). The house edge on the field is 5.5%.

**Proposition Bets:** All the proposition bets are booked in the grid in the middle of the layout by the stickman. "Hardways" means a pair of numbers on the dice (two 3s for a hardways 6, two 4s for a hardways 8, etc.). A hardways 4 or 10 pays 7 to 1 (11.1% edge), and 6 or 8 pays 9 to 1 (9.09%). If a 7 or a 4, 6, 8, or 10 is rolled the "easy way," hardways bets lose. "Any seven" is a one-roll wager on the 7, paying 4 to 1 with a whopping 16.6% edge. "Yo'leven" is also a one-roll wonder paying 14 to 1 with a 16.6% edge. "Any craps" is a one-roll bet on the 2, 3, or 12, paying 7 to 1 (11.1%). Other bad proposition bets include the "horn" (one-roll bet on 2, 3, 11, or 12 separately; 16.6%), and "c and e" (craps or 11; 11.1%).

Note: the players place their own pass line, field, Big 6 and 8, and come bets. Players must drop their chips on the table in front of the dealers and instruct them to make their place and buy bets, and to take or lay the odds on their come bets. Chips are tossed to the stickman, who makes the hardways, any craps, any seven, and c and e bets in the middle of the layout.

# Keno

Craps, blackjack, baccarat, and roulette arrived in Nevada casinos from Europe, but an early version of keno was brought over in the mid-1800s from China, where this bingo-type game was popular. It was rapidly Americanized in Reno casinos in the 1930s shortly after gambling was legalized.

Keno games are played once every seven or eight minutes. You participate by using a black crayon (provided) to mark a "ticket," imprinted with 80 boxes numbered 1 through 80, with 1 to 15 "spots" or numbers of your choice. You decide how many spots you want to mark based on how much money you're willing to bet. Eighty numbered Ping-Pong balls lying in a round plastic or wire bowl (the "goose") are mixed by an electric fan; the forced air blows the balls into two elongated tubes that hold 10 balls each. The numbers on the balls are announced over a public address system to the players in the keno "lounge" and are displayed on keno video monitors that hang all around the casino—in the coffee shop, restaurants, and bars. If enough of your numbers match the board's numbers, you win an amount enumerated in the keno payoff booklet (☞ Keno Payoffs chart).

You can bring your ticket to the central keno "counter," where a "writer" gives you a duplicate ticket and books your wager, or you can fill out a ticket at one of the casino's bars and restaurants, which are served by keno "runners," who collect tickets and bets and run them to the central counter where they are processed. The runners then deliver the duplicate tickets to you. After the game has been played and the winning numbers are displayed, the runner returns to check if there are any winners. If there are, the runner redeems the winning tickets for her customers—at which point it's customary to tip her.

There are six different types of keno tickets, the most common of which are the "straight," "replay," and "split" tickets. On a straight ticket, you mark off your chosen numbers—say, eight of them (remember, you're allowed to mark as many as 15). Looking at the payout chart, you can see that if four or fewer of your numbers match the called numbers, you lose. If five out of the eight match, you win $9 (on the $1 bet). If all eight match, you're an $18,000 winner. If you mark 15 spots and all 15 match (fat chance!), you win the big jackpot, usually $50,000.

A replay ticket uses the same numbers that you bet on with a previous ticket. Simply hand your bet (which doesn't have to be for the same amount) and the duplicate ticket from a prior game to the writer. A split ticket means that you're making two straight bets on a single ticket. Mark your numbers for the first straight bet and draw a line to separate them from the numbers for the second straight bet. Be sure to tell the writer that this is a split ticket.

Like the split ticket, "way" and "combination" wagers use one ticket to make what are often large and complex numbers of bets—a method

## Keno Payoffs (for a bet of $1)

| Numbers Marked | Winning Numbers | Pays $ | Numbers Marked | Winning Numbers | Pays $ |
|---|---|---|---|---|---|
| 1 | 1 number | 3 | | | |
| | | | 11 | 5 numbers | 1 |
| 2 | 2 numbers | 12 | | 6 numbers | 8 |
| | | | | 7 numbers | 72 |
| | | | | 8 numbers | 360 |
| | | | | 9 numbers | 1,800 |
| 3 | 2 numbers | 1 | | 10 numbers | 12,000 |
| | 3 numbers | 42 | | 11 numbers | 28,000 |
| 4 | 2 numbers | 1 | 12 | 6 numbers | 5 |
| | 3 numbers | 4 | | 7 numbers | 32 |
| | 4 numbers | 112 | | 8 numbers | 240 |
| | | | | 9 numbers | 600 |
| | | | | 10 numbers | 1,480 |
| 5 | 3 numbers | 2 | | 11 numbers | 8,000 |
| | 4 numbers | 20 | | 12 numbers | 36,000 |
| | 5 numbers | 480 | | | |
| | | | 13 | 6 numbers | 1 |
| 6 | 3 numbers | 1 | | 7 numbers | 16 |
| | 4 numbers | 4 | | 8 numbers | 80 |
| | 5 numbers | 88 | | 9 numbers | 720 |
| | 6 numbers | 1,480 | | 10 numbers | 4,000 |
| | | | | 11 numbers | 8,000 |
| | | | | 12 numbers | 20,000 |
| 7 | 4 numbers | 2 | | 13 numbers | 40,000 |
| | 5 numbers | 24 | | | |
| | 6 numbers | 360 | 14 | 6 numbers | 1 |
| | 7 numbers | 5,000 | | 7 numbers | 10 |
| | | | | 8 numbers | 40 |
| | | | | 9 numbers | 300 |
| 8 | 5 numbers | 9 | | 10 numbers | 1,000 |
| | 6 numbers | 92 | | 11 numbers | 3,200 |
| | 7 numbers | 1,480 | | 12 numbers | 16,000 |
| | 8 numbers | 18,000 | | 13 numbers | 24,000 |
| | | | | 14 numbers | 50,000 |
| 9 | 5 numbers | 4 | | | |
| | 6 numbers | 44 | 15 | 7 numbers | 8 |
| | 7 numbers | 300 | | 8 numbers | 28 |
| | 8 numbers | 4,000 | | 9 numbers | 132 |
| | 9 numbers | 20,000 | | 10 numbers | 300 |
| | | | | 11 numbers | 2,600 |
| | | | | 12 numbers | 8,000 |
| 10 | 5 numbers | 2 | | 13 numbers | 20,000 |
| | 6 numbers | 20 | | 14 numbers | 32,000 |
| | 7 numbers | 132 | | 15 numbers | 50,000 |
| | 8 numbers | 960 | | | |
| | 9 numbers | 3,800 | | | |
| | 10 numbers | 25,000 | | | |

of reducing paperwork. But these bets are really just a fancier and faster way to lose money at keno. If you want to try them out, most keno lounges have a booklet explaining the way and combination bets.

Keno has the highest house advantage in the casino, but this doesn't seem to have much of an effect on its popularity. Even though you can expect to lose 25¢ to 40¢ on every dollar you wager, many people like keno. Why? It's easy to play and slow-paced; you can sit in the lounge, drink, and visit with your fellow suckers. You can also maintain a level of action while eating or drinking in a restaurant or bar. But mostly it's a long-shot game, at which you can win $25,000; $50,000; and, at some places, even $100,000 by risking only a few dollars.

Video keno is played similarly to "live" keno. You drop your nickel or quarter into the machine, then use the attached "pen" to touch your numbers of choice. When you press the button that says "play" or "start," the machine illuminates the winning numbers, usually accompanied by a beep. If enough of your numbers match the machine's, you're paid off either in coins or credits.

# Poker Games

Over the last several years video poker has grown to be one of the most popular games in the casinos. Its no wonder that many of the newer table games that have made their way onto the casino floor are also based on poker. Let it Ride and Caribbean Stud are two of the fastest-growing table games, and Pai Gow Poker has been attracting new players to the tables. These games are fairly easy to learn; however, a player will need a general knowledge of the ranking of poker hands. From this, you'll understand what makes a winning hand and how to interpret the pay tables used for some of the bonus bets. Following is a hierarchy of poker hands, from strongest to weakest:

**Royal Flush:** This is the best poker hand, which is composed of a Ten (T), Jack (J), Queen (Q), King (K), and Ace (A) of the same suit.

**Straight Flush:** Five cards of the same suit that are in sequence.

**Four-Of-A-Kind:** Four cards of equal rank, one in each suit.

**Full House:** Three of a kind and a pair.

**Flush:** Any five cards of the same suit.

**Straight:** Five cards of any suit that are in sequence.

**Three-Of-A-Kind:** Any three cards of equal rank.

**Two Pair:** Two different pairs of the same rank.

**One Pair:** Two cards of the same rank.

## Let It Ride

Let It Ride was first introduced to the casinos in 1993. The game is popular because it offers a potential for high payouts, but also because the players are not playing against each other or trying to beat the dealer, camaraderie develops among the players creating a fun atmosphere. The game and the correct playing strategy can be learned quickly. In essence, each player is trying to put together a winning poker hand.

The game is played on a blackjack-size table. There are three circles on the table in front of each player. The circles are marked with the numbers 1 and 2, and a dollar sign ($). To start the game a player places three equal bets in each circle. The Shuffle Master machine deals out cards three at a time.

The dealer distributes a three-card hand to each player and retains the last hand. The dealer looks at the dealer's hand, discarding one of the three cards; the two remaining dealer's cards—still face down at this point—become the "community cards" for all the players. More about those in a moment.

The machine counts out the remaining cards into the discard tray. When this is finished, the players are all allowed to look at their three-card hands. At this point each player has the option to take back the bet in circle number one or "let it ride." To take back your bet, you scrape your cards on the table toward you or make a brushing motion with your hand. If you let your bet ride, then it becomes part of your cumulative bet for the hand.

After all the players have made their decisions, the dealer will turn up the first of the two community cards. This card is used as the fourth card for all the players' hands. The players now have the option of taking down their second bet or letting it ride. You may take down the second bet even if you let the first bet ride, but you cannot take down the first bet if you passed on the last round or put it back up if your hand now has more promise than you originally expected.

After all the players make their decisions, the dealer will turn up the second community card. This card completes the five-card hand for all players. At this point, the dealer will pay all the winning bets according to the following pay-out schedule:

| Let It Ride Payout Schedule | |
|---|---|
| **Hand** | **Payout** |
| Pair of Tens or Better | 1 to 1 |
| Two Pairs | 2 to 1 |
| Three of a Kind | 3 to 1 |
| Straight | 5 to 1 |
| Flush | 8 to 1 |
| Full House | 11 to 1 |
| Four of a Kind | 50 to 1 |
| Straight Flush | 200 to 1 |
| Royal Flush | 1,000 to 1 |

The "house edge" for the basic game is approximately 3.5% when you play the correct strategy. You must know which hands you should take down and when to "let it ride." Here is the proper strategy for the game:

**Let bet #1 ride if you have:**

1) A winning hand—one pair of tens or better.

2) A three-card royal flush.

3) A three-card straight flush.

**Let bet #2 ride if you have:**

1) A winning hand—one pair of tens or better.

2) A four-card royal flush or straight flush.

3) A four-card flush.

4) Four high cards (ten or better).

5) A four-card open-ended straight (any four cards in sequence, where you could have a straight by adding a card at either end).

There is a dollar side bet that can be made for a bonus payoff when certain hands are made. The pay tables for the bonus vary from casino to casino. The house edge ranges from 15% to 30% on these bets. As with most side bets offered by the casino, these should be avoided.

Let It Ride can be a fun game for the recreational player. The game is slower than blackjack. You will be dealt about 40 hands per hour, and some casinos offer lower-limit games. If you take the time to learn the simple strategy, you can enjoy the excitement of this table game.

## Caribbean Stud

Caribbean Stud is played on a blackjack-size table. It's another poker-based game, so you need to know the ranking of hands. You are playing against the dealer, and your hand must beat the dealer's hand. You do not have to worry about beating the other players' hands.

The game starts with each player making an ante bet equal to the table minimum. This is placed in the circle marked "ante" in front of the player. At this time the player also has the option of making an additional dollar side bet for the bonus jackpot. An automatic shuffler is used, and the dealer distributes a five-card hand to each player face down. The dealer retains a hand and turns one card face up.

Players look at their cards and decide to fold and forfeit their ante bet or call by making an additional bet, which is twice the size of the ante. For example, at a $5 table your ante bet would be $5 and your call bet would be $10.

After the players have made their decision to fold or call, the dealer's hand is turned over. The dealer must qualify by having a hand with ace plus king or better. If the dealer does not qualify, the players are paid even money for their original ante bet and the second call bet is a "push," which means it does not win or lose.

If the dealer qualifies and the player wins the hand, he or she is paid even money for the ante bet, and the call bet is paid based on the winning hand according to the table below:

| Caribbean Stud Payout Schedule | |
| --- | --- |
| **Hand** | **Payout** |
| One Pair or Less | 1 to 1 |
| Two Pairs | 2 to 1 |
| Three of a Kind | 3 to 1 |
| Straight | 4 to 1 |
| Flush | 5 to 1 |
| Full House | 7 to 1 |
| Four of a Kind | 20 to 1 |
| Straight Flush | 50 to 1 |
| Royal Flush | 100 to 1 |

The player must act before the dealer. This means there will be times when you fold a hand only to have the dealer not qualify. This does not mean you should play every hand. A simple strategy is to play your hand if it contains Ace-King or better, and fold anything else.

The house edge for the main game is about 5%, but the pace of the game is fairly slow. Because of this the house edge won't hurt your bankroll too much if you play for smaller stakes.

The same is not true of the side bet for the progressive jackpot. As with all so-called bonus bets, the bonus jackpot has a high house edge. You need a flush or higher to qualify for one of the bonus payouts, and the money you win when you receive one of these hands is not close to the odds of doing so. If you look at the chart below, you will see that you will make a flush once every 508 hands, and for this the casino will pay you $50 dollars. I think you can see why this is a bad bet.

| Caribbean Stud Progressive Jackpot Payout Schedule | | |
| --- | --- | --- |
| **Hand** | **Dollar Jackpot** | **Odds Against** |
| Flush | $50 | 508 to 1 |
| Full House | $75 | 693 to 1 |
| Four of a Kind | $100 | 4,164 to 1 |
| Straight Flush | 10% of progressive jackpot | 64,973 to 1 |
| Royal Flush | 100% of progressive jackpot | 649,740 to 1 |

If for some reason you decide to make the side bet, you should know that you are eligible for the jackpot even if the dealer's hand does not qualify. You must inform the dealer immediately before they pick up the cards. Normally the dealer will pick up all the cards without turning them over. Make sure you speak up.

That is about all you need to know to play Caribbean Stud. Give it a try, but stay away from the side bet.

## Caribbean Draw
The rules for Caribbean Draw are similar to those for Caribbean Stud. The payouts and betting strategies are the same. The difference is that after looking at their cards, the players have the option of discarding and drawing replacements for up to two cards.

The dealer must have a pair of eights or better to qualify. If not, only the ante bet will be paid. A simple strategy is to call with a pair of eights or better and fold all other hands.

## Pai Gow Poker
Pai Gow is played with a standard 52-card deck and one joker, which can be used as an ace or a wild card to complete only a straight, flush, or straight flush. The game is played on a blackjack-size table with up to six players and a banker. The players are playing against the banker. In most cases the casino acts as the banker although players can choose to bank the game if they wish to. This would require having enough money to cover all of the other player's bets. The casino collects a 5% commission on all winning bets.

To start the game, the players make their bets according to the table minimum. The dealer shuffles the cards and deals out seven stacks containing seven cards. This is done no matter how many players there are. The banker shakes a cup containing three dice to determine who gets the first hand.

You look at your seven cards and set them into a two-card hand and a five-card hand. There is a place marked on the table to place your hands. The two-card hand is placed in front and the five-card hand is placed behind it. If both hands beat the banker's two hands you win. If one of your hands beats the banker's and one loses, it is a "push," and there are no winners. If either of your hands has the exact same value as the banker's hand it is a tie, which is called a "copy," and the banker wins.

When you are setting your hands, your five-card hand must be a higher value than your two-card hand (based on the values of poker hands).

If you make a mistake and the two-card hand is higher it is a "foul," and you lose automatically. When the casino acts as the banker, the dealer must set the house hands according to certain rules, which is called the "House Way." If you are unsure of how to set your hand, you can ask the dealer to set it the "House Way." This will keep you from making a mistake.

Pai Gow is a slower-pace game than most table games. Since you must utilize only the seven cards dealt to you, there are many pushes. The banker has a slight edge because it wins the copies.

Here is a Pai Gow strategy:

The **Back** is the five-card hand; the **Front** is the two-card hand. A **complete hand** is a poker hand that requires all five cards to win (i.e., a straight, flush, or straight flush). A **set** is just a casino term for three of a kind.

**No Pair:** use the highest card in the Back and second- and third-highest in Front.

**One Pair:** place the pair in Back, the highest other two cards in Front.

**Two Pair:** if the "big" (i.e., higher-value) pair is **jack through ace,** place the "small" pair in Front. If the big pair is **7s through 10s,** place both pairs in Back if you can put Ace in Front. If the big pair is **2s through 6s,** place both pairs in Back if you can put King in Front. Otherwise, **split** the pairs, always putting the bigger pair in Back.

**Three Pair:** place the big pair in Front.

**Three of a kind:** if you have **aces,** place an ace and the next-highest card in Front. If you have **kings and below,** place the three of a kind in Back, the two highest remaining cards in Front.

**Two sets:** place the pair from the higher set in Front; the remaining set goes in the Back.

**Straight, flush, or straight flush:** if you have **no pair,** place the two highest cards in Front that leave a complete hand in Back. If you have **one pair,** place the two highest cards possible (pair or no pair) in Front that leave a complete hand in Back. If you have **two pair,** use "two-pair" strategy above. If you have **three of a kind,** place a complete hand in Back, a pair in Front.

**Full house:** put the pair in Front, the set in Back.

**Four of a kind:** If you have **jacks through aces,** always split the pairs, putting one in Front and one in Back. If you have **7s through 10s,** place the four of a kind in Back if you can put ace or king in front; otherwise split into two pair. If you have **6s or below,** never split. If you **also have a pair,** play four of a kind in Back, the pair in Front. If you **also have three of a kind,** put the highest pair in Front, a full house in Back.

**Five aces:** Place a pair of aces in front.

## Roulette

Roulette is a casino game that utilizes a perfectly balanced wheel with 38 numbers (0, 00, and 1 through 36), a small white ball, a large layout with 11 different betting options (☞ Roulette Table illustration), and special "wheel chips." The layout organizes the 11 different bets into six "inside bets" (the single numbers, or those closest to the dealer) and five "outside bets" (the grouped bets, or those closest to the players).

## Roulette Table

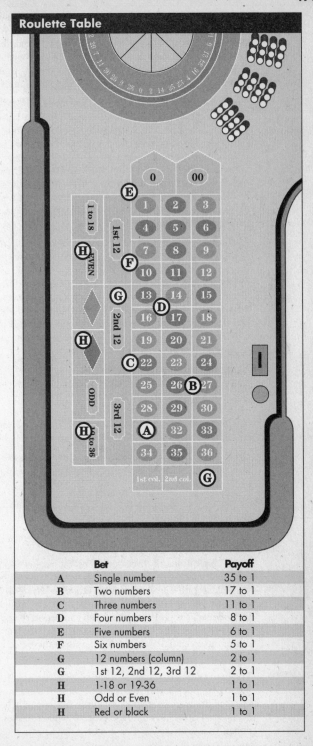

| | Bet | Payoff |
|---|---|---|
| A | Single number | 35 to 1 |
| B | Two numbers | 17 to 1 |
| C | Three numbers | 11 to 1 |
| D | Four numbers | 8 to 1 |
| E | Five numbers | 6 to 1 |
| F | Six numbers | 5 to 1 |
| G | 12 numbers (column) | 2 to 1 |
| G | 1st 12, 2nd 12, 3rd 12 | 2 to 1 |
| H | 1-18 or 19-36 | 1 to 1 |
| H | Odd or Even | 1 to 1 |
| H | Red or black | 1 to 1 |

The dealer stands between the layout and the roulette wheel, and chairs for five or six players are set around the roulette table. At crowded times, players also stand among and behind those seated, reaching over and around to place their bets. *Always* keep a close eye on your chips at these times to guard against "rack thieves," clever sleight-of-hand artists who can steal from your pile of chips right in front of your nose.

To buy in, place your cash on the layout near the wheel. Inform the dealer of the denomination of the individual unit you intend to play (usually 25¢ or $1, but it can go up as high as $500). Know the table limits (displayed on a sign in the dealer area); don't ask for a 25¢ denomination if the minimum is $1. The dealer gives you a stack of wheel chips of a different color from those of all the other players and places a chip marker atop one of your wheel chips on the rim of the wheel to identify its denomination. Note that you must cash in your wheel chips at the roulette table before you leave the game. Only the dealer can verify how much they're worth.

The dealer spins the wheel clockwise and the ball counterclockwise. When the ball slows, the dealer announces, "No more bets." The ball drops from the "back track" to the "bottom track," caroming off built-in brass barriers and bouncing in and out of the different cups in the wheel before settling into the cup of the winning number. Then the dealer, who knows the winning bettors by the color of their wheel chips, places a marker on the number and scoops all the losing chips into his or her corner. Depending on how crowded the game is, the casino can count on roughly 50 spins of the wheel per hour.

### How to Place Inside Bets

You can lay any number of chips (depending on the table limits) on a single number, 1 through 36 or 0 or 00. If the number hits, your payoff is 35 to 1, for a return of $36. You could, conceivably, place a $1 chip on all 38 numbers, but the return of $36 would leave you $2 short, which divides out to 5.26%, the house advantage.

If you place a chip on the line between two numbers and one of those numbers hits, you're paid 17 to 1 for a return of $18 (again, $2 short of the true odds).

Betting on three numbers returns 11 to 1, four numbers returns 8 to 1, five numbers pays 6 to 1 (this is the worst bet at roulette, with a 7.89% disadvantage), and six numbers pays 5 to 1.

### How to Place Outside Bets

Lay a chip on one of three "columns" at the lower end of the layout next to numbers 34, 35, and 36; this pays 2 to 1. A bet placed in the first 12, second 12, or third 12 boxes also pays 2 to 1. A bet on red or black, odd or even, and 1 through 18 or 19 through 36 pays off at even money, 1 to 1. If you think you can bet on red *and* black, or odd *and* even, in order to play roulette and drink for free all night, think again: the green 0 or 00, which fall outside these two basic categories, will come up on average once every 19 spins of the wheel.

The house advantage of 5.26% on every roulette bet (except, as noted, the five-number bet) is five times the best bets at craps and five times less than the average bet at keno. European-style wheels, including those at Monte Carlo, have a single green 0, which slashes the house edge in half to 2.7%.

## Slot Machines

Of all the games in the casino, slot machines are the most American: around the turn of the 20th century, Charlie Fey built the first mechanical slot in his San Francisco basement. Today, slot machines (along with video poker, keno, and blackjack machines) occupy more casino floor space and since 1992 have accounted for more gross casino winnings than all the table games combined. Once machine profits surpassed those of table games on the tony Las Vegas Strip, there's been no looking back. You'll soon realize that slot machines aren't confined to casinos, though. They're everywhere—in airports, supermarkets, bars, coin laundries, and minimarts.

Slot-machine technology has exploded in the past 20 years, and now there are hundreds of different models, which accept everything from pennies to specially minted $500 tokens. The old "mechanical" or "electromechanical" slots—all more than 30 years old—can still be found in some casinos, as antique or nostalgia pieces. They feature small skinny reels with fruit symbols; usually accept only one coin; don't have any lighting or sound effects; have a single pay line; and pay back minor amounts. "Multipliers" are machines that accept more than one coin (usually three to five, maximum) and are mostly electronically operated—with flashing lights, bells, and whistles, and spin, credit, and cashout buttons. Multipliers frequently have a variety of pay lines: three horizontal for example, or five horizontal and diagonal.

One advance in the game, however, has been the progressive jackpot. Banks of slots within a particular casino are connected by computer, and the jackpot total is displayed on a digital meter above the machines. Generally, the total increases by 5% of the wager. If you're playing a dollar machine, each time you pull the handle (or press the spin button), a nickel is added to the jackpot. Progressive slots in many casinos are also connected by modem to other casinos throughout the state, and these jackpots often reach into the millions of dollars. The largest slot jackpot ever paid—$34.9 million, won by a 34-year-old cocktail waitress from the Monte Carlo Hotel-Casino at the Desert Inn in January 2000—was on a Megabucks progressive, which is competitive with surrounding state lotteries. (One form of gambling that is specifically illegal in Nevada is the lottery.) Nevada Nickels and Quartermania are lower-denomination versions of the statewide progressive. Lately, super high-tech slot machines have been emerging from manufacturers at a rapid clip, with large video screens and high-resolution graphics, games-within-a-game bonusing, and video clips (such as on the hot Elvis machines). Some of the new machines have such gimmicky themes as 1960s television programs ("I Dream of Jeannie," "The Addams Family"); a Chinese-theme machine features firecrackers, fortune cookies, and MSG symbols. In addition, some slots are beginning to resemble video-poker machines, in which you choose symbols to hold or discard.

An innovation has been the introduction of the multi-denomination machines. Players can choose to play for pennies, nickels, quarters, or dollars without having to switch machines. Instead of dropping coins in a tray, these machines pay out in vouchers that can be redeemed at the casino cage.

Insert your coins or dollar tokens—or slip your paper dollars into the bill receptor. Pull the handle or press the spin button, then wait for the reels to spin and stop one by one, and for the machine to determine whether you're a winner (occasionally) or a loser (most of the time). It's pretty simple—but because there are so many different types of machines, be sure you know exactly how the one you're playing operates. If it's a progressive machine, you must play the maximum number of coins to qualify for the jackpot. For example, the maximum bet at Megabucks is $3. You can play $1; this limits the action to the first-coin pay line (usually the middle line across the reels). The same goes for $2 and the second-coin pay line (the top line). But to win the progressive total, the three Megabucks symbols must be lined up on the third-coin pay line (not surprisingly, the bottom line). Can you imagine lining up three Megabucks symbols on the third pay line with only a dollar or two played? Instead of winning at least $5 million, you wind up with bupkis!

**Slot candles:** Many people have placed a quarter in a slot machine only to see it drop through into the tray below. At that point they realize it was a dollar machine that they were putting the quarter in. The denomination of the slot machine is posted on the machine, although many times it is hard to see. There is an easy way to determine the denomination of a slot machine. Look at the circular light on the top of the machine. This light is called a **candle**. The top half of the candle is white and lights up when you press the change button. The bottom half of the candle is colored. The color denotes the denomination of the machine. The candles are blue for the dollar machines, yellow for quarters, and red for nickel machines. By knowing the color of the candles, you can spot the denomination of the machine you want to play from across the casino floor. This little bit of knowledge will save you a lot of time when searching for a slot machine.

The house advantage on slots varies widely from machine to machine, from 2% to 25%. Casinos that advertise a 97% payback are telling you that at least one of their slot machines has a house advantage of 3%. Which one? There's really no way of knowing. Generally, $1 machines pay back at a higher percentage than quarter or nickel machines. On the other hand, machines with smaller jackpots pay back more money more frequently, meaning that you'll be playing with more of your winnings. One good thing to keep in mind is this: in a recent nationwide study of slot-machine paybacks, a major gambling publication determined that downtown Las Vegas has the "loosest" slots. This means that from all the available data—specifically the ratio between the "handle" (total action wagered) and the "hold" (what the casino keeps) on slot machines (which is published by the Gaming Control Boards in most casino jurisdictions)—year after year downtown Las Vegas's is the lowest. In other words, they hold the smallest percentage of the total wagered.

One of the all-time great myths about slot machines is that they're "due" for a jackpot. Slots, like roulette, craps, keno, and the big six, are subject to the Law of Independent Trials, which means the odds are permanently and unalterably fixed. If the odds of lining up three sevens on a 25¢ slot machine have been set by the casino at 1 in 10,000, then those odds remain 1 in 10,000 whether the three 7s have been hit three times in a row or not hit for 90,000 plays. Don't waste a lot of time playing a machine that you suspect is "ready," and don't think that if someone hits a jackpot on a particular machine only minutes after you've finished playing on it that it was "yours."

If you have the hots for slots, remember to join as many slot clubs as you can. You're paying a pretty hefty commission for your romance with cherries, lemons, and 7s, so you might as well be rewarded with comps and perks.

## Sports Betting

In Las Vegas, the word "book" rarely denotes a work of literature. More often than not, book isn't even used as a noun, but when it is, book almost always refers to the large room attached to the casino, where sports wagers are made and paid, the odds on sporting events are displayed, and sports bettors (often called "wise guys") watch the main events on large TV screens and video monitors. Bookmakers (or book-

## Parlay Betting Odds

| Number of Teams | Payout Odds | True Odds |
|---|---|---|
| 2 | 13–5 | 3–1 |
| 3 | 6–1 | 7–1 |
| 4 | 10–1 | 15–1 |
| 5 | 20–1 | 31–1 |
| 6 | 35–1 | 63–1 |
| 7 | 50–1 | 127–1 |
| 8 | 100–1 | 225–1 |
| 9 | 200–1 | 511–1 |
| 10 | 400–1 | 1023–1 |

## Teaser Betting Odds

| Number of Teams | 6 points | 6¹/₂ points | 7 points |
|---|---|---|---|
| 2 | even | 10–11 | 1–12 |
| 3 | 9–5 | 8–5 | 3–2 |
| 4 | 3–1 | 5–2 | 2–1 |
| 5 | 9–2 | 4–1 | 7–2 |
| 6 | 7–1 | 6–1 | 5–1 |

ies) are people in the business of taking wagers. Book as a verb is the action of accepting and recording a wager, primarily on sporting and racing events, but also on casino games; the house books your black-jack, crap, and slot machine action.

The first race and sports book in a casino opened in 1975. Today nearly every major casino books race and sports bets. A book can be as small as a table with a clerk who quotes the odds and writes your receipt for a bet by hand, or as large as the Las Vegas Hilton's "super book," which boasts 46 video screens and 500 seats.

In Nevada you can bet on professional football, baseball, basketball, and hockey; college football and basketball; boxing matches; horse racing; and special events. But of all the sports, pro football draws the most action by far.

### Football Betting

A wager made on a football game is one of the best gambling (and entertainment) bargains in the business. It costs you all of $1 in commission to the house to place a $10 bet on a team; the return is several hours of heightened excitement while the game is played. As anyone who's made a casual bet with a friend or group of coworkers knows, having a little money riding on a game introduces a whole new level of energy and interest to it.

There are four ways to bet on a football game: point spread, money line, parlay, and teaser. A wager based on the "point spread" (or a "straight bet") means that you're not only betting that one team will beat the other, but that it will win by a predetermined number of points. The point spreads are calculated for all pro football games by an outside "handicapper" (or oddsmaker) based on the relative strengths or weaknesses of the teams playing. For example, when a strong team, such as the Jacksonville Jaguars, plays a weak team, such as the New York Jets, the spread will favor the Jags by, say, 17 points. This means that the Jags have to beat the Jets by 18 points in order for a wager placed on Jacksonville to win. If the Jags beat the Jets by 10 points, they didn't "cover" the spread, so a bet on the Jets would win. If the Jags win by 17 points exactly, it's a "push" or a tie, and the original bet (including the commission) is returned.

The "money line" bet on a pro football game uses odds instead of points and is determined simply by who wins and who loses. The money line for the Jacksonville-New York game might be a "minus 240 plus 180." This means you have to bet $24 to win $10 (for a total of $34) on the heavily favored Jags; conversely, a bet of $10 on the underdog Jets will win you $18 (for a total of $28).

A "parlay" is a bet on two, three, or four teams (sometimes more), all of which have to cover the point spread for you to win (☞ Parlay Betting Odds chart). If two out of the three teams cover and the third team wins but doesn't cover, you lose the whole bet. The payout on a two-team parlay is generally 13 to 5, on a three-team parlay 6 to 1, and on a four-team parlay 10 to 1.

A "teaser" is similar to a parlay, except that the point spreads are more variable than for a straight or parlay bet (☞ Teaser Betting Odds chart). If you win a three-team teaser after taking an additional 6 points on the spread, you're paid at 9 to 5; with 6½ additional points it's 8 to 5; and with 7 points, 3 to 2.

Football bets are usually made in denominations of $11, which includes the house's $1 commission for booking the bet. Winning bets pay off in denominations of $10. So, for example, you might bet $33 on the 49ers to cover the point spread. If the Jags cover, you win $30 (for a total payback of $63).

To make a football bet (or a bet on any sporting event), go to the sports book and step up to the counter. Study the board that lists all the games, and pick out the one(s) you want to put your money on. The teams are numbered. Give the team number, amount of the bet, and type of bet (points or money line) to the "writer," who inputs your bet into a computer and prints out your "ticket" or receipt. (Parlay and teaser cards are filled out and presented to the writer.) Check your ticket carefully to make sure the writer has given you the exact bet that you intended to make.

Then sit back and root for your money. If you lose, wallpaper your bathroom with the rest of your losing tickets. If you win, return to the casino where you made the bet, present the ticket to the sports book cashier, and receive your due.

## Video Poker

Like blackjack, video poker is a game of strategy and skill, and at select times on select machines, the player actually holds the advantage, however slight, over the house. Unlike with slot machines, you can determine the exact edge of video-poker machines (or in gambler's lingo, "handicap" the machine). Like slots, however, video poker machines are often tied into a progressive meter; when the jackpot total reaches high enough, you can beat the casino at its own game.

The variety of video-poker machines is already large, and it's steadily growing larger. All the different machines are played in a similar fashion, but the strategies are different. This section deals only with straight-draw video poker.

| 9/6 Video Poker Payout Schedule | | | | | |
|---|---|---|---|---|---|
| **Royal Flush** | 250 | 500 | 750 | 1000 | 4000 |
| **Straight Flush** | 50 | 100 | 150 | 200 | 250 |
| **Four of a Kind** | 25 | 50 | 75 | 100 | 125 |
| **Full House** | 9 | 18 | 27 | 36 | 45 |
| **Flush** | 6 | 12 | 18 | 24 | 30 |
| **Straight** | 4 | 8 | 12 | 16 | 20 |
| **Three of a Kind** | 3 | 6 | 9 | 12 | 15 |
| **Two Pair** | 2 | 4 | 6 | 8 | 10 |
| **Jacks or Better** | 1 | 2 | 3 | 4 | 5 |

You must first ascertain what denomination of coin a straight-draw video poker machine accepts. Thousands of penny, nickel, quarter, and dollar machines occupy casinos in Las Vegas. Five-dollar machines are becoming more popular around the state, and $25 and $100 machines can be played at places such as the Mirage, Golden Nugget, and Caesars Palace. Then there are the new multigame machines, where you can play 3, 5, 10, even 50 hands of video poker at the same time.

The schedule for the payback on winning hands is posted on the machine, usually above the screen. It lists the returns for a high pair (generally jacks or better), two pair, three of a kind, a straight, flush, full house, straight flush, four of a kind, and royal flush, depending on the number of coins played—usually 1, 2, 3, 4, or 5. (The machine assumes you're familiar with poker and its terminology.) Look for machines that pay with a single coin played: 1 coin for "jacks or better" (meaning a pair of jacks, queens, kings, or aces; any other pair is a stiff), 2 coins for two pair, 3 for three of a kind, 4 for a straight, 6 for a flush, 9 for a full house, 25 for four of a kind, 50 for a straight flush, and 250 for a royal flush. This is known as a 9/6 machine: one that gives a nine-coin payback for the full house and a six-coin payback for the flush with one coin played (☞ 9/6 Video Poker Payout Schedule chart). Some machines pay a unit for a pair of 10s but get you back by returning only one unit for two pair. Other machines are known as 8/5 (8 for the full house, 5 for the flush), 7/5, and 6/5.

The return from a standard 9/6 straight-draw machine (with a 4,000-coin "flattop" or royal-flush jackpot) is 99.5%; you give up a half percent to the house. An 8/5 machine with a 4,000 flattop returns 97.3%. On 6/5 machines (such as those you find in supermarkets, 7-Elevens, and coin laundries around the city), the figure drops to 95.1%, slightly better than roulette. The return from a 25¢, 8/5 progressive machine doesn't reach 100% until the meter hits $2,200—a rare sight. (You can figure nickel, $1, and $5 progressives by the $2,200 figure. A 100% payback on nickels is $440; on $1 it's $8,800, and on $5 it's $44,000.) Machines with varying paybacks are scattered throughout the casinos. In some you'll see an 8/5 machine right next to a 9/6, and someone will be blithely playing the 8/5 machine!

As with slot machines, it's always optimal to play the maximum number of coins in order to qualify for the jackpot. You insert five coins into the slot and press the "deal" button. Five cards appear on the screen—say, 5, J, Q, 5, 9. To hold the pair of 5s, you press the "hold" buttons under the first and fourth cards. The word "hold" appears underneath the two 5s. You then press the "draw" button (always the same button as "deal") and three new cards appear on the screen—say, 10, J, 5. You have three 5s; with five coins bet, the machine will give you 15 credits. If you want to continue playing, press the "max bet" button: five units will be removed from your number of credits, and five new cards will appear on the screen. You repeat the hold and draw process; if you hit a winning hand, the proper payback will be added to your credits. Those who want coins rather than credit can hit the "cash out" button at any time. Some older machines don't have credit counters and automatically dispense coins for a winning hand.

Like blackjack, video poker has basic strategies that have been formulated by the computer simulation of hundreds of millions of hands. The most effective way to learn it is with a video poker computer program that deals the cards on your screen, then tutors you in how to play each hand properly. The best program is *WinPoker,* available from **Huntington Press** (✉ 3687 S. Procyon Ave., Las Vegas, NV 89103, ☎ 702/252–0655 or 800/244-2444).

If you don't want to devote that much time to the study of video poker, memorizing these six rules will help you make the right decision for more than half the hands you'll be dealt:

1) If you're dealt a completely "stiff" hand (no like cards and no picture cards), draw five new cards.

2) If you're dealt a hand with no like cards but with one jack, queen, king, or ace, always hold on to the picture card; if you're dealt two different picture cards, hold both. But if you're dealt three different picture cards, only hold two (the two of the same suit, if that's an option).

3) If you're dealt a pair, always hold it, no matter what the face value.

4) Never hold a picture card or an ace ("kicker") with a pair of 2s through 10s.

5) Never draw two cards to try for a straight or flush.

6) Never draw one card to try for an inside straight.

# Wheel of Fortune (Big Six)

Prize wheels are among the oldest games of chance and among the easiest to play and lose. Nevada-style big six is modeled after the old carnival wheels that attracted suckers on the midway. The standard wheel, usually 6 feet across, is divided into nine sections and 54 individual slots or stops. Fifty-two of the stops are marked by dollar denominations: 23 $1, 15 $2, 8 $5, 4 $10, and 2 $20 stops. The other two stops are marked by a joker or the casino logo. A leather "flapper" mounted at the top of the wheel clicks as it hits the wood or metal pegs that separate each slot. When the wheel stops, the flapper falls between two pegs and indicates the winning number.

You lay your bet on a glass-covered table in front of the wheel. The layout display consists of the actual currency, which matches the numbers on the wheel (a Washington, Lincoln, Hamilton, Jackson, etc.). To play, you simply place a chip or cash atop the bill you think will be the winner. The payoff is a multiple of the denomination: a $1 bet on the $1 bill pays a buck; a $1 bet on the $2 bill pays $2; a $5 bet on the $20 pays $100. The joker, casino logo, or other nonnumerical symbol on the wheel, however, pays 40 to 1: a successful $1 bet on one of these will get you back $40.

The house advantage starts at 11.1% on the $5 bet and rockets to 22.2% on the $20 bet and 24% on the joker. This isn't a game you'll want to play all night, or for more than a few spins. But the big six often draws a crowd. Even hardened gamblers like to stop and watch and listen to the wheel spin, with its hypnotic clicking of flapper against pegs, to see where it stops. They'd probably even lay down a buck or two, but they'd be too embarrassed in front of the dealer!

# INDEX